KICK OFF
The F.A. Barclaycard Premiership Club Review
2002-2003

Publisher Simon Rosen
Editor John Ley
Contributing Editor Francesco Scimone
Football Statisticians Johanne Springett, Mark Peters
Designers Nick Thornton, Daniel Anim-Kwapong, Ian Bull
Statistics Programmers Karim Biria, Linden Davis,
Derek D'Urso, Darren Tang, Sean Cronin, Kam Varma

The publishers wish to confirm that the views expressed in articles and
reviews in this directory are not necessarily those of the F.A. Premier League
or its clubs. NB: The statistics relate to League matches only.

Every effort has been made to ensure that the information given in this guide
is as accurate and up-to-date as possible at the time of going to press,
1st June 2002. Details do change, however, and the publisher cannot accept
responsibility for any consequences arising from the use of this book.
If you come across an incorrect detail that we could amend for next year's
edition please let us know by sending an email to **info@sidanpress.com**.

This book is not an officially licensed F.A. Premier League publication.

Sidan Press Ltd
5 Callcott Road
Brondesbury
NW6 7EB

Tel: 0208 537 5288
info@sidanpress.com

Contents

 The heart of the Barclaycard Premiership - 4thegame.com

As well as being in his fourth year as Editor of Kick Off, John Ley has been a respected writer with the Daily Telegraph for 15 years. He is regarded as one of the leading statistical experts in the game, contributing to the internet, television and radio as well as being the longest serving football writer on the Daily Telegraph.

Welcome to Kick Off, the definitive fan's guide to the greatest league in the world. The F.A. Barclaycard Premiership continues to grow in importance and excitement and Kick Off, the superlative source of all the vital information you need to keep track of your team's progress, is every bit as exhilarating.

For this year's edition of Kick Off we have added greater detail and definition to aspects such as goalscoring. You can now find out exactly how your team managed to create and score their goals and determine where they need to improve to make the 2002-03 campaign even greater.

The latest edition of Kick Off, which is now regarded as the guide for the discerning supporter, provides every aspect of each F.A. Barclaycard Premiership club. For example, the manner in which each team's top scorer collected his goals is dissected in detail, while discipline is also explained carefully so you can see just why you favourite team collects so many – or so few – cards.

We have also charted the season, month by month, in detail to determine the defining moments; where it went right – or wrong – and just why your team endured agony or enjoyed ecstasy.

We want Kick Off to continue to grow and improve and therefore we value your comments. Please feel free to e-mail us at **info@sidanpress.com** with your thoughts, comments and ideas so that the next edition of Kick Off can be even better.

John Ley

Roll of Honour

Season	Champions	Runners-up	Relegated	Promoted
2001-2002	Arsenal	Liverpool FC	Ipswich Town Derby County Leicester City	Manchester City WBA Birmingham City
2000-2001	Manchester Utd	Arsenal	Manchester City Coventry City Bradford City	Fulham Blackburn Rovers Bolton Wanderers
1999-2000	Manchester Utd	Arsenal	Wimbledon Sheffield Wed Watford	Charlton Athletic Manchester City Ipswich Town
1998-1999	Manchester Utd	Arsenal	Charlton Athletic Blackburn Rovers Nottm Forest	Sunderland AFC Bradford City Watford
1997-1998	Arsenal	Manchester Utd	Bolton Wanderers Barnsley Crystal Palace	Nottm Forest Middlesbrough Charlton Athletic
1996-1997	Manchester Utd	Newcastle United	Sunderland AFC Middlesbrough Nottm Forest	Bolton Wanderers Barnsley Crystal Palace
1995-1996	Manchester Utd	Newcastle United	Manchester City QPR Bolton Wanderers	Sunderland AFC Derby County Leicester City
1994-1995	Blackburn Rovers	Manchester Utd	Crystal Palace Norwich City Leicester City Ipswich Town	Middlesbrough Bolton Wanderers
1993-1994	Manchester Utd	Blackburn Rovers	Sheffield United Oldham Athletic Swindon Town	Crystal Palace Nottm Forest Leicester City
1992-1993	Manchester Utd	Aston Villa	Crystal Palace Middlesbrough Nottm Forest	Newcastle United West Ham United Swindon Town

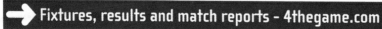

Fixtures, results and match reports - 4thegame.com

Half-Time/Full-Time Comparison Chart

Key ■ Win ■ Loss ■ Draw

Home				Away				Total			
Number of Home Half Time Wins	Full Time Result W	L	D	Number of Away Half Time Wins	Full Time Result W	L	D	Total number of Half Time Wins	Full Time Result W	L	D
4	3	-	1	2	1	-	1	6	4	-	2
Number of Home Half Time Losses	Full Time Result W	L	D	Number of Away Half Time Losses	Full Time Result W	L	D	Total number of Half Time Losses	Full Time Result W	L	D
6	-	3	3	10	-	10	-	16	-	13	3
Number of Home Half Time Draws	Full Time Result W	L	D	Number of Away Half Time Draws	Full Time Result W	L	D	Total number of Half Time Draws	Full Time Result W	L	D
9	4	2	3	7	2	3	2	16	6	5	5

The chart refers to the 2001-02 season only. It shows the number of times a team was winning, losing or drawing at half-time, and how many of those games they went on to win, lose or draw at the final whistle.

For example, this team was ahead at half-time in four of their home games and went on to win three and draw one of those four matches. Away from home, they were losing ten times and went on to lose all ten matches. Totals are displayed on the right-hand side of the chart. For example, this team won six, drew five and lost five out of the 16 they were drawing at half-time.

Results Table

Key 88 time of goal   88 time of assist
▲ player substituted   ● yellow card   ● red card

Arca	McCann	McCann 76	Schwarz	Laslandes ●	Quinn 74 76
Arca 82	McCann	Schwarz	Kilbane 77	Quinn
Arca	Thirlwell	Schwarz 82	Kilbane ▲	Quinn
McAteer	McCann	Schwarz ▲	Arca	Quinn ▲
Gray	McAteer	McCann ▲	Schwarz ●54	Arca
Gray	McAteer	McCann	Schwarz	Arca
McAteer ▲47	McCann	Thirlwell	Arca 47	Quinn ●▲55
McAteer ▲	McCann	Thirlwell ▲	Arca ▲	Quinn
McAteer ▲	McCann	Thirlwell ●	Arca 85	Quinn ▲
Arca ●	McCann	Thirlwell	Kilbane	Laslandes ▲
McAteer	McCann	Reyna	Thirlwell ▲	Kilbane ▲
McAteer ●76	McCann	Reyna 76	Arca	Quinn ▲
McAteer	McCann	Reyna	Arca ▲32	Quinn ▲17 32
McAteer ▲	McCann	Reyna	Arca	Quinn ▲
McAteer	McCann	Reyna ▲	Arca 86	Quinn
Arca ▲	McCann	McAteer ▲	Thirlwell	Kilbane
McAteer ▲	McCann ▲	Schwarz ●66	Kilbane	Quinn
McAteer ▲	Reyna	Schwarz	Kilbane	Quinn
Gray	McAteer ▲12	Reyna	Williams	Kilbane
McAteer	Reyna	Schwarz	Arca ▲	Quinn ▲80
McAteer ●	Reyna	Schwarz ▲	Kilbane ●	Quinn ▲

The team's League matches for 2001-02 are listed in chronological order. Home games are in white and away games in blue. The table headings are: Date; H/A – home or away; **Opponent**; H/T – half-time score (score of team in question first); **F/T** – full-time score; **Pos** – League position after match; **Referee**; **Team**; **Substitutes Used**. Cards are indicated by red and yellow circles besides a player's name. Times of goals are indicated by a black number alongside the goalscorer, while times of assists are represented by a pink number alongside the assistor. Assists are not always awarded. A substituted player has a coloured triangle alongside his name that can be matched with that of a teammate in the **Substitutes Used** column.

➡ **The heart of the Barclaycard Premiership – 4thegame.com**

Chart Explanations

Premiership Bookings Table 2001-2002

Key **M** matches refereed **Y** yellow cards **R** red cards

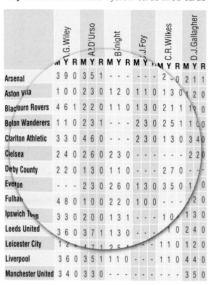

	A.G.Wiley			A.P.D'Urso			B.Knight			J.Foy			C.R.Wilkes			D.J.Gallagher		
	M	Y	R	M	Y	R	M	Y	R	M	Y	R	M	Y	R	M	Y	R
Arsenal	3	9	0	3	5	1	-	-	-	-	-	-	2	0		2	1	1
Aston Villa	1	0	0	2	3	0	1	2	0	1	1	0	1	3	0	2	0	
Blackburn Rovers	4	6	1	2	2	0	1	1	0	1	3	0	2	1	1	2	0	
Bolton Wanderers	1	1	0	2	3	1	-	-	-	2	3	0	2	5	1	1	0	0
Charlton Athletic	3	3	0	4	6	0	-	-	-	2	3	0	1	3	0	3	4	0
Chelsea	2	4	0	2	6	0	2	3	0	-	-	-	-	-	-	2	2	0
Derby County	2	2	0	1	3	0	1	1	0	-	-	-	2	7	0	-	-	-
Everton	-	-	-	2	3	0	2	6	0	1	3	0	3	5	0	1		0
Fulham	4	8	0	1	0	0	2	2	0	1	0	0	-	-	-	2	0	
Ipswich Town	3	3	0	2	0	0	1	3	1	-	-	-	1	0		1	3	0
Leeds United	3	6	0	3	7	1	1	3	0	-	-	-	1	0		2	4	0
Leicester City	1	2											1	1	0	1	2	0
Liverpool	3	6	0	3	5	1	1	1	0	-	-	-	1	1	0	4	4	0
Manchester United	3	4	0	3	3	0	-	-	-	-	-	-	-	-	-	3	5	0

This table shows the performance of referees against the teams in the F.A. Barclaycard Premiership whose games they have officiated at in the 2001-02 season.

Clubs are listed down the left-hand side while referees are shown along the top. Beneath each referee's name, the column is divided into **M** for Matches, **Y** for Yellow Cards and **R** for Red Cards.

Card totals for each team are shown on the right-hand side, while individual referee totals are written along the base of the table.

In this table, for example, A.P.D'Urso officiated at four Charlton matches and handed out six yellow and no red cards to Charlton players. B.Knight did not officiate at any Arsenal, Bolton Wanderers or Charlton matches in 2001-02.

Shot Efficiency

Key ■ Goals Scored ■ Other Shots On Target

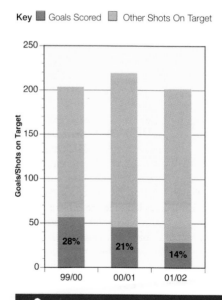

Season	Division	Shots Off Target	Shots On Target	Total Goals
1999 - 2000	P	n/a	204	57
2000 - 2001	P	n/a	220	46
2001 - 2002	P	224	202	29

This chart shows what percentage of a team's total Shots On Target have been converted to goals in each of the last three seasons. The overall bar height indicates how many Shots On Target a team has had, while the green section represents Goals Scored. The blue section shows other Shots On Target. For example, this team has managed 29 goals from 202 Shots On Target in 2001-02, equivalent to 14%. This team has also managed 224 Shots Off Target in the 2001-02 season as indicated in the table above.

 All the latest news, views and opinion - 4thegame.com

Team Performance Table

The chart refers to the 2001-02 season only and measures a team's success rate against four grades of opposition. The final League table is divided into sectors each containing five teams. The team in question is shown with their final points total. Other teams are shown with a score out of six reflecting the number of points that were earned in the two games against them. A score of 6/6 against Blackburn Rovers, for example, indicates home and away wins. The next three columns provide a measure of performance against teams in each sector: at home, away and overall. They are calculated by dividing the number of points earned by the number of points available. For example, this team earned five points out of a possible 30 – 17% – against the top five. They won 53% of the available points against teams in the second sector at home, and 50% away from home against teams in the bottom five.

League Position	Team	Points won from a possible six	Percentage of points won at home	Percentage of points won away	Overall percentage of points won
1	Arsenal	1/6			
2	Liverpool	0/6			
3	Manchester Utd	0/6	27%	7%	17%
4	Newcastle Utd	1/6			
5	Leeds United	3/6			
6	Chelsea	1/6			
7	West Ham Utd	3/6			
8	Aston Villa	2/6	53%	27%	40%
9	Tottenham H	0/6			
10	Blackburn R	6/6			
11	Southampton	1/6			
12	Middlesbrough	0/6			
13	Fulham	1/6	40%	7%	23%
14	Charlton Athletic	2/6			
15	Everton	3/6			
16	Bolton W	6/6			
17	**Sunderland**	**40**			
18	Ipswich Town	3/6	83%	50%	67%
19	Derby County	4/6			
20	Leicester City	3/6			

Goals by Position

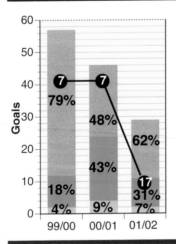

Key

Forward Midfield League Position
Defence Goalkeeper

The chart tracks a team's goalscoring record since the 1999-00 season. For each season, a team's goals are divided among Forwards (orange), Midfielders (green) and Defenders (blue). Compare the height of the columns with the scale on the left of the chart to calculate the number of goals scored. Percentage figures reveal the distribution of goals within a season throughout the team. This team's forwards, for example, claimed their greatest share of goals in 1999-00, dipped in 2000-01, and rose again in 2001-02. The black line graph reveals the team's League position at the end of each season.

➡ Fixtures, results and match reports – 4thegame.com

Bookings by Position

The chart tracks a team's disciplinary record since the 1999-00 season. For each season, a team's yellow cards are divided among Forwards (orange), Midfielders (green), Defenders (blue) and Goalkeepers (purple). Red cards for all positions are shown in the **Total Red** column immediately to the right of each **Yellow** column. Compare the height of the columns with the scale on the left of the chart to calculate the number of cards issued. Percentage figures reveal the distribution of yellow cards within a season. You can compare the relative disciplinary record of a group of players across seasons. This team's midfielders, for example, claimed the greatest share of bookings in 1999-00, dipped in 2000-01, and was back to a similar level in 2001-02.

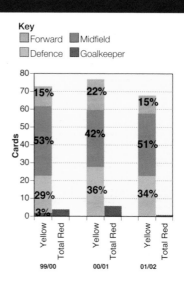

Goals Resulting From

Key ☐ Goals Scored ☐ Goals Conceded

| | Six Yard Area | | | | Inside Area | | | | Outside Area | | | | Total | | | |
| | Shots | | Headers | | Shots | | Headers | | Shots | | Headers | | Shots | | Headers | |
	Home	Away	Home	Away	Home	Away	Home	Away	Home	Away	Home	Away	Home	Away	Home	Away
Open Play	3	2	1	-	5	2	1	1	4	1	-	-	12	5	2	1
	-	1	2	2	5	16	1	1	3	4	-	-	8	21	3	3
Direct Free Kick									1	-			1	0		
									-	1			0	1		
Indirect Free Kick	-	-	-	-	-	-	2	3	-	-	-	-	0	0	2	3
	1	1	1	1	-	-	1	1	-	-	-	-	1	1	2	2
Penalty	-	-	-	-	1	-	-	-	-	-	-	-	1	0	0	0
	-	-	-	-	-	1	-	-	-	-	-	-	0	1	0	0
Corner	-	1	-	-	-	1	-	-	-	-	-	-	0	2	0	0
	-	1	-	1	-	1	1	1	-	-	-	-	0	2	1	2
Totals	3	3	1	0	6	3	3	4	5	1	0	0	14	7	4	4
	1	3	3	4	5	18	3	3	3	5	0	0	9	26	6	7

The chart refers to the 2001-02 season only. Goals scored and conceded are allocated according to how they were scored and where they were scored from at home and away.

Goals scored are in black text on a yellow background while goals conceded are in blue on white. Totals are shown at the far right and along the bottom of the chart and are picked out in bold.

This team, for example, scored three goals from Headers Inside the Area resulting from Indirect Free Kicks away from home. They conceded most goals from Shots Inside the Area in Open Play away from home.

Win Barclaycard Premiership tickets - 4thegame.com

Final F.A. Barclaycard Premiership Points and Positions 2001-02

Pos.	Teams	Points
1	Arsenal	87
2	Liverpool	80
3	Manchester United	77
4	Newcastle United	71
5	Leeds United	66
6	Chelsea	64
7	West Ham United	53
8	Aston Villa	50
9	Tottenham Hotspur	50
10	Blackburn Rovers	46
11	Southampton	45
12	Middlesbrough	45
13	Fulham	44
14	Charlton Athletic	44
15	Everton	43
16	Bolton Wanderers	40
17	Sunderland AFC	40
18	Ipswich Town	36
19	Derby County	30
20	Leicester City	28

There is a complete League table on page 132

The tenth Premier League campaign was one of the most exciting on record. In winning the title, Arsenal secured their first honours since 1998 at the end of Arsene Wenger's first full season in charge.

The Gunners won through thanks to their away record, becoming the first team to remain unbeaten on their travels since Preston North End in 1888-89.

Behind them, Liverpool finished second, their best final placing since 1990-91 when they also finished runners-up to Arsenal. While the Reds were unable to add to the five trophies won in 2001, they offered hope of success to come with some fine displays, especially in Europe where they reached the quarter-finals of the Champions League at their first attempt.

Manchester United, Champions for the last three seasons, had to settle for third place, the lowest they had finished since the launch of the Premier League in 1992.

Having gone out to Bayer Leverkusen in the Champions League semi-finals, the Red Devils finished empty-handed and will enter this year's tournament at the qualifying stage.

In fourth, Newcastle United continued to flourish under Bobby Robson. Having finished 11th in 2000-01, the Magpies shot up the table thanks to the combination of Robson's tactical nous and Alan Shearer's return to form.

It was a disappointing campaign for Leeds United. The Yorkshire club failed to build on the 2000-01 season when they finished fourth and made it to the semi-finals of the Champions League. Instead, with matters off the pitch dominating affairs at Elland Road, they slipped a place to fifth, earning entry to the UEFA Cup.

Chelsea qualified for the UEFA Cup as a result of their F.A. Cup exploits which took them all the way to Cardiff before losing to eventual League Champions Arsenal. Worthington Cup winners Blackburn Rovers will feature in Europe for the fourth time in eight seasons. Aston Villa and Fulham will try their luck via the Intertoto Cup, the former hoping to qualify for the UEFA Cup for the second season running via this route.

At the other end of the table, and for the first time ever in the Premier League, the three sides who came up – Fulham, Blackburn and Bolton – stayed up while Ipswich, Derby and Leicester dropped to Division One. Following the end of the seaason, Ipswich were awarded a place in the UEFA Cup via UEFA's Fair Play rankings. They become the first English club outside the top flight to play in Europe since West Ham in 1980-81.

Barclaycard Manager Of The Year
Arsene Wenger (Arsenal)

Barclaycard Player Of The Year
Fredrik Ljungberg (Arsenal)

Football Writers' Player of the Year
Robert Pires (Arsenal)

PFA Player Of The Year
Ruud van Nistelrooy
(Manchester United)

PFA Young Player Of The Year
Craig Bellamy (Newcastle United)

Champions Arsenal scooped three out of five end of season awards after completing the Double for the second time in five seasons.

Arsene Wenger claimed the Manager of the Year accolade after steering his charges to the F.A. Barclaycard Premiership title seven points clear of Liverpool.

Success in the F.A. Cup, beating London rivals Chelsea 2-0 in Cardiff, meant that the Gunners were able to celebrate the third Double in their long and illustrious history.

Arsenal's midfield dynamo Freddie Ljungberg claimed the corresponding Player of the Year prize. The Sweden international has proved to be another astute purchase by Wenger, having arrived for £3m in September 1998.

Ljungberg netted a number of crucial strikes in the run-in, netting six times in April before scoring a fine individual goal at the Millennium Stadium to seal Arsenal's F.A. Cup triumph.

His teammate and fellow midfielder Robert Pires was chosen by the nation's writers as their Player of the Year. The World Cup and European Championship winner was inspirational for Arsenal having taken a year to adjust to the pace of the Premier League after signing from Marseille in July 2000 for £6m.

Pires' fine season, which had seen him collect nine League goals in 28 appearances, was curtailed after damaging his knee ligaments in the F.A. Cup quarter-final replay with Newcastle in late March. Unfortunately for him, it meant he was out of the World Cup finals in Japan and Korea.

Manchester United's £19m summer signing Ruud van Nistelrooy had a brilliant first season in the F.A. Barclaycard Premiership, finishing with 23 League goals. After becoming the first United player to score more than 20 goals in a campaign since Brian McClair in 1987-88, he was acknowledged by his fellow professionals as the Player of the Year.

Craig Bellamy was chosen as the Young Player of the Year after helping Newcastle United to fourth place in the table, their best finish since 1996-97. Having joined in the summer from Coventry, he quickly formed a productive strike partnership with former England captain Alan Shearer.

Barclaycard Player and Manager of the Month Awards 2001-02
August Louis Saha (Fulham), Sam Allardyce (Bolton) **September** Juan Sebastian Veron (Manchester United), John Gregory (Aston Villa) **October** Rio Ferdinand (Leeds United), Glenn Hoddle (Spurs) **November** Danny Murphy (Liverpool), Gerard Houllier and Phil Thompson (Liverpool) **December** Ruud van Nistelrooy (Manchester United), Bobby Robson (Newcastle United) **January** Marcus Bent (Ipswich Town), Gordon Strachan (Southampton) **February** Ruud van Nistelrooy (Manchester United), Bobby Robson (Newcastle United) **March** Dennis Bergkamp (Arsenal), Gerard Houllier and Phil Thompson (Liverpool) **April** Fredrik Ljungberg (Arsenal), Arsene Wenger (Arsenal)

 The heart of the Barclaycard Premiership - 4thegame.com

Arsenal

F.A. Barclaycard Premiership	Final standing for the 2001-2002 season							
Final Position		Games Played	Games Won	Games Drawn	Games Lost	Goals For	Goals Against	Total Points
1	Arsenal	38	26	9	3	79	36	87
2	Liverpool	38	24	8	6	67	30	80
3	Manchester United	38	24	5	9	87	45	77

> "We want to improve. We have shown tremendous resilience and tremendous team spirit. We want to keep these qualities and to keep the players together."
>
> *Arsene Wenger (May 2002)*

Club Honours and Records

Premier League Champions: 1997-98, 2001-02

Football League Champions:

1930-31, 1932-33, 1933-34, 1934-35, 1937-38, 1947-48, 1952-53, 1970-71, 1988-89, 1990-91

FA Cup Winners:

1930, 1936, 1950, 1971, 1979, 1993, 1998, 2002

League Cup Winners: 1987, 1993

European Fairs Cup Winners: 1969-70

European Cup Winners' Cup Winners: 1993-94

Record victory:

12-0 v Loughborough Town, Division 2, 12 March, 1900

Record defeat:

0-8 v Loughborough Town, Division 2, 12 December, 1896

League goals in a season (team):

127, Division 1, 1930-31

League goals in a season (player):

42, Ted Drake, 1934-35

Career league goals: 150, Cliff Bastin, 1930 to 1947

League appearances: 558, David O'Leary, 1975 to 1993

Reported transfer fee paid: £13,000,000 to Bordeaux for Sylvain Wiltord, September 2000

Reported transfer fee received: £25,000,000 from Barcelona for Marc Overmars, July 2000

AFTER coming second three years in a row, Arsenal finally fulfilled their potential by winning the Double for the second time under Arsene Wenger. It was a wonderful, record-breaking season as they finally broke Manchester United's stranglehold on the Premier League.

Having signed Francis Jeffers, Giovanni van Bronckhorst, Richard Wright and Junichi Inamoto to swell the Highbury squad, Arsene Wenger made the short trip across North London to pinch Sol Campbell from their fierce rivals.

Spurs fans were furious but Wenger was delighted with his acquisition. His arrival prompted the question as to how Campbell would fit in alongside Tony Adams and Martin Keown, with some wondering whether Arsenal would break with tradition and go with a back three. Injuries, though, soon solved any such problems with Wenger sticking with his rigid, and trusted, back four.

Fears continued to persist over the future of Wenger, who had yet to sign a new contract at Highbury. Fans were also worried that Patrick Vieira could be on his way. Although Wenger made the Frenchman vice-captain, he continued to be linked with a move to Spanish giants Real Madrid throughout the season.

The heart of the Barclaycard Premiership - 4thegame.com

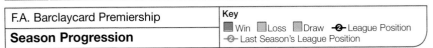

Arsenal

F.A. Barclaycard Premiership	Key
Season Progression	■ Win ■ Loss ■ Draw —❷— League Position —❷— Last Season's League Position

All Matches

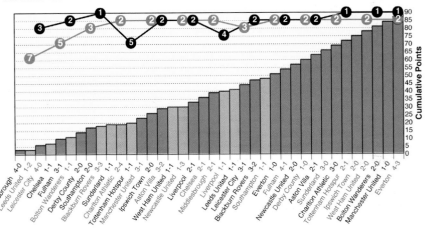

Home Matches

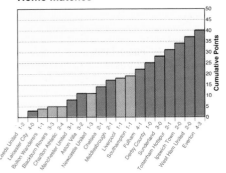

Away Matches

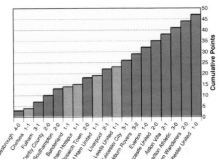

Chart Analysis

Arsenal's progress in the first half of the season was steady without being spectacular. Up until the New Year, they never fell below fifth, losing on just three occasions as they collected 30 points from their opening 17 matches.

Following the last of those games, a 3-1 home defeat to Newcastle in December, the Gunners went on a sensational unbeaten run that saw them storm to the title. Of 21 games played, 18 ended in victory, including a run of 13 consecutive wins between early February and May.

For the first time ever in the Premier League, Arsenal scored in every League fixture as well as not losing a game away from home all season.

BEST IN LEAGUE...
- **Longest unbeaten run overall, at home and away**
- **Most points away from home**
- **Longest scoring run overall, at home and joint away**

statistics powered by ◆ SUPERBASE™

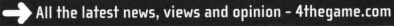

➡ All the latest news, views and opinion - 4thegame.com

> **"With an overwhelming majority of 34 in favour, the Club is delighted that Islington Council has given the go-ahead for the new stadium at Ashburton Grove."**
>
> *Arsenal Club Statement (December 2001)*

With the troops suitably reinforced, Arsenal started well, winning 4-0 at Middlesbrough, even if Ray Parlour was sent off. That result and the following game, the 2-1 home defeat by Leeds, immediately bucked the trend of the previous season when Arsenal had enjoyed the best home record but had managed only five away wins.

Wenger celebrated his fifth anniversary as manager with a 2-0 win over Derby. Despite the win, Martin Keown was sent off, a reminder of their poor disciplinary record. Even chairman Peter Hill-Wood criticised the number of cards collected by the Gunners.

Wenger had reason to feel better when, in December, permission was given for the club to go ahead with the £400m development of a new stadium at nearby Ashburton Grove. The news followed hot on the heels of the announcement that the manager had finally signed a new four-year deal worth £2m a year.

While results in the Champions League were satisfying, with home wins over Panathinaikos and Real Mallorca, in the League they fell behind, dropping seven points from a possible nine. Tony Adams and David Seaman, two of the 'old guard', as well as Campbell were all out injured.

November began uncomfortably on a Sunday afternoon, with a 4-2 home defeat by Charlton. For half-

It's a fact

When Arsenal won 2-0 at Southampton it was the first time since 1985 that their defence had been without any of the 'old guard' of Lee Dixon, Nigel Winterburn, Steve Bould, Tony Adams, Martin Keown or David Seaman.

F.A. Barclaycard Premiership
Half-Time/Full-Time Comparison

Key: ■ Win ■ Loss ■ Draw

Home				Away				Total			
Number of Home Half Time Wins	Full Time Result W	L	D	Number of Away Half Time Wins	Full Time Result W	L	D	Total number of Half Time Wins	Full Time Result W	L	D
6	4	1	1	12	11	-	1	18	15	1	2
Number of Home Half Time Losses	Full Time Result W	L	D	Number of Away Half Time Losses	Full Time Result W	L	D	Total number of Half Time Losses	Full Time Result W	L	D
6	4	1	1	-	-	-	-	6	4	1	1
Number of Home Half Time Draws	Full Time Result W	L	D	Number of Away Half Time Draws	Full Time Result W	L	D	Total number of Half Time Draws	Full Time Result W	L	D
7	4	1	2	7	3	-	4	14	7	1	6

Chart Analysis

statistics powered by ● SUPERBASE™

A clue to Arsenal's success can be found in the fact that they were strongest away from home where they never trailed at the interval. Of the 12 games they were leading at half-time on their travels, they held on to win 11.

At Highbury, they turned four out of six half-time defeats into full-time wins.

BEST IN LEAGUE...
- **Highest percentage of half-time deficits turned into wins overall and at home**

 Fixtures, results and match reports - 4thegame.com

F.A. Barclaycard Premiership Results Table

Key: 88 time of goal 88 time of assist ▲ player substituted ● player substituted ○ yellow card ● red card

DATE	H/A	OPPONENT	REFEREE	H/T	F/T	POS	Seaman	Lauren	Adams	Campbell	Cole	Ljungberg	Parlour	Vieira	Pires	Henry	Wiltord	SUBSTITUTES USED
18-08	H	Middlesbrough	G.P.Barber	1-1	4-0	2	Seaman	Lauren	Adams	Campbell	Cole 86 88	Ljungberg ▲	Parlour ●	Vieira	Pires 86 89	Henry ▲42	Wiltord ▲	Grimandi ▲, Bergkamp ▲88 89, Wiltord ▲
21-08	H	Leeds Utd	J.T.Winter	1-1	1-2	4	Seaman	Lauren	Adams	Campbell	Cole ○32	Ljungberg ▲	Parlour ▲	Vieira	Pires ●	Henry ●	Wiltord ○32	Bergkamp ●, Jeffers ○, Wiltord ▲32
25-08	H	Leicester City	A.P.D'Urso	2-0	4-0	3	Seaman	Lauren	Adams ▲	Campbell	Cole	Ljungberg ▲18	van Bronckhorst ▲	Vieira ●	Pires 16	Henry ▲16	Wiltord ▲28	Kanu ▲78 90, Bergkamp ▲, Henry ▲78 90
08-09	A	Chelsea	M.A.Riley	1-1	1-1	4	Seaman	Lauren ▲	Adams ▲	Keown	Cole ●	Wiltord ●	van Bronckhorst ● Grimandi	Vieira	Pires ◀	Henry ▲16 82	Bergkamp	Campbell ▲, Kanu ▲, Ljungberg ▲
15-09	H	Fulham	A.G.Wiley	1-0	3-1	1	Seaman	Lauren	Keown	Campbell	Cole	Ljungberg 16 82	Parlour ▲	Vieira	Pires ▲	Henry ▲16 82	Jeffers ▲	Bergkamp ▲90, Wiltord ▲90
22-09	H	Bolton	C.R.Wilkes	0-0	1-1	2	Seaman	Luzhny	Adams ▲	Grimandi ▲	Cole	Wiltord ▲	Parlour ●	Vieira ●	Pires ▲	Henry ●	Bergkamp	Pires ▲74, Jeffers ▲74
29-09	A	Derby County	R.Styles	1-0	2-0	1	Wright	Lauren	Keown ●	Upson	Cole	Ljungberg ▲	van Bronckhorst ▲	Vieira ○	Pires 5	Henry ▲21 62	Jeffers ▲21	Kanu ▲62, Luzhny ▲, Grimandi ▲
13-10	A	Southampton	G.P.Barber	1-0	2-0	2	Wright	Lauren	Keown ▲	Upson	Cole	Ljungberg ▲73	van Bronckhorst ▲	Vieira ○	Pires 5	Henry 73	Wiltord ▲5	Kanu ▲62, Bergkamp ▲, Grimandi ▲
20-10	H	Blackburn	U.D.Rennie	0-1	3-3	1	Wright	Lauren	Keown	Grimandi	Upson	Parlour	Parlour ▲	Vieira ●	Pires 48 52	Henry 79	Bergkamp 48 52	Kanu ▲40, Wiltord ▲79
27-10	A	Sunderland	M.A.Riley	1-0	1-1	3	Wright	Lauren	Keown	Campbell	Upson	Ljungberg	Parlour ▲	Vieira ○	van Bronckhorst ▲	Wiltord ▲40	Kanu ▲40	Kanu ▲40, Henry ▲
04-11	H	Charlton	M.R.Halsey	1-2	2-4	5	Wright	Lauren	Keown	Grimandi	Cole ▲	Ljungberg	van Bronckhorst	Vieira ○	Pires 6	Henry 6 60	Bergkamp	Wiltord ▲
17-11	A	Tottenham	J.T.Winter	0-0	1-1	5	Wright	Lauren	Keown	Campbell	Cole ◀	Parlour	Grimandi ▲	Vieira	Pires 81	Wiltord 81	Kanu ▲	Kanu ▲
25-11	H	Manchester Utd	P.Jones	0-1	3-1	3	Taylor	Upson ○	Keown	Cole	Cole	Ljungberg ●48	Parlour	Vieira 85	Pires ▲48	Henry 80 85	Bergkamp ▲	Bergkamp ▲, Grimandi ▲
01-12	A	Ipswich Town	D.R.Elleray	1-0	2-0	2	Taylor	Upson	Keown	Campbell	Cole	Ljungberg ▲56	Parlour	Vieira ▲	Pires ▲56	Henry 5 56	Kanu ▲	Edu ▲, van Bronckhorst ▲
09-12	A	Aston Villa	A.G.Wiley	0-2	3-2	2	Taylor	Luzhny ▲	Keown	Campbell	Cole	Ljungberg 47	Parlour 47	Vieira ○72	Pires 90	Henry ▲72 90	Bergkamp	Keown ▲, Wiltord ▲47
15-12	A	West Ham Utd	M.A.Riley	1-1	1-1	4	Taylor	Lauren	Keown	Campbell	Cole 37	Wiltord ▲	Grimandi	Vieira ○72	Pires ▲	Henry 37	Bergkamp	Edu ▲, Kanu ▲
18-12	H	Newcastle Utd	G.Poll	1-0	1-3	3	Taylor	Lauren	Keown	Campbell	Cole 20	Wiltord 40	Parlour ●	Vieira	Pires 20	Henry ●	Kanu	Kanu ▲
23-12	A	Liverpool	P.A.Durkin	1-0	2-1	2	Taylor	Lauren	Keown ▲	Campbell	Cole	Ljungberg 45 53	Parlour ▲	van Bronckhorst ●	Pires ▲53	Henry ▲45	Bergkamp ▲	Wiltord ▲, Upson ▲
26-12	H	Chelsea	G.P.Barber	0-1	2-1	2	Taylor	Lauren	Keown ○	Campbell 49	Cole	Ljungberg ▲	Parlour ▲	Vieira ●	Pires 49	Henry ●	Edu ▲	Bergkamp ▲, Wiltord ▲70
29-12	H	Middlesbrough	A.P.D'Urso	1-2	2-1	1	Taylor	Lauren	Keown ●	Campbell	Cole ●79	Ljungberg 62	Parlour	Vieira	Pires 56	Henry ▲72 90	Kanu ▲	Keown ▲, Bergkamp ▲79
13-01	H	Liverpool	S.W.Dunn	0-0	1-1	4	Taylor	Luzhny ▲	Keown	Campbell	Upson	Ljungberg 62	Grimandi	Vieira ●	Pires 62	Henry ●	Bergkamp ▲	Dixon ▲, Wiltord ▲
20-01	A	Leeds Utd	M.R.Halsey	1-1	1-1	4	Wright	Luzhny 32	Keown	Campbell	Cole	M.R.Halsey	Parlour	Vieira ●	Pires 45	Henry ▲45	Bergkamp ▲45	Wiltord ▲, van Bronckhorst ▲
23-01	A	Leicester City	D.R.Elleray	2-0	3-1	2	Wright	Luzhny ●	Keown ●	Campbell	Cole	Parlour ▲	van Bronckhorst ▲23	Vieira	Pires ▲20 74	Henry 42	Bergkamp ▲20	Grimandi ▲, Wiltord ▲90
30-01	A	Blackburn	D.J.Gallagher	2-2	3-2	2	Wright	Luzhny ●	Keown ▲	Campbell	Cole	Wiltord 40	Parlour	Vieira	Pires	Henry 20 74	Bergkamp 13 74	Upson ▲, van Bronckhorst ▲
02-02	A	Southampton	C.R.Wilkes	1-0	1-1	3	Wright	Lauren	Upson	Campbell	Cole ▲	Wiltord 40	Parlour	van Bronckhorst ▲	Pires	Henry ●	Bergkamp ▲40	Edu ●, van Bronckhorst ▲
10-02	H	Everton	J.T.Winter	0-0	1-0	2	Wright	Luzhny	Stepanovs	Campbell ●	Upson ▲	Parlour	Grimandi	Vieira 62	Pires	van Bronckhorst	Wiltord 62	Dixon ▲
23-02	H	Fulham	U.D.Rennie	3-1	4-1	2	Seaman	Luzhny	Stepanovs	Campbell	van Bronckhorst ▲	Lauren 5 59	Parlour	Vieira 15	Pires 11	Henry ▲15 39	Wiltord 5 39	Grimandi ▲, Aliadiere ▲
02-03	H	Newcastle Utd	N.S.Barry	2-0	2-0	2	Seaman	Dixon	Stepanovs 41	Campbell 41	Luzhny	Lauren	Grimandi	Vieira 15	Pires 11	Wiltord	Bergkamp ▲11 41	Edu ▲
05-03	A	Derby County	G.P.Barber	0-0	1-0	1	Seaman	Luzhny ▲	Stepanovs	Campbell	Lauren	Wiltord	Parlour ●	Vieira	Pires 69	Henry 69	Bergkamp 69	Dixon ▲
17-03	A	Aston Villa	S.W.Dunn	0-0	2-1	2	Seaman	Luzhny ▲	Adams	Campbell	Lauren	Ljungberg ▲61	Parlour ●	Vieira 15	Pires 61	Henry 61	Bergkamp ▲4 30	Kanu ▲, Grimandi ▲
30-03	H	Sunderland	P.A.Durkin	3-0	3-0	3	Seaman	Luzhny	Adams	Campbell	Lauren	Ljungberg ▲30	Edu	Vieira 2	Ljungberg 2	Henry 4	Bergkamp ▲4 30	Jeffers ▲30, Dixon ▲
01-04	A	Charlton	A.P.D'Urso	3-0	3-0	1	Seaman	Dixon	Keown	Campbell 16	Lauren	Wiltord 25	Edu	Vieira	Ljungberg 20	Henry 16 25	Bergkamp ▲20	Kanu ▲, Luzhny ▲
06-04	H	Tottenham	M.R.Halsey	1-0	2-1	1	Seaman	Luzhny	Adams	Campbell	Lauren 86	Edu ▲	Parlour	Vieira ●	Ljungberg 25	Henry 86	Bergkamp ▲25	Pires ▲, Dixon ▲
21-04	A	Ipswich Town	A.G.Wiley	0-0	2-0	1	Seaman	Lauren	Adams	Keown 69	Cole	Parlour ▲	Parlour	Vieira	Ljungberg 69 78	Henry ▲77 80	Bergkamp 78	Grimandi ▲78, Kanu ▲
24-04	H	West Ham Utd	S.W.Dunn	0-0	2-0	1	Seaman	Lauren	Adams	Campbell	Cole	Wiltord 40	Parlour	Vieira	Ljungberg 36	Henry ▲77 80	Bergkamp ▲36 44	Grimandi ▲, Kanu ▲80
29-04	A	Bolton	D.J.Gallagher	2-0	2-0	1	Seaman	Lauren	Adams	Keown	Cole	Edu ▲	Parlour	Vieira	Ljungberg 56	Wiltord 56	Bergkamp ▲36 44 83	Campbell ▲, Dixon ▲
08-05	A	Manchester Utd	P.A.Durkin	0-1	1-0	1	Seaman	Lauren	Luzhny	Keown	Campbell	Parlour	Edu	Vieira	Ljungberg 56	Kanu ▲	Wiltord 33 72 83	Kanu ▲
11-05	H	Everton	M.R.Halsey	2-2	4-3	1	Wright ▲	Dixon	Luzhny	Stepanovs	Cole 4	Wiltord ▲	Parlour ▲	Grimandi	Edu 72	Henry 33 72 83	Taylor ▲	Jeffers ▲83, Vieira ▲

F.A. Barclaycard Premiership
Squad List

Position	Name	Appearances	Appearances as Substitute	Goals or Clean Sheets	Goal Assists	Yellow Cards	Red Cards
G	D.Seaman	17		10			
G	S.Taylor	9	1	1	1		
G	R.Wright	12		3			
D	T.Adams	10				1	
D	S.Campbell	29	2	2	1	2	
D	A.Cole	29		2	5	6	
D	L.Dixon	3	10				
D	M.Keown	21	1		1	4	1
D	Lauren	27		2	1	8	
D	O.Luzhny	15	3		1	3	1
D	I.Stepanovs	6			1		
D	M.Upson	10	4			2	
M	Edu	8	6	1	1	3	
M	G.Grimandi	11	15		1	2	
M	F.Ljungberg	24	1	12	7	4	
M	R.Parlour	25	2		1	5	2
M	R.Pires	27	1	9	16	6	
M	G.van B'horst	13	8	1		4	1
M	P.Vieira	35	1	2	4	10	1
F	J.Aliadiere		1				
F	D.Bergkamp	22	11	9	13	2	
F	T.Henry	31	2	24	9	4	
F	F.Jeffers	2	4	2	1	1	
F	N.Kanu	9	14	3	2	2	
F	S.Wiltord	23	10	10	9		

an-hour Arsenal bombarded the Charlton goal yet had only Henry's early strike to show for their efforts. The Addicks replied and then an own goal from new goalkeeper Wright put the visitors ahead. Charlton went 3-1 up before half-time and then Jason Euell scored the visitors' fourth.

Following a visit to North London rivals Spurs which marked the return of Sol Campbell to his former club, Arsenal then faced Manchester United with Seaman, Adams and Keown all absent. In addition, Wright had been hurt against Deportivo La Coruna, meaning third choice goalkeeper Stuart Taylor, three days short of his 21st birthday, was given his F.A. Barclaycard Premiership debut.

Taylor's last League outing had been while on loan to Division Two Peterborough United, when he had conceded five goals at Port Vale, but he did not disappoint. Instead, World Cup winner Fabien Barthez was left red-faced, allowing Arsenal to secure a 3-1 win.

Paul Scholes had given United a first half lead but Freddie Ljungberg's equaliser was followed by two comical goals in the final nine minutes. Firstly, Henry rolled the ball home after Barthez had struck it straight at him. Then, with five minutes left, Henry was the beneficiary again when Barthez failed to reach Silvestre's back-pass.

December saw Arsenal ease into second spot with a 2-0 win at Ipswich, despite Sylvain Wiltord joining the growing list of walking wounded. Ljungberg and Henry, with his 18th goal in 19 appearances, secured the win. That was followed by a 3-2 win over Villa, the Gunners coming back from a two-goal deficit. Villa had netted twice in the opening 34 minutes but the returning Wiltord responded and then two more goals from Henry, in the final 17 minutes – including a very late winner –

F.A. Barclaycard Premiership
Top Goal Scorer

Thierry Henry

Total Premier League Goals Scored:	Percentage Of The Team's League Goals:
24	**30%**

Goals Scored From

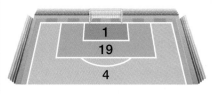

1
19
4

For the third season in succession, Henry finished as the Gunners' top marksman despite competition from Dennis Bergkamp and Sylvain Wiltord. The flying Frenchman continued to burgeon under Arsene Wenger, adding a further seven goals to his tally in Europe despite successive penalty misses in the Champions League against Deportivo La Coruna and Juventus. With a goal in the F.A. Cup, Henry took his tally to 32, six more than the 26 he claimed two seasons earlier, and ten more than last term. The only disappointment was a three-match ban following a bust-up with referee Graham Poll in the December loss to Newcastle United.

"Thierry is good, strong and level-headed and I think that the best is still to come from him."

Patrick Vieira

Goals Resulting From
Key
Open Play Corner Indirect Free Kick
Direct Free Kick Penalty

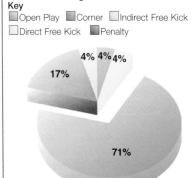

4% 4% 4%
17%
71%

	Right Foot	Left Foot	Header
Open Play	11	6	-
Set Piece	7	-	-

Goal Assists

Total number of goal assists	9

Teams Scored Against

Against	Home	Away
Charlton Athletic	2	2
Fulham	2	1
Aston Villa	2	0
Blackburn Rovers	1	1
Derby County	0	2
Everton	2	0
Leicester City	1	1
Manchester United	2	0
Chelsea	0	1
Ipswich Town	0	1
Liverpool	0	1
Middlesbrough	0	1
Southampton	0	1
Total goals scored	**12**	**12**

It's a fact

When Sylvain Wiltord scored in the 1-1 draw against Southampton in February, Arsenal broke Liverpool's Premier League record of scoring in 25 consecutive games.

"If it had been 11 v 11 we would have won this game comfortably...We lost a lot of energy when we were playing with ten men."

Arsene Wenger
post Newcastle
(December 2001)

secured a memorable victory.

Arsenal were showing a resilience which offered promising signs. However, just when they appeared to be in control of their own destiny, they responded with disappointments.

In mid-December, they drew at West Ham and followed that with a home defeat by Newcastle. Parlour was sent off again, in the first half, as the Gunners threw away a lead courtesy of Robert Pires' goal. Newcastle, who had gone 29 games without winning in London, won with goals from Andy O'Brien, Alan Shearer and Laurent Robert in the final half-hour. Craig Bellamy's dismissal did little to dent Newcastle's celebrations, particularly as the result took them to the top of the table.

Arsenal responded well, finishing 2001 with three victories, beginning with a defining moment, the 2-1 win at Anfield, a result secured despite the dismissal of van Bronckhorst. With Christmas Day just around the corner, they took the lead through Thierry Henry. Ljungberg made it two just after the break, before Jari Litmanen pulled one back for the home side. The win took Arsenal back into second and, on Boxing Day, they came from behind to beat

---

F.A. Barclaycard Premiership
Goals By Position

Key
Forward ■ Midfield ◼②◼ League Position
Defence ■ Goalkeeper

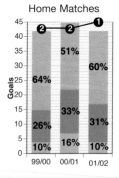
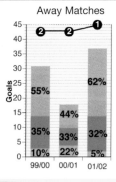
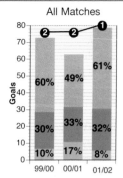

Chart Analysis

statistics powered by ◆ SUPERBASE™

Arsenal scored more goals than in either of the last two seasons when they finished second. Away from home, they scored 37, more than double last season's total of 18, while at home they scored less. The percentage of goals contributed by forwards rose, whilst that of the defence fell.

BEST IN LEAGUE...
• **Most goals scored by strikers overall and away from home**

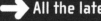 **All the latest news, views and opinion - 4thegame.com**

Chelsea at Highbury.

The 2-1 home win over Middlesbrough, courtesy of a late Ashley Cole winner, saw Arsenal come from behind again to enter the New Year perched atop the F.A. Barclaycard Premiership.

One fear for the Gunners was that impending suspensions might stretch Wenger's squad. For the visit of Liverpool just three weeks after the Anfield success, both Cole and Parlour were banned. With United top, this was a good chance to keep in sight of the leaders; instead they drew.

Henry scored again as Arsenal walked to an easy 3-1 win at Leicester and, having knocked Liverpool out of the F.A. Cup with nine men, won 3-2 at Blackburn. Arsenal also matched Liverpool's achievement of netting in 25 consecutive games.

The pool of striking talent at the Gunners' disposal was becoming the envy of the F.A. Barclaycard Premiership: Henry, Wiltord and Bergkamp were all scoring, and in some style.

They beat Liverpool's record in the next game, Wiltord scoring against Southampton, but it was not enough to prevent Arsenal dropping to fourth, three points behind leaders United.

After a memorable 4-1 win over Leverkusen in the Champions League the Gunners went to Newcastle seeking

F.A. Barclaycard Premiership
Team Performance Table

League Position	Team	Points Won From A Possible Six	Percentage Of Points Won At Home	Percentage Of Points Won Away	Overall Percentage Of Points Won
1	Arsenal	87			
2	Liverpool	4/6			
3	Manchester Utd	6/6	33%	83%	58%
4	Newcastle Utd	3/6			
5	Leeds United	1/6			
6	Chelsea	4/6			
7	West Ham Utd	4/6			
8	Aston Villa	6/6	87%	60%	73%
9	Tottenham H	4/6			
10	Blackburn R	4/6			
11	Southampton	4/6			
12	Middlesbrough	6/6			
13	Fulham	6/6	67%	100%	83%
14	Charlton Athletic	3/6			
15	Everton	6/6			
16	Bolton W	4/6			
17	Sunderland	4/6			
18	Ipswich Town	6/6	87%	87%	87%
19	Derby County	6/6			
20	Leicester City	6/6			

The table shows how many points out of a possible six Arsenal have taken off each of the teams in the four sections. The other columns show as a percentage how many points they have taken from those available.

Chart Analysis

statistics powered by SUPERBASE™

The Champions were one of only a few sides to take at least one point off every other team in the F.A. Barclaycard Premiership.

While they struggled at home against the other sides in the top five, they were clinical in seeing off teams in the bottom half of the table.

Their form away from home was exemplary as they powered their way to the title.

Leeds Utd were the only team to deny them a win in either of their two fixtures as Arsenal notched eight 'doubles', most notably against Manchester United.

It is interesting to note, though perhaps not surprising, that their overall percentage of points won rises steadily down the table.

Fixtures, results and match reports - 4thegame.com

> **"United will drop points. I've said that many times. They are winning easily against the teams down at the bottom but they are the team that has struggled most against the big sides."**
>
> *Arsene Wenger*
> *(February 2001)*

revenge and found it, winning 2-0 and achieving the important victory without Henry, who had a stomach strain. Bergkamp's goal of the season helped secure this massive win. They added another when struggling Derby were the visitors, although Arsenal had to wait until the 69th minute before Pires claimed the goal that fired his team two points clear of Manchester United.

Arsenal were on a roll. A fifth straight win in the F.A. Barclaycard Premiership was achieved at Villa and, though their Champions League aspirations had ended, they reached the F.A. Cup semi-final by beating Newcastle, in a replay. The Gunners were stunned when, in that game, Pires injured his knee and was ruled out for not only the rest of the season but France's World Cup campaign.

They were no fools at Charlton on 1 April, winning 3-0 and, when Spurs visited Highbury, Arsenal gained delight in winning again, albeit in tense and nervous circumstances. Arsenal led through Ljungberg but when referee Mark Halsey awarded Spurs a penalty, converted by Sheringham, hopes of a win seemed slim. Then, with four minutes left, Henry was fouled in the box and Lauren converted the spot-kick.

Arsenal reached the F.A. Cup final thanks to Gianluca Festa's own goal in the semi-final against Middlesbrough at

F.A. Barclaycard Premiership
Goals By Time Period

Key ■ Goals Scored ■ Goals Conceded

Home Matches

Time of Goal (mins)	Goals Scored	Goals Conceded
0-15	6	2
16-30	5	4
31-45	4	6
46-60	8	5
61-75	7	1
76-90	12	7

Away Matches

Time of Goal (mins)	Goals Scored	Goals Conceded
0-15	5	1
16-30	7	2
31-45	10	2
46-60	3	3
61-75	5	2
76-90	7	1

All Matches

Time of Goal (mins)	Goals Scored	Goals Conceded
0-15	11	3
16-30	12	6
31-45	14	8
46-60	11	8
61-75	12	3
76-90	19	8

Chart Analysis

statistics powered by ◆ SUPERBASE™

Arsenal were consistent scorers throughout games, with most goals coming in the last 15 minutes. The majority of goals at Highbury were scored in the second half of games. Away from home the opposite was true with most goals coming in the first half. Nearly half of the goals conceded came in the 15 minute intervals either side of half-time.

BEST IN LEAGUE...
• Joint most goals scored 16-30 and 76-90 minutes

 Fixtures, results and match reports - 4thegame.com

F.A. Barclaycard Premiership
Goals Resulting From

Key
☐ Goals Scored ☐ Goals Conceded

	Six Yard Area				Inside Area				Outside Area				Total			
	Shots		Headers		Shots		Headers		Shots		Headers		Shots		Headers	
	Home	Away	Home	Away	Home	Away	Home	Away	Home	Away	Home	Away	Home	Away	Home	Away
Open Play	6	4	2	-	23	20	1	1	2	4	-	-	31	28	3	1
	-	-	1	2	11	4	-	1	5	1	-	-	16	5	1	3
Direct Free Kick									-	1			0	1		
									1	-			1	0		
Indirect Free Kick	-	-	-	-	1	2	-	1	1	-	-	-	2	2	0	1
	-	-	-	-	1	-	2	-	-	-	-	-	1	0	2	0
Penalty	-	-	-	-	2	4	-	-	-	-	-	-	2	4	0	0
	-	-	-	-	2	1	-	-	-	-	-	-	2	1	0	0
Corner	1	-	1	-	1	-	1	-	-	-	-	-	2	0	2	0
	-	-	1	1	-	-	-	-	-	-	-	-	0	0	1	2
Totals	7	4	3	0	27	26	2	2	3	5	0	0	37	35	5	2
	0	0	2	3	14	5	2	2	6	1	0	0	20	6	4	5

How Goals Were Scored
Home & Away Matches

1% 8% 5% 6%
80%

Key
☐ Open Play
☐ Corner
☐ Indirect Free Kick
☐ Direct Free Kick
☐ Penalty

Charts do not include 1 own goal against.

How Goals Were Conceded
Home & Away Matches

3% 9% 9% 9%
71%

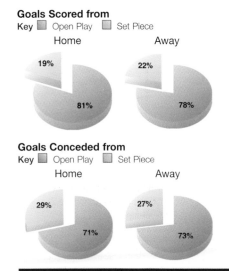

Goals Scored from
Key ☐ Open Play ☐ Set Piece

Home
19%
81%

Away
22%
78%

Goals Conceded from
Key ☐ Open Play ☐ Set Piece

Home
29%
71%

Away
27%
73%

Chart Analysis

Arsenal's scoring overall was pretty consistent, with almost identical splits for goals from Open Play and Set Pieces at home and away.

They managed just one goal from a Direct Free Kick, through Thierry Henry at Derby, while they conceded equal amounts from Penalties, Corners and Indirect Free Kicks.

BEST IN LEAGUE…
- Most goals scored from Open Play at home
- Most goals scored from Penalties overall and away

statistics powered by ◆ SUPERBASE™

 Win Barclaycard Premiership tickets - 4thegame.com

> **"We are going to miss him a lot – and we will try and win something for him. I was shocked about this news, it is very hard."**
>
> *Thierry Henry on Robert Pires (March 2002)*

It's a fact

Arsenal were the first team to reach 50 League cautions, with Ashley Cole and Robert Pires receiving bookings at Leeds in January.

Old Trafford. Pires was named the Football Writers' Asscociation Footballer of the Year, a fitting tribute for the injured but brilliant Frenchman.

On the pitch, Arsenal faced Ipswich and for 68 minutes the Gunners were stuck before Ljungberg, in a rich vein of form, struck twice. The Swede netted again late on against West Ham – Kanu added a second – to take Arsenal four points clear with two games to play.

Liverpool's defeat at Tottenham prompted the bookmakers to pronounce that Arsenal were now favourites to win the F.A. Barclaycard Premiership.

Just five days before the F.A. Cup final, they went to Bolton and won 2-0 with first half goals from Ljungberg – his sixth in five games – and Wiltord helping the Gunners to put one hand on the F.A. Barclaycard Premiership trophy. It was Arsenal's 11th straight win in the competition, a club record, and left them needing one point from the final two games to clinch the title.

The Gunners began May by completing the first leg of the Double, goals from Parlour and Ljungberg accounting for Chelsea 2-0 in the F.A. Cup final. Four days later, they went to Old Trafford – and left with the title, thanks to another vital goal from Wiltord – before returning to Highbury for a celebratory 4-3 win over Everton.

F.A. Barclaycard Premiership
Shot Efficiency

Key
■ Goals Scored   ■ Other Shots On Target

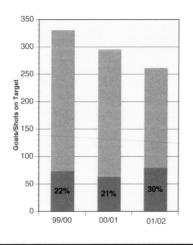

Season	Division	Shots Off Target	Shots On Target	Total Goals
1999-2000	P	n/a	330	73
2000-2001	P	n/a	295	63
2001-2002	P	239	261	79

Chart Analysis

Arsenal scored nearly a third of their efforts on target, up considerably on each of the two previous seasons. They managed it despite registering significantly less Shots On Target.

BEST IN LEAGUE...
• **Most Shots On Target**

statistics powered by **SUPERBASE**™

➡ The heart of the Barclaycard Premiership - 4thegame.com

F.A. Barclaycard Premiership	Key	
Team Discipline	■ Forward ■ Midfield	
	□ Defence ■ Goalkeeper	

Total Number Of Bookings

Total number of red cards	6
Total number of yellow cards	71

Referee Performance

Referee	Games Refereed	Red Cards	Yellow Cards
M.A.Riley	3	-	11
J.T.Winter	3	-	10
A.G.Wiley	3	-	9

Type of Yellow Cards Received

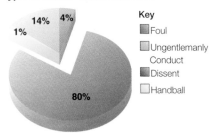

Key

■ Foul
□ Ungentlemanly Conduct
■ Dissent
□ Handball

14% 4% 1% 80%

Bookings by Position 1999/2000 - 2001/2002

Home Matches

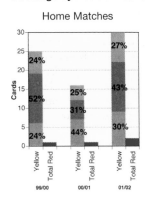

Away Matches

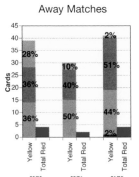

All Matches

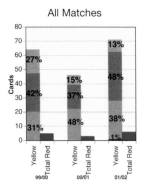

Chart Analysis

Arsenal collected more cards of both colours than in either of the two previous seasons. Midfielders were the chief offenders as they had been two seasons ago.

In goal, rookie keeper Stuart Taylor became the first Arsenal stopper to pick up a booking in the last three seasons.

All six Red Cards received by Arsenal were for second bookable offences. Although the reds were brandished by six different referees, most disciplinary points were incurred when Messrs Riley, Winter and Wiley were officiating.

WORST IN LEAGUE...
• Joint most Red Cards away from home

"What is rarely mentioned is that we have improved a lot in the past three or four months. I believe we have mastered the nervous situations in the games much better."
Arsene Wenger
(May 2002)

statistics powered by ◆ SUPERBASE™

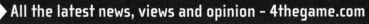

→ All the latest news, views and opinion - 4thegame.com

Aston Villa

F.A. Barclaycard Premiership Final standing for the 2001-2002 season

Final Position		Games Played	Games Won	Games Drawn	Games Lost	Goals For	Goals Against	Total Points
7	West Ham United	38	15	8	15	48	57	53
8	Aston Villa	38	12	14	12	46	47	50
9	Tottenham Hotspur	38	14	8	16	49	53	50

> "We've got to want the League and we've got to act like that but we've got to do it within the range of our income. Now it's about the next step. But the next step just doesn't mean throwing money everywhere."
>
> *Graham Taylor (February 2002)*

Club Honours and Records

Football League Champions: 1893-94, 1895-96, 1896-97, 1898-1899, 1899-1900, 1909-1910, 1980-81

Division 2 Champions: 1937-38, 1959-60

Division 3 Champions: 1971-72

FA Cup Winners: 1887, 1895, 1897, 1905, 1913, 1920, 1957,

League Cup Winners: 1961, 1975, 1977, 1994, 1996

European Cup Winners: 1981-82

European Super Cup Winners: 1982-83

Record victory: 13-0 v Wednesbury Old Athletic, FA Cup 1st Round, 30 October, 1886

Record defeat: 1-8 v Blackburn Rovers, FA Cup 3rd Round, 16 February, 1889

League goals in a season (team):
128, Division 1, 1930-31

League goals in a season (player):
49, Tom Waring, Division 1, 1930-31

Career league goals: 215, Harry Hampton, 1904 to 1920; 215, Billy Walter, 1919 to 1934

League appearances:
561, Charlie Aitken, 1961 to 1976

Reported Transfer fee paid: £9,500,000 to River Plate for Juan Pablo Angel, January 2001

Reported Transfer fee received: £12,600,000 from Manchester United for Dwight Yorke, August 1998

IT was a disappointing season for Aston Villa, who finished with a place in the Intertoto Cup. Villa were seventh when John Gregory walked out in January; they finished only marginally worse, in eighth, under Graham Taylor and will expect much more this term.

The shock arrival of Peter Schmeichel in the summer gave Villa a pre-season boost; the former Manchester United goalkeeper could not resist the lure of the F.A. Barclaycard Premiership and agreed to join new signings Bosko Balaban, Moustapha Hadji, Olof Mellberg and Hassan Kachloul.

Off the pitch, and throughout the first half of the season, a split between chairman Doug Ellis and manager John Gregory was simmering as the £15m that had allegedly been promised for new players failed to materialise

On the field, the early signs were encouraging. Villa started with a seven-game unbeaten run, their best opening sequence for three years. It included the visit of Manchester United on what could have been a perfect day for Schmeichel; Darius Vassell offered early signs of things to come with a goal after just four minutes and Villa held strong for most of the game until an own goal by Alpay in the final

 Fixtures, results and match reports - 4thegame.com

Aston Villa

Key
■ Win ■ Loss ■ Draw —❷— League Position
—❷— Last Season's League Position

All Matches

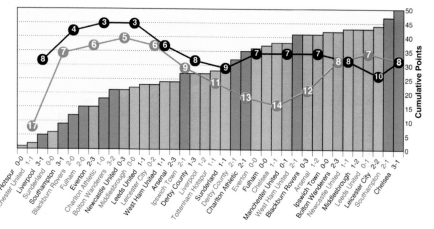

Home Matches

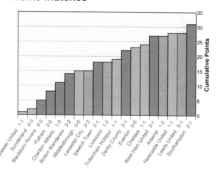

Away Matches

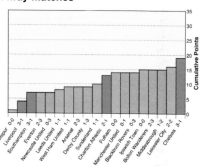

Chart Analysis

A fine start to the season which left Villa with 21 points from a possible 30 gave way to a run of just one win in 11 that saw them slide to mid-table by the turn of the year.

Following John Gregory's departure in January after the win at Charlton, Graham Taylor was installed as manager for the visit of Chelsea in February.

Once in charge, the new gaffer presided over an initial sequence of one win in eleven games, including a run of eight matches without a victory.

A disappointing finish in eighth place had much to do with a miserable away sequence which saw them pick up a measly four wins on the road all season.

statistics powered by ◆ SUPERBASE™

 Win Barclaycard Premiership tickets – 4thegame.com

> **"Everything is fine at the moment but December, January and February is a cold time for an old body and you don't know what's around the corner."**
>
> *Peter Schmeichel*
> *(October 2001)*

It's a fact

Villa scored just 22 goals in 19 home games, their lowest return in the Premier League.

minute earned United a lucky point.

Villa continued their impressive start with a stunning 3-1 win at Anfield. They failed to repeat that heady performance at home to Sunderland and had to make do with a goalless draw.

The Villans returned to form with three straight wins, at Southampton, and at home to Blackburn and Fulham. With seven goals scored – Vassell and Angel had netted two apiece – and only one conceded, John Gregory's men were setting out their stall. Villa even had Dublin sent off at Southampton, who had Rory Delap dismissed. Dublin's red card was later rescinded. The forward pairing of Vassell and Angel eased Villa into fourth place with a 2-0 win over Blackburn and Ian Taylor – in his first appearance of the season – and Vassell secured a similar score against Fulham.

The Midlanders were beginning to consider themselves as serious title challengers and Gregory was named September manager of the month.

Their first defeat of the season, in October, was a surprise 3-2 loss at Everton. Villa were 3-0 down after an hour but Hadji offered some hope. When Schmeichel raced up field to smash a tremendous volley beyond Paul Gerrard, the goalkeeper's real worth to Villa was

F.A. Barclaycard Premiership
Half-Time/Full-Time Comparison

Key: ■ Win ■ Loss ■ Draw

Home				Away				Total			
Number of Home Half Time Wins	Full Time Result W L D			Number of Away Half Time Wins	Full Time Result W L D			Total number of Half Time Wins	Full Time Result W L D		
6	4	-	2	7	4	1	2	13	8	1	4
Number of Home Half Time Losses	Full Time Result W L D			Number of Away Half Time Losses	Full Time Result W L D			Total number of Half Time Losses	Full Time Result W L D		
4	-	3	1	4	-	4	-	8	-	7	1
Number of Home Half Time Draws	Full Time Result W L D			Number of Away Half Time Draws	Full Time Result W L D			Total number of Half Time Draws	Full Time Result W L D		
9	4	1	4	8	-	3	5	17	4	4	9

Chart Analysis

statistics powered by SUPERBASE™

The Villans were strongest at home, where four out of nine half-time draws were turned into wins. However, they did conspire to drop points when two games they were leading at half-time finished as draws.

Away from home, Villa had to be in the lead at half-time to stand any chance of winning the game. Similarly, all four matches in which Villa trailed at the break ended in defeat.

The heart of the Barclaycard Premiership – 4thegame.com

key: 88=time of goal 88=time of... ▲=player substituted ▲=player substituted ▲=yellow card ●=red card

SUBSTITUTES USED

DATE	H/A	OPPONENT	H/T	F/T	POS	REFEREE	TEAM											SUBSTITUTES USED		
18-08	H	Tottenham	0-0	0-0	8	D.J.Gallagher	Schmeichel	Delaney	Mellberg	Alpay	Wright	Merson ▲	Hendrie	Boateng	Kachloul	Angel ▲	Vassell ▲	Hadji ▲	Stone ▲	Ginola ▲
26-08	A	Manchester Utd	1-0	1-1	15	G.P.Barber	Schmeichel	Delaney	Mellberg	Alpay	Wright	Merson ▲	Hendrie	Boateng	Kachloul	Angel ▲	Vassell 4	Hadji ▲	Balaban ▲	
08-09	A	Liverpool	3-1	0-0	8	A.P.D'Urso	Schmeichel	Delaney	Mellberg ○86	Alpay	Wright	Merson ▲31	Hendrie ▲55	Boateng	Kachloul	Dublin 31:55	Vassell 86	Hadji ▲	Staunton ▲	
16-09	H	Sunderland	0-0	0-0	9	U.D.Rennie	Schmeichel	Delaney	Mellberg	Alpay	Wright	Merson 79	Hendrie	Boateng	Kachloul	Dublin	Vassell	Ginola ▲	Balaban ▲	
24-09	A	Southampton	2-1	3-1	5	S.W.Dunn	Schmeichel	Stone	Staunton	Alpay	Wright	Hadji 79	Hendrie ▲79	Boateng 9	Kachloul ▲	Angel ▲15	Dublin ●9:15	Stone ▲	Staunton ▲	Balaban ▲
30-09	H	Blackburn	0-0	2-0	4	M.R.Halsey	Schmeichel	Stone	Staunton	Alpay	Wright	Hadji ○50	Hendrie 46:72	Boateng	Kachloul ○	Angel ▲46:72	Vassell 50	Staunton ▲	Dublin ▲	Balaban ▲
14-10	A	Fulham	0-0	2-0	4	P.A.Durkin	Schmeichel	Stone	Staunton	Alpay	Wright	Hadji ○50	Hendrie	Boateng	Kachloul	Angel ▲61	Vassell 50	Taylor ▲61	Dublin ▲	Balaban ▲
20-10	A	Everton	0-1	2-3	5	R.Styles	Schmeichel 90	Delaney	Staunton	Alpay	Wright 68	Hadji 68	Taylor	Boateng	Hendrie	Angel ▲	Vassell 90	Ginola ▲	Samuel ▲	Dublin ▲
24-10	H	Charlton	1-0	1-0	3	D.Pugh	Schmeichel	Delaney	Staunton	Alpay	Wright	Hadji	Hendrie ▲	Boateng	Kachloul 9	Dublin	Vassell 9	Taylor ▲	Samuel ▲	
27-10	H	Bolton	2-1	3-2	1	E.K.Wolstenholme	Schmeichel	Delaney	Staunton 12	Alpay	Wright	Hadji 46	Hendrie ▲	Boateng	Kachloul ○	Angel ▲12:42:46	Vassell ▲42	Merson ▲	Taylor ▲	Dublin ▲
03-11	A	Newcastle Utd	0-1	0-3	1	C.R.Wilkes	Schmeichel	Delaney ▲	Staunton	Alpay	Wright	Hadji 46	Hendrie ▲	Boateng	Kachloul	Angel ▲	Vassell	Ginola ▲	Taylor ▲	Dublin ▲
17-11	H	Middlesbrough	0-0	0-0	3	P.Jones	Schmeichel	Delaney ▲	Mellberg	Alpay	Wright	Stone	Hendrie ▲	Boateng	Kachloul	Angel ▲	Vassell	Ginola ▲	Taylor ▲	Dublin ▲
25-11	A	Leeds Utd	1-1	1-1	5	N.S.Barry	Schmeichel	Stone	Mellberg 35	Alpay	Wright	Merson 35	Hendrie ▲	Boateng	Kachloul 35	Angel ▲	Vassell	Taylor ▲	Dublin ▲	Ginola ▲
01-12	H	Leicester City	0-1	0-2	6	S.G.Bennett	Schmeichel	Delaney ▲	Mellberg	Alpay	Wright	Stone ▲	Hendrie	Boateng	Merson	Angel	Vassell ▲	Dublin ●▲	Ginola ●▲	Staunton ▲
05-12	A	West Ham Utd	1-1	1-1	6	M.L.Dean	Enckelman	Delaney ▲	Mellberg	Staunton	Wright	Stone 1	Hendrie	Boateng	Barry ▲	Merson 1	Dublin 1	Vassell ▲	Samuel ▲	
09-12	A	Arsenal	2-0	2-3	6	A.G.Wiley	Enckelman	Samuel	Mellberg	Staunton	Wright	Stone 34	Hendrie 34	Boateng	Barry ▲	Merson 21	Dublin 21	Vassell ▲	Samuel	
17-12	H	Ipswich Town	1-1	1-3	8	M.L.Dean	Schmeichel	Samuel	Staunton 44	Staunton	Wright	Stone 70	Hendrie ▲	Boateng	Barry	Angel ▲44:70	Merson 45	Hendrie ▲	Vassell ▲	Kachloul ▲
22-12	A	Derby County	1-1	1-2	8	D.R.Elleray	Schmeichel	Samuel ▲	Staunton	Staunton	Wright	Stone	Hendrie	Boateng ▲	Barry ▲	Angel ▲45	Dublin 45	Hendrie ▲	Balaban ▲	Kachloul ▲
26-12	H	Liverpool	1-1	1-2	9	A.P.D'Urso	Schmeichel	Samuel ▲	Mellberg	Staunton	Wright	Merson	Hendrie ▲20	Boateng ▲	Kachloul	Angel 20	Vassell	Hendrie ▲	Stone ▲	Taylor ▲
29-12	H	Tottenham	0-1	1-1	9	E.K.Wolstenholme	Schmeichel	Samuel	Mellberg	Staunton	Wright ▲	Merson	Hendrie	Boateng ▲	Kachloul	Angel 89	Vassell	Taylor ▲	Stone ▲	Taylor ▲
01-01	A	Sunderland	0-0	1-1	9	M.A.Riley	Schmeichel	Samuel	Mellberg	Staunton	Wright	Stone	Hendrie	Taylor 59	Kachloul ▲	Dublin	Vassell 59	Barry ▲	Stone ▲	Taylor ▲
12-01	H	Derby County	2-1	2-1	7	M.R.Halsey	Schmeichel	Delaney	Mellberg ○	Staunton	Samuel ○	Merson ▲26	Taylor ▲26	Boateng 42	Hendrie ▲	Angel 11:26	Vassell 11	Barry ▲	Kachloul ▲	Hadji ▲
21-01	A	Charlton	2-0	2-1	7	R.Styles	Schmeichel	Delaney	Mellberg	Staunton	Samuel 8	Merson	Hendrie ▲	Boateng 42	Hadji	Angel ▲42	Vassell 8	Barry ▲	Kachloul ▲	
30-01	H	Everton	0-0	0-0	7	C.J.Foy	Enckelman	Delaney	Mellberg	Staunton	Samuel	Merson	Hendrie	Boateng	Hadji	Angel ▲	Vassell	Kachloul ▲	Dublin ▲	
02-02	A	Fulham	0-0	0-0	7	M.D.Messias	Enckelman	Delaney	Mellberg	Staunton	Samuel	Merson 28	Hendrie ▲	Boateng	Barry	Angel	Vassell ▲28	Stone ▲	Kachloul ▲	
09-02	H	Chelsea	1-0	0-1	7	P.A.Durkin	Enckelman	Delaney ▲	Mellberg ▲	Staunton	Samuel ○	Merson	Hendrie ▲	Boateng	Hadji	Angel	Vassell ▲28	Stone ▲	Dublin ▲	Barry ▲
23-02	A	Manchester Utd	0-0	0-1	7	J.T.Winter	Schmeichel	Delaney ▲	Mellberg	Staunton	Samuel ▲	Hadji ▲	Stone	Boateng	Barry ▲	Angel	Dublin ▲	Dublin ▲	Hitzlsperger ▲	
02-03	H	West Ham Utd	1-1	2-1	7	G.P.Barber	Schmeichel	Delaney	Mellberg ○	Staunton	Barry 26	Hadji ▲	Hitzlsperger	Boateng	Barry 23	Angel 23	Vassell 89	Merson ▲	Dublin ▲	Hadji ▲
05-03	A	Blackburn	0-1	0-3	7	S.G.Bennett	Schmeichel	Delaney	Mellberg	Staunton	Barry	Hadji ▲	Hitzlsperger	Boateng ○	Barry	Angel ▲	Vassell	Merson ▲	Kachloul ▲	
17-03	H	Arsenal	1-1	1-2	7	S.W.Dunn	Enckelman	Delaney	Mellberg	Staunton	Samuel	Merson ▲	Hendrie ▲	Boateng ▲	Barry	Angel ●	Vassell	Hendrie ▲	Dublin ▲	Balaban ▲
30-03	H	Bolton	2-2	2-3	7	D.Pugh	Enckelman	Delaney ▲	Mellberg	Staunton	Barry	Taylor 17	Hitzlsperger 17	Boateng 15	Hadji	Angel	Vassell ▲	Taylor ▲	Hadji ▲69	Dublin ▲69
02-04	A	Newcastle Utd	1-1	1-1	8	S.W.Dunn	Enckelman	Delaney ▲	Mellberg	Staunton	Barry 26	Taylor	Hitzlsperger	Boateng	Hadji ▲	Crouch ▲06	Stone ▲	Angel ▲	Samuel ▲	Vassell ▲
06-04	A	Middlesbrough	0-1	1-2	10	G.P.Barber	Schmeichel	Delaney	Mellberg	Staunton	Barry	Taylor	Hitzlsperger	Boateng	Hadji ▲	Angel 60	Crouch 60	Angel 60	Balaban ▲	
13-04	H	Leeds Utd	0-1	1-0	10	B.Knight	Enckelman	Delaney	Mellberg	Staunton	Barry	Taylor ○	Hitzlsperger	Boateng ▲	Kachloul ▲	Angel ●	Crouch	Kachloul ▲	Dublin ▲	Vassell ▲
20-04	A	Leicester City	2-1	2-2	7	G.Poll	Enckelman	Delaney ▲	Mellberg	Staunton	Samuel ▲	Stone	Hitzlsperger 27	Boateng	Barry	Crouch 22	Vassell ▲22	Kachloul ▲	Balaban ▲	Samuel ▲
27-04	H	Southampton	2-0	2-1	9	D.R.Elleray	Enckelman	Delaney	Mellberg ○	Staunton	Samuel ▲	Stone	Hitzlsperger 7	Boateng	Barry ○41	Crouch ▲	Vassell 7:41	Hadji ▲	Samuel ▲	Angel ▲
11-05	A	Chelsea	1-0	3-1	8	S.G.Bennett	Enckelman	Delaney	Mellberg	Staunton	Wright 88	Stone 21:63	Hitzlsperger ▲	Boateng	Barry	Crouch ▲21	Vassell ▲63	Dublin ▲88	Angel ▲	Hendrie ▲

F.A. Barclaycard Premiership
Squad List

Position	Name	Appearances	Appearances as Substitute	Goals or Clean Sheets	Goal Assists	Yellow Cards	Red Cards
G	P.Enckelman	9		2			
G	P.Schmeichel	29		1 7			
D	Alpay	14				3	
D	G.Barry	16	4		3		
D	M.Delaney	30				3	
D	O.Mellberg	32			1	3	
D	J.Samuel	17	6		2	3	
D	S.Staunton	30	3		2	1	
D	A.Wright	23			2	2	
M	G.Boateng	37		1	2	5	
M	D.Ginola		5				1
M	M.Hadji	17	6	2	3	3	
M	L.Hendrie	25	4	2	4	3	
M	T.Hitzlsperger	11	1	1	2	1	
M	H.Kachloul	17	5	2	1	3	
M	P.Merson	18	3	2	2		
M	S.Stone	14	8	1	4	2	
M	I.Taylor	7	9	3	1	2	
F	J.Angel	26	3	12	4	3	
F	B.Balaban		8				
F	P.Crouch	7		2	2		
F	D.Dublin	9	12	4	5	2	1
F	D.Vassell	30	6	12	4	3	

highlighted, even if it was too little too late.

Villa finished the month of October with successive wins to take their place at the top of the table; at that stage, even Gregory could not have envisaged what was to follow just three months later.

Kachloul's first goal for Villa earned his new club a 1-0 win over Charlton and two more from Angel against Bolton pointed them to a 3-2 win and a lofty position at the top of the table, the first time the club had led the Premier League since December 1998.

The joy, though, was short-lived as Villa embarked on a run of six games without a win and, from being a hero, Gregory was suddenly the chief villain. Banners began to appear calling for chairman Doug Ellis to step down and, more surprisingly, Gregory. Gareth Barry also put in a transfer request as the cracks began to show.

November was a poor month. Villa began with a 3-0 defeat at Newcastle, where Alan Shearer scored a scintillating goal, and then came a disappointing goalless draw at home to Middlesbrough, for whom former Villa defender Gareth Southgate enjoyed an outstanding performance to deny his old club. By now, Gregory had fallen out with new skipper Paul Merson, leaving him out of the Boro game.

A 2-0 defeat by Leicester saw the dismissal of David Ginola, who was later punished for man-handling one of the assistant referees and never played for the club again. The fans were unhappy, one fan running onto the pitch and throwing his club scarf in a puddle in protest.

Merson scored at his old club Arsenal along with Steve Stone to give Villa a two-goal first half lead but the visitors collapsed, allowing the Gunners to win 3-2 thanks to Thierry Henry's last-gasp winner.

Villa were now sixth and though Angel

All the latest news, views and opinion – 4thegame.com

F.A. Barclaycard Premiership

Top Goal Scorer

Juan Pablo Angel

Total Premier League Goals Scored:	Percentage Of The Team's League Goals:
12	26%

Goals Scored From

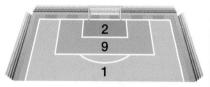

2
9
1

Following his arrival at Villa Park midway through the previous season, the Colombian international struggled to find his feet, scoring just once in nine League outings. Yet John Gregory stuck by him and he repaid the faith shown in him by finding the net on a regular basis in 2001-02. With the previous season's top scorer Dion Dublin marginalised before being sent on loan to Millwall, Angel forged a telling partnership with Darius Vassell – the pair struck 24 F.A. Barclaycard Premiership goals between them. Despite the arrival of Peter Crouch late in the season, the Colombian's return was a personal triumph in what proved to be an ultimately disappointing season for Villa.

> "He's certainly paid his money back. He's well in credit now in my opinion."
>
> *John Gregory*

Goals Resulting From

Key
- Open Play
- Corner
- Indirect Free Kick
- Direct Free Kick
- Penalty

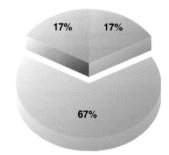

17% 17%

67%

	Right Foot	Left Foot	Header
Open Play	6	3	-
Set piece	1	1	1

Goal Assists

Total number of goal assists	4

Teams Scored Against

Against	Home	Away
Bolton Wanderers	2	0
Derby County	1	1
Ipswich Town	2	0
Blackburn Rovers	1	0
Charlton Athletic	0	1
Middlesbrough	0	1
Southampton	0	1
Tottenham Hotspur	1	0
West Ham United	1	0
Total goals scored	**8**	**4**

 Fixtures, results and match reports - 4thegame.com

> "John's resignation is sad, was most unexpected but has been amicable. I can understand how John feels regarding his need for a break."
>
> *Chairman Doug Ellis*
> *(January 2002)*

scored twice against Ipswich, a 3-1 defeat at struggling Derby before Christmas was another setback.

Fresh signs that all was not well with Gregory and Ellis were witnessed when the manager admitted he had wanted to sign Andy Cole before the Manchester United striker joined Blackburn. Villa also failed in attempts to sign Leicester's Muzzy Izzet and Gregory admitted he was frustrated at being unable to spend any money.

Having lost at home to Liverpool and been held to a 1-1 draw by Spurs, Villa were now eighth going into the New Year. Gregory was later charged with misconduct after clashing with referee Andy D'Urso in the Liverpool game but the subsequent ban came after he had left the club.

A 1-1 draw against Sunderland was followed by a 2-1 win over Derby, down to ten men after 24 minutes, and a 2-1 win at Charlton. On both occasions Angel and Vassell were on hand to secure the points, with Schmeichel saving a penalty from Graham Stuart in the latter game only for the midfielder to convert the rebound.

Gregory had challenged his team to win nine of their remaining 16 games to qualify for Europe but soon after the win at the Valley, he resigned. Ellis claimed the pressure

F.A. Barclaycard Premiership
Goals By Position

Key: Forward | Midfield | League Position | Defence | Goalkeeper

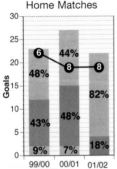

Home Matches

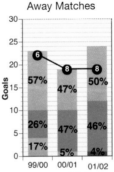

Away Matches

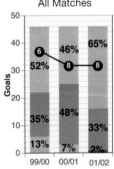

All Matches

Chart Analysis

statistics powered by **SUPERBASE**™

Villa finished with exactly the same number of goals – 46 – as they had done in the previous two seasons. The final tally included a contribution from their goalkeeper Peter Schmeichel – his strike against Everton the only goal scored at the right end by a goalkeeper in 2001-02. They may take some encouragement from the fact that the contribution from forwards rose to 65% compared to 46% the previous season.

 Win Barclaycard Premiership tickets - 4thegame.com

had got to his manager but, from a holiday break in New York, Gregory rang a Birmingham radio station to insist that was not the case. He soon returned to management at Derby, and a list of potential successors emerged, with Lothar Matthaeus, Alan Curbishley and George Graham all linked to the Villa Park post.

Instead, Ellis turned to former boss Graham Taylor, who had left Villa 12 years earlier to manage England and could not resist the chance to return to the F.A. Barclaycard Premiership. Stuart Gray and John Deehan had been in charge for two games, against Everton and Fulham, and both ended in goalless draws before Taylor was installed.

Villa under Taylor started with a 1-1 draw against Chelsea before Schmeichel made an emotional return to Old Trafford, only to leave with a 1-0 defeat.

When Ellis belatedly promised funds for Taylor, with £20m in the kitty, how Gregory must have smiled. While Taylor had to wait to spend Ellis' money, at least he managed to find his first win, beating West Ham 2-1 at home thanks to a late, late goal from Vassell.

Successive defeats followed, a dismal 3-0 reverse at Blackburn and 2-1 loss at home to Arsenal, when Barry saw his penalty saved by David Seaman. Villa had dropped to eighth, with European

F.A. Barclaycard Premiership
Team Performance Table

League Position	Team	Points Won From A Possible Six	Percentage Of Points Won At Home	Percentage Of Points Won Away	Overall Percentage Of Points Won
1	Arsenal	0/6			
2	Liverpool	3/6			
3	Manchester Utd	1/6	13%	27%	20%
4	Newcastle Utd	1/6			
5	Leeds United	1/6			
6	Chelsea	4/6			
7	West Ham Utd	4/6			
8	**Aston Villa**	**50**	67%	42%	54%
9	Tottenham H	2/6			
10	Blackburn R	3/6			
11	Southampton	6/6			
12	Middlesbrough	1/6			
13	Fulham	4/6	73%	47%	60%
14	Charlton Athletic	6/6			
15	Everton	1/6			
16	Bolton W	3/6			
17	Sunderland	2/6			
18	Ipswich Town	4/6	67%	20%	43%
19	Derby County	3/6			
20	Leicester City	1/6			

The table shows how many points out of a possible six Aston Villa have taken off each of the teams in the four sections. The other columns show as a percentage how many points they have taken from those available.

Chart Analysis

statistics powered by **SUPERBASE**™

As well as being unique in doing the 'double' over Villa, Arsenal were one of nine teams whom the Midlanders failed to beat.

For their part, while Villa only managed to do the 'double' over Charlton Athletic and Southampton, they did at least remain unbeaten against a further six teams. Against two of those, Tottenham and Sunderland, they drew both encounters.

They garnered least points at home to teams in the top five, while away from home, the 3-1 win at Liverpool was their only success against teams in this sector.

Particularly shocking was their form away from home against teams in the bottom five, where they registered three draws and two defeats.

The heart of the Barclaycard Premiership - 4thegame.com

qualification appearing less likely. With that in mind, Villa again applied to enter the Intertoto Cup.

The latest losses set the alarm bells ringing again and seasoned professional Steve Staunton admitted: "There is a cloud over everyone."

The cloud refused to shift at Portman Road where Ipswich, fighting for F.A. Barclaycard Premiership survival, held Villa to a goalless draw. But for the acrobatics of Schmeichel, Villa could have been embarrassed further.

Ellis finally released some funds for Taylor. A day before the transfer deadline, the former England manager signed Portsmouth's six foot, seven inch striker Peter Crouch for an initial £4m, with another £1m to follow if Villa were to qualify for the Champions League.

Villa went to struggling Bolton and lost 3-2, with Crouch making his debut. The visitors actually led 2-1 but threw it away to finish once again with nothing.

Spring arrived, but Villa's fortunes did not improve. A 1-1 home draw against Newcastle was followed by successive defeats, at Middlesbrough and at home to Leeds.

Schmeichel's short affair with Villa came to an end when Taylor decided against taking up a second season's option on the former Manchester United goalkeeper.

It's a fact

The win against Derby at Villa Park was Aston Villa's 150th Premier League win from 376 games.

"When you're as tall as Peter, it's not easy for other people to recognise your level of skill – but he undoubtedly has this."

Graham Taylor on Peter Crouch (March 2002)

F.A. Barclaycard Premiership

Goals By Time Period

Key   ■ Goals Scored   ■ Goals Conceded

Home Matches

Time of Goal (mins)

0-15	5	6
16-30	5	3
31-45	3	1
46-60	3	2
61-75	4	4
76-90	2	1

Goals

Away Matches

Time of Goal (mins)

0-15	5	2
16-30	5	3
31-45	5	5
46-60	3	5
61-75	2	6
76-90	4	9

Goals

All Matches

Time of Goal (mins)

0-15	10	8
16-30	10	6
31-45	8	6
46-60	6	7
61-75	6	10
76-90	6	10

Goals

Chart Analysis

statistics powered by ◆ SUPERBASE™

Villa proved to be most dangerous in the first half of matches. The opening 30 minutes were particularly fruitful, spawning 20 out of 46 goals.

Most goals were conceded in the first 15 and last 30 minutes of games. Interestingly, the Villa defence was breached just once in the last 15 minutes at home, compared to nine times on their travels.

 All the latest news, views and opinion - 4thegame.com

F.A. Barclaycard Premiership
Goals Resulting From

Key
☐ Goals Scored ☐ Goals Conceded

	Six Yard Area				Inside Area				Outside Area				Total			
	Shots		Headers		Shots		Headers		Shots		Headers		Shots		Headers	
	Home	Away	Home	Away	Home	Away	Home	Away	Home	Away	Home	Away	Home	Away	Home	Away
Open Play	3	-	2	2	6	9	2	2	2	1	-	-	11	10	4	4
	2	1	-	-	9	14	-	1	2	2	-	-	13	17	0	1
Direct Free Kick									-	-			0	0		
									-	1			0	1		
Indirect Free Kick	-	1	-	1	1	3	-	1	-	-	-	-	1	4	0	2
	-	-	-	1	1	2	-	1	-	-	-	-	1	2	0	2
Penalty	-	-	-	-	2	-	-	-	-	-	-	-	2	0	0	0
	-	-	-	1	1	2	-	-	-	-	-	-	1	2	0	1
Corner	1	1	1	1	-	-	2	1	-	-	-	-	1	1	3	2
	-	1	1	2	-	-	-	-	-	-	-	-	0	1	1	2
Totals	4	2	3	4	9	12	4	4	2	1	0	0	15	15	7	8
	2	2	1	4	11	18	0	2	2	3	0	0	15	23	1	6

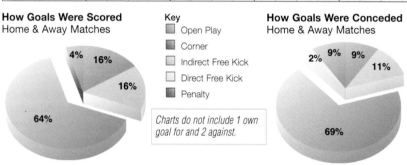

How Goals Were Scored
Home & Away Matches

4% 16% 16% 64%

Key
☐ Open Play
☐ Corner
☐ Indirect Free Kick
☐ Direct Free Kick
☐ Penalty

Charts do not include 1 own goal for and 2 against.

How Goals Were Conceded
Home & Away Matches

2% 9% 9% 11% 69%

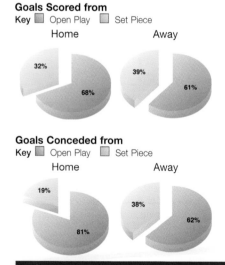

Goals Scored from
Key ☐ Open Play ☐ Set Piece

Home — 32% 68%
Away — 39% 61%

Goals Conceded from
Key ☐ Open Play ☐ Set Piece

Home — 19% 81%
Away — 38% 62%

Chart Analysis

Villa scored a large proportion of goals from Corners and Indirect Free Kicks. Their tallies for shots and headers scored were almost identical at home and away.

They were particularly resilient at defending headers, conceding just one at home all season.

However, they suffered from shots inside the area away from home, where they shipped 18 goals. Equally, they conceded more from Set Pieces on their travels than they did at Villa Park.

BEST IN LEAGUE...
- **Most goals scored from Indirect Free Kicks overall and away**

statistics powered by ◆ SUPERBASE™

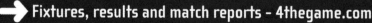

➡ **Fixtures, results and match reports – 4thegame.com**

> **"It's not just the media that affected him. All of a sudden there are agents hovering about and now he's wearing bright blue boots, for goodness sake."**
>
> *Graham Taylor on Darius Vassell (May 2002)*

Amazingly, Schmeichel opted for a move back to Manchester – with newly promoted Manchester City – in time for this season.

Clearly Taylor had his sights set on making changes. Balaban's future seemed in doubt though he was given the chance to prove himself by December if he wanted a future at Villa Park.

The manager gave a new contract to the improving Jloyd Samuel but then told both Steve Stone and Alan Wright that they could leave Villa Park.

On the field there was some cheer with the end of the season approaching.

Leicester were down but still held on for a 2-2 draw at Filbert Street where Thomas Hitzlsperger, the young German, scored his first goal. Vassell then scored twice to end Villa's home programme with a rare win, over Southampton.

Following that win, Villa added another victory, at beaten F.A. Cup finalists Chelsea. Fittingly, Crouch and Vassell scored, as did Dublin, back after a loan spell at Millwall. It was only Villa's 12th win of a disappointing season, their fewest number of Premier League wins for seven years.

F.A. Barclaycard Premiership **Shot Efficiency**	Key ■ Goals Scored ■ Other Shots On Target

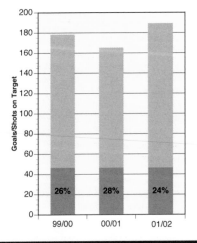

Season	Division	Shots Off Target	Shots On Target	Total Goals
1999 - 2000	P	n/a	178	46
2000 - 2001	P	n/a	165	46
2001 - 2002	P	184	189	46

Chart Analysis

Villa managed their most Shots On Target in the last three seasons, yet still they scored the same amount of goals.

Encouragingly, in 2001-02 they displayed some composure, hitting the target on more occasions than not.

statistics powered by ◆ **SUPERBASE**™

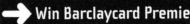

F.A. Barclaycard Premiership

Team Discipline

Key
- Forward
- Midfield
- Defence
- Goalkeeper

Total Number Of Bookings

Total number of red cards	2
Total number of yellow cards	42

Referee Performance

Referee	Games Refereed	Red Cards	Yellow Cards
S.G.Bennett	3	1	3
S.W.Dunn	3	1	3
M.R.Halsey	2	-	4

Type of Yellow Cards Received

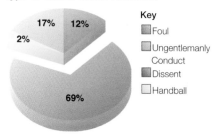

Key
- Foul
- Ungentlemanly Conduct
- Dissent
- Handball

17% 12% 2% 69%

Bookings by Position 1999/2000 - 2001/2002

Home Matches

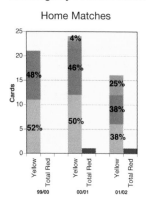

Away Matches

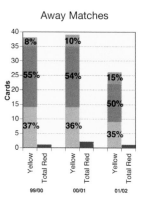

All Matches

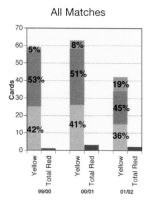

Chart Analysis

Villa collected considerably less cautions than they had in the previous two seasons – 42 this year compared to 59 and 63 in 1999-2000 and 2000-2001 respectively.

The number of Yellow Cards attributed to forwards has almost tripled since 1999-2000 from three to eight. The percentage of yellow cards received for Fouls was relatively low, while the figures for Ungentlemanly Conduct and Dissent were high.

Although Villa picked up two Red Cards during the campaign – one down from last year – they weren't a particularly dirty side. In fact, Graham Barber officiated three of their games without handing out a single card to Villa players.

> "David is very disappointed. He has had a great career in England and he has been a role model."
> *Graham Taylor after David Ginola was found guilty of misconduct (January 2002)*

statistics powered by **SUPERBASE**™

 The heart of the Barclaycard Premiership - 4thegame.com

Blackburn Rovers

	F.A. Barclaycard Premiership Final standing for the 2001-2002 season							
Final Position		Games Played	Games Won	Games Drawn	Games Lost	Goals For	Goals Against	Total Points
9	Tottenham Hotspur	38	14	8	16	49	53	50
10	Blackburn Rovers	38	12	10	16	55	51	46
11	Southampton	38	12	9	17	46	54	45

"We wanted to do it for our supporters. Obviously finishing tenth will also please the board, the Chairman, John Williams and the Directors."

Graeme Souness (May 2002)

Club Honours and Records

Premier League Champions: 1994-95
Football League Champions: 1913-14, 1991-92
Division 2 Champions: 1938-39
Division 3 Champions: 1974-75
FA Cup Winners: 1884, 1885, 1886, 1890, 1891, 1928
League Cup Winners: 2002
Full Members' Cup: 1987
Record Victory: 11-0 v Rossendale,
FA Cup 1st Round, 13 October, 1884
Record Defeat:
0-8 v Arsenal, Division 1, 25 February, 1933
League goals in a season (team):
114, Division 2 1954-55
League goals in a season (player):
43 Ted Harper, Division 1 1925-26
Career League goals:
Simon Garner 168, 1978 to 1992
League Appearances:
Derek Fazackerley, 596, 1970 to 1986
Reported transfer fee paid: £7,500,000 to
Southampton for Kevin Davies, June 1998.
£7,500,000 to Manchester United for Andy Cole,
December 2001
Reported transfer fee received: £15,000,000 from
Newcastle for Alan Shearer, July 1996

BLACKBURN enjoyed a successful first season back in the top flight. Victory in the Worthington Cup final, against Tottenham, saw Rovers claim a place in the UEFA Cup, while finishing tenth in the League was a satisfying return after a strong finish.

Promotion from Division One as runners-up to champions Fulham was no more than Blackburn deserved after an absence from the Premier League of two years. Although they were sensible enough not to expect a repeat of their success in 1995, they were optimistic of consolidating their position.

Graeme Souness may have secretly harboured hopes of rediscovering the success he enjoyed with Rangers and Liverpool; after all, he had already reached the top and was hoping to get there again.

Souness was counting on Matt Jansen repeating his great achievement of scoring 23 Division One goals but he also invested £6.75m in striker Corrado Grabbi. The Italian proved to be a huge flop, taking six games to score his first goal before a knee injury limited his performances.

Injury affected Blackburn from their first game, at Derby, where David Dunn was felled by Fabrizio Ravanelli. Although the Italian apologised, Dunn came off at

 All the latest news, views and opinion - 4thegame.com

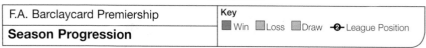

F.A. Barclaycard Premiership

Season Progression

Key
■ Win ■ Loss ■ Draw **➋** League Position

All Matches

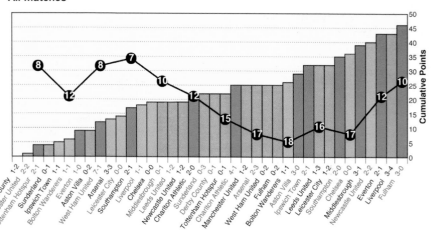

Home Matches

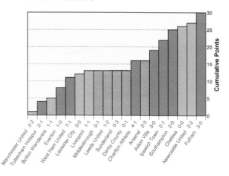

Away Matches

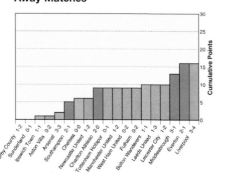

Chart Analysis

Blackburn adjusted well to life back in the top flight, losing just three times in their opening 14 matches to find themselves safely in mid-table come the start of December.

However, defeat at home to Middlesbrough heralded a dismal run that saw Rovers plummet into the drop zone with ten defeats from their next 12 outings prior to the Worthington Cup Final.

Interestingly, the two wins in this period both came against Charlton Athletic.

Victory in Cardiff at the end of February not only saw Rovers claim their first major trophy since the Premier League title in 1995, it also prompted a fightback which saw them pull away from danger.

Following the triumph in Cardiff, they went on to win six out of their last 11 games to finish a very creditable tenth in the table.

statistics powered by **SUPERBASE**™

> **"If you have got one Garry Flitcroft in your dressing room then you are a lucky manager. I don't have to do any shouting, I don't have to do any barking because it's all done for me."**
>
> *Graeme Souness*
> *(October 2001)*

It's a fact

When Blackburn were awarded a penalty in their 34th game of the season, at Middlesbrough in April, it was their first spot-kick of the campaign.

half-time and missed the next six League games.

Rovers lost 2-1 at Derby, where Jansen was denied his first top flight goal by an assistant referee's flag, but they were satisfied with a 2-2 draw at home to Manchester United where David Beckham scored an own goal for Rovers before stealing an equaliser from a free kick.

Blackburn bounced back with their first Premier League win since March 1999, beating Tottenham 2-1 at Ewood Park in late August with goals from Mahon – a summer arrival from Sporting Lisbon – and Damien Duff.

Clearly, the challenge of stepping up a division was proving difficult for Rovers and Souness warned his troops to become 'streetwise'. Nathan Blake was sold to Wolves and another striker, Marcus Bent, defected to Ipswich later in the season. With Jason McAteer also leaving for Sunderland, Rovers were looking to increase their squad strength and turned to Germany, and Nuremberg, for Nils-Eric Johansson.

However, results did not improve. In September they drew 1-1 at Ipswich and at home to Bolton thanks to an 85th minute equaliser from defender Lucas Neill, who had arrived earlier in the month from Millwall. Rovers claimed a valuable win at home to Everton, with Grabbi finally scoring. They then travelled to Villa Park for a Sunday

---

F.A. Barclaycard Premiership
Half-Time/Full-Time Comparison

Key ■ Win ■ Loss ■ Draw

Home				Away				Total			
Number of Home Half Time Wins	Full Time Result W	L	D	Number of Away Half Time Wins	Full Time Result W	L	D	Total number of Half Time Wins	Full Time Result W	L	D
8	7	-	1	4	2	1	1	12	9	1	2
Number of Home Half Time Losses	Full Time Result W	L	D	Number of Away Half Time Losses	Full Time Result W	L	D	Total number of Half Time Losses	Full Time Result W	L	D
5	-	3	2	10	-	8	2	15	-	11	4
Number of Home Half Time Draws	Full Time Result W	L	D	Number of Away Half Time Draws	Full Time Result W	L	D	Total number of Half Time Draws	Full Time Result W	L	D
6	1	2	3	5	2	2	1	11	3	4	4

Chart Analysis

statistics powered by ◆ **SUPERBASE**™

At home, Blackburn were good value for the three points if they had their noses in front at half-time. The only time they surrendered a half-time lead out of eight occasions was to Newcastle late in the season.

When Rovers were down at half-time – which happened in nearly half of their matches – they struggled to get anything out of the game, managing to convert just four of the 15 defeats into points.

 Fixtures, results and match reports – 4thegame.com

F.A. Barclaycard Premiership Results Table

Key: 88 time of goal · 88 time of assist · ▲ player substituted · ● yellow card · ● red card

DATE	H/A	OPPONENT	H/T	F/T	POS	REFEREE	TEAM											SUBSTITUTES USED		
18-08	A	Derby County	0-1	1:2	14	P.A.Durkin	Friedel	Curtis	Short	Berg	Bjornebye	Gillespie	Filcroft	Dunn	Duff	Jansen	Grabbi	Bent ▲	Hignett ▲72	Blake ▲72
22-08	H	Manchester Utd	0-1	2:2	15	A.G.Wiley	Friedel	Curtis	Short ●	Berg	Bjornebye	Gillespie ▲69	Filcroft ●69	Mahon 49	Duff	Jansen	Grabbi	Bent ▲	Taylor ▲	Blake ▲
25-08	H	Tottenham	1-0	2:1	8	S.G.Bennett	Friedel	Neill	Short	Berg	Taylor	Gillespie ▲	Filcroft	Mahon ▲6	Duff 70	Jansen 6	Grabbi	Bent ▲	Hignett ▲	Blake ▲
08-09	A	Sunderland	0-0	0-1	13	M.L.Dean	Friedel	Neill	Taylor	Berg	Bjornebye	Gillespie ▲	Filcroft	Mahon	Duff	Jansen	Bent ▲	Bent ▲	McAleer ▲	Hughes ▲
16-09	A	Ipswich Town	0-1	1:1	13	G.Poll	Friedel	Gillespie	Neill	Berg	Taylor	Duff	Filcroft	Tugay -54	Mahon	Jansen 54	Grabbi	Bent ▲	Bent ▲	
19-09	H	Bolton	0-0	1:1	12	J.T.Winter	Friedel	Johnson ▲	Short	Berg	Bjornebye	Duff 85	Filcroft	Tugay	Mahon	Jansen	Grabbi	Hughes ▲	Hignett ▲	Bent ▲
22-09	H	Everton	1-0	1-0	6	G.P.Barber	Friedel	Johnson ●	Short	Berg	Bjornebye	Duff ▲	Filcroft	Tugay 38	McAleer ▲	Jansen	Grabbi ▲38	Hughes ▲	Hignett ▲	Hughes ▲
30-09	A	Aston Villa	0-0	0-2	11	M.R.Halsey	Friedel	Johnson ▲	Neill	Berg	Bjornebye	Mahon	Filcroft	Tugay	Mahon	Jansen	Hughes ▲	Osterstad ▲	McAleer ▲	Hughes ▲
14-10	H	West Ham Utd	3-1	7:1	8	A.P.D'Urso	Friedel	Neill	Johansson	Berg ▲26	Bjornebye	Johnson ▲28	Filcroft 18	Tugay 63 80	Dunn 26 82	Jansen 82 90	Grabbi ▲18 28	Short ▲	Hignett ▲80 90	Hignett ▲
20-10	A	Arsenal	1-0	3:3	10	U.D.Rennie	Friedel	Neill	Short	Berg	Bjornebye	Gillespie ▲41	Filcroft 88	Tugay	Johnson ▲58	Jansen ▲41	Dunn 58 88	Bent ▲	Hughes ▲	Hignett ▲
29-10	H	Leicester City	0-0	0-0	10	R.Styles	Friedel	Neill	Johansson	Berg	Bjornebye	Johnson	Filcroft	Tugay	Duff	Jansen	Grabbi ▲	Gillespie ▲	Hignett ▲	Bent ▲
03-11	A	Southampton	1-1	2:1	7	A.G.Wiley	Friedel	Johansson	Johansson	Berg	Taylor	Gillespie	Filcroft	Tugay 44	Dunn 44	Jansen ▲89	Hughes ▲	Bent ▲89	Bent ▲89	Johnson ▲
17-11	H	Liverpool	0-1	1:1	7	M.A.Riley	Friedel	Neill ▲	Short	Berg	Bjornebye	Gillespie 52	Filcroft ▲	Tugay	Duff	Jansen 52	Bent	Hignett ▲	Hignett ▲	
24-11	H	Chelsea	0-0	0-0	10	G.Poll	Friedel	Curtis	Short ▲	Berg ▲	Bjornebye	Gillespie ▲	Mahon	Tugay	Duff	Jansen	Duff	Johansson ▲	Hughes ▲	
01-12	H	Middlesbrough	0-1	0-1	10	B.Knight	Friedel	Neill	Short ▲	Berg 82	Taylor	Gillespie	Mahon	Tugay	Duff ▲	Jansen	Osterstad	Mahon ▲	Johansson ▲	Grabbi ▲
09-12	H	Leeds Utd	0-0	1:2	14	A.P.D'Urso	Friedel	Neill	Short	Berg 82	Neill	Gillespie	Mahon	Tugay	Duff	Jansen	Duff	Johansson ▲	Johansson ▲	
15-12	A	Newcastle Utd	1-0	1:2	15	S.W.Dunn	Friedel	Curtis ▲	Short	Berg	Neill	Gillespie 56 90	Filcroft	Tugay 34	Dunn 34	Jansen ▲90	Duff 56	Taylor ▲	Hughes ▲	Grabbi ▲
22-12	A	Charlton	0-0	2:0	12	A.G.Wiley	Friedel	Neill	Curtis ▲	Berg	Neill	Gillespie	Filcroft	Tugay ▲	Mahon	Grabbi ▲	Grabbi	Duff 90	Hughes ▲	
26-12	A	Sunderland	0-2	0:3	14	C.R.Wilkes	Friedel	Neill ●	Short ●	Berg ▲	Johansson	Gillespie	Filcroft	Mahon	Osterstad ▲	Jansen	Osterstad	Grabbi ▲	Taylor ▲	Hughes ▲
29-12	H	Fulham	0-1	0:2	18	P.Jones	Friedel	Neill ▲	Short ▲	Berg	Bjornebye	Gillespie ▲	Filcroft	Tugay	Duff	Jansen	Duff ▲	Dunn ▲	Hignett ▲	Taylor ▲
01-01	A	Tottenham	0-1	0:1	15	J.T.Winter	Friedel	Neill	Short	Berg	Bjornebye	Gillespie ▲	Filcroft	Tugay	Cole	Jansen ▲	Cole	Cole ▲	Dunn ▲	Osterstad ▲
12-01	H	Charlton	2-0	4:1	14	N.S.Barry	Friedel	Curtis	Taylor	Berg	Bjornebye	Hignett 84	Dunn 45 88	Tugay 5	Cole 5 45 84	Cole	Duff	Cole 88	Gillespie ▲	Duff ▲88
19-01	A	Manchester Utd	0-1	1:2	15	U.D.Rennie	Friedel	Neill	Taylor	Johansson	Bjornebye ▲	Hignett 49	Dunn ▲	Tugay	Cole	Cole 49	Duff	Cole 49	Grabbi ▲	Filcroft ▲
30-01	H	Arsenal	2-2	2:3	17	D.J.Gallagher	Friedel	Neill	Taylor	Johansson	Bjornebye	Hignett ▲30	Filcroft ▲	Tugay	Duff 38	Grabbi ▲	Cole	Duff 38	Grabbi ▲	Gillespie ▲
02-02	A	West Ham Utd	0-1	0:2	17	P.Jones	Friedel	Neill	Taylor	Johansson	Bjornebye	Hignett ▲	Filcroft	Hughes	Cole	Grabbi	Mahon 30 38	Cole	Mahon ▲30 38	Gillespie ▲
09-02	A	Fulham	0-1	1:1	18	M.R.Halsey	Friedel	Curtis ▲	Short ●	Berg	Taylor	Neill	Dunn	Tugay	Cole	Jansen ▲	Hughes	Cole	Hignett ▲	Gillespie ▲
02-03	A	Bolton	1-1	3:0	18	P.A.Durkin	Friedel	Neill	Johansson	Berg	Bjornebye ▲	Dunn	Filcroft ▲	Hughes	Unsal ▲	Jansen	Duff	Yordi ●	Johansson ▲	Duff ▲68
05-03	H	Aston Villa	1-0	3:0	18	S.G.Bennett	Friedel	Neill	Johansson	Berg	Unsal ▲7	Hignett 7 88	Filcroft 84	Tugay 84	Duff 84	Jansen 68	Cole 88	Yordi 84	Gillespie ▲49	Gillespie ▲
13-03	H	Ipswich Town	2-0	2:1	15	P.Dowd	Friedel	Neill	Johansson	Berg	Unsal	Dunn 4:3	Filcroft	Tugay	Duff 20	Jansen ▲	Cole 43	Yordi 20	Gillespie 30 38	Hughes ▲
17-03	H	Leeds Utd	0-2	1:3	16	G.Poll	Friedel	Neill	Short	Berg	Unsal	Dunn ▲	Filcroft	Tugay	Duff	Jansen 49	Yordi	Yordi	Gillespie ▲	Hughes ▲
30-03	A	Leicester City	0-1	1:2	17	G.P.Barber	Friedel	Neill	Short	Johansson	Bjornebye ▲	Tugay	Filcroft	Tugay	Unsal 46	Jansen	Yordi 46	Yordi 46	Gillespie ▲	Taylor ▲
01-04	H	Southampton	2-0	2:0	17	C.R.Wilkes	Friedel	Neill	Short	Berg	Bjornebye	Gillespie	Filcroft	Hughes 46	Unsal 46	Jansen	Yordi ▲29	Yordi ▲29	Jansen	Hignett ▲
10-04	H	Chelsea	0-0	0:0	17	S.W.Dunn	Friedel	Neill	Short	Berg	Bjornebye	Gillespie	Dunn	Tugay	Cole	Jansen	Cole	Cole	Jansen	Hughes ▲
20-04	A	Middlesbrough	1-0	2:1	16	N.S.Barry	Friedel	Neill ▲	Short	Berg	Unsal	Gillespie 28 67	Dunn 82 82	Tugay	Cole 28 67	Yordi ▲33	Cole 28 67	Yordi ▲33	Jansen 10	Filcroft ▲
23-04	H	Newcastle Utd	1-0	2:2	15	U.D.Rennie	Friedel	Neill ▲	Short	Berg	Unsal	Gillespie 28 67	Dunn	Tugay	Cole 63	Cole 28 67	Cole 63	Cole 74	Yordi 33 74	Hughes ▲
28-04	A	Everton	1-2	1:2	12	A.G.Wiley	Friedel	Taylor	Taylor	Berg ▲29	Unsal ▲	Dunn 50	Dunn	Tugay	Cole 63	Jansen 10	Cole 63	Yordi 74	Johansson ▲	
08-05	A	Liverpool	1-2	3:4	12	A.G.Wiley	Kelly	Curtis ▲	Short	Berg ▲29	Johansson	Gillespie	Dunn	Tugay ▲	Cole 50	Jansen 81	Cole 50	Jansen 81	Johansson ▲81	Gillespie ▲81
11-05	H	Fulham	0-0	0:3	10	C.J.Foy	Kelly	Neill ●	Johansson ▲	Berg	Taylor	Gillespie	Dunn	Tugay ●82	Cole 52 82	Jansen ▲66	Cole 52 82	Yordi 66	Hughes ▲	Unsal ▲

F.A. Barclaycard Premiership
Squad List

Position	Name	Appearances	Appearances as Substitute	Goals or Clean Sheets	Goal Assists	Yellow Cards	Red Cards
G	B.Friedel	36		7			
G	A.Kelly	2		1			
D	H.Berg	34		1	2	2	
D	S.Bjornebye	23				3	
D	J.Curtis	10					
D	N.Johansson	14	6				
D	L.Neill	31		1	1	9	
D	C.Short	21	1			3	3
D	M.Taylor	12	7				
M	D.Duff	31	1	7	7	3	
M	D.Dunn	26	3	7	8	4	
M	G.Flitcroft	26	3	1	3	7	
M	K.Gillespie	21	11	3	5	3	
M	C.Hignett	4	16	4	3	3	
M	D.Johnson	6	1	1	1	1	
M	A.Mahon	10	3	1	1		
M	J.McAteer	1	3				
M	K.Tugay	32	1	3	5	8	
M	H.Unsal	7	1		2	2	
F	M.Bent	1	8		1	2	
F	N.Blake		3	1			
F	A.Cole	15		9	3	2	1
F	C.Grabbi	10	4	1	3	1	
F	M.Hughes	4	17	1		3	
F	M.Jansen	34	1	10	5	2	
F	E.Ostenstad	2	2				
F	Yordi	5	3	2			

fixture and lost 2-0.

One of the highlights of the F.A. Barclaycard Premiership season was to follow, however, when Rovers began October with a stunning 7-1 home win over West Ham. With England coach Sven-Goran Eriksson in attendance, Blackburn blew the Hammers apart They followed that with a 3-3 thriller at Highbury, where David Dunn claimed a brace.

Results were improving with Rovers putting together a six-game run without defeat. They were unbeaten in October and November while progressing nicely in the Worthington Cup.

Souness was quick to spot the warning signs and after a goalless home draw against Leicester, accused his players of believing their own publicity. Not for the first time, the Scot felt the need to put a halt to the celebrations with the club having reached seventh spot in the table.

His warnings were to prove right and December heralded Blackburn's dip in form. In six F.A. Barclaycard Premiership games, they lost five. A 4-0 Worthington Cup win over Arsenal did little to paper over the cracks of their poor League form. Middlesbrough won 1-0 at Ewood Park and then Rovers suffered another home defeat, against Leeds. They then went a goal up at Newcastle through Dunn, before the Magpies responded to win 2-1.

The trend halted briefly when Blackburn won 2-0 at the Valley, where Duff and Dunn maintained Rovers' impressive midfield goalscoring record in the absence of leading scorer Jansen.

Rovers needed to strengthen and it was no surprise when they admitted that talks had started with Liverpool over signing Robbie Fowler. They failed, but success in the transfer market soon followed.

The year ended with successive home defeats, against Sunderland and Derby.

➡ Win Barclaycard Premiership tickets – 4thegame.com

F.A. Barclaycard Premiership

Top Goal Scorer

Matt Jansen

Total Premier League Goals Scored:	Percentage Of The Team's League Goals:
10	18%

Goals Scored From

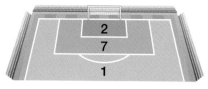

2
7
1

A year after scoring 23 goals to propel Blackburn into the F.A. Barclaycard Premiership, Matt Jansen hit double figures in a season which saw him break into the England set-up. The arrivals of Corrado Grabbi and, later in the season, Andy Cole, did not prevent him from scoring invaluable goals, despite the fact he was troubled all season with a hernia problem. Although it was the first time for three years that the club's top scorer had finished with so few goals, it was understandable given Rovers' battle with relegation. His continued success received international recognition with a call-up for England's friendly against Paraguay only for illness to rule him out of the squad.

"Matt's blessed with natural fitness because his genes have been kind to him. He has shown where he wants to be next season because he has worked his socks off."

Graeme Souness

Goals Resulting From

Key

□ Open Play ■ Corner □ Indirect Free Kick
□ Direct Free Kick ■ Penalty

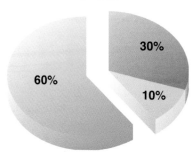

30%
60%
10%

	Right Foot	Left Foot	Header
Open Play	-	6	-
Set piece	-	2	2

Goal Assists

Total number of goal assists	5

Teams Scored Against

Against	Home	Away
Arsenal	2	0
Liverpool	1	1
Bolton Wanderers	0	1
Charlton Athletic	1	0
Everton	0	1
Ipswich Town	0	1
Leeds United	0	1
West Ham United	1	0
Total goals scored	**5**	**5**

 The heart of the Barclaycard Premiership - 4thegame.com

**"It was a big decision.
When you leave a
club like Manchester
United it's always
going to be a
big decision."**

*Andy Cole
(December 2001)*

Sunderland won 3-0 against a Blackburn side reduced to ten men when Short was sent off for the second time this season. Something had to be done and, before the Derby game, Souness introduced new signing Andy Cole to the crowd. The £7.5m arrival from Manchester United wanted regular football and he got it at Rovers, beginning on New Year's Day at Tottenham. The result, though, was disappointing with Spurs winning 1-0.

Rovers were dropping down the table and their concentration was not helped by success in both domestic cup competitions. In the Worthington Cup, they overcame Sheffield Wednesday to reach the final for the first time. Back in the League, they enjoyed a rare win with Cole scoring his first F.A. Barclaycard Premiership goal for Rovers in a 4-1 win over Charlton.

It was their first home win since October but four successive defeats highlighted fears of a relegation battle. The worries began with a 2-1 loss at Old Trafford. Jansen set up a goal for Hignett but Roy Keane claimed an 80th minute winner. Arsenal were the visitors next. Two goals behind, Blackburn responded through a brace from Jansen but Arsenal, despite having Oleg Luzhny sent off, stole the

F.A. Barclaycard Premiership
Goals By Position

Key
■ Forward ■ Midfield –❷– League Position
■ Defence ■ Goalkeeper

Home Matches

	99/00 Div 1	00/01 Div 1	01/02
Forward	36%	67%	39%
Defence	61%	21%	55%
	3%	12%	6%

League Position: ⑪ (99/00), ❷ (00/01), ⑩ (01/02)

Away Matches

	99/00 Div 1	00/01 Div 1	01/02
Forward	50%	48%	50%
Defence	32%	39%	50%
	18%	12%	

League Position: ⑪ (99/00), ❷ (00/01), ⑩ (01/02)

All Matches

	99/00 Div 1	00/01 Div 1	01/02
Forward	42%	59%	44%
Defence	49%	29%	53%
	9%	12%	4%

League Position: ⑪ (99/00), ❷ (00/01), ⑩ (01/02)

Chart Analysis

statistics powered by ◆ SUPERBASE™

Following promotion, Blackburn scored fewer goals than they did last season.

They managed 11 more goals at Ewood Park than on their travels in keeping with the figures for the previous two seasons.

Over half of their goals were scored from midfield – well up on last season – while the contribution from the defence dwindled.

BEST IN THE LEAGUE...
• **Most goals scored from midfield at home**

points through Dennis Bergkamp.

Rovers were still in the market for big names with Souness moving for former Aston Villa forward Savo Milosevic and Celta Vigo striker Catanha. He failed to lure either and successive London defeats, at West Ham and Fulham provided their tenth loss in 12 games and hardly the best preparation for the Worthington Cup final, which was to be against another London side, Spurs. The defeat at Fulham saw Rovers drop into the relegation zone.

Having lost Short for a third time to a red card, at Craven Cottage, the defender was denied a place at the Millennium Stadium. Regardless, Rovers won 2-1, Cole snatching the winner to take Rovers to glory and into Europe. The marvellous win in Cardiff seemed to inspire Rovers who returned to the business of the League with greater determination and confidence.

Rovers faced Bolton in their next game and drew 1-1. Crucially, they lost Cole, who was sent off for stamping on Bolton's Mike Whitlow. Although Cole protested vehemently, Souness said: "Andy deserved to go. He simply fell for the three-card trick when Whitlow clattered into him."

The red card, the third of Cole's career, earned him a three-match ban but he went out in some style, scoring in the 3-0 win over Villa and adding his seventh for the club in the 2-1 win over Ipswich.

F.A. Barclaycard Premiership
Team Performance Table

League Position	Team	Points Won From A Possible Six	Percentage Of Points Won At Home	Percentage Of Points Won Away	Overall Percentage Of Points Won
1	Arsenal	1/6			
2	Liverpool	1/6			
3	Manchester Utd	1/6	20%	7%	13%
4	Newcastle Utd	1/6			
5	Leeds United	0/6			
6	Chelsea	2/6			
7	West Ham Utd	3/6			
8	Aston Villa	3/6	83%	8%	46%
9	Tottenham H	3/6			
10	**Blackburn R**	**46**			
11	Southampton	6/6			
12	Middlesbrough	3/6			
13	Fulham	3/6	80%	80%	80%
14	Charlton Athletic	6/6			
15	Everton	6/6			
16	Bolton W	2/6			
17	Sunderland	0/6			
18	Ipswich Town	4/6	33%	13%	23%
19	Derby County	0/6			
20	Leicester City	1/6			

The table shows how many points out of a possible six Blackburn Rovers have taken off each of the teams in the four sections. The other columns show as a percentage how many points they have taken from those available.

Chart Analysis

statistics powered by  SUPERBASE™

Rovers' results were erratic throughout the season. They struggled in particular away from home against the top five teams, managing to garner just one point from a possible 15.

More surprising, though, they collected just two points on their travels against teams in the bottom five. In fact, their record against the relegation-battlers was poor overall, managing just one win – at home to Ipswich – out of ten fixtures.

Against teams in their own sector, they fared best at home but struggled again away from Ewood Park.

They showed their best form against teams in the third sector, where they registered their only 'doubles' against Southampton, Charlton and Everton.

➡ Fixtures, results and match reports – 4thegame.com

"I have been very, very fortunate to have won a fair bit but I can tell you this is as sweet as any."

Graeme Souness after Blackburn claimed the Worthington Cup (February 2002)

Another star of that show was Dunn, whose outside chance of making the senior England squad for the World Cup finals was increasing with each impressive performance.

Rovers added two new faces to their squad before the transfer deadline in March, with Turkish internatonal Hakan Unsal, an experienced international midfielder, arriving from Galatasaray for around £1m. In addition, Yordi, a former Spanish international, arrived from Real Zaragoza and actually made his bow in Cardiff.

Unsal made his debut against Bolton and featured in the two victories which went a long way to ensuring that Rovers would be staging UEFA Cup football as an F.A. Barclaycard Premiership, rather than a Nationwide, team. However, with Cole absent, Rovers suffered their first defeat in four League games when they lost 3-1 at Leeds.

Another defeat followed. Rovers went to struggling Leicester, already on the verge of relegation, and handed Dave Bassett's men their first win in 17 League games. The defeat left Rovers in 17th place.

The response in early April was promising. Rovers started the month with a 2-0 home win over Southampton, courtesy of Duff and Jansen. The former scored a goal and the latter turned in a performance which did not go

F.A. Barclaycard Premiership
Goals By Time Period

Key
■ Goals Scored ■ Goals Conceded

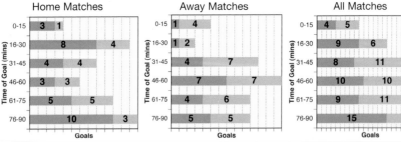

Home Matches

Time of Goal (mins)	Goals Scored	Goals Conceded
0-15	3	1
16-30	8	4
31-45	4	4
46-60	3	3
61-75	5	5
76-90	10	3

Away Matches

Time of Goal (mins)	Goals Scored	Goals Conceded
0-15	1	4
16-30	1	2
31-45	4	7
46-60	7	7
61-75	4	6
76-90	5	5

All Matches

Time of Goal (mins)	Goals Scored	Goals Conceded
0-15	4	5
16-30	9	6
31-45	8	11
46-60	10	10
61-75	9	11
76-90	15	8

Chart Analysis

statistics powered by ◆ SUPERBASE™

Blackburn were sluggish starters, scoring just three goals in the first 15 minutes at Ewood Park. Away from home, they struggled even more, netting just twice in the opening half-hour.

They threatened more as the game wore on, and were particularly strong in the last quarter-hour, scoring almost twice as many goals as they conceded.

F.A. Barclaycard Premiership
Goals Resulting From

Key
☐ Goals Scored ☐ Goals Conceded

	Six Yard Area				Inside Area				Outside Area				Total			
	Shots		Headers		Shots		Headers		Shots		Headers		Shots		Headers	
	Home	Away	Home	Away	Home	Away	Home	Away	Home	Away	Home	Away	Home	Away	Home	Away
Open Play	2	2	-	1	12	8	2	1	10	4	-	-	24	14	2	2
	3	1	1	-	7	21	1	2	2	2	-	-	12	24	2	2
Direct Free Kick									-	-			0	0		
									1	1			1	1		
Indirect Free Kick	1	-	-	1	1	1	-	-	-	-	-	-	2	1	0	1
	-	-	-	-	-	-	1	1	-	-	-	-	0	0	1	1
Penalty	-	-	-	-	-	1	-	-	-	-	-	-	0	1	0	0
	-	-	-	-	-	1	-	-	-	-	-	-	0	1	0	0
Corner	-	-	1	1	1	-	1	2	-	-	-	-	1	0	2	3
	2	1	-	1	-	-	2	-	-	-	-	-	2	1	2	1
Totals	3	2	1	3	14	10	3	3	10	4	0	0	27	16	4	6
	5	2	1	1	7	22	4	3	3	3	0	0	15	27	5	4

How Goals Were Scored
Home & Away Matches

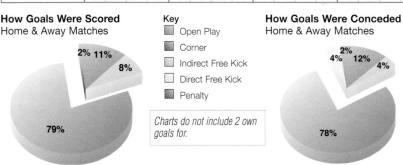

Key
■ Open Play
■ Corner
☐ Indirect Free Kick
☐ Direct Free Kick
■ Penalty

Charts do not include 2 own goals for.

2% 11%
8%
79%

How Goals Were Conceded
Home & Away Matches

2%
4% 12%
4%
78%

Goals Scored from
Key ■ Open Play ☐ Set Piece

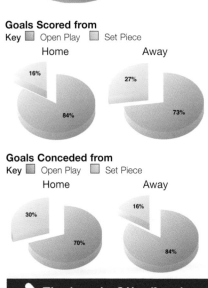

Home
16%
84%

Away
27%
73%

Goals Conceded from
Key ■ Open Play ☐ Set Piece

Home
30%
70%

Away
16%
84%

Chart Analysis

These charts reflect Blackburn's mid-table status in the final F.A. Barclaycard Premiership table.

Rovers scored just two more goals from Open Play than they conceded. Similarly, they scored just one more header than they conceded.

They were particularly susceptible to shots Inside Area away from home.

WORST IN LEAGUE…
- **Most goals conceded from Corners at home**

statistics powered by ● SUPERBASE™

> "I'm reluctant to play the two wide men any more because it leaves us far too vulnerable at times. That's OK when you're bossing a game and scoring plenty of goals, but when you find yourself under the cosh it's not ideal."
>
> *Graeme Souness*
> *(April 2002)*

It's a fact

When Craig Short was sent off at Fulham in February, he became the first F.A. Barclaycard Premiership player to be sent off three times during a League campaign.

unnoticed by England manager Sven-Goran Eriksson.

Souness was in trouble soon afterwards. He was banned from the touchline for a game and fined £10,000 after being found guilty of misconduct by the F.A. for using 'offensive and insulting language' towards referee Graham Barber during Rovers' 1-0 F.A. Cup fifth round defeat by Middlesbrough in February.

That was, perhaps, the lowest point of an encouraging April, which began with a 2-0 home win over Southampton. A draw against Chelsea was followed by a win at the Riverside which as good as cemented Rovers' place in the top flight. Alan Shearer returned with Newcastle to score twice in the 2-2 Ewood Park draw and Stig Inge Bjornebye injured his eye in a freak training ground accident.

Rovers took their tally to 11 points from a possible 15, and with it safety, with a 2-1 win at Everton, thanks to a winner from Cole.

In May, Rovers lost a seven-goal thriller at Anfield, where Cole scored again. Having announced his retirement from international football after failing to make England's World Cup squad, the striker scored twice more, taking his Rovers total to 13 in 20 games, as Blackburn completed the season with a 3-0 win over Fulham.

F.A. Barclaycard Premiership
Shot Efficiency

Key: ■ Goals Scored ■ Other Shots On Target

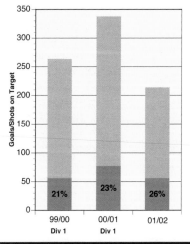

Season	Division	Shots Off Target	Shots On Target	Total Goals
1999 - 2000	1	n/a	263	55
2000 - 2001	1	n/a	337	76
2001 - 2002	P	210	213	55

Chart Analysis

As would be expected following their promotion, Blackburn scored less goals than they had done in finishing second in Division One the previous season.

Nevertheless, they improved their Shot Efficiency, converting 3% more of Shots On Target into goals.

statistics powered by **SUPERBASE**™

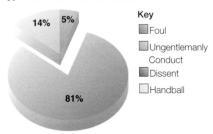

F.A. Barclaycard Premiership		Key
Team Discipline		■ Forward ■ Midfield ■ Defence ■ Goalkeeper

Total Number Of Bookings

Total number of red cards	4
Total number of yellow cards	58

Referee Performance

Referee	Games Refereed	Red Cards	Yellow Cards
A.G.Wiley	4	1	6
M.R.Halsey	2	1	4
R.Styles	1	-	6

Type of Yellow Cards Received

Key
■ Foul
■ Ungentlemanly Conduct
■ Dissent
■ Handball

14% 5% 81%

Bookings by Position 1999/2000 - 2001/2002

Home Matches
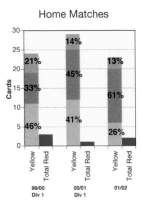

Away Matches
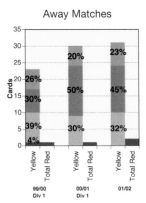

All Matches
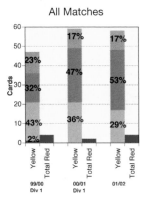

Chart Analysis

Despite playing eight fewer matches than the previous season, Blackburn still managed to collect 58 Yellow Cards, just one fewer than in 2000-01.

They also doubled their Red Card tally to four – the same as two seasons ago – in a hard-fought campaign which eventually saw them finish well clear of relegation.

The number of cautions awarded to defenders was at its lowest for three years, while midfielders claimed the bulk of bookings.

"Everybody wants to play at the highest level, so it's not a question of not wanting it. It's individuals making errors which are costing us – and that's the story of our season."
Graeme Souness
(April 2002)

statistics powered by **SUPERBASE**™

Fixtures, results and match reports - 4thegame.com

Bolton Wanderers

F.A. Barclaycard Premiership Final standing for the 2001-2002 season

Final Position		Games Played	Games Won	Games Drawn	Games Lost	Goals For	Goals Against	Total Points
15	Everton	38	11	10	17	45	57	43
16	Bolton Wanderers	38	9	13	16	44	62	40
17	Sunderland AFC	38	10	10	18	29	51	40

"Everybody had written us off at the start of the season. Most people thought we would not only be relegated, but finish bottom of the division."

Sam Allardyce (April 2002)

Club Honours and Records

Division 1 Champions: 1996-97

Division 2 Champions: 1908-09, 1977-78

Division 3 Champions: 1972-73

FA Cup Winners: 1923, 1926, 1929, 1958

Sherpa Van Trophy Winners: 1989

Record Victory:
13-0 v Sheffield United, FA Cup 2nd Round,
1 February, 1890

Record Defeat:
1-9 v Preston North End, FA Cup 2nd Round,
10 December, 1887

League goals in a season (team):
100, Division 1, 1996-97

League goals in a season (player):
38, Joe Smith, Division 1, 1920-21

Career league goals:
255, Nat Lofthouse, 1946 to 1961

League appearances:
519, Eddie Hopkinson, 1956 to 1970

Reported transfer fee paid: £3,500,000 to
Wimbledon for Dean Holdsworth, October 1997

Reported transfer fee received: £4,500,000 from
Liverpool for Jason McAteer, September 1995

DESPITE spending less than a million pounds to improve his squad, Sam Allardyce still kept Bolton in the F.A. Barclaycard Premiership. It was a remarkable achievement given the way in which Wanderers had gone up.

Having secured promotion via the play-offs, Bolton wasted little time in making their mark on the new season.

After an audacious move to sign German star Oliver Bierhoff failed to materialise, they started the new campaign with much the same squad as they had finished with.

Kevin Nolan scored the new season's first goal as Bolton romped to a remarkable 5-0 opening day win at Leicester. Allardyce had a dig at those who had predicted an immediate return, saying: "The experts have written us off. We use that as motivation."

Bolton continued to respond to their critics by winning their next two games to become early table-toppers.

Ricketts, later to be rewarded with his first England cap, scored the winner over Middlesbrough at the Reebok Stadium but possibly the most surprising result of Bolton's good start came at home to Liverpool. Allardyce's men showed scant regard for the Reds' treble-winning season

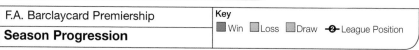

Bolton Wanderers

F.A. Barclaycard Premiership
Season Progression

Key
■ Win ■ Loss ■ Draw ●—League Position

All Matches

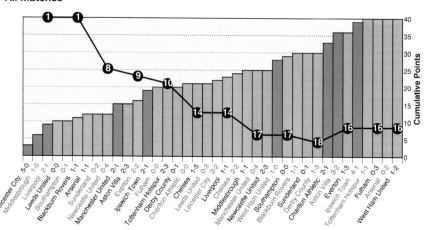

Home Matches

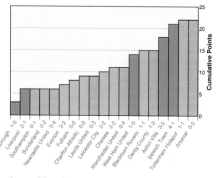

Away Matches

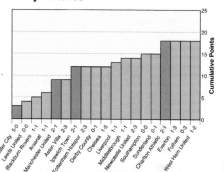

Chart Analysis

After gaining promotion via the play-offs, Bolton had a dream start in the F.A. Barclaycard Premiership, beating Leicester, Middlesbrough and Liverpool to be top of the table by the end of August.

However, reality soon hit home as the Trotters managed just three victories in their next 27 outings, including a 12-match sequence without winning between November and February.

With the spectre of relegation looming large, they claimed three priceless wins in four games in and around Easter to boost their points' tally.

It meant that they were able to take their foot off the pedal and in fact they went on to lose their last three games of the season.

WORST IN THE LEAGUE...
• **Most games without winning at home**

statistics powered by SUPERBASE™

→ **The heart of the Barclaycard Premiership – 4thegame.com**

It's a fact

Kevin Nolan scored the first goal of the season in the F.A. Barclaycard Premiership, netting the first of Bolton's five at Leicester after 15 minutes.

by stealing their third successive victory. Ricketts scored again and, after Emile Heskey had responded, the experienced Dean Holdsworth stole an 89th minute winner.

Although only Silkeborg's Henrik Pedersen had been added in the summer for just £650,000, Bolton impressed, taking another point from a goalless encounter at Elland Road in early September. The draw kept Wanderers at the top of the table, where they stayed despite the fact that they failed to win in their next three games.

They suffered their first defeat of the season at home to Southampton in mid-September. Twice Bolton hit the woodwork but a late goal from Marian Pahars burst Wanderers' bubble. They remained hard to beat, however, and took a point from 1-1 away draws at Blackburn and Arsenal. At Ewood Park, they were denied a win by Lucas Neill's late leveller and then, at Highbury three days later, Ricketts won a point with a goal seven minutes from the end. Even the dismissal, after half-an-hour, of Ricardo Gardner could not deter the visitors.

On the bench that day was Djibril Diawara, a late call up for the injured Nicky Southall. Diawara only took part after a fan, a 34-year-old postman, loaned his shirt, which was taken to the Highbury shop so that Diawara's name

F.A. Barclaycard Premiership
Half-Time/Full-Time Comparison

Key: ■ Win ■ Loss ■ Draw

Home				Away				Total			
Number of Home Half Time Wins	W	L	D	Number of Away Half Time Wins	W	L	D	Total number of Half Time Wins	W	L	D
5	4	-	1	4	3	1	-	9	7	1	1
Number of Home Half Time Losses	W	L	D	Number of Away Half Time Losses	W	L	D	Total number of Half Time Losses	W	L	D
7	-	5	2	7	-	6	1	14	-	11	3
Number of Home Half Time Draws	W	L	D	Number of Away Half Time Draws	W	L	D	Total number of Half Time Draws	W	L	D
7	1	2	4	8	1	2	5	15	2	4	9

Chart Analysis

statistics powered by ◆ SUPERBASE™

Not surprisingly, Bolton's best chance of taking all three points hinged on their being in front at the break.

Out of 14 games they were losing at half-time, they won none, salvaging a point on just three occasions.

They were consistent both home and away when level at half-time, going on to secure at least a point 11 out of 15 times.

F.A. Barclaycard Premiership Results Table

Key: 88 time of goal 88 time of assist ▲ player substituted ● yellow card ● red card

DATE	H/A	OPPONENT	H/T	F/T	POS	REFEREE	TEAM											SUBSTITUTES USED		
18-08	A	Leicester City	4-0	5-0	1	R.Styles	Jaaskelainen	Barness	Bergsson ▲41	Whitlow ●	Charlton	Nolan 15 41	Warhurst ▲	Frandsen 15 45 83	Gardner ▲33	Hansen 83	Ricketts 33	Southall ▲	Marshall ▲	Pedersen ▲
21-08	H	Middlesbrough	1-0	1-0	1	S.W.Dunn	Jaaskelainen	Barness	Bergsson	Whitlow ●	Charlton	Nolan ▲	Warhurst ●	Frandsen ▲	Gardner	Hansen 39	Ricketts ▲39	Southall ▲	Holdsworth ▲	Marshall ▲
27-08	H	Liverpool	1-0	2-1	1	G.Poll	Jaaskelainen	Barness	Bergsson	Whitlow ●	Charlton ●	Nolan ▲	Warhurst 26	Frandsen ▲	Gardner 89	Hansen ▲	Ricketts ▲26	Farrelly ▲	Holdsworth ▲89	Diawara ▲
08-09	A	Leeds Utd	0-0	0-0	1	S.G.Bennett	Jaaskelainen	Barness	Bergsson	Whitlow ●	Charlton ●	Nolan	Farrelly	Frandsen	Pedersen	Hansen ▲	Ricketts ▲	Holdsworth ▲	Richardson ▲	Diawara ▲
15-09	H	Southampton	0-0	0-1	2	D.Pugh	Jaaskelainen	Barness	Bergsson	Whitlow ●	Charlton	Nolan ▲	Warhurst ●	Frandsen	Pedersen	Hansen	Ricketts ▲	Southall ▲	Holdsworth ▲	Gardner ▲
19-09	A	Blackburn	0-0	1-1	1	J.T.Winter	Jaaskelainen ●	Barness	Bergsson	Whitlow ●	Charlton ●	Nolan ▲	Warhurst ●	Gardner 68	Pedersen ▲	Hansen ▲	Ricketts ▲	Wallace ▲▲68	Holdsworth ▲	Gardner ▲
22-09	A	Arsenal	0-0	1-1	1	C.R.Wilkes	Jaaskelainen ●	Barness	Bergsson	Whitlow ●	Charlton	Nolan ●	Warhurst ●	Johnson ●	Gardner ●	Hansen ▲	Holdsworth ▲	Diawara ▲	Holdsworth ▲	N'Gotty ▲
29-09	H	Sunderland	0-0	0-2	4	D.R.Elleray	Jaaskelainen ●	Barness	Bergsson	Whitlow ●	Charlton	Nolan ▲	Warhurst	Johnson ●	Gardner ●	Wallace ▲	Holdsworth ▲	Diawara ▲	Ricketts ▲83	Hansen ▲
13-10	H	Newcastle Utd	0-1	0-2	4	M.A.Riley	Jaaskelainen ●	Barness ▲	Bergsson	Whitlow ●	Southall ▲	Nolan ▲	Warhurst	Johnson ●	Gardner	Hansen	Holdsworth ●	Diawara ▲	N'Gotty ▲	Hansen ▲
20-10	A	Manchester Utd	1-1	2-1	6	G.P.Barber	Jaaskelainen 83	Barness ▲	Bergsson	Whitlow	Charlton ●	Nolan 35	Warhurst ▲	Frandsen	Gardner	Hansen ▲	Ricketts 35 83	Johnson ▲	Barness ▲	Ricketts ▲
27-10	A	Aston Villa	1-2	2-3	8	E.K.Wolstenholme	Banks	N'Gotty ▲	Bergsson ●	Diawara ●	Charlton ●	Nolan	Farrelly ▲	Frandsen 1	Gardner 74	Hansen ▲	Ricketts ● 174	Holdsworth ▲	Wallace ▲	Barness ▲
03-11	H	Everton	1-1	2-2	9	A.P.D'Urso	Poole	N'Gotty ●	Bergsson ● 90	Whitlow	Charlton ●	Nolan ● 10	Warhurst ●	Frandsen 10	Gardner ●	Wallace ●	Holdsworth 90	Holdsworth ▲	Farrelly ▲	Diawara ●▲
18-11	A	Ipswich Town	2-1	2-3	8	S.G.Bennett	N'Gotty	Bergsson 6 25	Whitlow	Charlton ●	Nolan	Warhurst ●▲	Frandsen 6	Gardner ●	Wallace ●	Ricketts 25	Holdsworth ▲	Farrelly ▲	Holdsworth ●	
24-11	H	Fulham	0-0	0-0	9	M.L.Dean	Jaaskelainen	N'Gotty	Bergsson	Whitlow	Charlton	Nolan	Warhurst	Frandsen	Gardner ▲	Wallace	Ricketts	Farrelly ▲	Holdsworth ●▲	
03-12	A	Tottenham	1-0	2-3	10	P.A.Durkin	Jaaskelainen	N'Gotty ▲	Bergsson	Whitlow	Charlton	Nolan ▲ 8	Warhurst ▲	Frandsen ▲	Gardner ▲	Wallace 56	Ricketts ▲8 56	Hansen ▲	Johnson ▲	Holdsworth ▲
08-12	H	Derby County	0-0	0-1	12	M.D.Messias	Jaaskelainen	Barness	Bergsson	Whitlow	Charlton	Nolan	Warhurst ●▲	Frandsen ●	Gardner ▲	Wallace ▲	Ricketts	Hansen ▲	Johnson ▲	Farrelly ▲
15-12	H	Charlton	0-0	0-0	12	C.J.Foy	Jaaskelainen	N'Gotty	Bergsson	Whitlow	Charlton	Nolan 3	Warhurst ●	Frandsen ▲	Gardner	Wallace ▲	Ricketts	Hansen ▲	Holdsworth ▲	
23-12	A	Chelsea	1-2	1-5	14	U.D.Rennie	Jaaskelainen	Barness ▲	Hendry	Whitlow	Charlton	Nolan	Warhurst ●	Frandsen	Johnson ▲	Gardner	Johnson ▲	Hansen ▲	Farrelly ▲	Holdsworth ▲
26-12	H	Leeds Utd	0-2	0-3	15	A.G.Wiley	Jaaskelainen	Barness ▲	Diawara	Whitlow	Charlton	Nolan	Warhurst ●	Frandsen ▲3	Farrelly ●	Holdsworth	Ricketts	Johnson ▲	Pedersen ▲	Southall ▲
29-12	H	Leicester City	1-2	2-2	15	M.A.Riley	Jaaskelainen	Barness ▲	Hendry ▲▲34	N'Gotty	Charlton ●	Nolan 34	Warhurst ●	Frandsen	Farrelly ▲	Holdsworth 90	Ricketts ●90	Pedersen ▲	Southall ▲90	Diawara ▲
01-01	A	Liverpool	0-0	1-1	14	C.R.Wilkes	Southall	Bergsson	Diawara	Charlton ▲	Nolan .78	Warhurst	Frandsen	Holdsworth ●	Holdsworth ▲	Ricketts ●	Farrelly ▲	Pedersen ▲78		
12-01	H	Chelsea	0-0	2-2	16	J.T.Winter	Jaaskelainen	Southall	N'Gotty ▲	Diawara	Charlton ●	Nolan 55 78	Farrelly	Frandsen ▲	Nolan 55 78	Pedersen ▲	Ricketts 55	Farrelly ▲	Gardner ▲	Barness ▲
19-01	A	Middlesbrough	0-2	0-4	17	A.P.D'Urso	Jaaskelainen	Southall ▲	N'Gotty ▲	Charlton ●	Charlton	Farrelly	Charlton ▲	Bobic ●▲74	Pedersen ▲	Ricketts	Gardner ▲	Barness ▲	Bobic ▲	
29-01	H	Manchester Utd	0-2	0-4	17	D.R.Elleray	Jaaskelainen ●	Barness	Whitlow	Barness	Nolan	Farrelly	Gardner	Bobic ▲74	Hansen ▲74	Ricketts	Hansen ▲74	Charlton ●	Pedersen ▲
02-02	A	Newcastle Utd	2-2	2-3	18	D.R.Elleray	Jaaskelainen ●	Barness ●	Bergsson	Whitlow	Charlton 34	Southall 34	Farrelly	Gardner 19	Hansen ▲	Bobic ▲	Johnson ▲	Charlton ●	Pedersen ▲	Holdsworth ▲
09-02	H	West Ham Utd	1-0	1-0	17	D.Pugh	Jaaskelainen	N'Gotty	Bergsson	Whitlow 37	Charlton	Nolan	Warhurst ●▲	Tofting	Gardner 37	Bobic ▲	Ricketts	Southall ▲	Holdsworth ▲	Hansen ▲
23-02	A	Southampton	0-0	0-0	17	E.K.Wolstenholme	Jaaskelainen	Barness	Bergsson	Whitlow ●	Charlton ▲	Nolan ●	Djorkaeff ▲	Tofting	Gardner	Bobic ●	Ricketts	Hansen ▲	Wallace ▲	Espartero ▲
23-02	H	Blackburn	1-0	1-1	17	P.A.Durkin	Jaaskelainen	Southall ▲	Bergsson	N'Gotty	Djorkaeff	Nolan	Djorkaeff ▲	Tofting	Gardner ▲	Bobic ▲45	Wallace ▲45	Hansen ▲	Barness ▲	Ricketts ●
05-03	H	Sunderland	0-1	0-1	17	G.Poll	Jaaskelainen ●	Barness ▲	Bergsson	Southall ▲	Gardner	Gardner 46	Warhurst ▲	Tofting	Djorkaeff	Bobic ▲45	Wallace ▲45	Espartero ▲	Barness ▲	Ricketts ▲
16-03	A	Derby County	0-1	1-3	18	D.R.Elleray	Jaaskelainen	N'Gotty	Bergsson ▲	Whitlow ▲	Gardner	Gardner 46	Warhurst 46	Tofting	Djorkaeff	Wallace	Ricketts	Frandsen ▲	Southall ▲	Bobic ▲
23-03	A	Charlton	2-0	2-1	16	C.J.Foy	Jaaskelainen	Barness	Bergsson ▲	Charlton	Gardner	Nolan ●	Warhurst ▲	Djorkaeff 15 39	Djorkaeff 15 39	Holdsworth ▲15	Southall ▲	Ricketts ▲		
30-03	H	Aston Villa	2-2	3-2	15	R.Styles	Poole	N'Gotty 75	Konstantinidis	Charlton	Gardner ●76	Nolan 8 .76	Farrelly	Djorkaeff ▲40	Bobic 40	Holdsworth ●	Whitlow ▲	Ricketts ▲	Bobic ▲	
01-04	A	Everton	1-3	2-3	16	S.G.Bennett	Poole	Konstantinidis ●	Whitlow	Charlton	Nolan	Warhurst	Djorkaeff ▲	Gardner	Bobic 40	Holdsworth ▲	Frandsen ▲75	Wallace ▲	Ricketts ▲	
06-04	H	Ipswich Town	4-0	4-1	13	J.T.Winter	Jaaskelainen	N'Gotty	Bergsson	Charlton 2	Nolan	Warhurst ▲	Gardner ▲38	Djorkaeff 35	Bobic ▲2 30 38	Wallace ▲2 30 38	Frandsen ▲75	Wallace ▲	Ricketts ●
20-04	H	Tottenham	0-1	1-1	15	M.D.Messias	Jaaskelainen	N'Gotty	Bergsson	Whitlow ●	Nolan	Southall	Gardner ▲38	Djorkaeff 70	Bobic ▲	Wallace ▲	Ricketts ▲	Holdsworth ▲70	Holdsworth ●
23-04	A	Fulham	0-1	0-3	16	P.A.Durkin	Jaaskelainen	Barness	Bergsson	Charlton ●	Nolan	Southall ▲	Frandsen	Djorkaeff	Bobic ▲	Wallace ▲	Ricketts ▲	Espartero ▲	Holdsworth ●
29-04	H	Arsenal	0-2	0-2	16	D.J.Gallagher	Jaaskelainen	Barness	Bergsson	Charlton	Nolan	Farrelly	Frandsen	Djorkaeff	Bobic ▲	Wallace ▲	Ricketts ●	Johnson ▲	Ricketts ▲
11-05	A	West Ham Utd	0-1	1-2	16	M.L.Dean	Jaaskelainen	Barness	Bergsson	Konstantinidis ▲	Tofting ▲	Tofting ●	Frandsen	Djorkaeff 66	Bobic ▲	Ricketts ▲	Smith ▲	Holdsworth ▲	Nolan ▲

F.A. Barclaycard Premiership
Squad List

Position	Name	Appearances	Appearances as Substitute	Goals or Clean Sheets	Goal Assists	Yellow Cards	Red Cards
G	S.Banks	1					
G	J.Jaaskelainen	34		7	1	2	2
G	K.Poole	3					
D	A.Barness	19	6			1	
D	G.Bergsson	30		1	3	1	
D	S.Charlton	35	1		1	3	
D	C.Hendry	3			1	2	
D	B.N'Gotty	24	2	1			
D	L.Richardson		1				
D	M.Whitlow	28	1		1	9	
M	D.Diawara	4	5			1	1
M	Y.Djorkaeff	12		4	2		
M	M.Espartero		3				
M	G.Farrelly	11	7				
M	P.Frandsen	25	4	3	6	4	
M	R.Gardner	29	2	3	6	3	1
M	J.Johnson	4	6			2	
M	K.Konstantinidis	3				1	1
M	K.Nolan	34	1	8	4	5	
M	J.Smith		1				
M	N.Southall	10	8	1	1	1	
M	S.Tofting	6				1	
M	P.Warhurst	25			2	7	1
F	F.Bobic	14	2	4	3	2	
F	B.Hansen	10	7	1	2	1	
F	D.Holdsworth	9	22	2		4	1
F	I.Marshall		2				
F	H.Pedersen	5	6		1		
F	M.Ricketts	26	11	12	2	4	
F	R.Wallace	14	5	3	3	2	

could be printed on it!

Newcastle handed the Trotters a third successive home loss in October. The game was hanging in the balance, with Newcastle leading 1-0, when, with an hour gone, goalkeeper Jussi Jaaskelainen was sent off for deliberate handball.

Without a goalkeeper on the bench, Bo Hansen went in goal and, from the free kick, Laurent Robert scored. Bolton were struggling but they were earning a reputation for being resilient and determined and there was no better way to bounce back than to win at Old Trafford.

The season's biggest shock so far came after Juan Sebastian Veron had given Manchester United the lead. Nolan replied and, with seven minutes remaining, Ricketts claimed a shock winner.

Rod Wallace joined Bolton on a free from Rangers in September but, after scoring on his debut at Blackburn, had to wait until December for his next goal.

Goals were forthcoming but the results were not; Bolton lost 3-2 at Villa Park despite a goal in the first minute from Ricketts, and then they were held to a 2-2 draw at home to Everton in early November, with Ricketts scoring his ninth goal of the season in the final minute.

Rovers were continually looking to boost their squad; Allardyce failed to sign Barcelona goalkeeper Richard Dutruel, Spanish superstar Kiko and Rangers striker Kenny Miller.

They found some solace in their away form, winning 2-1 at Ipswich with Ricketts claiming goal number ten and yet another winner.

What followed threatened to ruin Bolton's season. Their wonderful start was all but forgotten as they set off on a 12-game run without a win, beginning with a goalless draw against Fulham. The sequence was finally ended with a 1-0

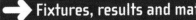

Fixtures, results and match reports - 4thegame.com

F.A. Barclaycard Premiership

Top Goal Scorer

Michael Ricketts

Total Premier League Goals Scored:	Percentage Of The Team's League Goals:
12	27%

Goals Scored From

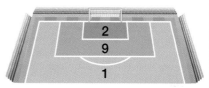

2
9
1

R icketts had been magnificent in helping Bolton to promotion, with 19 Division One goals. He continued his improvement with vital strikes in the F.A. Barclaycard Premiership, including three in his first three games and ten by the end of the year, earning him an England call-up against Holland in Amsterdam. He scored vital goals such as the winner against Middlesbrough, an equaliser at Highbury and, perhaps most importantly, the late winner over Manchester United at Old Trafford. Ricketts seemed to tire towards the end of the season and spent most of the last two months on the substitutes' bench.

"I've probably surprised myself with the amount of goals I've scored in a short space of time."
Michael Ricketts

Goals Resulting From
Key
☐ Open Play ☐ Corner ☐ Indirect Free Kick
☐ Direct Free Kick ■ Penalty

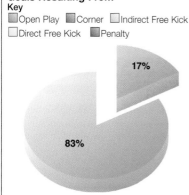

17%

83%

	Right Foot	Left Foot	Header
Open Play	6	2	2
Set piece	1	-	1

Goal Assists

Total number of goal assists	2

Teams Scored Against

Against	Home	Away
Aston Villa	0	2
Leicester City	1	1
Arsenal	0	1
Chelsea	1	0
Everton	1	0
Ipswich Town	0	1
Liverpool	1	0
Manchester United	0	1
Middlesbrough	1	0
Tottenham Hotspur	0	1
Total Goals Scored	**5**	**7**

 Win Barclaycard Premiership tickets - 4thegame.com

"Signing a player of Youri Djorkaeff's calibre and class underlines our determination to stay in the top flight. He is an outstanding player and World Cup winner, and perhaps the biggest signing in the club's history."

Sam Allardyce
(February 2002)

home win over West Ham in February.

A 1-0 loss at Derby was followed by a goalless home draw against Charlton and a 5-1 thrashing at Chelsea, not the best way for Allardyce to celebrate his 100th League game in charge.

More woe was to follow with nine man Bolton held to a 2-2 draw by struggling Leicester. For once, Ricketts scored an own goal to give Leicester the lead and Brian Deane added a second for the visitors. By then, Bolton had lost both Paul Warhurst (18 minutes) and Holdsworth (21), dismissed by referee Mike Riley.

Leicester also had Muzzy Izzet sent off but Bolton rallied, with Nolan scoring before half-time and Ricketts heading an equaliser in the last minute of added time. The decisions of the referee infuriated Allardyce, who had been wired up to a heart monitor for a documentary; the results made interesting television.

Three successive draws in the New Year saw Bolton drop into 16th place. The first came at Anfield, where Nolan levelled with 12 minutes left. They followed that with a home 2-2 draw against Chelsea, where Nolan was on hand again to claim a late equaliser, in the 79th minute.

F.A. Barclaycard Premiership
Goals By Position

Key
🟦 Forward ⬛ Midfield –❷– League Position
⬜ Defence ⬛ Goalkeeper

Home Matches
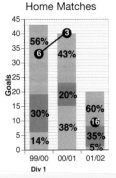

Away Matches
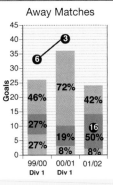

All Matches
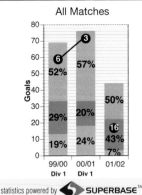

Chart Analysis

statistics powered by **SUPERBASE**™

Bolton scored significantly less goals than they had in Division One, although they also played less games.

The percentage of goals scored from midfield was more than double compared to the previous season while the contribution from defence tailed off dramatically.

Away from home, they scored most of their goals from midfield.

➡️ **The heart of the Barclaycard Premiership – 4thegame.com**

A 1-1 draw at Middlesbrough was again eked out with a late leveller; this time it was Hansen's turn to claim a point, in the 74th minute, but Wanderers were the subject of revenge at the end of January when Manchester United, still seething from their home defeat, won 4-0 at the Reebok.

Bolton signed German international striker Fredi Bobic on loan from Borussia Dortmund in January, while defender Bruno N'Gotty completed a £500,000 transfer. In February, Allardyce added Tahiti-born French midfielder Gerald Forchelet from Cannes, Danish international midfielder Stig Tofting and French star Youri Djorkaeff, the latter arriving on a free transfer.

February began with a 3-2 defeat at Newcastle where Bolton again gave up a lead. Gardner and Nicky Southall gave Wanderers a 2-1 advantage but Alan Shearer and Craig Bellamy sent the Trotters home with nothing. Although the defeat put Wanderers into the relegation zone, the rest of February was more satisfying with Allardyce's team winning at home for the first time since August, against West Ham United.

The next results, though, were disappointing. Draws against Southampton and Blackburn were followed by successive defeats, firstly at Sunderland and then at home to rivals Derby. The poor results

F.A. Barclaycard Premiership
Team Performance Table

League Position	Team	Points Won From A Possible Six	Percentage Of Points Won At Home	Percentage Of Points Won Away	Overall Percentage Of Points Won
1	Arsenal	1/6			
2	Liverpool	4/6			
3	Manchester Utd	3/6	20%	40%	30%
4	Newcastle Utd	0/6			
5	Leeds United	1/6			
6	Chelsea	1/6			
7	West Ham Utd	3/6			
8	Aston Villa	3/6	60%	7%	33%
9	Tottenham H	1/6			
10	Blackburn R	2/6			
11	Southampton	1/6			
12	Middlesbrough	4/6			
13	Fulham	1/6	40%	33%	37%
14	Charlton Athletic	4/6			
15	Everton	1/6			
16	**Bolton W**	**40**			
17	Sunderland	0/6			
18	Ipswich Town	6/6	33%	50%	42%
19	Derby County	0/6			
20	Leicester City	4/6			

The table shows how many points out of a possible six Bolton Wanderers have taken off each of the teams in the four sections. The other columns show as a percentage how many points they have taken from those available.

Chart Analysis

statistics powered by SUPERBASE™

Despite finishing in the bottom five, Bolton acquitted themselves well against the teams at the other end of the table, picking up twice as many points away from home as they did at the Reebok.

They didn't fare so well on their travels against teams in the second sector, picking up just one point from a possible 15 thanks to a 1-1 draw at Blackburn.

Although they did the 'double' over Ipswich in their sector, they failed to take any points off Sunderland or relegated Derby County.

They failed to do the 'double' over any other team in the F.A. Barclaycard Premiership while Newcastle were the only other side that Bolton failed to take any points off.

 All the latest news, views and opinion – 4thegame.com

coincided with the news that Allardyce had sent a circular to clubs, asking if they may be interested in signing any of his players. Allardyce was angry that news of the circular had been leaked. He qualified the decision by saying: "The list is one of several I have circulated this year. The disappointing thing this time is that confidential information has been disclosed to our players and the media by managers at other clubs."

The 3-1 loss at home to Derby also saw goalkeeper Jaaskelainen sent off for the second time but Bolton, knowing that they faced a difficult end to the season, produced a vital win when they travelled to London to face Charlton.

By now, they were without Bergsson after the defender damaged ankle ligaments in a challenge with Fabrizio Ravanelli in the Derby defeat. He missed the rest of the season but Wanderers defied the odds to win at the Valley.

Architect of the 2-1 win was Djorkaeff who scored both goals, his first in England, to earn Bolton only their second win in 18 League outings. His reward was to be recalled to France's squad in place of the injured Robert Pires.

After that came another win, the 3-2 home victory over Villa, lifting Bolton into 15th place, a game which featured another new signing, Greek international defender Kostas

It's a fact

Bolton had something to show for their 3-2 defeat against Spurs in December; the second goal, by Rod Wallace, was the club's 100th in the Premier League.

"We are all determined to stay in the F.A. Barclaycard Premiership and it will be a good challenge."

Youri Djorkaeff
(February 2002)

F.A. Barclaycard Premiership
Goals By Time Period

Key: ▪ Goals Scored ▫ Goals Conceded

Home Matches

Time of Goal (mins)	Goals Scored	Goals Conceded
0-15	3	4
16-30	2	5
31-45	7	5
46-60	2	4
61-75	1	5
76-90	5	8

Away Matches

Time of Goal (mins)	Goals Scored	Goals Conceded
0-15	6	1
16-30	2	2
31-45	6	10
46-60	1	7
61-75	5	4
76-90	4	7

All Matches

Time of Goal (mins)	Goals Scored	Goals Conceded
0-15	9	5
16-30	4	7
31-45	13	15
46-60	3	11
61-75	6	9
76-90	9	15

Chart Analysis

statistics powered by ◆ SUPERBASE™

Bolton were good starters, especially away from home where they managed to score six in the opening 15 minutes. They also scored six on their travels in the period before half-time, although they conceded ten too.

Overall, they had a higher tendency to score in the first half and concede in the second. In particular, they managed just three goals in the half-hour after the break at the Reebok.

 Fixtures, results and match reports – 4thegame.com

Bolton Wanderers

F.A. Barclaycard Premiership

Goals Resulting From

Key
☐ Goals Scored   ☐ Goals Conceded

	Six Yard Area				Inside Area				Outside Area				Total			
	Shots		Headers		Shots		Headers		Shots		Headers		Shots		Headers	
	Home	Away	Home	Away	Home	Away	Home	Away	Home	Away	Home	Away	Home	Away	Home	Away
Open Play	1	2	-	-	6	7	3	2	3	2	-	-	10	11	3	2
	1	2	-	2	14	10	2	2	2	6	-	-	17	18	2	4
Direct Free Kick									2	4			2	4		
									1	1			1	1		
Indirect Free Kick	-	-	-	1	1	2	-	-	-	-	-	-	1	2	0	1
	-	-	1	-	1	2	1	1	1	-	-	-	2	2	2	1
Penalty	-	-	-	-	-	-	-	-	-	-	-	-	0	0	0	0
	-	-	-	-	1	1	-	-	-	-	-	-	1	1	0	0
Corner	1	-	1	1	-	-	1	2	-	1	-	-	1	1	2	3
	-	-	1	1	1	-	2	2	-	-	-	-	1	0	3	3
Totals	2	2	1	2	7	9	4	4	5	7	0	0	14	18	5	6
	1	2	2	3	17	13	5	5	4	7	0	0	22	22	7	8

How Goals Were Scored
Home & Away Matches

14%   16%   9%   60%

Key
- Open Play
- Corner
- Indirect Free Kick
- Direct Free Kick
- Penalty

How Goals Were Conceded
Home & Away Matches

3% 3%   12%   12%   69%

Charts do not include 1 own goal for and 3 against.

Goals Scored from
Key ☐ Open Play   ☐ Set Piece

Home — 32% / 68%   Away — 46% / 54%

Goals Conceded from
Key ☐ Open Play   ☐ Set Piece

Home — 34% / 66%   Away — 27% / 73%

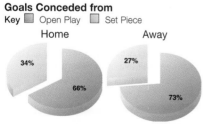

Chart Analysis

Bolton scored nearly twice as many goals from Set Pieces away from home as they did at home.

The percentage of goals scored from Open Play was low, compensated by the number of goals scored – ten – from Free Kicks, Direct or Indirect.

BEST IN THE LEAGUE...
- **Most goals scored from Direct Free Kicks overall and away**

statistics powered by **SUPERBASE**™

➡ **Win Barclaycard Premiership tickets - 4thegame.com**

It's a fact

Bolton's 5-0 win at Filbert Street was their best ever opening day victory.

Konstantinidis, on loan from Hertha Berlin.

If safety appeared likely at the start of April, nerves crept in with a 3-1 defeat at Everton where Bobic was allegedly punched in the ribs by Everton's Duncan Ferguson, who was dismissed. Optimism returned with the 4-1 win over Ipswich in which Bobic scored a first half hat-trick but a 1-1 draw at home to Tottenham was followed by a dismal display at Fulham. The Cottagers won 3-0 and secured their own safety but Allardyce was left with a nervous disposition, admitting: "I'm a bag of nerves."

However, by the time Bolton faced title-chasing Arsenal, they were safe. Ipswich's defeat by Manchester United and Sunderland's draw at Charlton meant that the Trotters could not be relegated, and they lost 2-0 at the Reebok as Arsenal moved closer to the Championship. Indeed, there was a strange feel about the game because, with safety secured, some Bolton fans were delighted that, by losing to Arsenal, the prospect of the trophy remaining at nearby Old Trafford was now slim.

With safety assured, it mattered little that Bolton ended the season with three defeats, finishing at West Ham with a 2-1 loss, albeit because of the F.A. Barclaycard Premiership's final goal of the season, from the Hammers' Ian Pearce.

F.A. Barclaycard Premiership
Shot Efficiency

Key
■ Goals Scored ■ Other Shots On Target

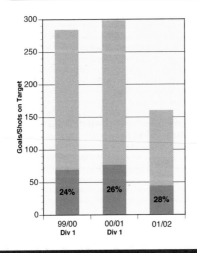

Season	Division	Shots Off Target	Shots On Target	Total Goals
1999 - 2000	1	n/a	284	69
2000 - 2001	1	n/a	298	76
2001 - 2002	P	195	160	44

Chart Analysis

Bolton continue to get better at converting their shots on target into goals with their success rate increasing by 2% year-on-year.

Although they played eight less games than last season in Division One, not including the play-offs, they managed just over half as many shots on target as in the previous term.

F.A. Barclaycard Premiership	
Team Discipline	

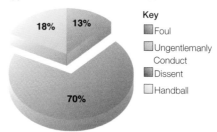

Key
- ■ Forward
- ■ Midfield
- ■ Defence
- ■ Goalkeeper

Total Number Of Bookings

Total number of red cards	7
Total number of yellow cards	56

Referee Performance

Referee	Games Refereed	Red Cards	Yellow Cards
M.A.Riley	2	3	4
C.R.Wilkes	2	1	5
R.Styles	2	-	6

Type of Yellow Cards Received

18% 13%
70%

Key
- ■ Foul
- □ Ungentlemanly Conduct
- ■ Dissent
- □ Handball

Bookings by Position 1999/2000 - 2001/2002

Home Matches

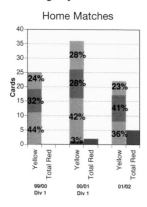

Away Matches

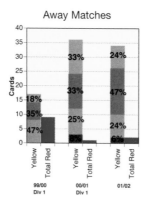

All Matches

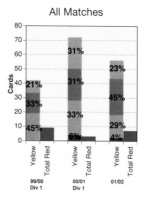

Chart Analysis

For the first time in the last three seasons, midfielders were Bolton's chief villains when it came to collecting Yellow Cards, amassing 45% of the total.

Despite playing less games than in the previous season in Division One, over twice as many Bolton players were dismissed.

The Trotters suffered at the hands of Mike Riley, clocking up 52 disciplinary points in the two games in which the Yorkshire official handed them three Red Cards.

WORST IN THE LEAGUE...
- **Most red cards at home and joint overall**

statistics powered by **SUPERBASE**™

> "It's hard enough for us in the F.A. Barclaycard Premiership without having to suffer those cruel blows against us."
> *Sam Allardyce after seeing two of his players sent off at home to Leicester (December 2001)*

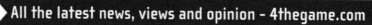

All the latest news, views and opinion - 4thegame.com

Charlton Athletic

F.A. Barclaycard Premiership		Final standing for the 2001-2002 season						
Final Position		Games Played	Games Won	Games Drawn	Games Lost	Goals For	Goals Against	Total Points
13	Fulham	38	10	14	14	36	44	44
14	Charlton Athletic	38	10	14	14	38	49	44
15	Everton	38	11	10	17	45	57	43

"I think at the outset, when you consider the injuries we've had, if you told me we'd be comfortable with a few games to go, I would have taken that."

Alan Curbishley (May 2002)

Club Honours and Records

Division 1 Champions: 1999-00

Division 3 Champions: 1928-29, 1934-35

FA Cup Winners: 1947

Record victory:

8-1 v Middlesbrough, Division 1, 12 September, 1953

Record defeat:

1-11 v Aston Villa, Division 2, 14 November, 1959

League goals in a season (team):

107, Division 2, 1957-58

League goals in a season (player):

32, Ralph Allen, Division 3 (South), 1934-35

Career league goals:

153, Stuart Leary, 1953 to 1962

League appearances:

583, Sam Bartram 1934 to 1956

Reported transfer fee paid:

£4,750,000 to Wimbledon for Jason Euell, July 2001

Reported transfer fee received: £4,375,000 from Leeds United for Danny Mills, June 1999

CHARLTON had finished ninth in 2000-01 and though they finished five places further down the table, they were rarely threatened by relegation despite adversity.

Addicks boss Alan Curbishley, wanted by West Ham before the start of the 2001-02 season, admitted that the new campaign had filled him with concern. Yet even he could not have predicted the number of injuries to key players.

He signed Wimbledon striker Jason Euell – who tipped his new team to make Europe – and Spurs defender Luke Young, while making Shaun Bartlett's move from FC Zurich permanent. Having enjoyed such a good first campaign back in the top flight the previous season, there were fears in South East London that Charlton would struggle to hold on to their coveted spot in the F.A. Barclaycard Premiership.

Even before a ball had been kicked, defender Radostin Kishishev faced the prospect of missing most of the season. He eventually returned in late January. The next crock was Richard Rufus, so important to Charlton's back line. In early September, he suffered knee ligament damage and did not reappear until March. Claus Jensen, Mark Kinsella and John Robinson were also injured early on but Charlton chairman Richard Murray

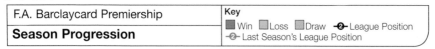

Charlton Athletic

F.A. Barclaycard Premiership

Season Progression

All Matches

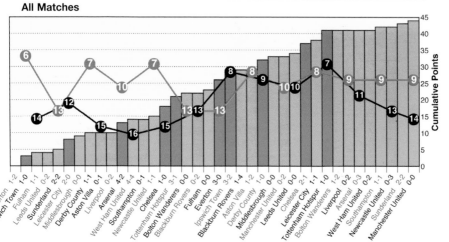

Home Matches

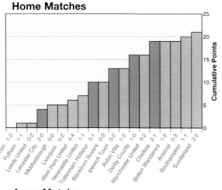

Away Matches

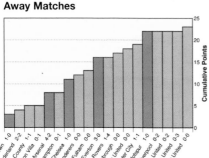

Chart Analysis

Charlton started the season slowly, registering just three wins in their opening 14 matches. They then picked up four in their next seven to propel themselves into eighth place on New Year's Day.

The next nine games produced an even split of results, and with the win at Spurs in March, they reached 41 points and almost certain safety

Just three points from their final eight games then saw Charlton drop to 14th as the season petered out.

In stark contrast to last season when their home form sustained their campaign, there was little to choose between home and away form this time around, with no less than eight teams leaving the Valley victorious.

statistics powered by ◆ **SUPERBASE**™

➡ **All the latest news, views and opinion - 4thegame.com**

> **"It was an unsavoury situation for us and I'm very disappointed in it. It happens sometimes in football and it will be dealt with."**
>
> *Alan Curbishley following the training ground bust-up between Andy Todd and Dean Kiely (October 2001)*

It's a fact

When Chris Powell claimed the winner against Spurs, in March, it was his first League goal for Charlton and his first since September 1997, while with Derby.

warned Curbishley he had no funds to buy his way out of the crisis.

Thus it was that an opening day defeat by Everton at the Valley, followed by draws against Fulham and Sunderland, and another loss at home to Leeds, in which Graham Stuart was sent off, gave Addicks fans grave cause for concern.

On the plus side, there were signs that Charlton's well-organised youth policy was beginning to produce results. Scott Parker and Paul Konchesky both settled and Curbishley saw only his second win of the season when Charlton beat Leicester 2-0 at the Valley, despite losing Steve Brown, the second Charlton player to see red.

A training ground bust-up between Andy Todd and keeper Dean Kiely did little to boost team spirit with the defender later put on the transfer list.

Jensen's return, in October, helped to inspire the Addicks but losses to Aston Villa and Liverpool saw them slump to 16th. They responded in truly magnificent style, a memorable 4-2 win at Highbury easing their relegation fears.

The Gunners dominated early on but Charlton responded in a game that saw four goals in 18 minutes either side of the interval, earning the visitors a 4-1

F.A. Barclaycard Premiership
Half-Time/Full-Time Comparison

Key: ■ Win ■ Loss ■ Draw

Home

Number of Home Half Time Wins	Full Time Result W	L	D
3	2	-	1

Number of Home Half Time Losses	Full Time Result W	L	D
7	-	6	1

Number of Home Half Time Draws	Full Time Result W	L	D
9	3	2	4

Away

Number of Away Half Time Wins	Full Time Result W	L	D
3	2	-	1

Number of Away Half Time Losses	Full Time Result W	L	D
6	-	5	1

Number of Away Half Time Draws	Full Time Result W	L	D
10	3	1	6

Total

Total number of Half Time Wins	Full Time Result W	L	D
6	4	-	2

Total number of Half Time Losses	Full Time Result W	L	D
13	-	11	2

Total number of Half Time Draws	Full Time Result W	L	D
19	6	3	10

Chart Analysis

statistics powered by ◆ SUPERBASE™

Charlton fared well on the road, where ten half-time draws were turned into three wins and just one defeat.

Overall, the Addicks did not lose any of the six matches in which they led at the break, although they did drop points in two.

In common with other teams in the League, they failed to win any of the games that they were losing at half-time.

Fixtures, results and match reports - 4thegame.com

F.A. Barclaycard Premiership **Results Table**

Key: 88 time of goal 88 time of assist ● yellow card ▲ player substituted ● red card

The results table records each fixture with half-time (H/T) and full-time (F/T) scores, league position (POS), referee, the starting eleven (TEAM) and the SUBSTITUTES USED. Goal and assist times, cards and substitution markers appear next to player names.

DATE	H/A	OPPONENT	H/T	F/T	POS	REFEREE	TEAM											SUBSTITUTES USED		
18-08	H	Everton	0-0	1-2	15	N.S.Barry	Kiely	Young	Fish	Brown	Powell	Stuart	Parker ▲	Euell	Salako ●	Bartlett	Johansson 57	Fortune ▲	Peacock ▲	Lisbie ▲
25-08	A	Ipswich Town	0-0	1-0	12	S.W.Dunn	Kiely 85	Young	Rufus	Todd	Powell	Stuart	Parker	Euell	Konchesky	Euell	Johansson	Lisbie ▲85	Brown ▲	Konchesky ▲
09-09	H	Fulham	1-1	1-1	14	J.T.Winter	Kiely	Young	Fish	Brown ●	Todd	Powell	Parker	Euell	Konchesky	Lisbie	Bartlett ●24	Robinson ▲	Konchesky ●24	Salako ▲
16-09	H	Leeds Utd	0-1	0-2	15	M.R.Halsey	Kiely	Young ◢	Fish	Brown	Powell	Robinson	Parker	Euell	Konchesky	Euell	Kinsella	Kinsella ▲	Lisbie ▲	Lisbie ▲
22-09	A	Sunderland	1-0	2-2	15	A.P.D'Urso	Kiely	Young 61	Fish	Brown 61	Powell	Stuart	Parker ▲	Euell	Konchesky ●10	Bartlett 10	Johansson ▲	Robinson ▲	Todd ▲	Euell ▲
29-09	H	Leicester City	1-0	2-0	12	M.L.Dean	Kiely	Young	Fish	Brown ●	Powell ▲44	Stuart	Parker	Euell	Konchesky	Bartlett ▲56	Johansson 44 56	Todd ▲	Robinson ▲	Euell ▲
13-10	H	Middlesbrough	0-0	0-0	11	D.R.Elleray	Kiely	Young	Fish	Todd ●	Robinson ▲	Powell	Parker ●	Kinsella	Konchesky	Bartlett ●	Johansson	Jensen ▲	Euell ▲	Euell ▲
20-10	A	Derby County	0-1	1-1	13	A.P.D'Urso	Kiely 73	Young	Todd	Todd	Konchesky	Robinson ▲	Parker ●	Kinsella	Konchesky	Bartlett ●	Johansson	Robinson ▲	Peacock ▲	Euell ▲73
24-10	A	Aston Villa	0-1	0-2	15	D.Pugh	Kiely	Young	Fish	Brown	Powell	Powell	Parker ●	Kinsella	Jensen ●	Bartlett ●	Robinson ●	Robinson ▲	Robinson ▲	Euell ▲
27-10	H	Liverpool	0-2	0-2	16	P.Jones	Kiely	Young	Fish	Brown	Robinson	Parker	Jensen ●	Euell	Bartlett	Parker ●	Parker ●	Parker ▲	Parker ▲	-
04-11	A	Arsenal	2-1	4-2	15	M.R.Halsey	Kiely	Young	Fish	Brown 35	Konchesky 35 42	Powell	Parker ▲51	Kinsella 49 53	Jensen 49 53	Euell 53	Johansson 49	Bartlett ●	Bartlett ●	Robinson ●
19-11	H	West Ham Utd	2-2	4-4	16	A.G.Wiley	Kiely	Young ▲	Fish 90	Brown	Powell	Konchesky	Jensen 21	Kinsella 21	Euell 21 28	Euell 21 28	Johansson 28 51 90	Robinson ▲	Robinson ●	-
24-11	A	Southampton	0-0	0-1	16	D.J.Gallagher	Kiely	Young	Fish	Brown ▲	Powell ▲	Jensen	Konchesky ●	Bartlett	McDonald ●83	Parker ●	Robinson ●	Parker ▲	Parker ▲	Robinson ▲
01-12	H	Newcastle Utd	0-0	1-1	15	A.P.D'Urso	Kiely	Young	Fish ▲	Powell	Stuart ▲	Robinson 83	Bartlett	McDonald ●83	Bartlett	Bartlett ●	Peacock ●	Bartlett ▲	Bartlett ▲	Lisbie ▲
05-12	A	Chelsea	1-0	1-0	15	D.J.Gallagher	Kiely	Young ●	Fish	Fortune	Powell	Stuart ▲4	Jensen	Robinson ●	Costa	Euell ●89	Costa	Costa ▲	Costa ▲	Lisbie ▲89
08-12	H	Tottenham	2-0	3-1	10	S.W.Dunn	Kiely ●	Young ●19	Fish	Fortune	Stuart ▲19 78	Jensen	Jensen	Stuart ▲4	Euell ▲4	Lisbie ●19 78	Bart-Williams ▲	Bart-Williams ▲	Bart-Williams ▲	Konchesky ▲
15-12	A	Bolton	0-0	0-0	11	C.J.Foy	Kiely	Young	Fish	Fortune ●	Costa	Jensen	Konchesky	Stuart ●	Lisbie	Euell	Lisbie	Konchesky ▲	Johansson ▲	Johansson ▲
22-12	H	Blackburn	0-0	0-2	13	A.G.Wiley	Kiely	Young	Fish ●	Fortune	Powell ▲	Jensen	Konchesky ●	Stuart	Lisbie	Euell	Lisbie	Johansson ▲	Johansson ▲	Johansson ▲
26-12	A	Fulham	1-0	1-0	12	S.G.Bennett	Kiely	Young	Fish	Fortune ●	Costa	Jensen ▲	Costa	Euell ▲	Bart-Williams	Euell ▲4	Bart-Williams ●	Costa ●	Bart-Williams ●	Bart-Williams ▲
29-12	H	Everton	1-0	3-0	9	G.P.Barber	Kiely	Young ●	Fish ●	Powell ▲28	Stuart ▲28	Jensen ▲	Peacock ●68	Konchesky ●	Robinson ●16	Euell 68	Konchesky ●88	Konchesky ▲88	Bart-Williams ▲88	Bart-Williams ▲88
01-01	H	Ipswich Town	2-2	3-2	8	U.D.Rennie	Kiely	Young ●	Fish 32	Robinson ●16	Powell ▲70	Parker ▲32	Konchesky 68	Euell 68	Parker ●	Euell 68	Peacock ●	Bartlett ●	Bartlett ●	Bart-Williams ●
12-01	A	Blackburn	0-2	1-4	10	N.S.Barry	Kiely	Robinson	Fish	Fortune ▲	Powell	Parker ●	Jensen ▲	Lisbie ●	Parker ●	Euell 51	Svensson ●	Svensson ▲	Svensson ▲	Lisbie 88
21-01	H	Aston Villa	0-2	1-2	10	R.Styles	Kiely	Young ◢	Fish	Powell 88	Stuart 88	Robinson	Jensen ▲	Fortune	Kishishev	Euell	Fortune	Fortune ▲	Kishishev ▲	Lisbie 77
29-01	H	Derby County	0-0	1-0	9	D.Pugh	Kiely	Young	Fortune	Konchesky	Powell	Svensson 77	Jensen ▲	Stuart 77	Bart-Williams 77	Euell ▲	Konchesky ●	Kishishev ●	Svensson ●	Lisbie ▲
03-02	A	Middlesbrough	0-1	0-2	10	A.G.Wiley	Kiely	Robinson	Fish ▲	Fortune	Powell	Stuart	Jensen ●	Bart-Williams	Bart-Williams	Euell	Johansson	Johansson ▲	Johansson ▲	Konchesky ▲
10-02	H	Manchester Utd	0-0	0-0	10	M.L.Dean	Kiely	Young ◢	Fish	Powell	Stuart ▲28	Robinson	Jensen ▲	Bart-Williams	Bart-Williams	Euell	Kishishev 72	Kishishev ●	Kishishev ▲	-
24-02	A	Leeds Utd	0-0	0-2	10	M.L.Dean	Kiely	Young	Fish	Powell	Stuart	Robinson ●	Parker	Kinsella ●	Bart-Williams	Euell	Svensson ●	Brown ●	Brown ●	-
02-03	H	Chelsea	0-2	2-1	9	G.Poll	Kiely	Young	Fortune	Powell	Stuart 42	Konchesky ●	Parker ▲	Kinsella	Bart-Williams 89	Euell 72 89	Kishishev ●	Kishishev ▲	Kishishev ▲	Robinson ▲
09-03	A	Leicester City	1-1	1-1	7	C.R.Wilkes	Kiely	Young ●	Fortune	Powell	Stuart ▲70	Brown ●	Parker ●	Kinsella	Bart-Williams	Euell 42	Brown	Svensson ▲72	Brown ◢	Johansson ▲
18-03	A	Tottenham	0-2	0-2	8	J.T.Winter	Kiely	Young	Fortune	Rufus	Powell ▲70	Stuart 70	Parker	Kinsella	Bart-Williams	Euell	Stuart ●	Brown ●	Kishishev ●	-
23-03	H	Bolton	1-2	1-2	8	C.J.Foy	Kiely	Young	Fortune	Powell	Stuart	Parker	Kinsella	Bart-Williams	Euell	Stuart ●	Johansson ▲52	Konchesky ●	Konchesky ●	-
30-03	A	Liverpool	0-2	0-2	9	P.Dowd	Kiely	Young ●	Fortune	Powell	Stuart	Parker	Kinsella	Bart-Williams	Robinson	Euell 52	Robinson ●	Johansson ▲	Johansson ●	Robinson ▲
01-04	H	Arsenal	0-3	0-3	11	A.P.D'Urso	Kiely	Young	Fortune	Konchesky	Powell	Parker	Kinsella	Bart-Williams	Robinson	Euell	Listie	Johansson ●	Robinson ●	Johansson ▲
06-04	A	West Ham Utd	0-2	0-2	12	M.A.Riley	Kiely	Young ●	Rufus	Fortune	Stuart	Parker	Kinsella	Bart-Williams	Stuart	Euell	Listie ●	Konchesky ●	Konchesky ●	-
13-04	H	Southampton	1-0	1-1	12	P.Dowd	Kiely	Robinson	Rufus 16	Fortune	Stuart 42	Parker	Kinsella	Bart-Williams	Stuart 70	Euell 16	Listie ●	Listie ●	Konchesky ●	Listie ●
20-04	H	Newcastle Utd	0-3	1-3	13	M.L.Dean	Kiely	Young	Rufus	Konchesky	Powell ▲70	Parker	Kinsella	Bart-Williams	Robinson	Euell	Johansson	Johansson ●	Listie ●	-
27-04	A	Sunderland	1-2	2-2	13	E.K.Wolstenholme	Kiely	Young	Rufus	Konchesky ●	Stuart 82	Parker	Kinsella	Bart-Williams	Robinson	Euell 1	Svensson 1	Svensson ●	Svensson ▲	Lisbie ▲82
11-05	A	Manchester Utd	0-0	0-0	14	G.Poll	Kiely	Young	Fortune	Powell	Stuart	Parker	Kinsella	Bart-Williams	Konchesky ▲	Euell	Listie ●	Jensen ▲	Svensson ●	Johansson ▲

F.A. Barclaycard Premiership
Squad List

Position	Name	Appearances	Appearances as Substitute	Goals or Clean Sheets	Goal Assists	Yellow Cards	Red Cards
G	D.Kiely	38		12	2	2	
D	S.Brown	11	3	2		3	1
D	J.Costa	22	2			9	
D	M.Fish	25			2	3	
D	J.Fortune	14	4			2	
D	R.Kishishev		3				
D	P.Konchesky	22	12	1	4	4	
D	C.Powell	35	1	1	1	3	
D	R.Rufus	10		1		1	
D	A.Todd	3	2			2	
D	L.Young	34			2	5	
M	C.Bart-Williams	10	6	1	2	2	
M	C.Jensen	16	2	1	1		
M	M.Kinsella	14	3		1	2	
M	S.Parker	36	2	1	2	9	1
M	G.Peacock	1	4				
M	J.Robinson	16	12	1	2	4	
M	J.Salako	2	1				
M	G.Stuart	31		3	3	3	1
F	S.Bartlett	10	4	2	1	2	
F	J.Euell	31	5	11	3	3	
F	J.Johansson	21	9	5	4	1	
F	K.Lisbie	10	12	5	4	2	
F	C.McDonald		2	1			
F	M.Svensson	6	6		1	1	

advantage. Arsenal replied but Charlton held on for a famous win.

After the joy came the comedy, with Charlton and West Ham sharing eight Valley goals in a bizarre 4-4 draw in which former Charlton striker Jermain Defoe, barracked for his defection across the Thames, claimed an equaliser after former Valley loanee Paul Kitson had struck a hat-trick for the Hammers. Euell scored twice but a family bereavement ruled him out for the next two games, the defeat at Southampton and the draw at home to Newcastle United.

Curbishley knew he had to take steps to halt the decline and made two signings. In came Portuguese defender Jorge Costa and Nottingham Forest's Chris Bart-Williams, both on loan. Bart-Williams was later to make the move permanent.

Euell returned to action as the Addicks won 1-0 at Chelsea, thanks to another youngster, Kevin Lisbie. He was to prosper again when Charlton faced Spurs at the Valley. Lisbie had lost his boots, stolen from his car, but in borrowed footwear he netted twice in the 3-1 win.

Curbishley looked for fresh ways to inspire his side and turned to Joe Dunbar, Lennox Lewis' trainer, to add a new look to training. Charlton responded and appeared fighting fit as they tried to get over the prolonged absentees.

With so many injuries, consistency was always going to be difficult. However, successive wins at the turn of the year, at Everton and at home to Ipswich, showed the spirit Curbishley had demanded from those players still fit.

Jorge Costa soon proved a hit at the Valley. His arrival and subsequent partnership with young Jonathan Fortune coincided with a marked improvement in the New Year. Charlton reluctantly lost Bartlett for the early part of the year when

➡ Win Barclaycard Premiership tickets – 4thegame.com

F.A. Barclaycard Premiership

Top Goal Scorer

Jason Euell

Total Premier League Goals Scored:	Percentage Of The Team's League Goals:
11	**29%**

Goals Scored From

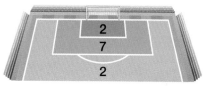

E uell arrived in the summer of 2001 from Wimbledon, having clocked up 19 Division One goals in 2000-01. The Addicks paid a club record fee of £4.75m to secure his services but Euell took time to settle. He had to wait until mid-October to claim his first League goal for Charlton. Once he did start scoring, he suffered the tragic death of his young daughter. Still he returned and kept Charlton in the safety zone with valuable goals, including a brace in the 4-4 draw with West Ham and another pair in the 2-1 win over Chelsea at the Valley. By the end of the season, it started to look like money well spent with the striker scoring more than twice as many goals as any other teammate.

"I brought Jason Euell in as an addition to our strike-force, but one of the attractions of him is that he can play in a number of different positions."

Alan Curbishley

Goals Resulting From

Key

 Open Play ■ Corner ☐ Indirect Free Kick
☐ Direct Free Kick ■ Penalty

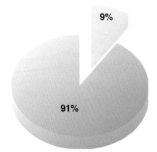

9%

91%

	Right Foot	Left Foot	Header
Open Play	8	2	-
Set piece	-	1	-

Goal Assists

Total number of goal assists	3

Teams Scored Against

Against	Home	Away
Chelsea	2	0
West Ham United	2	0
Arsenal	0	1
Blackburn Rovers	0	1
Derby County	0	1
Everton	0	1
Ipswich Town	1	0
Leicester City	0	1
Sunderland	1	0
Total Goals Scored	**6**	**5**

 The heart of the Barclaycard Premiership - 4thegame.com

> **"It's a little bit do-or-die at the moment and one or two players are trying a bit too hard because they are all desperate to play well. I'm disappointed because a few things are creeping into our game, and that is not natural for us."**
>
> *Alan Curbishley*
> *(February 2002)*

they were forced to release the South African striker for the African Nations Cup in Mali.

After disappointing results at Blackburn, where Scott Parker was sent off, and at home to Villa, Charlton rallied. They overcame the shock of a home F.A. Cup defeat by Division One Walsall, by beating Derby in January, only their fourth success at the Valley.

Curbishley, one of the brightest managers in the country, was a wanted man again when he was linked with the Aston Villa job following John Gregory's resignation. The manager insisted he was not interested in leaving, claiming his job at Charlton was far from complete.

Curbishley was concerned at the disappointing home results; the Valley was growing, with a capacity increased to more than 26,000, from 20,000, and the Addicks boss said: "We have not given our fans anything to cheer about for some time. Their support has been brilliant but we have lost more games than we did in the previous season."

Just as they seemed to be turning the corner with their injury problems, the jinx struck again when Mark Fish had to undergo a knee operation in February. Elsewhere, others were returning to fitness. Mark Kinsella and Matthias

F.A. Barclaycard Premiership
Goals By Position

Key: Forward ■ Midfield ■ League Position ■ Defence ■ Goalkeeper

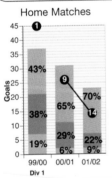

Home Matches

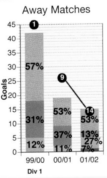

Away Matches

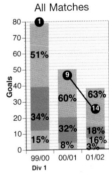

All Matches

Chart Analysis

statistics powered by **SUPERBASE**™

Charlton's goal total dropped to one goal per game. As in the previous campaign, while the strikers contributed the lion's share of goals, the rest of the team struggled to pitch in with a significant contribution.

The goal credited to a goalkeeper was an own goal by Richard Wright in the Addicks' 4-2 win at Highbury.

Away from home, the defence weighed in with twice as many goals as the midfield.

Svensson, who had agreed new deals, were back in action and things began to look up.

Goalkeeper Dean Kiely, playing for a place in Mick McCarthy's Republic of Ireland World Cup squad, was putting in performances that deserved international recognition as Charlton started to edge up the table.

Two goalless draws, against Middlesbrough and Leeds, and a 2-0 home defeat by Manchester United did not affect the Addicks' League position too drastically. After three games without a goal they began the month of March with a memorable victory, the 2-1 win over Chelsea at the Valley completing a 'double' over the Blues.

The victory owed much to Euell, who claimed a brace to take his tally in his first season at the Valley, to 11, both goals coming in the last 20 minutes.

Another crowd in excess of 26,000 crammed into the Valley for the match, keeping the Addicks on course for an impressive attendance record. Indeed, 2001-02 provided Charlton with 20,000 plus crowds at every home League game for the first time since the 1948-49 season.

Perhaps the success Charlton enjoyed was difficult for some people to accept; after a 1-1 draw at Leicester, Chris Powell admitted that the club was still wary of the threat of relegation, even though they were

F.A. Barclaycard Premiership
Team Performance Table

League Position	Team	Points Won From A Possible Six	Percentage Of Points Won At Home	Percentage Of Points Won Away	Overall Percentage Of Points Won
1	Arsenal	3/6			
2	Liverpool	0/6			
3	Manchester Utd	1/6	7%	33%	20%
4	Newcastle Utd	1/6			
5	Leeds United	1/6			
6	Chelsea	6/6			
7	West Ham Utd	1/6			
8	Aston Villa	0/6	47%	40%	43%
9	Tottenham H	6/6			
10	Blackburn R	0/6			
11	Southampton	1/6			
12	Middlesbrough	2/6			
13	Fulham	2/6	25%	42%	33%
14	**Charlton Athletic**	44			
15	Everton	3/6			
16	Bolton W	1/6			
17	Sunderland	2/6			
18	Ipswich Town	6/6	67%	47%	57%
19	Derby County	4/6			
20	Leicester City	4/6			

The table shows how many points out of a possible six Charlton Athletic have taken off each of the teams in the four sections. The other columns show as a percentage how many points they have taken from those available.

Chart Analysis

statistics powered by SUPERBASE™

Charlton managed to take just one point off the top five teams at home – a 1-1 draw with Newcastle. Their shortcomings at the Valley were also exposed by teams within their own sector, where they failed to win any of their fixtures.

They did however manage home wins over both Chelsea and Spurs in the second sector, as well as over the bottom three.

Whilst eight teams failed to beat the Addicks,

Curbishley's side could not defeat eleven of their F.A. Barclaycard Premiership opponents.

In general, they managed to take something off all the teams during the course of the season, with just three teams – Liverpool, Aston Villa and Blackburn –- doing the 'double' over them.

 Fixtures, results and match reports - 4thegame.com

now ninth and 20 points clear of the bottom.

Powell said: "Yes, we are in the top half and it may sound strange me saying this but you just have to look how close it is among the teams below us."

Any lingering fears of relegation were put to bed in the next outing, at White Hart Lane, where Young returned against his former club. Powell, having voiced his fears, was the man who secured another three points. How ironic that he remains a Spurs fan – he plans to buy a White Hart Lane season ticket when he retires – and that his only previous Charlton goal had come a season earlier against Spurs in the F.A. Cup.

The win took Charlton into seventh; rather than worry about the drop, they could afford to dream about Europe. Perhaps they let such a lofty position get to their heads, with their worst run of the season to follow.

It began at home to Bolton, who were fighting for F.A. Barclaycard Premiership survival and left with a 2-1 win. Charlton might have stolen a point but Euell sent his penalty wide early in the game.

Away from the first team, forgotten man Martin Pringle, on loan to Grimsby, suffered a double fracture of his leg and there were initial fears that his career could be over.

If March finished badly, April started horribly. Charlton

It's a fact

Charlton reached a century of Premier League points when they won at Arsenal, taking their total to 101 from a possible 261.

"**The London games have been a good source of points and when people tell you about these quirks or stats you want to keep them going.**"

Alan Curbishley
(March 2002)

F.A. Barclaycard Premiership
Goals By Time Period

Key
■ Goals Scored ■ Goals Conceded

Home Matches

Time of Goal (mins)

0-15	2	8
16-30	5	5
31-45	3	5
46-60	5	1
61-75	1	5
76-90	7	6

Goals

Away Matches

Time of Goal (mins)

0-15	1	4
16-30	1	4
31-45	3	3
46-60	3	3
61-75	4	1
76-90	3	4

Goals

All Matches

Time of Goal (mins)

0-15	3	12
16-30	6	9
31-45	6	8
46-60	8	4
61-75	5	6
76-90	10	10

Goals

Chart Analysis

statistics powered by ◆ SUPERBASE™

Charlton were poor starters, scoring just three goals and conceding 12 in the opening 15 minutes of all matches.

They managed 50% more goals in the second half than in the first, scoring the most in the final 15 minutes (although they conceded as many too).

The only time they outscored their opponents was in the opening 15 minutes after the restart.

 Win Barclaycard Premiership tickets - 4thegame.com

Charlton Athletic

F.A. Barclaycard Premiership
Goals Resulting From

Key ☐ Goals Scored ☐ Goals Conceded

	Six Yard Area				Inside Area				Outside Area				Total			
	Shots		Headers		Shots		Headers		Shots		Headers		Shots		Headers	
	Home	Away	Home	Away	Home	Away	Home	Away	Home	Away	Home	Away	Home	Away	Home	Away
Open Play	3	2	2	1	9	8	2	-	2	-	-	-	**14**	**10**	**4**	**1**
	3	2	-	2	17	2	-	1	2	4	-	-	**22**	**8**	**0**	**3**
Direct Free Kick									1	-			**1**	**0**		
									1	-			**1**	**0**		
Indirect Free Kick	1	-	-	1	1	-	-	1	-	-	-	-	**2**	**0**	**0**	**2**
	-	-	1	-	1	1	1	2	-	-	-	-	**1**	**1**	**2**	**2**
Penalty	-	-	1	-	-	-	-	-	-	-	-	-	**0**	**0**	**1**	**0**
	-	-	-	-	1	2	-	-	-	-	-	-	**1**	**2**	**0**	**0**
Corner	-	-	-	-	-	-	-	1	-	-	-	-	**0**	**0**	**0**	**1**
	-	1	-	-	2	-	-	2	-	-	-	-	**2**	**1**	**0**	**2**
Totals	4	2	3	2	10	8	2	2	3	0	0	0	**17**	**10**	**5**	**4**
	3	3	1	2	21	5	1	5	3	4	0	0	**27**	**12**	**2**	**7**

How Goals Were Scored
Home & Away Matches

3%
3% 3% 11%

81%

Key
- ☐ Open Play
- ☐ Corner
- ☐ Indirect Free Kick
- ☐ Direct Free Kick
- ☐ Penalty

Charts do not include 2 own goals for and 1 against.

How Goals Were Conceded
Home & Away Matches

2% 6% 10%
13%

69%

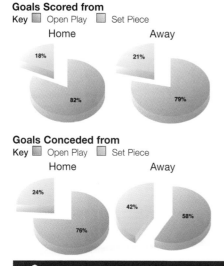

Goals Scored from
Key ☐ Open Play ☐ Set Piece

Home
18%
82%

Away
21%
79%

Goals Conceded from
Key ☐ Open Play ☐ Set Piece

Home
24%
76%

Away
42%
58%

Chart Analysis

The Addicks conceded close to a third of their goals from Set Pieces. This was particularly evident away from home.

Nevertheless, they conceded most goals from Open Play Inside Area.

Their success from Set Pieces was limited, with solitary goals scored from Corners, Direct Free Kicks and Penalties, although they had more success from Indirect Free Kicks.

The one Penalty Charlton scored was interesting in that Graham Stuart's initial shot was parried and he scored from the rebound with his head.

statistics powered by **SUPERBASE**™

➡ The heart of the Barclaycard Premiership – 4thegame.com

It's a fact

The 1-0 win over Derby, in January, allowed the Addicks to celebrate their 100th Premier League game in style.

lost to three early goals as Arsenal announced their title challenge was on full throttle, and a fourth successive loss at West Ham, in which Paul Konchesky missed a penalty, left Curbishley wanting the season to end a month early.

Rufus scored a rare goal to earn Charlton a point at home to Southampton but the win-less run was extended to six games when they were unfortunate enough to face another team with something to prove. Newcastle were on fire, claiming their 5,000th home goal, while Alan Shearer broke the 200 Premier League goal barrier as the Addicks slumped to another 3-0 loss.

They finished their home programme against Sunderland and left the visitors still fearing for their safety when Lisbie netted an 82nd minute equaliser in a 2-2 draw.

They ended the season at Old Trafford where Manchester United had a slim chance of finishing second. Jorge Costa made his final appearance after deciding to return to Portugal. The Addicks secured a goalless draw, a low-key finish to an otherwise satisfying season.

F.A. Barclaycard Premiership
Shot Efficiency

Key ◼ Goals Scored ◻ Other Shots On Target

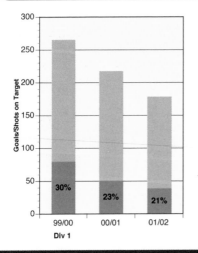

Season	Division	Shots Off Target	Shots On Target	Total Goals
1999 - 2000	1	n/a	265	79
2000 - 2001	P	n/a	217	50
2001 - 2002	P	182	178	38

Chart Analysis

Both the number of Shots On Target and goals scored fell dramatically compared to the previous season.

The Shot Efficiency also went down for the second season running, with Charlton converting 2% less of their chances.

statistics powered by **SUPERBASE**™

➡ **All the latest news, views and opinion - 4thegame.com**

F.A. Barclaycard Premiership

Team Discipline

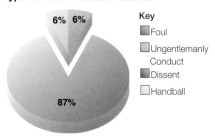

Key
- ☐ Forward ■ Midfield
- ☐ Defence ■ Goalkeeper

Total Number Of Bookings

Total number of red cards	3
Total number of yellow cards	63

Referee Performance

Referee	Games Refereed	Red Cards	Yellow Cards
M.L.Dean	3	1	6
S.W.Dunn	2	-	9
M.R.Halsey	2	1	4

Type of Yellow Cards Received

6% 6%

87%

Key
- ■ Foul
- ☐ Ungentlemanly Conduct
- ■ Dissent
- ☐ Handball

Bookings by Position 1999/2000 - 2001/2002

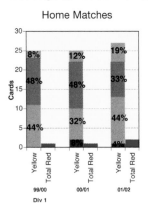

Home Matches

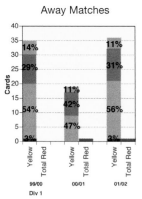

Away Matches

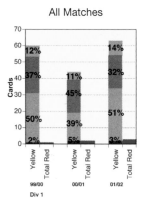

All Matches

Chart Analysis

The number of Yellow Cards dished out to Charlton players rose sharply, even outstripping their tally from two seasons ago when they were in Division One and played eight more League matches.

The worst offenders were defenders, who clocked 32 yellow cards compared to 17 in 2000-01

A staggering 87% of their cautions were for committing Fouls, while all three Red Cards received by Charlton players were for direct sending off offences.

"I just wonder if it's time there was someone sitting up in the stand. Perhaps there should be someone like the third umpire at cricket."
Alan Curbishley
(September 2001)

statistics powered by SUPERBASE™

→ **Fixtures, results and match reports - 4thegame.com**

Chelsea

	F.A. Barclaycard Premiership Final standing for the 2001-2002 season							
Final Position		Games Played	Games Won	Games Drawn	Games Lost	Goals For	Goals Against	Total Points
5	Leeds United	38	18	12	8	53	37	66
6	Chelsea	38	17	13	8	66	38	64
7	West Ham United	38	15	8	15	48	57	53

> **"I don't know if we can do it, but we want to do it, it will be difficult but that is what I want to do. In my mind this target is available."**
> *Claudio Ranieri on winning the Championship (May 2002)*

Club Honours and Records

Football League Champions: 1954-55

Division 2 Champions: 1983-84, 1988-89

FA Cup Winners: 1970, 1997, 2000

League Cup Winners: 1965, 1998

Full Members' Cup Winners: 1986

Zenith Data Systems Cup Winners: 1990

European Cup Winners' Cup Winners: 1997-98

European Super Cup Winners: 1998

Record victory: 13-0 v Jeunesse Hautcharage, European Cup Winners' Cup, 29 September, 1971

Record defeat: 1-8 v Wolverhampton Wanderers, Division 1, 26 September, 1953

League goals in a season (team): 98, Division 1, 1960-61

League goals in a season (player): 41, Jimmy Greaves, 1960-61

Career league goals: 164, Bobby Tambling, 1958 to 1970

League appearances: 655, Ron Harris, 1962 to 1980

Reported transfer fee paid: £15,000,000 to Atletico Madrid for Jimmy Floyd Hasselbaink, June 2000

Reported transfer fee received: £12,000,000 from Rangers for Tore-Andre Flo, November 2000

CHELSEA flattered to deceive in the 2001-02 campaign. An F.A. Cup final meant that they qualified for the UEFA Cup but chairman Ken Bates will no doubt expect more.

As had happened previously, inconsistency was to derail the Blues' season, not to mention several episodes off the park. Still, some of their football, particularly at Stamford Bridge, was sublime.

Newcomers included Frank Lampard, Emmanuel Petit, Boudewijn Zenden and William Gallas, at a combined cost of more than £32m. In the other direction, the Chelsea career of Dennis Wise came to an end as the former England man left for Leicester City.

Although Ranieri had spent the summer learning English, there were times when confusion still seemed to reign at Chelsea.

Stamford Bridge had a new look, with rebuilding work completed to increase the capacity to more than 40,000, and Chelsea started with a 1-1 home draw against Newcastle, Zenden getting off the mark with a debut goal. A howler by Ed de Goey, who had surprisingly been given the nod as Chelsea's goalkeeper, ruined the day.

 Win Barclaycard Premiership tickets - 4thegame.com

Chelsea

Key
■ Win ■ Loss ■ Draw —❷— League Position
—❷— Last Season's League Position

All Matches

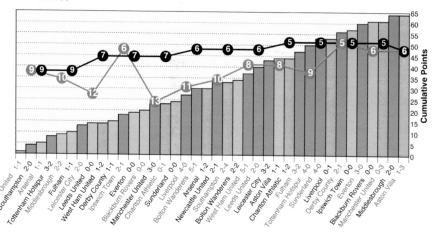

Home Matches

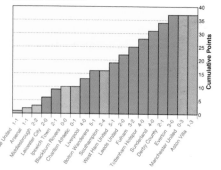

Away Matches

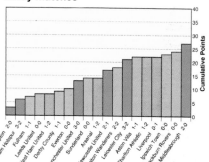

Chart Analysis

Chelsea's decent start saw them lose just once in their opening 14 matches – the 2-1 defeat at West Ham United.

There followed an inconsistent eight game spell when defeats to Charlton and Southampton were balanced with wins against Liverpool and Newcastle.

A 5-1 thumping of West Ham towards the end of January kicked off a fine home run which saw them pick up seven wins on the spin.

However, their form on the road meant that they failed to stake a decisive claim for a Champions League spot.

Although their away form was an improvement on the previous season, their inability to win more than one game on the trot away from home – the first two excepted – ultimately cost them dear.

statistics powered by SUPERBASE™

➡ **The heart of the Barclaycard Premiership - 4thegame.com**

It's a fact

Chelsea won in their first away game of the season, at Southampton – a far cry from the previous campaign, when they took 17 away games to secure a win.

Chelsea, though, looked hard to beat. They won 2-0 at Southampton and then drew 1-1 at home to Arsenal where Jimmy Floyd Hasselbaink was sent off. Although Hasselbaink later had the red card rescinded, Chelsea were drawing too many games. In the next match, at Tottenham, feelings ran high again. Chelsea extended their run of poor discipline as, despite winning 3-2, Lampard was sent off.

An incident off the field did little to improve Chelsea's image. Lampard, Jody Morris, Eidur Gudjohnsen and John Terry were all fined two weeks' wages for 'drunken and insulting behaviour' that upset grieving Americans in a Heathrow hotel a day after the September 11 terrorist attacks. On the day Chelsea discovered the incidents, they threw away a 2-0 lead against Middlesbrough at home, finishing with just a point.

To add insult to injury, Jesper Gronkjaer needed knee surgery with the season just four games old but Chelsea, having negotiated the first round of the UEFA Cup on the first anniversary of Ranieri's Stamford Bridge tenure, were beginning to believe they could mount a positive campaign.

Then came another moment which seemed to suggest team unity was not what it should be. Chelsea were drawn against Hapoel Tel Aviv in the UEFA Cup. With political unrest beginning to rear its head in Israel, Chelsea made an

F.A. Barclaycard Premiership
Half-Time/Full-Time Comparison

Key: ■ Win ■ Loss ■ Draw

Home				Away				Total			
	Full Time Result				**Full Time Result**				**Full Time Result**		
Number of Home Half Time Wins	W	L	D	Number of Away Half Time Wins	W	L	D	Total number of Half Time Wins	W	L	D
13	10	1	2	7	5	1	1	20	15	2	3
Number of Home Half Time Losses	W	L	D	Number of Away Half Time Losses	W	L	D	Total number of Half Time Losses	W	L	D
2	-	2	-	4	1	1	2	6	1	3	2
Number of Home Half Time Draws	W	L	D	Number of Away Half Time Draws	W	L	D	Total number of Half Time Draws	W	L	D
4	1	1	2	8	-	2	6	12	1	3	8

Chart Analysis

The Blues had a good record of winning matches when they were in front at half-time, picking up 48 out of a possible 60 points.

Their record in matches when they were on level terms or down at the break was not so great, winning just two out of 18.

Away from home, they failed to convert any half-time draws into wins.

DATE	H/A	OPPONENT	H/T	F/T	POS	REFEREE	TEAM											SUBSTITUTES USED		
19-08	H	Newcastle Utd	1-0	1-1	9	A.P.D'Urso	de Goey	Melchiot ●	Desailly	Terry	Le Saux	Gronkjaer	Lampard	Petit	Zenden ▲8	Hasselbaink	Zola 8	Jokanovic ▲	Gallas ▲	Jokanovic ▲
25-08	A	Southampton	1-0	2-0	5	D.R.Elleray	de Goey	Gallas	Desailly	Terry	Le Saux 32	Gronkjaer ▲	Lampard 90	Petit ▲	Jokanovic	Hasselbaink 32	Zenden	Morris ▲	Stanic ▲90	Zola
08-09	H	Arsenal	1-1	1-1	9	M.A.Riley	de Goey	Gallas	Desailly	Terry	Le Saux ●	Gronkjaer ●	Lampard	Petit	Zenden ▲	Hasselbaink 30	Zola 30	Morris ▲	Stanic ▲	-
16-09	A	Tottenham	2-0	3-2	6	S.W.Dunn	de Goey	Melchiot ●	Desailly ●	Terry ▲	Le Saux ●	Gronkjaer ●	Lampard ●45	Petit	Zenden ▲	Hasselbaink 45 80 80	Zola ▲	Gudjohnsen ▲90	Gallas ▲	Jokanovic ▲
23-09	H	Middlesbrough	2-2	2-2	6	R.Styles	de Goey	Melchiot ●	Desailly ●	Terry ▲	Gallas	Gronkjaer ▲	Lampard	Petit	Zenden ▲37	H'baink ●3 37	Gudjohnsen 3	Morris ▲	Le Saux ▲	Zola ▲
30-09	A	Fulham	1-0	1-1	9	G.Poll	de Goey	Melchiot ●	Desailly	Terry	Babayaro	Jokanovic ●	Jokanovic	Petit	Zenden ▲32	Hasselbaink 32	Zola ●	Ferrer ▲	Gudjohnsen ▲	Dalla Bona ▲
13-10	H	Leicester City	2-0	2-0	5	J.T.Winter	Cudicini	Gallas	Desailly	Terry	Babayaro	Zola 45	Jokanovic ●	Petit	Zenden ▲42	Hasselbaink 32	Gudjohnsen ▲21 45	Lampard ▲20	Ferrer ▲	Melchiot ▲
21-10	A	Leeds Utd	0-0	0-0	7	P.A.Durkin	Bosnich	Melchiot	Gallas	Terry	Babayaro ▲	Lampard	Dalla Bona	Petit	Zenden ▲	Hasselbaink	Gudjohnsen ▲	Zenden ▲	Forssell ▲	Forssell ▲
28-10	A	West Ham Utd	1-2	1-2	7	D.J.Gallagher	Bosnich	Melchiot ▲	Gallas	Terry	Le Saux	Lampard ▲	Dalla Bona	Petit	Zola 22	Hasselbaink 22	Gudjohnsen ▲	Forssell ▲	Forssell ▲	Zenden ▲
28-10	H	Derby County	0-1	1-1	8	S.G.Bennett	Bosnich	Melchiot ▲	Desailly	Terry ●	Le Saux	Lampard ▲	Dalla Bona	Petit	Zenden	Hasselbaink 48	Stanic ●	Dalla Bona ▲	Forssell ▲	Lampard ▲
04-11	H	Ipswich Town	0-1	2-1	7	R.Styles	Bosnich ▲	Melchiot ▲	Desailly	Terry	Babayaro	Stanic ●	Dalla Bona 90	Petit	Forssell ▲36	Zola 36	Gudjohnsen ▲	Hasselbaink ▲	Stanic ●	Gallas ▲
18-11	A	Everton	0-0	0-0	7	M.R.Halsey	Bosnich ●	Melchiot ●	Gallas	Terry	Babayaro ●	Lampard	Dalla Bona	Petit	Zenden	Zola 36	Gudjohnsen ▲	Cudicini ▲	Stanic ●	Zenden ▲
24-11	H	Blackburn	0-0	0-0	8	G.Poll	Cudicini	Melchiot	Gallas	Terry	Le Saux	Stanic ●	Lampard	Petit	Zenden ●	Hasselbaink	Zola ●	Gudjohnsen ▲	Dalla Bona ▲	Zola ▲
01-12	A	Manchester Utd	1-0	3-0	5	A.G.Wiley	Cudicini	Melchiot 6	Gallas	Terry	Babayaro ●86	Dalla Bona ▲86	Lampard	Jokanovic ●	Le Saux ●	H'baink ▲6 64	Gudjohnsen ●86	Stanic ●	Forssell ▲	Zola ▲
05-12	H	Charlton	0-0	0-1	7	D.J.Gallagher	Cudicini	Melchiot	Gallas	Terry	Babayaro	Dalla Bona ●	Lampard	Jokanovic ●	Zenden ●	Hasselbaink ●	Gudjohnsen ▲	Forssell ▲	Zola ▲	-
09-12	A	Sunderland	0-0	0-0	5	N.S.Barry	Cudicini	Melchiot	Melchiot	Terry	Le Saux	Dalla Bona ●	Lampard	Jokanovic ●	Stanic	Hasselbaink	Gudjohnsen ▲	Forssell ▲	Forssell ▲	-
16-12	H	Liverpool	2-0	4-0	5	M.R.Halsey	Cudicini	Melchiot	Gallas	Terry	Babayaro	Stanic ●	Lampard 71	Petit	Le Saux ▲3	Hasselbaink ▲328	Gudjohnsen ●2590	Zola ▲90	Zola ▲90	Jokanovic ▲
23-12	H	Bolton	2-1	5-1	6	U.D.Rennie	Cudicini	Melchiot	Gallas	Terry ●	Babayaro	Stanic ●	Lampard 87	Dalla Bona 75	Zenden ▲3	Hasselbaink 45 41	Gudjohnsen ●41 45	Zola ▲87	Ferrer ▲	Petit ▲
26-12	A	Arsenal	1-0	1-2	6	G.P.Barber	Cudicini ●	Melchiot	Melchiot	Terry ▲	Babayaro ●	Dalla Bona	Lampard 31	Petit	Le Saux ▲3	Hasselbaink 31	Gudjohnsen ●35 45	Zola ▲	Forssell ▲	Dalla Bona ▲
29-12	H	Newcastle Utd	2-1	2-1	6	S.G.Bennett	Cudicini ●	Melchiot	Gallas	Terry ●	Babayaro ●	Stanic ●	Lampard	Dalla Bona	Le Saux 35	Hasselbaink 45	Gudjohnsen 35 45	Zola ▲	Forssell ▲	Jokanovic ▲
01-01	A	Southampton	0-0	2-2	6	E.K.Wolstenholme	Cudicini	Melchiot ●	Gallas	Terry ▲	Babayaro ▲	Dalla Bona ●	Lampard	Dalla Bona	Le Saux ●	Hasselbaink 19 44	Gudjohnsen 19 44	Zola ▲	Forssell ▲	Jokanovic ▲
12-01	A	Bolton	0-0	2-2	6	J.T.Winter	Cudicini	Melchiot	Desailly	Terry	Le Saux 66	Dalla Bona ●61	Lampard	Morris ▲	Stanic ▲53	Zola ▲53	Gudjohnsen 53	Jokanovic ▲	Forssell ▲66	Forssell ▲87 90
20-01	H	West Ham Utd	1-0	5-1	6	A.P.D'Urso	Cudicini	Melchiot	Desailly	Terry 51	Gallas	Zola ●61	Lampard	Petit ●	Stanic ● 90	H'baink ▲45 61	Gudjohnsen ●51 81	H'baink ▲45 61	Morris ▲	Forssell ▲87 90
30-01	H	Leeds Utd	2-0	2-0	6	S.G.Bennett	Cudicini	Melchiot	Desailly	Terry	Le Saux	Dalla Bona 31	Lampard	Petit 2	Stanic ●	Hasselbaink 31	Gudjohnsen 90	Zola ▲79	Forssell ▲	-
02-02	A	Leicester City	0-1	3-2	5	G.P.Barber	Cudicini	Melchiot	Desailly	Terry ▲	Le Saux 61	Dalla Bona ●	Lampard	Petit ▲	Stanic ▲	Hasselbaink 61 90	Gudjohnsen ●2	Zola ▲79	Hasselbaink 61 90	Forssell ▲79 90
09-02	A	Aston Villa	0-1	1-2	5	P.A.Durkin	Cudicini	Ferrer ▲	Gallas	Terry ●	Le Saux	Dalla Bona 64	Lampard 64	Petit ●	Stanic ●	Hasselbaink 64	Gudjohnsen ●	Zola ▲	Keenan ▲	Gronkjaer ▲
02-03	H	Charlton	0-0	1-2	6	P.Jones	Cudicini	Melchiot 17	Desailly	Gallas	Babayaro ●	Stanic ▲	Lampard 85	Morris ▲	Le Saux 28	Hasselbaink 85	Gudjohnsen ●	Zola ▲	Forssell ▲	Forssell ▲83
06-03	A	Fulham	2-1	3-2	6	A.G.Wiley	Cudicini	Melchiot	Desailly 24	Gallas	Babayaro	Zola ▲	Lampard 90	Petit	Le Saux 28	Gudjohnsen ●28	Gudjohnsen ●28	Gronkjaer ▲ ●	Forssell ▲	Forssell ▲83
13-03	H	Tottenham	1-0	4-0	5	B.Knight	Cudicini	Melchiot	Desailly 24	Gallas 24	Babayaro ●	Gronkjaer ●69	Lampard ●90	Petit	Le Saux 23	H'baink ▲23 69 81	H'baink ▲23 69 81	Zola ▲	Zola ▲	Stanic ▲85
16-03	A	Sunderland	1-0	4-0	5	M.R.Halsey	Cudicini	Melchiot	Desailly 24	Gallas	Babayaro ●	Gronkjaer ▲73	Lampard 73	Dalla Bona ●90	Le Saux ▲	Hasselbaink	Dalla Bona ●90	Forssell ▲73	Forssell ▲85	Stanic ▲85
24-03	A	Liverpool	0-0	0-1	5	M.L.Dean	Cudicini	Melchiot	Desailly	Gallas ▲	Babayaro ●	Gronkjaer	Lampard	Petit 86	Stanic	Hasselbaink	Gudjohnsen	Zola ▲	Zola ▲	-
30-03	H	Derby County	0-0	2-1	5	E.K.Wolstenholme	Cudicini	Melchiot	Desailly ●	Terry ●	Le Saux ●50	Gronkjaer	Lampard	Petit 86	Le Saux ●50	Hasselbaink	Forssell ▲	Forssell ▲66	Terry ▲50	Terry ▲50
01-04	A	Ipswich Town	0-0	0-0	5	D.R.Elleray	Cudicini	Melchiot	Desailly	Terry ▲	Le Saux	Zola	Lampard	Dalla Bona	Stanic	Hasselbaink	Forssell ▲	Forssell ▲66	Gudjohnsen ▲	Zenden ▲
06-04	H	Everton	2-0	3-0	4	S.W.Dunn	Cudicini	Melchiot	Desailly	Terry ▲	Le Saux	Zola 44 90	Lampard	Petit ▲	Gudjohnsen 90	Hasselbaink	Gudjohnsen 90	Jokanovic ▲	Cole ▲	Zenden ▲
10-04	H	Blackburn	0-0	0-0	4	G.P.Barber	Cudicini	Melchiot	Desailly	Terry ▲	Gallas	Zola ●	Lampard	Petit	Stanic	Gudjohnsen	Gudjohnsen	Zenden ▲	Zenden ▲	-
20-04	H	Manchester Utd	0-2	0-3	5	B.Knight	Cudicini	Melchiot	Desailly	Terry	Gallas ●	Gronkjaer ▲	Lampard	Petit ▲38 43	Stanic ●	Hasselbaink	Gudjohnsen ●	Dalla Bona ▲	Dalla Bona ▲	Zenden ▲
27-04	A	Middlesbrough	0-1	1-3	5	S.G.Bennett	Cudicini	Melchiot	Desailly ▲	Terry	Gallas	Gronkjaer ▲	Lampard	Petit ▲38 43	Zenden ▲43	Zola	Zola	Cole ▲38	Dalla Bona ▲	Staniс ▲70
11-05	H	Aston Villa	0-1	1-3	6	S.G.Bennett	Cudicini	Terry	Terry	Gallas	Le Saux ▲	Gronkjaer ▲	Lampard	Petit	Zenden ▲43	Cole	Zola	Huth ▲	Gudjohnsen ▲70	Dalla Bona ▲70

F.A. Barclaycard Premiership
Squad List

Position	Name	Appearances	Appearances as Substitute	Goals or Clean Sheets	Goal Assists	Yellow Cards	Red Cards
G	M.Bosnich	5		2			
G	C.Cudicini	27	1	12		1	
G	E.de Goey	6		1			
D	C.Babayaro	18			1	6	
D	M.Desailly	24		1	1	5	
D	A.Ferrer	2	2				
D	W.Gallas	27	3	1		4	
D	R.Huth		1				
D	G.Le Saux	26	1	1	7	6	
D	M.Melchiot	35	2	2		4	
D	J.Terry	32	1	1	1	4	
M	S.Dalla Bona	16	8	4	2	7	
M	J.Gronkjaer	11	2		3	5	
M	S.Jokanovic	12	8			4	1
M	J.Keenan		1				
M	F.Lampard	34	3	5	4	1	1
M	J.Morris	2	3			1	
M	E.Petit	26	1	1	3	3	
M	M.Stanic	18	9	1	3	8	
M	B.Zenden	13	9	3	2	1	
F	C.Cole	2	1	1			
F	M.Forssell	2	20	4	5	1	
F	E.Gudjohnsen	26	6	14	9	2	
F	J.Hasselbaink	35		23	10	5	1
F	G.Zola	19	16	3	8	1	

open offer to let any reluctant players stay behind. No fewer than six players decided not to travel and Chelsea, having lost 2-0 in Israel, went out of Europe after drawing 1-1 in the return. Another early exit did little for Chelsea's strained finances.

The Blues' inability to finish off teams they had dominated was, according to Ranieri, a 'little problem', as he admitted: "My team tend to lose concentration and it has cost us some results."

In defence, Gallas was beginning to look a bargain while Terry was flowering. Between the sticks, Mark Bosnich had finally got his chance after de Goey needed a cartilage operation.

In October, Chelsea revealed losses of £11m over the previous season, highlighting further the need for success on the field. Instead, three games without a win, including their first F.A. Barclaycard defeat of the season at West Ham, which was Ranieri's 50th game in charge, did little to inspire confidence.

Lampard echoed the sentiments of his teammates when he claimed Chelsea needed to be more ruthless. A win over Ipswich, though, was followed by successive goalless draws, at Everton and at home to Blackburn, when the players were booed off the Stamford Bridge pitch by their restless fans.

There were even rumours, later denied, that Ranieri had offered his resignation. The players responded in a rare, public show of unity, by hitting back at suggestions of discontent. With the club finding its way into seventh place on a list of the world's richest clubs, the players wanted to prove they were worth it.

The response was impressive, Chelsea winning 2-0 at Leeds in the Worthington Cup, and then, a week after rumours that Ranieri was on his way, he led his team to a wonderful 3-0 victory at Old Trafford.

 Fixtures, results and match reports – 4thegame.com

F.A. Barclaycard Premiership
Top Goal Scorer

Jimmy Floyd Hasselbaink

Total Premier League Goals Scored:	Percentage Of The Team's League Goals:
23	35%

Goals Scored From

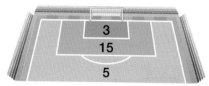

3
15
5

To Chelsea fans, Jimmy Floyd Hasselbaink really is worth his weight in goals. Having notched 23 strikes in his first season at Stamford Bridge, not only did he repeat the feat, he thrilled the crowds with some spectacular efforts. These included a fantastic hat-trick in the 4-0 home League win over Tottenham. The Dutchman netted 29 goals in all competitions including three apiece in each of the two domestic cups. During the course of the campaign, he forged a telling partnership with Eidur Gudjohnsen, who finished the season with 14 in the League. If they keep it up, the pair could well prove to be the driving force to fire Chelsea to glory.

"You have to aim as high as possible. I want to score goals every week."

Jimmy Floyd Hasselbaink

Goals Resulting From
Key
- ■ Open Play ■ Corner □ Indirect Free Kick
- □ Direct Free Kick ■ Penalty

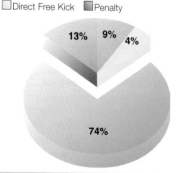

13% 9% 4%

74%

	Right Foot	Left Foot	Header
Open Play	10	3	4
Set piece	6	-	-

Goal Assists

Total number of goal assists	10

Teams Scored Against

Against	Home	Away
Tottenham Hotspur	3	2
Leicester City	1	2
West Ham United	2	1
Everton	2	0
Middlesbrough	2	0
Southampton	1	1
Arsenal	1	0
Bolton Wanderers	1	0
Derby County	0	1
Fulham	0	1
Liverpool	1	0
Manchester United	0	1
Total Goals Scored	**14**	**9**

➡ Win Barclaycard Premiership tickets – 4thegame.com

> "The coach has given me the chance and I owe him a lot. I would love to see him remain here and the lads feel the same. We are all together – it is a good atmosphere."
>
> *John Terry*
> *(November 2001)*

Mario Melchiot gave Chelsea a sixth minute lead and Hasselbaink netted his 11th goal of the season as Chelsea won at a canter. Le Saux struck the woodwork before a third from Gudjohnsen confirmed Chelsea's ultimately easy win. Chelsea were now fifth in the F.A. Barclaycard Premiership but, as if to encapsulate their season, they followed that resounding success with setbacks, losing at home to Charlton and drawing at Sunderland.

Chelsea continued to flourish in the Worthington Cup, beating Newcastle to reach the semi-finals, and then came another performance in which the very best Chelsea had to offer was there for all to witness.

Liverpool arrived at Stamford Bridge in mid-December as F.A. Barclaycard Premiership leaders; they left with a 4-0 defeat. The result announced Chelsea as realistic Championship contenders after a stunning victory which began with a third minute goal from Le Saux.

Hasselbaink scored a lucky 13th of the season before Sam Dalla Bona and Gudjohnsen completed the rout. With rivals Arsenal and Leeds managing only to draw, Chelsea were in the hunt. Another one-sided affair, the 5-1 thrashing of Bolton, maintained their challenge but

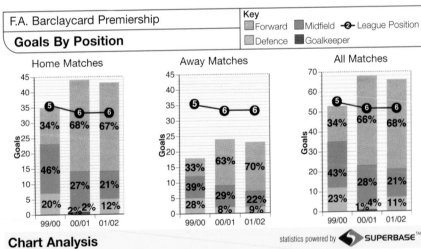

F.A. Barclaycard Premiership
Goals By Position

Key
Forward Midfield —❷—League Position
Defence Goalkeeper

Chart Analysis

statistics powered by **SUPERBASE**™

While the distribution of goals throughout the team remained pretty consistent, the majority of Chelsea's goals came courtesy of their burgeoning strike partnership of Hasselbaink and Gudjohnsen. The goal attributed to the goalkeeper last season was for an own goal scored by Liverpool's Sander Westerveld.

BEST IN LEAGUE...
- **Most goals scored at home**
- **Most goals scored by strikers at home**

➤ **The heart of the Barclaycard Premiership - 4thegame.com**

they slipped up on Boxing Day at Highbury, losing 2-1 to Arsenal after taking the lead through Lampard.

Problems off the field persisted with Terry and Morris fined two weeks' wages after an incident outside a nightclub in London.

In the Worthington Cup, Chelsea won the first leg of the semi-final, beating Spurs 2-1, while in the League a 5-1 win over West Ham saw Hasselbaink take his tally for the season to 19.

Chelsea were becoming a Jekyll and Hyde side. After the West Ham game, they crossed London for the return with Spurs and lost by the same score, their first defeat by Tottenham for 12 years.

The players held a team meeting and the response was perfect. A 2-0 win over Leeds at the end of January and a 3-2 success at Leicester took them into fifth place with an eye on qualification for the Champions League.

Terry broke a toe in February while Roberto Di Matteo was forced to retire after a year of trying to recover from a broken leg.

Disappointment in the Worthington Cup was balanced by their continued success in the F.A. Cup; wins over Norwich, West Ham and Preston had taken Chelsea into the quarter-finals and yet another match with Tottenham.

F.A. Barclaycard Premiership
Team Performance Table

League Position	Team	Points won from a possible six	Percentage of points won at home	Percentage of points won away	Overall percentage of points won
1	Arsenal	1/6			
2	Liverpool	3/6			
3	Manchester Utd	3/6	53%	47%	50%
4	Newcastle Utd	4/6			
5	Leeds United	4/6			
6	Chelsea	64			
7	West Ham Utd	3/6			
8	Aston Villa	1/6	58%	42%	50%
9	Tottenham H	6/6			
10	Blackburn R	2/6			
11	Southampton	3/6			
12	Middlesbrough	4/6			
13	Fulham	4/6	47%	53%	50%
14	Charlton Athletic	0/6			
15	Everton	4/6			
16	Bolton W	4/6			
17	Sunderland	4/6			
18	Ipswich Town	4/6	100%	47%	73%
19	Derby County	4/6			
20	Leicester City	6/6			

The table shows how many points out of a possible six Chelsea have taken off each of the teams in the four sections. The other columns show as a percentage how many points they have taken from those available.

Chart Analysis

Overall, Chelsea were equally successful in the top three sectors, collecting on average 50% of the points available at home and away.

Compared to the previous season, there was a significant improvement in their ability to bag points away from home – in fact, they performed better against teams in the third sector on the road than they did at Stamford Bridge.

Nevertheless, they were strong at home, as can be seen from their performance against teams in the bottom five, where they collected maximum points.

Chelsea managed to pick up points off most teams, London rivals Charlton being the only side to do the 'double' over them.

➡ **All the latest news, views and opinion - 4thegame.com**

Before that tie, they suffered a disappointing result at Charlton, who completed a 'double' over the Blues by winning 2-1 at the Valley where Lampard's goal was of little comfort. The result put a dent in their Champions League aspirations.

Chelsea did find some solace, in a 3-2 win against closest neighbours Fulham at Stamford Bridge. Tempers were high at times and, when Fulham were awarded a controversial penalty, Gianfranco Zola became a hero, preventing an irate fan from getting to referee Peter Jones and ushering him diplomatically off the pitch.

Chelsea owed the win to their 'third man', striker Mikael Forssell, who had been reduced to a bit-part player by the continued success of the Hasselbaink-Gudjohnsen partnership. Forssell, a 74th minute substitute, claimed the winner – the seventh time in 12 games that he had risen from the bench to score for Chelsea.

Next came Tottenham in the F.A. Cup. Despite having Le Saux sent off, Chelsea won 4-0 to re-ignite their good record against Spurs. The teams met for a sixth time three days later in the F.A. Barclaycard Premiership, at Stamford Bridge, and Chelsea repeated the score with a wonderful hat-trick from Hasselbaink.

Chelsea were in the mood to follow Ranieri's

It's a fact

Gianfranco Zola made his 250th appearance for Chelsea in the 3-2 win at Leicester in February and celebrated with a goal.

"At this moment, Chelsea have to win every game if we are to keep our little chance of arriving in the Champions League."

Claudio Ranieri
(March 2002)

F.A. Barclaycard Premiership
Goals By Time Period

Key
■ Goals Scored □ Goals Conceded

Home Matches

Time of Goal (mins)	Scored	Conceded
0-15	4	3
16-30	9	3
31-45	9	1
46-60	3	2
61-75	6	5
76-90	12	7

Away Matches

Time of Goal (mins)	Scored	Conceded
0-15	1	3
16-30	1	2
31-45	8	1
46-60	2	3
61-75	4	4
76-90	7	4

All Matches

Time of Goal (mins)	Scored	Conceded
0-15	5	6
16-30	10	5
31-45	17	2
46-60	5	5
61-75	10	9
76-90	19	11

Chart Analysis

statistics powered by ◆ SUPERBASE™

Chelsea struggled to get off the mark away from home, notching just two goals in the opening half-hour on their travels. They compensated by scoring most of their goals away from home in the last 15 minutes of the first half.

BEST IN LEAGUE...
• **Joint most goals scored 31-45 and 76-90 minutes**

 Fixtures, results and match reports - 4thegame.com

F.A. Barclaycard Premiership
Goals Resulting From

Key ☐ Goals Scored ☐ Goals Conceded

	Six Yard Area				Inside Area				Outside Area				Total			
	Shots		Headers		Shots		Headers		Shots		Headers		Shots		Headers	
	Home	Away	Home	Away	Home	Away	Home	Away	Home	Away	Home	Away	Home	Away	Home	Away
Open Play	4	2	1	2	18	10	-	1	9	3	-	-	31	15	1	3
	2	2	-	-	5	6	1	-	-	4	-	-	7	12	1	0
Direct Free Kick									-	1			0	1		
									1	-			1	0		
Indirect Free Kick	1	-	-	-	-	-	-	1	2	-	-	-	3	0	0	1
	1	-	2	1	1	1	-	-	1	-	-	-	3	1	2	1
Penalty	-	-	-	-	3	1	-	-	-	-	-	-	3	1	0	0
	-	-	-	-	3	-	-	-	-	-	-	-	3	0	0	0
Corner	-	-	-	2	2	-	1	-	1	-	-	-	3	0	1	2
	-	-	1	2	1	-	2	1	-	-	-	-	1	0	3	3
Totals	5	2	1	4	23	11	1	2	12	4	0	0	40	17	2	6
	3	2	3	3	10	7	3	1	2	4	0	0	15	13	6	4

How Goals Were Scored
Home & Away Matches

2% 9% 6% 6% 77%

Key
- ☐ Open Play
- ☐ Corner
- ☐ Indirect Free Kick
- ☐ Direct Free Kick
- ☐ Penalty

Charts do not include 1 own goal for.

How Goals Were Conceded
Home & Away Matches

3% 8% 18% 18% 53%

Goals Scored from
Key ☐ Open Play ☐ Set Piece

Home — 24% 76%
Away — 22% 78%

Goals Conceded from
Key ☐ Open Play ☐ Set Piece

Home — 38% 62%
Away — 29% 71%

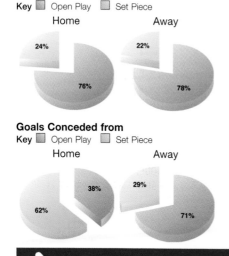

Chart Analysis

While Chelsea's scoring from Open Play and Set Pieces was pretty consistent home and away, the manner in which they conceded goals, especially at Stamford Bridge, raised a few eyebrows. Although they struggled from Set Pieces, they still managed to score a lot more than they conceded.

WORST IN THE LEAGUE...
- **Most goals conceded from Indirect Free Kicks overall and at home**

statistics powered by ◆ SUPERBASE™

→ Win Barclaycard Premiership tickets – 4thegame.com

> **"We haven't got that staying power, that will to drag out a result from nowhere and hold onto it. Our biggest problem is our inconsistency."**
>
> *Graeme Le Saux*
> *(March 2002)*

It's a fact

The 5-1 thrashing of Bolton, in December, was Chelsea's 150th victory in the Premier League.

instruction and win every game. The next victims were Sunderland, with a third successive 4-0 victory putting the visitors' League future in doubt. The impressive run ended briefly at Anfield, where Vladimir Smicer scored the game's only goal, before resuming with a 2-1 home win over Derby.

In the next four games, Chelsea scored in only one, and any hope of sneaking into the fourth Champions League spot was fast beginning to evaporate. They bucked the trend when Hasselbaink scored twice, in the 3-0 win over Everton – a result which took them into fourth spot for a brief spell – but clearly the F.A. Cup was on their minds.

Chelsea won the semi-final, with Terry scoring the only goal at Villa Park against Fulham, while back in the League Manchester United, their eyes still on the title, won 3-0 against a lacklustre Blues. At least they went into the F.A. Cup final on the back of a 2-0 win at Middlesbrough.

In Cardiff, Chelsea faced an Arsenal side set for the Double and, with Terry and Hasselbaink not fully fit, were beaten 2-0 at the Millennium Stadium. The League season ended with another defeat, at home to Aston Villa, Chelsea's fourth at Stamford Bridge.

F.A. Barclaycard Premiership	Key
Shot Efficiency	■ Goals Scored ■ Other Shots On Target

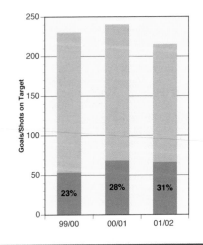

Season	Division	Shots Off Target	Shots On Target	Total Goals
1999 - 2000	P	n/a	230	53
2000 - 2001	P	n/a	240	68
2001 - 2002	P	259	215	66

Chart Analysis

Chelsea's ability to convert 31% of their Shots On Target was one of the best returns in the F.A. Barclaycard Premiership and continued the upward trend of previous seasons. This success came despite them registering their lowest total of Shots On Target for three seasons.

statistics powered by ◆ SUPERBASE™

The heart of the Barclaycard Premiership - 4thegame.com

Chelsea

F.A. Barclaycard Premiership
Team Discipline

Key
- ■ Forward
- ■ Midfield
- □ Defence
- ■ Goalkeeper

Total Number Of Bookings

Total number of red cards	3
Total number of yellow cards	69

Referee Performance

Referee	Games Refereed	Red Cards	Yellow Cards
G.P.Barber	3	-	11
S.G.Bennett	4	-	8
A.P.D'Urso	2	-	6

Type of Yellow Cards Received

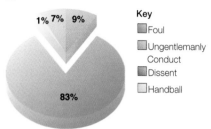

Key
- ■ Foul
- ■ Ungentlemanly Conduct
- ■ Dissent
- □ Handball

1% 7% 9%
83%

Bookings by Position 1999/2000 - 2001/2002

Home Matches
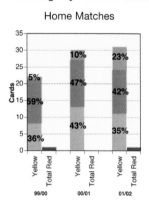

Away Matches
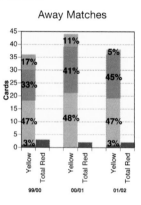

All Matches
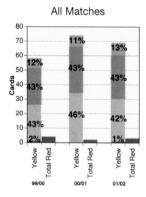

Chart Analysis

Chelsea accrued five less Yellow and one more Red Card compared to last season. While they added one yellow at home, they dropped six on the road.

The distribution of bookings across the team followed the pattern of the previous two seasons. For the third year running, midfielders received 43% of the team's overall cautions.

Forwards were least likely to offend away from home, where they picked up just 2 out of 38 Yellow Cards.

Most of Chelsea's cautions were picked up for Fouls, followed by Dissent.

> "For Chelsea, this year has been a period of transition. It has been a good year and I think we have found the right blend for progress."
>
> *Claudio Ranieri*
> *(April 2002)*

statistics powered by ◆ SUPERBASE™

➡ All the latest news, views and opinion - 4thegame.com

KICK OFF: THE F.A. BARCLAYCARD PREMIERSHIP CLUB REVIEW   **83**

Derby County

F.A. Barclaycard Premiership Final standing for the 2001-2002 season

Final Position		Games Played	Games Won	Games Drawn	Games Lost	Goals For	Goals Against	Total Points
18	Ipswich Town	38	9	9	20	41	64	36
19	Derby County	38	8	6	24	33	63	30
20	Leicester City	38	5	13	20	30	64	28

"Anyone who is not 100% will not be needed. I have to do as much wheeling and dealing as I can to get this club back into the F.A. Barclaycard Premiership."

John Gregory (April 2002)

Club Honours and Records

Football League Champions: 1971-72, 1974-75

Division 2 Champions: 1911-12, 1914-15, 1968-69, 1986-87

Division 3 Champions (North): 1956-57

FA Cup Winners: 1946

Record victory: 12-0 v Finn Harps, UEFA Cup, 1st Round, 1st Leg, 15 September, 1976

Record defeat:
2-11 v Everton, FA Cup 1st Round, 1889-90

League goals in a season (team):
111, Division 3 (North), 1956-57

League goals in a season (player):
37, Jack Bowers, Division 1, 1930-31;
37, Ray Straw, Division 3 (North), 1956-57

Career league goals:
292, Steve Bloomer, 1892 to 1906 and 1910 to 1914

League appearances:
486, Kevin Hector, 1966 to 1978 and 1980 to 1982

Reported transfer fee paid: £3,000,000 to Sheffield Utd for Lee Morris (rising to £4,000,000 with appearances), October 1999

Reported transfer fee received: £7,000,000 from Leeds United for Seth Johnson, October 2001

AFTER just managing to stay up the previous season, Derby had a problematic campaign which saw the Rams suffer relegation.

Jim Smith embarked on what many believed would be his final season as Derby manager, after which he was expected to move upstairs to make way for Colin Todd. In the event, neither manager could have predicted such short tenures.

There was much excitement around Pride Park following the announcement that the Bald Eagle would be joined by the White Feather, with Fabrizio Ravanelli returning to England after his successful spell with Middlesbrough in 1996-97.

Rory Delap was sold to Southampton but Stefano Eranio, having said sad goodbyes at the end of the previous season, did a U-turn and re-signed, although he never actually played for Derby again. An opening day win over Blackburn, with Ravanelli and the ever-improving Malcolm Christie scoring the goals, offered some hope that Derby, a year older and wiser, would not be sucked into another relegation dogfight.

Ravanelli announced on his arrival that his aim was to win a trophy, having lost in two cup finals with Boro. That he was in the Boro side that was relegated was not

 Fixtures, results and match reports – 4thegame.com

F.A. Barclaycard Premiership
Season Progression

Key
■ Win ■ Loss ■ Draw –❷– League Position
–❷– Last Season's League Position

All Matches

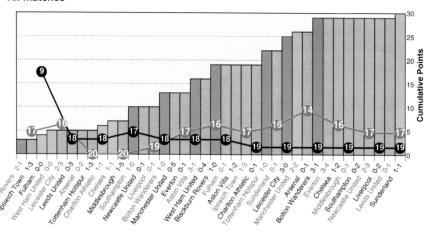

Home Matches

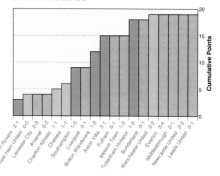

Away Matches

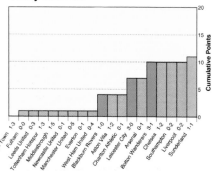

Chart Analysis

Derby's season never really got started following an opening day win at home to newly-promoted Blackburn Rovers.

They lost six out of their next ten games before winning again, at home to Southampton. By then, the damage was done. Stuck in 17th – the position in which they had finished the previous season – they began their descent to Division One.

Away from home – where they took just a solitary point from their opening nine fixtures – they managed to collect just 11 points from a possible 57.

The arrival of John Gregory at the end of January seemed to spur them on as the Rams collected three wins in six matches.

It proved to be a false dawn as seven straight defeats condemned Derby County to relegation.

statistics powered by ◆ SUPERBASE™

 Win Barclaycard Premiership tickets – 4thegame.com

> "Without making light of our position, though, it's worth noting that, after half a dozen games, we're only four points behind Aston Villa in sixth place."
>
> *Jim Smith*
> *(September 2001)*

It's a fact

When Derby started the season with a 2-1 victory against Blackburn, it was the first time for eight years that they had managed to register an opening day victory.

mentioned when he left Lazio for Derby and Smith hailed him as a role model for younger players such as Christie and Seth Johnson.

Early signs of problems were on show when, in the second game, Derby lost 3-1 at Ipswich. Branko Strupar was still suffering from a worrying groin problem but that was the least of the manager's worries.

Smith set out his stall at Fulham where he was delighted to be tagged boring as he masterminded a goalless draw. Another stalemate, against West Ham, was followed by successive defeats by Leicester, Leeds and Arsenal. The Leicester loss left a bitter taste, the visitors winning with a penalty secured by Robbie Savage, whose exuberant celebrations did not go down well with the home fans.

Smith's cause was not helped by the club's financial plight. Still paying off the £24m it cost to build Pride Park, the manager was ordered to sell a player. Yet by the time Johnson went to Leeds for £7m, Smith had also departed.

After the 2-0 defeat at Highbury, he paid the price for three years of struggle when he left by mutual consent after rejecting the post of Director of Football. A club manager since 1972 – including six years at Derby – he later emerged as assistant to Roland Nilsson at Coventry. That left Todd with the unenviable task of lifting Derby out of

F.A. Barclaycard Premiership
Half-Time/Full-Time Comparison

Key: ■ Win ■ Loss ■ Draw

Home				Away				Total			
Number of Home Half Time Wins	Full Time Result W	L	D	Number of Away Half Time Wins	Full Time Result W	L	D	Total number of Half Time Wins	Full Time Result W	L	D
5	3	-	2	2	2	-	-	7	5	-	2
Number of Home Half Time Losses	Full Time Result W	L	D	Number of Away Half Time Losses	Full Time Result W	L	D	Total number of Half Time Losses	Full Time Result W	L	D
5	-	5	-	10	-	9	1	15	-	14	1
Number of Home Half Time Draws	Full Time Result W	L	D	Number of Away Half Time Draws	Full Time Result W	L	D	Total number of Half Time Draws	Full Time Result W	L	D
9	2	5	2	7	1	5	1	16	3	10	3

Chart Analysis

statistics powered by ◆ SUPERBASE™

Derby always took something from a match which they were leading at half-time. However, the picture was not so rosy when they were behind at the break.

At Pride Park, they lost five out five after being behind at half-time, while away from home, they fared only marginally better – losing nine and drawing one out of ten.

Of the 16 games they were drawing at half-time, they managed to convert three into wins.

 The heart of the Barclaycard Premiership – 4thegame.com

F.A. Barclaycard Premiership Results Table

Key: ● time of goal ▲ time of substituted ▲ player substituted ● yellow card ● red card

DATE	H/A	OPPONENT	H/T	F/T	POS	REFEREE	TEAM											SUBSTITUTES USED
18-08	H	Blackburn	2-1	2-1	4	P.A.Durkin	Poom	O'Neal	Daino	Riggott	Higginbotham	Boertien	Powell ●	Morris ▲	Burley 45 65	Christie 65	Ravanelli 45	Kinkladze ▲
21-08	A	Ipswich Town	0-1	1-3	9	E.K.Wolstenholme	Poom	O'Neal ●	Daino ▲	Riggott	Higginbotham ●	Boertien	Powell ●	Johnson ●	Burley	Christie	Ravanelli 84	Burton ▲84, Murray ▲
25-08	A	Fulham	0-0	0-0	9	M.L.Dean	Oakes	Mawene ▲	Mawene	Riggott	Higginbotham	Boertien	Powell	Johnson	Burley	Christie ●	Burton	Kinkladze ● ▲, Murray ▲
08-09	H	West Ham Utd	0-0	0-0	10	C.R.Wilkes	Oakes	Burley ●	Burley	Riggott	Higginbotham	Boertien	Powell ●	Johnson ●	Kinkladze	Burton ●	Ravanelli ●	Morris ▲
15-09	H	Leicester City	1-1	2-3	13	G.P.Barber	Oakes	Mawene 24	Mawene ▲	Riggott	Higginbotham	Boertien ●	Burley ●	Johnson ●	Kinkladze	Burton 4 86	Ravanelli ▲86	Christie ●
23-09	A	Leeds Utd	0-1	0-3	18	A.G.Wiley	Oakes	O'Neal	Mawene ▲	Riggott	Higginbotham ●	Boertien ●	Burley ●	Johnson ●	Murray ▲	Christie	Burton ▲	Kinkladze ▲
29-09	H	Arsenal	0-1	0-2	19	R.Styles	Oakes ●	Jackson ▲	Riggott	Higginbotham ●	Boertien	Powell ●	Johnson ●	Murray ▲	Christie	Burton ▲	Ravanelli ●	Kinkladze ▲
15-10	A	Tottenham	1-2	1-3	18	M.R.Halsey	Feuer	Burley	Burley 15	Riggott	Higginbotham	Mawene	Powell ●	Valakari	Murray ▲	Burton ▲15	Christie ●	Kinkladze ▲
20-10	H	Charlton	1-0	1-1	18	A.P.D'Urso	Feuer	Burley 15	Burley	Riggott	Higginbotham ●	Zivagno	Powell ●	Cartone	Ravanelli 15	Christie ●	Burton ▲	Valakari ▲
28-10	H	Chelsea	1-0	1-1	18	S.G.Bennett	Poom	Burley	Burley	Riggott	Higginbotham	Zivagno	Powell ●	Cartone 7	Ravanelli ●7	Burton ●	Christie ▲	Christie ▲
03-11	A	Middlesbrough	0-0	1-5	20	N.S.Barry	Poom	Burley	Burley	Riggott	Higginbotham	Zivagno ▲	Powell	Cartone	Ravanelli 89	Burton	Christie ▲	Boertien ▲
17-11	H	Southampton	0-1	0-1	17	P.A.Durkin	Poom	Grenet ▲	Grenet	Riggott	Higginbotham	Zivagno ▲	Powell	Burley	Cartone	Burton	Ravanelli	Boertien ▲
24-11	A	Newcastle Utd	0-1	0-1	18	R.Styles	Poom	Mawene 24	Grenet	Riggott	Higginbotham	Zivagno ▲	Powell	Burley	Cartone	Cartone	Ravanelli	—
01-12	H	Liverpool	0-1	0-1	19	G.P.Barber	Poom	Grenet	Grenet	Riggott	Higginbotham	Zivagno	Powell	Cartone	Cartone	Christie	Ravanelli	Burton ▲
08-12	H	Bolton	0-0	1-0	18	M.D.Messias	Poom	Grenet	Grenet	Riggott	Higginbotham	Zivagno	Powell	Cartone ▲66	Cartone ▲66	Christie ▲66	Ravanelli	Bolder ▲
12-12	A	Manchester Utd	0-2	0-5	18	M.R.Halsey	Oakes	Grenet ▲	Grenet	Riggott	Higginbotham	Zivagno	Bolder	Cartone	Cartone	Christie ▲	Ravanelli	Burton ▲, Murray ▲
15-12	A	Everton	0-0	0-1	18	C.R.Wilkes	Oakes	Grenet ▲	Grenet	Elliott	Higginbotham	Zivagno	Powell ▲	Cartone	Cartone	Bolder	Ravanelli	Kinkladze ▲, Boertien ▲
22-12	A	Aston Villa	1-1	3-1	18	D.R.Elleray	Poom	Mawene	Grenet ▲	Riggott 45	Higginbotham	Zivagno	Boertien	Kinkladze ▲	Cartone ▲67	Cartone ▲67	Ravanelli 45 67	Burton ▲87, Christie ▲87, Bolder ▲
26-12	H	West Ham Utd	0-1	0-4	19	G.Poll	Poom	Mawene	Grenet	Riggott	Higginbotham	Zivagno	Powell	Boertien	Cartone ●	Cartone ●	Ravanelli	Kinkladze ▲, Bolder ▲
29-12	A	Blackburn	1-0	1-0	18	D.Pugh	Poom	Carbonari ●	Grenet ●	Riggott	Higginbotham	Zivagno	Powell	Cartone ▲40	Cartone ▲40	Christie 40	Ravanelli	Boertien ▲
01-01	H	Fulham	0-0	0-1	18	B.Knight	Poom	Carbonari ● ▲	Riggott	Higginbotham	Zivagno	Powell	Cartone ▲	Cartone ▲	Christie	Ravanelli	Burton ▲	Bolder ▲
12-01	A	Aston Villa	1-2	1-2	19	M.R.Halsey	Oakes	Elliott ▲	Jackson	Riggott	Higginbotham	Zivagno ▲	Powell 23	Boertien	Burton	Christie 23	Ravanelli	Kinkladze ▲, Bolder ▲
19-01	H	Ipswich Town	0-0	1-3	19	P.A.Durkin	Oakes	Carbonari ▲	Jackson	Riggott	Higginbotham	Zivagno ▲	Powell	Valakari	Christie 79	Christie 79	Ravanelli 79	Kinkladze ▲
29-01	A	Charlton	0-0	0-1	19	D.Pugh	Oakes	Mawene	Jackson	Higginbotham	Boertien	Powell	Ducrocq ▲	Valakari	Christie	Ravanelli ▲	Kinkladze ▲	—
02-02	H	Tottenham	1-0	1-0	19	U.D.Rennie	Oakes	Riggott	Zivagno ▲	Higginbotham	Zivagno	Powell ●	Morris ▲43	Morris ▲43	Christie ●	Ravanelli ▲43	Boertien ▲	O'Neal ▲
09-02	H	Sunderland	0-0	0-1	19	G.Poll	Oakes	Riggott	Powell ▲	Zivagno	Powell ●	Lee ●	Ducrocq ●	Morris ▲	Christie	Ravanelli	Boertien ▲	Burton ▲
03-02	A	Leicester City	0-0	3-0	19	M.A.Riley	Foletti	Barton	Zivagno	Barton	Kinkladze ▲53	Lee ●	Ducrocq ●	Boertien	Christie 53 89	Stupar ▲64	Ravanelli	Foletti ▲, Valakari ▲
03-03	H	Manchester Utd	1-1	2-2	19	S.W.Dunn	Oakes	Barton	Zivagno ●77	Higginbotham	Kinkladze ▲	Lee ●	Ducrocq ●	Boertien	Christie 9 77	Ravanelli ▲9	Christie ▲	Morris ▲
05-03	A	Arsenal	0-0	0-2	19	G.P.Barber	Oakes	Barton	Zivagno	Higginbotham	Kinkladze ▲	Lee ▲	Ducrocq ●	Morris	Stupar ▲	Stupar ▲	Ravanelli ●	Valakari ▲, Grenet ▲
16-03	H	Bolton	1-0	3-1	19	D.R.Elleray	Oakes	Riggott	Higginbotham 87	Zivagno	Kinkladze ▲	Lee ●	O'Neal	Boertien 53	Christie ▲22	Ravanelli ▲22 53	Morris ▲87	Stupar ▲
23-03	H	Everton	0-1	3-4	19	N.S.Barry	Oakes	Barton	Zivagno ● ▲	Kinkladze ▲	Lee 81	O'Neal ●	Boertien 76	Christie ▲22	Ravanelli	Morris ▲76	Stupar ▲57 81	—
30-03	A	Chelsea	0-0	1-2	19	M.L.Dean	Oakes	Barton 60	Zivagno ● ▲	Kinkladze ▲	Lee ▲	Valakari	Boertien	Stupar ▲60	Stupar ▲	Ravanelli	Morris ▲76	Elliott ▲
06-04	H	Middlesbrough	0-1	0-2	19	S.G.Bennett	Oakes	Barton	Zivagno ▲	Morris	Valakari	Boertien	Stupar ▲	Stupar ●	Ravanelli	Grenet ▲	Elliott ▲, Bolder ▲
13-04	A	Southampton	0-2	2-3	19	H.Styles	Oakes	Barton 53	Higginbotham	Kinkladze ▲	Lee ●	Boertien ●	Morris ▲46 53	Christie ▲46	Stupar	Ravanelli ▲	Stupar ▲	Elliott ▲
20-04	A	Liverpool	0-1	0-2	19	M.A.Riley	Poom	Jackson	Higginbotham	Kinkladze ▲	Lee ●	Boertien ●	Morris ▲	Christie	Stupar	Evatt ▲	Ravanelli ▲	—
27-04	H	Leeds Utd	0-1	1-1	19	G.Poll	Poom	Jackson	Higginbotham	Kinkladze ▲	Lee ●	Boertien ●	Morris ▲	Christie	Stupar ▲	Bolder ▲	Evatt ● ▲	Robinson ▲68
11-05	A	Sunderland	1-1	1-1	19	A.G.Wiley	Poom	Barton	Zivagno ▲	Evatt	Lee	Bolder	Boertien ●	Christie	Stupar ▲68	Twigg ▲68	Robinson ▲68	Jackson ▲

F.A. Barclaycard Premiership
Squad List

Position	Name	Appearances	Appearances as Substitute	Goals or Clean Sheets	Goal Assists	Yellow Cards	Red Cards
G	I.Feuer	2					
G	P.Foletti	1	1				
G	A.Oakes	20		4		1	
G	M.Poom	15		3			
D	W.Barton	14			2	1	
D	P.Boertien	23	9		2	7	
D	H.Carbonari	3				2	
D	D.Daino	2					
D	S.Elliott	2	4				
D	I.Evatt	1	2			1	
D	F.Grenet	12	3			2	1
D	D.Higginbotham	37		1		7	
D	R.Jackson	6	1				
D	Y.Mawene	17		1		4	
D	B.O'Neil	8	2			2	1
D	C.Riggott	37			1	7	
D	L.Zavagno	26			1	8	
M	A.Bolder	2	9				
M	C.Burley	11			3	3	
M	P.Ducrocq	19				3	
M	S.Johnson	7				3	
M	G.Kinkladze	13	11	1		3	
M	R.Lee	13			1	2	
M	A.Murray	3	3				
M	D.Powell	23		1		4	
M	G.Twigg		1			1	
M	S.Valakari	6	3				
F	D.Burton	8	9	1	4	1	
F	B.Carbone	13		1	3		1
F	M.Christie	27	8	9	3	2	
F	L.Morris	9	6	4	2	1	
F	F.Ravanelli	30	1	9	6	6	
F	M.Robinson		2	1			
F	B.Strupar	8	4	4			

the relegation zone.

Todd began with defeat in the Worthington Cup at Fulham followed by a 3-1 loss at Tottenham, where Johnson made his farewell appearance. At least he was able to bring players in. With goalkeeper Mart Poom injured, he signed Wimbledon's Ian Feuer on loan while adding Argentinian Luciano Zavagno and Frenchman Pierre Ducrocq. Benito Carbone teamed up with Ravanelli, on loan from Bradford, before £3m was invested in another Frenchman, Francois Grenet.

The signings made little improvement as an air of depression descended on Pride Park. Successive draws, against Charlton and Chelsea, were followed by a 5-1 defeat at Middlesbrough, where Ravanelli scored a late consolation effort against his former club, now managed by Smith's former assistant Steve McClaren.

The Rams finally won against Southampton in mid-November to move off the foot of the F.A. Barclaycard Premiership, but only thanks to one of the strangest goals of the season. James Beattie sliced a Craig Burley cross high into the grey Derby sky and chaos reigned. Paul Jones, the Saints goalkeeper, thought the ball had gone to safety, only for it to bounce in off Youl Mawene.

Two more defeats followed, against Newcastle and Liverpool, Ravanelli missing penalties in both. He vowed never to take another spot-kick while, off the pitch, unrest among the players was beginning to show.

Georgi Kinkladze, unable to claim a first team spot under Todd, drafted in a lawyer to discuss his absence with the manager. After one start, he injured his neck and was out again.

Derby enjoyed a 1-0 win over Bolton thanks to a goal from Christie. Unfortunately for them, the Rams were not

→ All the latest news, views and opinion - 4thegame.com

F.A. Barclaycard Premiership

Top Goal Scorer

Fabrizio Ravanelli

Total Premier League Goals Scored:	Percentage Of The Team's League Goals:
9	27%

Goals Scored From

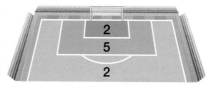

2
5
2

A t one stage, following the departure of Colin Todd in January, it looked as if Ravanelli would be installed as manager of Derby County. The Italian striker denied any interest in wanting to be manager, but continued to hunt for goals. Although he finished level on nine F.A. Barclaycard Premiership goals with Malcolm Christie, he played less games than the England Under-21 international. His tally might have been better but for successive penalty misses against Newcastle and Liverpool. Overall, the first half of the season proved more profitable with eight of his nine goals coming in the opening 18 games.

> "When I was at Juventus, the mentality was to put the team first and that's how it should be here. If the manager wants to drop me, that's fine with me."
>
> *Fabrizio Ravanelli*

Goals Resulting From

Key
- Open Play
- Corner
- Indirect Free Kick
- Direct Free Kick
- Penalty

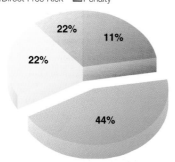

22%
11%
22%
44%

	Right Foot	Left Foot	Header
Open Play	2	1	1
Set piece	-	4	1

Goal Assists

Total number of goal assists	6

Teams Scored Against

Against	Home	Away
Aston Villa	1	0
Blackburn Rovers	1	0
Bolton Wanderers	0	1
Charlton Athletic	1	0
Chelsea	1	0
Ipswich Town	0	1
Leicester City	1	0
Middlesbrough	0	1
Tottenham Hotspur	0	1
Total Goals Scored	**5**	**4**

 Fixtures, results and match reports – 4thegame.com

> **"Since Colin's appointment we have lost 11 games in 17, are second bottom of the Premier League and were knocked out of the F.A. Cup. Clearly, things have not improved."**
>
> *Chief executive*
> *Keith Loring*
> *(January 2002)*

scoring in other areas; 90 per cent of Derby's goals had come from their strikers, and they were unable to stop the rot at Old Trafford, where they were beaten 5-0 by Manchester United.

Todd bemoaned a lack of desire but, despite the odd success, results were deteriorating at an alarming rate. Another defeat, at Everton, was followed by a shock 3-1 win over Villa. After losing 4-0 at West Ham, where Carbone was sent off, Derby bounced back again, winning 1-0 at Blackburn.

By the turn of the year, Derby was a pretty gloomy place to be. Knocked out of the F.A. Cup by struggling Division Three club Bristol Rovers, the Rams lost against Fulham and Villa, and Todd's position became untenable.

In January, after just three months in the job, he was sacked. Coach Billy McEwan took temporary control but successive losses did little to help his cause.

Ravanelli had been linked with the vacancy, a suggestion which was regarded by captain Darryl Powell as ridiculous. Ravanelli himself called a press conference to deny he wanted the job so the search went on for Derby's third manager of the campaign.

F.A. Barclaycard Premiership

Goals By Position

Key
Forward ■ Midfield League Position
Defence ■ Goalkeeper

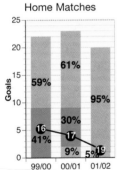

Home Matches

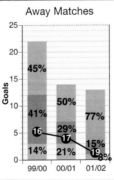

Away Matches

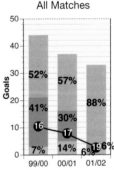

All Matches

Chart Analysis

statistics powered by **SUPERBASE**™

Derby scored their least amount of goals in three years in the top flight and paid the price.

Their final goal tally of 33 was not enough to keep them in the F.A. Barclaycard Premiership.

They suffered from an over-reliance on their strikers, who bagged a staggering 88% of their goals. At home, that figure rose to 95% – 19 out of 20 goals.

Defenders and midfielders scored just four out of 33 goals between them.

Win Barclaycard Premiership tickets - 4thegame.com

Former Blackburn boss Roy Hodgson was linked with the post but, as Derby slumped to defeat at Charlton, John Gregory was spotted in the Valley stands. Having just left Villa, the former Derby player was available and the Rams wasted little time in appointing him, with the carrot of a £1m bonus for keeping the club in the F.A. Barclaycard Premiership.

Gregory could not have asked for a better start. He went for experience, signing Newcastle's veteran pair Warren Barton and Rob Lee, and Derby beat Spurs 1-0 in early February with Lee Morris netting the winner.

The new manager switched from the 3-5-2 formation preferred by Todd to a more rigid 4-4-2 and it worked. Derby lost 1-0 at home to Sunderland but another important win, at Leicester, offered hope. Gregory wasn't helped by a three-game touchline ban following a misconduct charge left over from his time at Villa, but still Pride Park was buzzing with optimism for the first time.

The 3-0 victory at Filbert Street was followed by another impressive response even though the 2-2 draw against Manchester United at Pride Park was shrouded in controversy. Malcolm Christie had given the Rams a shock early lead and though Paul Scholes and Juan Sebastian Veron had responded, Christie scored

F.A. Barclaycard Premiership
Team Performance Table

League Position	Team	Points won from a possible six	Percentage of points won at home	Percentage of points won away	Overall percentage of points won
1	Arsenal	0/6			
2	Liverpool	0/6			
3	Manchester Utd	1/6	7%	0%	3%
4	Newcastle Utd	0/6			
5	Leeds United	0/6			
6	Chelsea	1/6			
7	West Ham Utd	1/6			
8	Aston Villa	3/6	73%	20%	47%
9	Tottenham H	3/6			
10	Blackburn R	6/6			
11	Southampton	3/6			
12	Middlesbrough	0/6			
13	Fulham	1/6	27%	7%	17%
14	Charlton Athletic	1/6			
15	Everton	0/6			
16	Bolton W	6/6			
17	Sunderland	1/6			
18	Ipswich Town	0/6	25%	58%	42%
19	**Derby County**	**30**			
20	Leicester City	3/6			

The table shows how many points out of a possible six Derby County have taken off each of the teams in the four sections. The other columns show as a percentage how many points they have taken from those available.

Chart Analysis

statistics powered by  SUPERBASE™

Relegated Derby managed to take just one point out of a possible 30 off the top five teams, drawing 2-2 at home to Manchester United in a game they felt they should have won following Malcolm Christie's late goal which was disallowed by the referee.

They performed very well at home to teams in the second sector, picking up three wins and two draws, but were suspect on the road, losing four out of five matches.

Their away form continued to disappoint against teams in the third sector. while at home they fared little better.

Conversely, they did better against teams in their own sector away from home, picking up over twice as many points as they did at home.

Derby failed to take any points off seven teams and did the 'double' over just two, Blackburn and Bolton, both of them newly-promoted to the top flight.

 The heart of the Barclaycard Premiership – 4thegame.com

again with 13 minutes remaining.

In the final minute, Christie was denied a hat-trick when United keeper Fabien Barthez tried to grab the ball and it appeared to run out his grasp. Christie took the chance to score but referee Steve Dunn blew for a foul. Gregory was furious but the F.A. took the unprecedented step of issuing a statement backing the official.

It was a stunning blow to Derby, whose hopes of surviving would have been considerably helped by two more points. As it was, the draw left them on 26 points, and, in 19th place. Two days later they went to Highbury and, though Arsenal showed some nerves, the Rams could hold out for only 69 minutes before Robert Pires netted the game's only goal.

The boost they needed arrived at the Reebok Stadium where they overcame relegation rivals Bolton, winning 3-1. The victory featured Ravanelli's first headed goal of the year, though their cause was helped by the sending off of Bolton keeper Jussi Jaaskelainen.

Ravanelli was so pleased with his goal that police had to calm him down as he raced to the travelling Derby fans to celebrate.

County scored three for the second time in successive games, against Everton at Pride Park, but this time it was

It's a fact

When Derby lost at home to Newcastle in April, it was their fifth successive defeat – the club's worst League run for 11 years.

> **"There is a Chinese proverb that says when you set out on a 1,000-mile journey, the first step is the hardest. The pressure at Derby starts now and I don't want to be associated with any form of failure."**
>
> *John Gregory*
> *(January 2002)*

F.A. Barclaycard Premiership
Goals By Time Period

Key ■ Goals Scored □ Goals Conceded

Home Matches

Time of Goal (mins)

0-15	4	2
16-30	1	3
31-45	3	3
46-60	3	5
61-75	3	8
76-90	6	5

Goals

Away Matches

Time of Goal (mins)

0-15	1	8
16-30	2	4
31-45	1	1
46-60	3	8
61-75	2	5
76-90	4	11

Goals

All Matches

Time of Goal (mins)

0-15	5	10
16-30	3	7
31-45	4	4
46-60	6	13
61-75	5	13
76-90	10	16

Goals

Chart Analysis

statistics powered by **SUPERBASE**™

Derby scored most frequently in the final 15 minutes of their matches, although that was when they conceded most too.

On the road, there was never a period when they were scoring more goals than they were conceding.

Their resilience seemed to fade as the game wore on, conceding twice as many goals in the second half as they did in the first – 42 compared to 21.

 All the latest news, views and opinion - 4thegame.com

F.A. Barclaycard Premiership
Goals Resulting From

Key ☐ Goals Scored ☐ Goals Conceded

	Six Yard Area				Inside Area				Outside Area				Total			
	Shots		Headers		Shots		Headers		Shots		Headers		Shots		Headers	
	Home	Away	Home	Away	Home	Away	Home	Away	Home	Away	Home	Away	Home	Away	Home	Away
Open Play	3	1	1	-	8	7	1	1	1	1	-	-	12	9	2	1
	6	4	-	1	10	15	-	2	3	4	-	-	19	23	0	3
Direct Free Kick									1	1	-	-	1	1		
									3	1			3	1		
Indirect Free Kick	-	-	-	-	-	1	-	-	-	-	-	-	0	1	0	0
	-	2	-	1	-	1	-	-	1	2	-	-	1	5	0	1
Penalty	-	-	-	-	1	1	-	-	-	-	-	-	1	1	0	0
	-	-	-	-	2	1	-	-	-	-	-	-	2	1	0	0
Corner	3	-	-	-	-	-	1	-	-	-	-	-	3	0	1	0
	-	-	-	-	-	1	-	2	-	-	-	-	0	1	0	2
Totals	6	1	1	0	9	9	2	1	2	2	0	0	17	12	3	1
	6	6	0	2	12	18	0	4	7	7	0	0	25	31	0	6

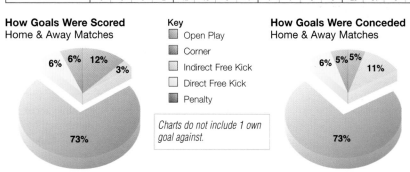

How Goals Were Scored
Home & Away Matches

6% 6% 12% 3% 73%

Key
☐ Open Play
☐ Corner
☐ Indirect Free Kick
☐ Direct Free Kick
☐ Penalty

Charts do not include 1 own goal against.

How Goals Were Conceded
Home & Away Matches

6% 5% 5% 11% 73%

Goals Scored from
Key ☐ Open Play ☐ Set Piece

Home — 30% / 70%
Away — 23% / 77%

Goals Conceded from
Key ☐ Open Play ☐ Set Piece

Home — 24% / 76%
Away — 30% / 70%

Chart Analysis

As a share of the total goals, Derby conceded as many as they scored from Open Play. They were most vulnerable from Shots Inside Area where they conceded nearly half of their goals.

They proved to be more adept at defending Headers at home, where they conceded none compared to six on their travels.

From Set Pieces, they scored most goals from Corners, while they conceded most from Indirect Free Kicks.

WORST IN THE LEAGUE...
- **Most goals conceded from Indirect Free Kicks away**
- **Most goals conceded from Direct Free Kicks overall and at home**

statistics powered by SUPERBASE™

Fixtures, results and match reports - 4thegame.com

> **"I have told Ravanelli to look for another club because there is no future for him at Derby."**
>
> *John Gregory (May 2002)*

not enough as the visitors, inspired by new boss David Moyes, ran out 4-3 winners. A 2-1 loss at Chelsea at the end of March suggested any hopes of surviving were going out of the window.

Indeed, April spelled the end for Derby, with a sixth successive defeat, at Liverpool, confirming what had appeared the inevitable relegation for some time. The month began with a 1-0 defeat at home to Middlesbrough followed by a 2-0 loss at Southampton.

Newcastle were the next visitors. Inspired by Dyer, the Magpies won 3-2 although Gregory was furious with a linesman, accusing him of missing two obvious offside goals. The manager was later charged with misconduct after being sent away from the dug-out by referee Rob Styles.

Liverpool sent Derby down with a 2-0 win at Anfield and they ended their Pride Park programme with their seventh successive defeat, against Leeds.

Gregory announced that Ravanelli had no future at Pride Park and, without the Italian, the Rams ended the season with a 1-1 draw at Sunderland, Marvin Robinson scoring his first goal for the club, a promising sign for life in Division One.

It's a fact

When the Rams lost at Chelsea in March, it extended their sequence in London without a win to 24 games.

F.A. Barclaycard Premiership
Shot Efficiency

Key
■ Goals Scored   ■ Other Shots On Target

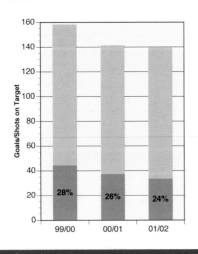

Season	Division	Shots Off Target	Shots On Target	Total Goals
1999 - 2000	P	n/a	158	44
2000 - 2001	P	n/a	141	37
2001 - 2002	P	150	140	33

Chart Analysis

In what was a difficult season, Derby had one less Shot On Target than they managed last time around.

Their ability to convert these into goals declined slightly, continuing a drop of 2% year-on-year since 1999-00.

statistics powered by **SUPERBASE**™

F.A. Barclaycard Premiership
Team Discipline

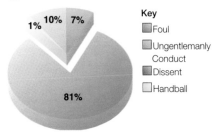

Key
- ■ Forward
- ■ Midfield
- ■ Defence
- ■ Goalkeeper

Total Number Of Bookings

Total number of red cards	3
Total number of yellow cards	70

Type of Yellow Cards Received

Key
- ■ Foul
- ■ Ungentlemanly Conduct
- ■ Dissent
- ■ Handball

1% 10% 7% 81%

Referee Performance

Referee	Games Refereed	Red Cards	Yellow Cards
M.R.Halsey	3	1	7
R.Styles	3	-	8
M.L.Dean	2	-	7

Bookings by Position 1999/2000 - 2001/2002

Home Matches
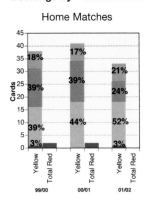

Away Matches
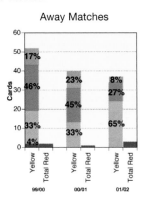

All Matches
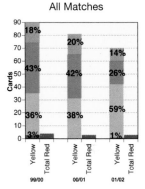

Chart Analysis

Although the number of cards picked up by Derby players fell by 11 compared to the previous season, the Rams were still one of the biggest offenders in the League.

In contrast with previous seasons, their defenders picked up the majority of the cautions while forwards and midfielders registered significant declines.

Although P.A.Durkin refereed four Derby matches, he showed Rams players just two Yellow Cards in total.

WORST IN THE LEAGUE...
- **Most Yellow Cards at home**

"On the playing side there has been an unprofessional culture that I will not allow to continue. We are in a privileged position and those privileges won't be abused any longer."
John Gregory (April 2002)

statistics powered by **SUPERBASE**™

Everton

F.A. Barclaycard Premiership	Final standing for the 2001-2002 season							
Final Position		Games Played	Games Won	Games Drawn	Games Lost	Goals For	Goals Against	Total Points
14	Charlton Athletic	38	10	14	14	38	49	44
15	Everton	38	11	10	17	45	57	43
16	Bolton Wanderers	38	9	13	16	44	62	40

"Let's be fair, when I took over, if somebody had said to me you can come to Arsenal on the last day safe, I would have taken it."

David Moyes (May 2002)

Club Honours and Records

Football League Champions: 1890-91, 1914-15, 1927-28, 1931-32, 1938-39, 1962-63, 1969-70, 1984-85, 1986-87

Division 2 Champions: 1930-31

FA Cup Winners: 1906, 1933, 1966, 1984, 1995

European Cup Winners' Cup Winners: 1984-85

Record victory: 11-2 v Derby County, FA Cup 1st Round, 18 January, 1890

Record defeat: 4-10 v Tottenham Hotspur, Division 1, 11 October, 1958

League goals in a season (team):
121, Division 2, 1930-31

League goals in a season (player):
60, William Ralph 'Dixie' Dean, Division 1, 1927-28

Career league goals:
349, William Ralph 'Dixie' Dean, 1925 to 1937

League appearances:
578, Neville Southall, 1981 to 1998

Reported transfer fee paid: £5,750,000 to Middlesbrough
for Nick Barmby, October 1996

Reported transfer fee received: £8,000,000 from Arsenal for Francis Jeffers, June 2001

OPTIMISM is high at Goodison Park every August and with David Moyes now settled as manager, the 2002-03 campaign can only be better than last term.

Everton were reeling even before the season started with Francis Jeffers moving to Arsenal for £8m while Michael Ball joined Rangers, for £6.5m.

Walter Smith invested £4.5m in Canadian international Tomasz Radzinski from Anderlecht, while Alan Stubbs, the Celtic defender, joined his favourite club on a free transfer.

Everton had a golden vision for a new £150m stadium on the Kings Dock Waterfront site, close to the Liverpool city centre. First, though, the Toffees had to be transformed on the pitch after just about a decade of struggle. It was a good start, Duncan Ferguson scoring his 100th career goal – a penalty, at Charlton – to earn his team a 2-1 opening day win.

That was followed by a draw at home to Spurs and a 2-0 win over Middlesbrough. Everton were top of the F.A. Barclaycard Premiership, albeit after just three games, and there was a level of optimism rarely experienced in recent years at Goodison Park. Injuries had denied Radzinski his debut. He finally started at the end of September while Paul Gascoigne

All the latest news, views and opinion - 4thegame.com

Everton

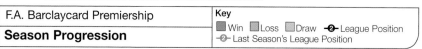

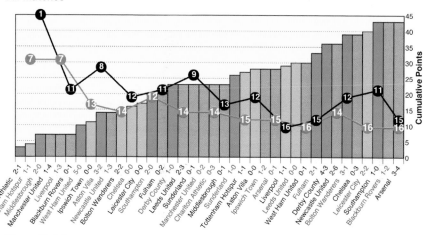

F.A. Barclaycard Premiership
Season Progression

All Matches

Key
■ Win ■ Loss ■ Draw ❷ League Position
❷ Last Season's League Position

Home Matches

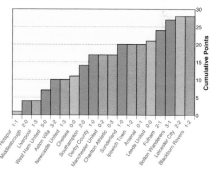

Away Matches

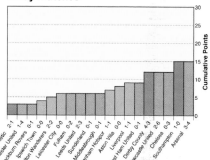

Chart Analysis

Everton got off to a great start. Despite losing three games on the spin in September, they were sitting comfortably in mid-table come the middle of December with 23 points from 16 games.

Then, a 3-2 defeat at Leeds seemed to knock them off their stride, heralding a sequence of five straight defeats which turned into a run of one win in 13 matches.

The last of those, a 1-0 defeat at West Ham United, was Walter Smith's last League game in charge.

His replacement David Moyes was quickly drafted in and presided over a mini-revival which saw the Toffees pull away from the drop zone with four wins in their last nine matches.

WORST IN THE LEAGUE...
• **Longest run without winning away**

statistics powered by ◆ SUPERBASE™

➜ **Fixtures, results and match reports – 4thegame.com**

> ## "If the fans choose to boo then it's part and parcel of the game and I do not find it unacceptable."
>
> *Walter Smith*
> *(September 2001)*

It's a fact

The second goal scored by Fulham's Barry Hayles in the 2-0 defeat at Craven Cottage in December was the 500th to be conceded by Everton in the Premier League. It was also their 150th defeat.

promised to put his past behind him by showing Smith and Everton that he should be a first choice midfielder.

Everton soon reverted to type. A 4-1 thrashing at Old Trafford was followed by a 3-1 home defeat in the 165th Merseyside derby. Then came the 1-0 reverse at Blackburn, where Gascoigne returned. Fortunes improved at the end of September and into October, when the Toffeemen swamped West Ham, winning 5-0 at Goodison Park.

Optimism grew when Everton, losers in nine of 11 previous games against Aston Villa, won 3-2 at home. Defensively, they were benefiting from the arrival of Stubbs and the continued improvement of David Weir.

Kevin Campbell had started encouragingly, with four goals from his first seven League appearances, while Radzinski also started to look impressive in place of Ferguson upfront. Further injuries coincided with a poor run which began the alarm bells ringing once again at Goodison Park.

As winter beckoned, so did Everton's problems: Campbell suffered a back injury which was to keep him out until after the New Year while Ferguson and, later on, Mark Pembridge, were also ruled out for lengthy periods.

A 2-2 draw against Bolton saw Paul Gerrard, the first choice goalkeeper, dropped in favour of Steve Simonsen,

---

F.A. Barclaycard Premiership
Half-Time/Full-Time Comparison

Key: ■ Win ■ Loss ■ Draw

Home				Away				Total			
Number of Home Half Time Wins	W	L	D	Number of Away Half Time Wins	W	L	D	Total number of Half Time Wins	W	L	D
6	6	-	-	2	2	-	-	8	8	-	-
Number of Home Half Time Losses	W	L	D	Number of Away Half Time Losses	W	L	D	Total number of Half Time Losses	W	L	D
7	-	5	2	5	-	5	-	12	-	10	2
Number of Home Half Time Draws	W	L	D	Number of Away Half Time Draws	W	L	D	Total number of Half Time Draws	W	L	D
6	2	2	2	12	1	5	6	18	3	7	8

Chart Analysis

statistics powered by ◆ SUPERBASE™

Everton boasted a 100% record in matches that they were leading at half-time, winning eight out of eight.

It was another story when they were behind at the break, managing to salvage just two draws from 12 matches.

Their form faltered in games they were drawing at half-time, dropping points in nearly 40% of the 18 games.

➤ **Win Barclaycard Premiership tickets - 4thegame.com**

Key: **88** time of goal   88 time of assist   ▲ player substituted   ○ yellow card   ● red card

DATE	H/A	OPPONENT	H/T	F/T	POS	REFEREE	TEAM (starting XI)	SUBSTITUTES USED
18-08	A	Charlton	0-0	2-1	5	N.S.Barry	Gerrard · Watson · Stubbs · Weir 77 · Pistone ○ · Alexandersson ▲ · Gemmill · Gravesen ○77 · Pembridge · Ferguson ○65 · Campbell 65	Unsworth ▲ · Moore ▲ · —
20-08	H	Tottenham	0-1	1-1	10	D.R.Elleray	Gerrard · Watson ● · Stubbs · Weir · Pistone ● · Alexandersson ▲ · Gemmill · Gravesen · Naysmith · Ferguson ○64 · Campbell 64	Pembridge ▲17 · Moore ○ · Unsworth ▲ · Tal ▲
25-08	A	Middlesbrough	1-0	2-0	1	U.D.Rennie	Gerrard · Watson · Stubbs · Weir · Pistone ● · Alexandersson ▲52 · Gemmill ▲17 · Unsworth · Naysmith · Ferguson ▲17 · Campbell 52	Pembridge ▲17 · Tal ▲ · Naysmith ▲
08-09	A	Manchester Utd	0-2	1-4	5	D.J.Gallagher	Gerrard · Watson · Stubbs ▲ · Weir ◀ · Pistone · Alexandersson ▲ · Gemmill 68 · Unsworth · Pembridge · Ferguson · Campbell 68	Tal ▲ · Moore ▲ · Xavier ▲
15-09	H	Liverpool	1-2	1-3	7	P.A.Durkin	Gerrard · Watson · Stubbs · Weir · Xavier · Naysmith · Unsworth ▲ · Gravesen · Gemmill · Ferguson 5 · Campbell 5	Gascoigne ▲ · Hibbert ▲ · Radzinski ▲
22-09	A	Blackburn	0-1	0-1	11	G.P.Barber	Gerrard · Hibbert ▲ · Xavier · Weir · Xavier · Naysmith · Gascoigne · Gravesen ◀ · Gemmill · Ferguson ◀ · Campbell	Unsworth ▲ · Moore ● ▲ · —
29-09	H	West Ham Utd	1-0	5-0	7	P.A.Durkin	Gerrard · Watson 75 · Xavier · Weir · Pistone · Alexandersson 45 · Gascoigne · Gravesen 55 · Pembridge · Naysmith 75 · Radzinski ▲78	Campbell 45 · Pembridge ▲▲52 · Hibbert ▲ · Moore ◀
13-10	A	Ipswich Town	1-0	0-0	10	C.R.Wilkes	Gerrard · Watson ◀ · Xavier ● · Weir · Pistone ● · Alexandersson · Gemmill ◀ · Pembridge · Naysmith · Naysmith · Campbell	Radzinski · Stubbs ▲ · Unsworth ◀
20-10	H	Aston Villa	1-0	3-2	8	R.Styles	Gerrard · Watson 30 · Xavier · Weir · Pistone · Alexandersson · Pembridge ▲ · Gravesen ▲61 · Alexandersson · Radzinski ▲58 · Campbell	Gemmill ▲61 · Gascoigne ▲ · Ferguson ▲
27-10	H	Newcastle Utd	0-1	1-3	10	J.T.Winter	Gerrard · Pistone · Weir 50 · Stubbs ▲44 · Unsworth ▲ · Alexandersson 50 · Gemmill ● · Naysmith · Naysmith · Radzinski · Campbell ▲	Ferguson ▲ · Gascoigne ▲ · Stubbs ▲
03-11	A	Bolton	1-1	2-2	11	A.P.D'Urso	Gerrard · Pistone · Stubbs · Weir · Unsworth · Alexandersson · Gemmill · Gravesen ●44 · Gascoigne ▲57 · Radzinski · Campbell ▲	Ferguson ▲ · Cleland ▲ · Cadamarteri ▲
18-11	H	Chelsea	0-0	0-0	12	U.D.Rennie	Gerrard · Pistone · Stubbs ● · Weir · Unsworth · Alexandersson ▲ · Gemmill · Gravesen ● · Naysmith · Watson · Radzinski	Radzinski · Gascoigne ▲ · Pentridge ▲ · —
24-11	A	Leicester City	0-0	0-0	12	U.D.Rennie	Gerrard · Pistone · Stubbs · Weir · Unsworth ▲ · Alexandersson ▲ · Gemmill · Gravesen ● · Naysmith · Watson · Radzinski	Radzinski · Gascoigne ▲ · Gascoigne ▲
02-12	H	Southampton	0-0	2-0	9	J.T.Winter	Gerrard · Pistone · Stubbs ● · Weir · Unsworth · Alexandersson ▲ · Gemmill · Gravesen 86 · Naysmith · Naysmith 50 · Radzinski	Pembridge ▲36 · Gascoigne ▲ · —
08-12	A	Fulham	0-1	0-2	11	P.Dowd	Simonsen ● · Pistone ● · Stubbs ● · Weir ● · Naysmith · Gemmill · Gascoigne ▲ · Gravesen ▲ · Pembridge · Watson · Radzinski	Alexandersson ▲ · Moore ▲ · —
15-12	H	Derby County	0-0	1-0	9	C.R.Wilkes	Simonsen · Pistone ▲ · Stubbs ▲ · Weir 76 · Naysmith · Alexandersson · Gemmill ● · Gravesen ▲ · Pembridge · Watson 84 · Radzinski	Unsworth ▲ · Moore ▲76 · Gascoigne ▲
19-12	A	Leeds Utd	0-2	2-3	9	P.Jones	Simonsen · Pistone ▲ · Xavier · Weir 90 · Unsworth · Alexandersson ▲ · Gemmill · Pembridge · Naysmith 84 · Watson 84 · Radzinski	Gascoigne ▲ · Moore ▲84 · Tal ▲90
22-12	A	Sunderland	0-0	0-1	13	B.Knight	Simonsen · Xavier · Xavier · Unsworth · Naysmith · Gascoigne ● · Gemmill · Gravesen ● · Tal ◀ · Moore · Radzinski	Alexandersson ▲ · Gascoigne ◀ · Tal ▲90
26-12	H	Manchester Utd	0-0	0-2	13	U.D.Rennie	Simonsen · Watson · Xavier · Weir · Naysmith · Alexandersson ▲ · Gemmill · Gravesen ● · Naysmith · Blomqvist ▲ · Radzinski	Gascoigne ▲ · Ferguson ▲ · Moore ◀
29-12	A	Charlton	0-1	0-3	13	G.P.Barber	Simonsen · Watson · Xavier · Weir · Naysmith · Alexandersson ▲ · Gemmill · Unsworth · Naysmith · Blomqvist ▲ · Radzinski	Gascoigne ▲ · Tal ▲ · Ferguson ▲
01-01	A	Middlesbrough	0-0	0-1	13	R.Styles	Simonsen · Watson ● · Stubbs ● · Weir · Xavier · Naysmith · Alexandersson ▲27 · Unsworth ● · Alexandersson ▲ · Blomqvist · Cadamarteri ▲	Ferguson ▲ · Hibbert ▲ · Moore ▲ · Blomqvist ▲
12-01	H	Sunderland	1-0	1-0	13	D.R.Elleray	Simonsen · Hibbert · Stubbs · Weir · Naysmith · Alexandersson ▲27 · Gascoigne · Unsworth ● · Unsworth · Blomqvist ▲27 · Campbell	Cleland ▲ · Chadwick ▲ · Moore ◀
19-01	A	Tottenham	1-1	1-1	13	C.R.Wilkes	Simonsen · Hibbert ▲ · Stubbs · Weir 7 · Unsworth · Alexandersson ▲ · Gemmill ● · Gascoigne ▲ · Naysmith · Ferguson ● · Campbell	Moore ▲ · Chadwick ▲ · —
30-01	A	Aston Villa	0-0	0-0	12	C.J.Foy	Simonsen · Hibbert ▲ · Clarke ● · Clarke ● · Unsworth ● · Cadamarteri ▲ · Gemmill · Moore · Naysmith · Campbell · Chadwick ▲	Chadwick ▲ · Cleland ▲ · —
02-02	H	Ipswich Town	1-2	1-2	14	S.W.Dunn	Simonsen ● · Clarke ▲ · Stubbs ● · Weir · Unsworth ▲26 · Blomqvist · Gemmill · Gascoigne · Naysmith · Campbell 26 · Radzinski	Moore ▲ · Linderoth ▲ · —
10-02	H	Arsenal	0-0	0-1	15	J.T.Winter	Simonsen · Clarke ● · Stubbs ● · Weir · Unsworth · Blomqvist ▲ · Linderoth · Carsley · Naysmith · Ginola · Campbell	Gascoigne ▲ · Pembridge ▲ · Moore ▲
23-02	A	Liverpool	0-0	1-1	16	D.R.Elleray	Simonsen · Clarke ○ · Stubbs · Weir · Pistone 52 · Gemmill · Linderoth · Carsley · Naysmith · Ginola · Campbell	Gascoigne ○ · Radzinski ▲52 · Gravesen ● ▲
03-03	H	Leeds Utd	0-0	0-0	15	A.P.D'Urso	Simonsen ○ · Clarke ▲ · Stubbs ● · Weir · Unsworth · Linderoth · Gemmill · Carsley · Blomqvist ● · Radzinski · Campbell 41	Radzinski ▲ · Gravesen ▲ · Tal ▲90
06-03	A	West Ham Utd	0-0	0-0	15	B.Knight	Simonsen · Pistone ● · Stubbs · Weir · Unsworth · Alexandersson ▲ · Gemmill · Carsley · Blomqvist ● · Radzinski ● · Campbell	Linderoth ▲ · Gravesen ● ▲ · Ginola ▲
16-03	A	Fulham	2-0	2-1	15	G.P.Barber	Simonsen · Hibbert · Stubbs · Weir · Pistone · Carsley · Gemmill · Gravesen ● · Unsworth ▲1 · Radzinski ▲1 · Campbell	Blomqvist ▲ · Moore ▲ · —
23-03	A	Derby County	1-4	4-3	13	N.S.Barry	Simonsen · Hibbert ● · Stubbs ▲52 · Weir · Unsworth 38 · Naysmith · Gemmill 54 · Carsley · Blomqvist · Ferguson 12 · Radzinski ▲1	Clarke ▲ · Watson ▲52 54 71 · Campbell ▲
29-03	H	Newcastle Utd	2-2	2-6	13	G.Poll	Simonsen · Hibbert ▲ · Watson · Weir · Pistone ●46 · Gemmill 34 · Alexandersson 34 · Gravesen 38 · Naysmith · Ferguson 6 · Radzinski ▲46	Blomqvist ▲ · Chadwick ▲ · Watson ◀
01-04	H	Bolton	1-0	3-1	13	S.G.Bennett	Simonsen · Hibbert · Watson · Weir 7 · Unsworth · Alexandersson ▲27 · Gemmill 56 · Unsworth ● · Naysmith · Ferguson ● · Radzinski ▲56 85	Chadwick ▲56 85 · Linderoth ▲85 · —
06-04	A	Tottenham	0-2	1-1	13	D.R.Elleray	Simonsen · Watson ● · Clarke ● · Weir · Pistone · Cadamarteri ▲ · Gemmill · Moore · Blomqvist ▲ · Campbell · Chadwick ●	Chadwick ● · Cleland ▲ · —
13-04	A	Chelsea	0-2	0-3	13	U.D.Rennie	Gerrard · Watson · Stubbs ● · Weir · Pistone · Alexandersson ▲ · Gemmill · Gravesen 62 · Unsworth 85 · Ferguson 85 · Radzinski ▲	Moore ▲ · Campbell ▲ · Linderoth ▲
20-04	H	Leicester City	0-2	2-2	13	J.T.Winter	Gerrard · Watson 41 · Stubbs · Weir · Pistone · Alexandersson ▲ · Gemmill · Gravesen ●62 · Unsworth · Chadwick · Campbell 41	Radzinski ▲ · Campbell ▲62 · Chadwick ▲62
20-04	A	Southampton	1-0	1-0	11	J.T.Winter	Gerrard · Watson · Stubbs 52 · Weir · Pistone · Gemmill · Carsley · Gravesen · Unsworth ● · Chadwick 52 · Campbell	Radzinski ▲ · Campbell · —
28-04	H	Blackburn	0-1	1-2	—	M.R.Halsey	Gerrard · Watson · Stubbs · Weir · Pistone · Alexandersson ▲ · Linderoth · Gravesen · Unsworth ● · Radzinski 20 31 · Campbell	Blomqvist ▲ · Radzinski ▲62 · —
11-05	A	Arsenal	2-3	3-4	15	M.R.Halsey	Simonsen · Watson 89 · Stubbs · Weir · Unsworth ● · Linderoth · Carsley 20 · Pembridge 31 89 · Blomqvist ◀ · — · Campbell	Ginola ▲ · —

F.A. Barclaycard Premiership

Squad List

Position	Name	Appearances	Appearances as Substitute	Goals or Clean Sheets	Goal Assists	Yellow Cards	Red Cards
G	P.Gerrard	13		4			
G	S.Simonsen	25		7		1	
D	P.Clarke	5	2			2	
D	A.Cleland		3				
D	T.Hibbert	7	3		1	1	
D	G.Naysmith	23	1		4	3	
D	A.Pistone	25		1	2	7	
D	A.Stubbs	29	2	2	1	5	
D	D.Unsworth	28	5	3	1	5	
D	S.Watson	24	1	4	2	1	
D	D.Weir	36		4	1	5	1
D	A.Xavier	11	1			1	
M	N.Alexandersson	28	3	2	6	1	
M	J.Blomqvist	10	5	1		2	
M	L.Carsley	8		1			
M	P.Gascoigne	8	10	1	3	2	
M	S.Gemmill	31	1	1	5	3	
M	D.Ginola	2	3				
M	T.Gravesen	22	3	2	5	7	1
M	T.Linderoth	4	4				
M	M.Pembridge	10	4	1	4		
M	I.Tal	1	6		1		
F	D.Cadamarteri	2	1				
F	K.Campbell	21	2	4	4	1	
F	N.Chadwick	2	7	3			
F	D.Ferguson	17	5	6	1	6	1
F	J.Moore	3	13	2		1	
F	T.Radzinski	23	4	6	3	1	

while Gascoigne returned, with a goal. That was followed by stalemates against Chelsea and Leicester.

Smith bolstered his squad with the addition of Manchester United winger Jesper Blomqvist. Troubled by injuries for the previous two seasons, he was prepared to gamble with the Swede insisting he was back to full fitness. Ironically, he made his debut at home to Manchester United on Boxing Day.

By then, Everton were tumbling down the table. Six defeats in seven games including a four-game spell without a goal put Smith's position in doubt. Already Campbell had questioned how Smith had not resigned over a lack of funds, but suddenly fans were wondering whether he should just go full stop.

Everton lost 2-0 in a controversial game at Fulham where Weir was sent off and players from both teams clashed, eventually leading to a £25,000 fine – Fulham were fined £30,000 for their involvement – and a Football Association warning.

Ferguson underwent surgery on a troublesome ankle problem in late November and with Campbell still troubled with a back strain, Smith was forced to switch Steve Watson, ordinarily a defender, into attack. His first game upfront was against Chelsea and the flame-haired defender did his best to make up for the squad's deficiencies.

The makeshift striker suffered the fate of so many teammates, however, when he was injured during the 1-0 loss at Middlesbrough. Everton went into an F.A. Cup tie at Division Two Stoke under huge pressure. The feeling that defeat would end Smith's tenure persisted but Stubbs stole a winner as the manager survived.

Matters improved when Blomqvist scored his first goal in the League for three

F.A. Barclaycard Premiership

Top Goal Scorer

Duncan Ferguson

Total Premier League Goals Scored:	Percentage Of The Team's League Goals:
6	13%

Goals Scored From

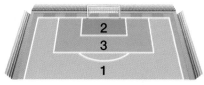

Everton's disappointing season was mirrored by their lack of a dominating leading scorer. The six goals Ferguson scored was the lowest total by Everton's top marksman in their F.A. Barclaycard Premiership history, three less than the nine claimed by Kevin Campbell a season earlier. Injuries limited Campbell to just four League goals, and Ferguson, after scoring successive penalties in the opening two games of the season, then went 14 games without a goal. His return to scoring coincided with the arrival of new manager David Moyes. He immediately installed the Scot as his skipper and Ferguson responded with three goals in as many games.

"He has trained non-stop since I took over and the more games he gets in, the fitter he'll become. He has thought about his situation and decided it is time to show what he is all about."

David Moyes

Goals Resulting From

Key
■ Open Play ■ Corner □ Indirect Free Kick
□ Direct Free Kick ■ Penalty

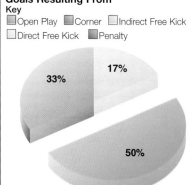

33% 17% 50%

Goal Assists

Total number of goal assists	1

Teams Scored Against

Against	Home	Away
Charlton Athletic	0	1
Derby County	0	1
Fulham	1	0
Leicester City	1	0
Newcastle United	0	1
Tottenham Hotspur	1	0
Total Goals Scored	**3**	**3**

	Right Foot	Left Foot	Header
Open Play	1	2	-
Set piece	-	3	-

➡ **All the latest news, views and opinion – 4thegame.com**

> "Walter Smith brought a stability and dignity to Everton when it desperately needed it most. This decision was not taken lightly, but it was felt it was in the best interests of the club."
>
> *Deputy chairman*
> *Bill Kenwright*
> *(March 2002)*

years, at home to Sunderland, but that was to be Smith's last F.A. Barclaycard Premiership success.

The injury list was worsening: Blomqvist, Thomas Gravesen, Watson, Pembridge, Alessandro Pistone and Radzinski were all injured for a period in January which was to prove defining for the luckless Smith.

In addition, Everton lost Portuguese international Abel Xavier to Liverpool when the defender jumped ship at a cost of just £800,000.

Smith made more signings with Swedish midfielder Tobias Linderoth arriving in late January, and, a week later he made a double swoop, signing Coventry's Lee Carsley and, more surprisingly, Aston Villa's wayward genius, David Ginola.

Ferguson returned to fitness and had to sit out the home game against Arsenal through suspension, which Everton lost 1-0.

The club secured a loan of £25m, raising the funds against predicted future season ticket sales, but team spirit was showing signs of cracking with Gravesen allegedly at the centre of a dressing-room rift.

Spirits were lifted with a 4-1 F.A. Cup win over Leyton

F.A. Barclaycard Premiership
Goals By Position

Key
■ Forward ■ Midfield ➋ League Position
□ Defence ■ Goalkeeper

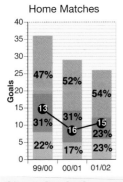

Home Matches

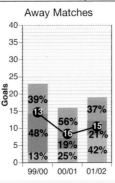

Away Matches

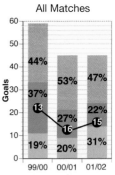

All Matches

Chart Analysis

statistics powered by ◆ **SUPERBASE**™

Everton managed the same amount of goals overall as last season although they did finish higher in the final table. Whilst the contribution from the forwards and midfielders declined, the defence weighed in with more than their fair share, particularly away from home.

BEST IN THE LEAGUE...
- **Most goals scored by defence overall and away**

 Fixtures, results and match reports - 4thegame.com

Orient in which Campbell scored twice. While League form continued to drop, a win over Crewe, in a replay at Gresty Road, took Everton into the quarter-finals of the F.A. Cup.

In the League, meanwhile, Everton had dropped to 15th with a 1-1 draw against Liverpool, a goalless affair against Leeds and a 1-0 loss at West Ham.

In many ways, the success of the season depended on Everton's cup date at Middlesbrough, with a place in the semi-finals of the F.A. Cup beckoning. The Toffees responded miserably, losing 3-0. Gazza played what was to be his final Everton game and it was also to prove the end of the road for Smith.

On the morning of 12 March, two days after the F.A. Cup disappointment, Smith was sacked and Everton responded immediately by approaching Preston for permission to talk to their promising Scot, David Moyes. The Division One Club's first reaction was to try and hold on to their manager, who had taken North End to the previous season's play-off final.

Nevertheless, two days after the departure of Smith, Moyes was confirmed as the man given the unenviable task of securing Everton's F.A. Barclaycard position and turning the club's long term prospects around. Moyes agreed a four-year contract worth £3.2m and

F.A. Barclaycard Premiership
Team Performance Table

League Position	Team	Points won from a possible six	Percentage of points won at home	Percentage of points won away	Overall percentage of points won
1	Arsenal	0/6			
2	Liverpool	1/6			
3	Manchester Utd	0/6	7%	7%	7%
4	Newcastle Utd	0/6			
5	Leeds United	1/6			
6	Chelsea	1/6			
7	West Ham Utd	3/6			
8	Aston Villa	4/6	53%	13%	33%
9	Tottenham H	2/6			
10	Blackburn R	0/6			
11	Southampton	6/6			
12	Middlesbrough	3/6			
13	Fulham	3/6	75%	50%	63%
14	Charlton Athletic	3/6			
15	**Everton**	**43**			
16	Bolton W	4/6			
17	Sunderland	3/6			
18	Ipswich Town	1/6	67%	40%	53%
19	Derby County	6/6			
20	Leicester City	2/6			

The table shows how many points out of a possible six Everton have taken off each of the teams in the four sections. The other columns show as a percentage how many points they have taken from those available.

Chart Analysis

statistics powered by SUPERBASE™

Everton struggled against the top five teams both at home and away, winning none of the ten fixtures as they collected a measly two points from a possible 30.

Although they fared better at home against teams in the second sector, they still failed to win any of the five away matches.

They collected the biggest share of points against teams in their own sector, where five wins out of eight helped them secure 15 valuable points.

Everton's form tailed off disappointingly against teams in the bottom five of the table, where they were able to secure just over half the points available.

The Toffees did the 'double' over Derby and Southampton while failing to take any points off four teams, including three out of the top five.

➡ Win Barclaycard Premiership tickets - 4thegame.com

immediately spoke of Everton as the club of the people. It was a phrase that soon grew on the blue half of the city.

Gascoigne as anticipated, left to join Burnley on the day Moyes took charge of his first match at home to Fulham.

What a start it proved to be for Moyes. A team that had managed just two goals in their previous six League games doubled that figure within 13 minutes. Having received a hero's welcome beforehand, Moyes looked on in shock as David Unsworth scored after 32 seconds. When Ferguson, given the captaincy, scored a second, Everton started to believe in miracles.

That Gravesen was sent off and Fulham responded with a goal did little to dampen the party celebrations. Everton followed that with another win, 4-3 at fellow relegation sufferers Derby, where Ferguson scored again.

Moyes was still pinching himself when Everton went to Newcastle on Good Friday looking for a third successive win. At St James' Park, Moyes was given a reality check. Ferguson may have scored for a third time in three games, against his former club, but Newcastle responded to win 6-2 and put the Moyes revolution into perspective.

Two wins and a draw in early April secured safety for another season. Everton returned to winning ways at Goodison Park against Bolton where Ferguson was sent off

It's a fact

Everton won eight games at home, their highest number of Goodison Park victories for six seasons.

"Everton have given me the best opportunity I have had and I am going to try and grab it with both hands."

David Moyes
(March 2002)

F.A. Barclaycard Premiership
Goals By Time Period

Key
■ Goals Scored ■ Goals Conceded

Home Matches

Time of Goal (mins)	Goals Scored	Goals Conceded
0-15	3	3
16-30	4	5
31-45	2	2
46-60	8	3
61-75	4	5
76-90	5	5

Away Matches

Time of Goal (mins)	Goals Scored	Goals Conceded
0-15	2	5
16-30	1	4
31-45	5	5
46-60	4	7
61-75	3	5
76-90	4	8

All Matches

Time of Goal (mins)	Goals Scored	Goals Conceded
0-15	5	8
16-30	5	9
31-45	7	7
46-60	12	10
61-75	7	10
76-90	9	13

Chart Analysis

statistics powered by ◆ SUPERBASE™

Everton were at their most dangerous just after half-time, scoring 12 goals overall during this period. That contributed to a second half tally of 28 compared to 17 for the first.

The Toffees were vulnerable in the opening half-hour of matches when they conceded 17 goals and scored just ten in reply. They were equally under pressure away from home, where they consistently conceded more than they scored throughout their match.

➡ **The heart of the Barclaycard Premiership - 4thegame.com**

Everton

F.A. Barclaycard Premiership
Goals Resulting From

Key
☐ Goals Scored ☐ Goals Conceded

	Six Yard Area				Inside Area				Outside Area				Total			
	Shots		Headers		Shots		Headers		Shots		Headers		Shots		Headers	
	Home	Away	Home	Away	Home	Away	Home	Away	Home	Away	Home	Away	Home	Away	Home	Away
Open Play	3	2	3	-	7	7	1	-	3	4	-	-	13	13	4	0
	5	1	-	2	8	15	3	4	1	4	-	-	14	20	3	6
Direct Free Kick									-	1	-	-	0	1		
									-	1	-	-	0	1		
Indirect Free Kick	1	-	1	-	1	1	-	-	-	1	-	-	2	2	1	0
	-	-	1	-	-	-	-	1	1	1	-	-	1	1	1	1
Penalty	-	-	-	-	2	1	-	-	-	-	-	-	2	1	0	0
	-	-	-	-	1	-	-	-	-	-	-	-	1	0	0	0
Corner	1	-	1	-	-	1	1	1	-	-	-	-	1	1	2	1
	1	5	1	-	-	-	-	1	-	-	-	-	1	5	2	0
Totals	5	2	5	0	10	10	2	1	3	6	0	0	18	18	7	1
	6	6	2	2	9	15	4	5	2	6	0	0	17	27	6	7

How Goals Were Scored
Home & Away Matches

Key
☐ Open Play
☐ Corner
☐ Indirect Free Kick
☐ Direct Free Kick
☐ Penalty

Charts do not include 1 own goal for.

How Goals Were Conceded
Home & Away Matches

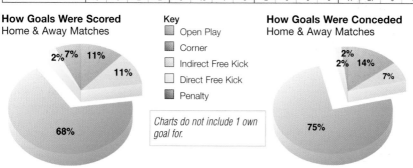

2% 7% 11%
11%
68%

2%
2% 14%
7%
75%

Goals Scored from
Key ☐ Open Play ☐ Set Piece

Home
32%
68%

Away
32%
68%

Goals Conceded from
Key ☐ Open Play ☐ Set Piece

Home
26%
74%

Away
24%
76%

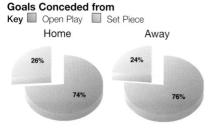

Chart Analysis

Not only was Everton's percentage of goals from Set Pieces well above the average, it was also identical both home and away.

Conversely, they conceded most from Open Play. They were also vulnerable to Corners, where they shipped more goals – eight – than they did from all other Set Pieces put together.

From headers, they scored eight goals but conceded 13.

However, they did just manage to score more goals from Free Kicks, both Direct and Indirect, than they conceded.

statistics powered by **SUPERBASE**™

All the latest news, views and opinion - 4thegame.com

> **"The tension started for me on the first day I joined the club but you only have to look at our record now, four wins in seven matches. That's exceptional when wins are so tight at this stage of the season."**
>
> *David Moyes (May 2002)*

It's a fact

Duncan Ferguson has notched 12 League strikes since re-signing for Everton but has failed to net a single goal from a header.

for allegedly punching Fredi Bobic in the ribs. That they won 3-1 was of some comfort but the captain was carpeted by Moyes and was fined.

Everton were beaten 3-0 by Chelsea, the latter inspired by two goals from Jimmy Floyd Hasselbaink, but drew 2-2 at home to Leicester, where Ferguson made amends for his red card by scoring the equaliser in what was his final game of the season before he served a three-match ban.

Steve Watson netted the winner at St Mary's against Southampton and that win confirmed Everton's safety and went some way to justifying the Board's decision to gamble on bringing Moyes to Goodison Park.

Sadly, their last game at home was a defeat, a 2-1 loss against Blackburn.

That they finished the season at Arsenal was always going to be of concern to Everton and though the Gunners had already secured the Double, Everton were sucked into the party, losing 4-3. How ironic it was that what proved to be the winner was scored by none other than Francis Jeffers.

F.A. Barclaycard Premiership
Shot Efficiency

Key ■ Goals Scored ■ Other Shots On Target

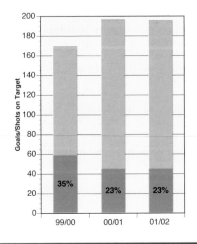

Season	Division	Shots Off Target	Shots On Target	Total Goals
1999 - 2000	P	n/a	169	59
2000 - 2001	P	n/a	196	45
2001 - 2002	P	179	195	45

Chart Analysis

Everton managed almost identical figures to the previous season – scoring the same amount of goals from just one less Shot On Target.

However, there is still a long way to go before they get back to the efficiency levels of two seasons ago.

statistics powered by **SUPERBASE**™

 Fixtures, results and match reports - 4thegame.com

F.A. Barclaycard Premiership

Team Discipline

Key
■ Forward ■ Midfield
□ Defence ■ Goalkeeper

Total Number Of Bookings

Total number of Red Cards	3
Total number of Yellow Cards	55

Referee Performance

Referee	Games Refereed	Red Cards	Yellow Cards
D.R.Elleray	4	-	7
B.Knight	2	-	6
N.S.Barry	2	-	6

Type of Yellow Cards Received

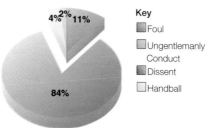

Key
■ Foul
□ Ungentlemanly Conduct
■ Dissent
□ Handball

4% 2% 11%
84%

Bookings by Position 1999/2000 - 2001/2002

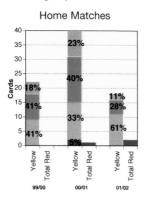

Home Matches

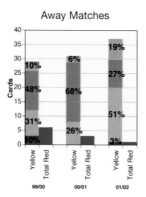

Away Matches

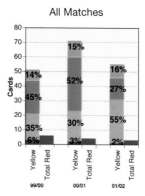

All Matches

Chart Analysis

The Toffees were handed 16 fewer Yellow Cards than in the previous campaign, as the number of Red Cards also declined.

More than half their cautions were picked up by defenders while the number given to midfielders almost halved. The percentage contribution from forwards remained consistent with the previous two seasons.

While discipline at home seemed much improved, with less than half as many Yellow Cards picked up compared to the previous season, away from home, where they picked up over two thirds of all bookings, there was a slight increase.

Interestingly, they have had Yellow Cards shown to goalkeepers in each of the last three seasons.

> "Duncan deserved to be sent off, no question. He was stupid and I told him so."
>
> *David Moyes following Duncan Ferguson's dismissal at home to Bolton (April 2002)*

statistics powered by ◆ SUPERBASE™

Fulham

F.A. Barclaycard Premiership Final standing for the 2001-2002 season

Final Position		Games Played	Games Won	Games Drawn	Games Lost	Goals For	Goals Against	Total Points
12	Middlesbrough	38	12	9	17	35	47	45
13	Fulham	38	10	14	14	36	44	44
14	Charlton Athletic	38	10	14	14	38	49	44

"It was presumptuous of people to say we would get into the top six because the whole season has been a discovery for us."

Assistant manager Christian Damiano (April 2002)

Club Honours and Records

Division 1 Champions: 2000-01

Division 2 Champions: 1948-49, 1998-99

Div 3 (South) Champions: 1931-32

Record victory:

10-1 v Ipswich Town, Division 1, 26 December, 1963

Record defeat: 0-10 v Liverpool, League Cup 2nd Round, 23 September, 1986

League goals in a season (team):

111, Division 3 (South), 1931-32

League goals in a season (player):

43, Frank Newton, Division 3 (South), 1931-32

Career league goals:

159, Gordon Davies, 1978 to 1991

League appearances:

594, Johnny Haynes, 1952 to 1970

Reported transfer fee paid:

£11,500,000 to Lyon for Steve Marlet, August 2001

Reported transfer fee received: £2,225,000 from Birmingham for Geoff Horsfield, July 2000

FULHAM were tipped to succeed in their first season in the F.A. Barclaycard Premiership after they cruised to the Division One title the previous season. That they only secured safety as late as April proves that the gap between the top two divisions has developed into a chasm.

Fulham arrived in the top flight with the kind of optimism reserved for more experienced participants. That they were new kids on the Premier League block and playing top flight football for the first time in 33 years did little to dissuade the self-belief that ability, talent and, above all, money can nurture.

After all, they had clinched promotion with 101 points and 90 goals with the trio of Louis Saha, Luis Boa Morte and Barry Hayles netting 63 goals between them. What's more, in the summer of 2001, Tigana spent more than £31m to make certain that Fulham would not join the past ranks of also-rans usually occupied by promoted clubs.

They persuaded Holland's first choice goalkeeper Edwin van der Sar to leave Juventus for Craven Cottage while more than £11m alone was spent on Lyon striker Steve Marlet. The addition of Steed Malbranque, Jon Harley and Abdeslam Ouaddou suggested Fulham would more

 The heart of the Barclaycard Premiership – 4thegame.com

F.A. Barclaycard Premiership

Season Progression

All Matches

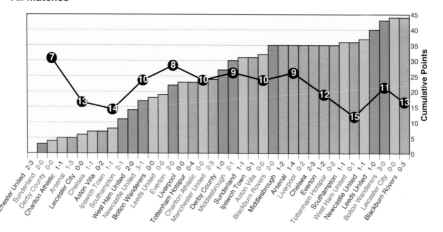

Home Matches

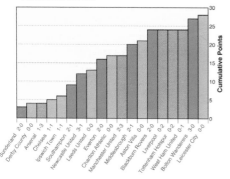

Away Matches

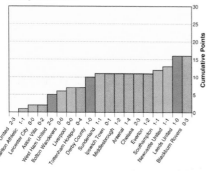

Chart Analysis

Having cruised into the top flight as runaway Division One champions, Fulham struggled to acclimatise to life in the F.A. Barclaycard Premiership.

The Cottagers only beat Sunderland in their opening nine games to leave them languishing in 14th.

Their form then improved with three wins on the spin and Fulham continued to pick up points throughout the rest of November and early December to leave them in the top half of the table.

Fulham's worst run of results started in mid-February, when a 2-1 loss at Middlesbrough kicked off a sequence of seven defeats in eight which saw them slump to 15th in the table.

Two wins and two draws in the last five matches ensured that the Cottagers did not return whence they came at the first time of asking.

➡ **All the latest news, views and opinion - 4thegame.com**

> "The atmosphere at Fulham is terrific. The fans are so close to the pitch and I like the stadium very much."
>
> *Edwin van der Sar (September 2001)*

It's a fact

Fulham started the season with a 3-2 defeat at Manchester United – their first opening day loss for ten years, when they were beaten at Chester.

than hold their own. Tigana was linked with moves for many others, including Arsenal's Kanu, but the start of the season was not what Fulham had hoped for.

Starting at the home of the Champions is not the best way to announce your arrival on the scene. Mohamed Al Fayed, Fulham's owner and chairman, claimed he wanted his club to become the next Manchester United and the early signs at Old Trafford suggested that he might just get his wish.

Certainly the man who usually gets what he wants could be proud of his Premier League debutants. Saha started as he had finished, with a goal, after just four minutes. David Beckham responded, Saha scored again, but as if to confirm that money counts, United's £19m newcomer Ruud van Nistelrooy scored twice to secure the points.

It was an auspicious start and Fulham got their first win when they beat Sunderland 2-0 at Craven Cottage, Saha and Hayles both scoring. Draws against Derby and Charlton followed.

Another defeat, at home to Arsenal, was followed by draws against Leicester and Chelsea. October was similarly hard, with a 2-0 loss at Aston Villa followed by a draw with Ipswich. In that game, Tigana used Hayles and Boa Morte in attack – his sixth different striking pairing in six games.

F.A. Barclaycard Premiership
Half-Time/Full-Time Comparison

Key: ■ Win ■ Loss ■ Draw

Home				Away				Total			
Number of Home Half Time Wins	W	L	D	Number of Away Half Time Wins	W	L	D	Total number of Half Time Wins	W	L	D
7	6	-	1	2	1	-	1	9	7	-	2
Number of Home Half Time Losses	W	L	D	Number of Away Half Time Losses	W	L	D	Total number of Half Time Losses	W	L	D
6	-	5	1	7	-	6	1	13	-	11	2
Number of Home Half Time Draws	W	L	D	Number of Away Half Time Draws	W	L	D	Total number of Half Time Draws	W	L	D
6	1	-	5	10	2	3	5	16	3	3	10

Chart Analysis

statistics powered by **SUPERBASE**™

Fulham were strongest at home, not losing any of the 13 matches in which they either led or were level in at the interval.

Of the six remaining games in which they were behind at half-time, they went on to salvage a solitary point. It was a similar story away from home.

Overall, the Cottagers drew ten out of 16 games in which they were level at the break.

 Fixtures, results and match reports - 4thegame.com

F.A. Barclaycard Premiership Results Table

Key: 88 time of goal   88 time of assist   ● player substituted   ▲ player substituted   ● yellow card   ● red card

DATE	H/A	OPPONENT	H/T	F/T	POS	REFEREE	TEAM											SUBSTITUTES USED		
19-08	A	Manchester Utd	1-1	2-3	13	P.Jones	Van der Sar	Finnan	Goma ●	Melville	Harley	Goldbaek	Malbranque ▲48	Davis 4	Collins	Saha 4 48	Hayes ▲48	Stobers ▲	Betsy ▲	Ouaddou ▲
22-08	H	Sunderland	0-0	2-0	6	B.Knight	Van der Sar	Finnan	Goma	Melville	Brevett ▲	Goldbaek 84	Malbranque 70	Davis	Legwinski ▲	Saha 84	Hayes 70	Harley ▲	Saha 84	—
25-08	H	Derby County	0-0	0-0	7	M.L.Dean	Van der Sar	Finnan	Goma ▲	Melville	Brevett ● ▲	Goldbaek ● ▲	Malbranque ● ▲	Davis	Legwinski ● ▲	Saha ●	Saha ●	Legwinski ▲	Legwinski ▲	Symons ▲
09-09	A	Charlton	1-1	1-1	10	J.T.Winter	Van der Sar	Finnan	Symons	Melville	Brevett	Legwinski 37	Malbranque 37	Knight	Davis	Saha	Boa Morte 37	Malbranque ▲	Hayes ▲	Hayes ▲
15-09	H	Arsenal	0-1	1-3	12	A.G.Wiley	Van der Sar	Finnan	Symons	Melville	Brevett	Legwinski ▲	Malbranque 48	Davis	Knight ▲	Saha	Boa Morte ▲48	Marlet ▲	Marlet ▲	—
22-09	A	Leicester City	0-0	0-0	13	E.K.Wolstenholme	Van der Sar	Finnan	Knight ▲	Melville	Brevett	Boa Morte ● ▲	Malbranque ▲	Davis ●	Collins	Saha	Market	Legwinski ▲▲	Symons ▲	Malbranque ▲
30-09	H	Chelsea	0-1	1-1	14	G.Poll	Van der Sar	Finnan	Knight ▲	Melville	Brevett	Goldbaek ▲	Malbranque ▲	Davis ●	Collins ●	Saha 55	Hayes 55	Malbranque ▲	Marlet ▲	Boa Morte ▲
14-10	A	Aston Villa	0-0	0-2	15	P.A.Durkin	Van der Sar	Finnan	Knight ▲	Melville	Brevett	Legwinski	Malbranque ▲22	Davis ● ▲	Collins	Saha	Market ▲22	Boa Morte ▲	Goma ▲	Hayes ▲
21-10	H	Ipswich Town	1-0	1-1	14	M.A.Riley	Van der Sar	Finnan	Goma ▲	Melville	Brevett	Legwinski 22	Clark ▲	Collins 22	Davis	Saha	Hayes	Saha ▲	Saha	Malbranque ▲
27-10	A	Southampton	2-1	2-1	13	A.P.D'Urso	Van der Sar	Finnan 32	Goma	Melville	Brevett	Legwinski	Malbranque 24 32	Collins	Davis	Marlet ▲24	Hayes	Market ▲24	Saha	—
03-11	A	West Ham Utd	1-0	2-0	12	G.P.Barber	Van der Sar	Finnan	Goma ●	Melville ●	Brevett	Legwinski 43	Malbranque ▲63 63	Collins ▲	Davis	Saha ▲63	Hayes ▲63	Goldbaek ▲	Davis ▲	Stobers ▲
17-11	H	Newcastle Utd	2-0	3-1	10	E.K.Wolstenholme	Van der Sar	Finnan	Goma	Melville 70	Brevett ●	Legwinski 20 28	Malbranque ▲28	Davis	Collins	Saha 20	Hayes 70	Clark ▲	Boa Morte ▲	Clark ▲
24-11	A	Bolton	0-0	0-0	11	M.L.Dean	Van der Sar	Finnan	Goma	Melville	Brevett ●	Legwinski ●	Malbranque ▲	Davis	Collins	Saha	Hayes	Boa Morte ▲	Davis ▲	Clark ▲
02-12	H	Leeds Utd	0-0	0-0	12	G.Poll	Van der Sar	Finnan	Goma	Melville	Brevett	Legwinski ● ▲	Malbranque	Collins ▲	Davis	Saha	Collins	Davis ▲	Davis ▲	—
08-12	A	Everton	1-0	2-0	8	P.Dowd	Van der Sar	Finnan	Goma	Melville ●	Brevett 36	Legwinski 36	Malbranque 50	Collins	Davis ●	Saha ▲	Hayes ●36 50	Legwinski ▲	Saha ▲	Marlet ●
12-12	A	Liverpool	0-0	0-0	9	J.T.Winter	Van der Sar	Finnan	Goma	Melville	Brevett	Boa Morte ●	Malbranque	Davis ▲	Collins ▲	Saha ●	Hayes	Legwinski ▲	Davis ▲	—
15-12	A	Tottenham	0-2	0-4	10	N.S.Barry	Van der Sar	Finnan	Goma	Melville	Brevett	Legwinski ▲	Malbranque ▲	Collins ●	Davis	Saha ●	Hayes	Clark ▲	Clark ▲	Stobers ▲
26-12	H	Charlton	0-0	0-0	10	S.G.Bennett	Van der Sar	Finnan	Goma	Melville	Brevett 89	Legwinski ▲45	Malbranque 45	Knight	Davis	Saha	Hayes ●	Boa Monte ▲	Market ▲89	Saha ▲
30-12	H	Manchester Utd	1-2	2-3	12	D.J.Gallagher	Van der Sar	Finnan 69	Goma	Melville	Brevett	Davis	Malbranque 45	Davis	Legwinski ●	Saha	Hayes	Market ▲89	Saha ▲40 45	Boa Monte ▲▲
02-01	A	Derby County	0-0	0-0	12	B.Knight	Van der Sar	Finnan 72	Goma	Melville	Brevett	Legwinski	Malbranque 40	Davis	Knight ▲	Saha ▲15	Market 45	Knight ▲	Knight ▲	Boa Monte ▲
12-01	H	Middlesbrough	2-1	2-1	9	M.L.Dean	Van der Sar	Finnan	Goma ●	Melville	Brevett	Legwinski 7	Malbranque 15	Knight ▲	Davis	Saha ▲15	Hayes ●15	Stobers ▲	Market 45	Stobers ▲
19-01	A	Sunderland	1-0	1-1	10	P.Jones	Van der Sar	Finnan	Goma	Melville ●	Harley	Legwinski	Malbranque ●	Knight ●	Saha	Saha	Hayes ▲15	Goldbaek ▲	Collins ▲	Ouaddou ▲
30-01	H	Ipswich Town	0-1	0-1	10	A.G.Wiley	Van der Sar	Finnan	Goma	Melville	Brevett	Legwinski	Malbranque ▲	Knight ▲	Davis 76	Hayes	Saha 52	Collins ▲	Goldbaek ▲	—
02-02	H	Aston Villa	0-0	0-0	9	M.D.Messias	Van der Sar	Finnan	Goma	Melville	Brevett	Legwinski ●	Malbranque 63	Knight ▲	Saha	Saha	Market 56	Goldbaek ▲	Goldbaek ▲	—
09-02	A	Blackburn	1-0	2-0	9	M.R.Halsey	Van der Sar	Finnan	Goma	Melville	Harley	Legwinski	Malbranque ●	Davis	Hayes 31	Hayes 31	Saha 76	Willock ▲	Willock ▲	—
19-02	A	Middlesbrough	0-1	1-2	9	D.J.Gallagher	Van der Sar	Finnan	Goma 56	Melville	Brevett ▲10	Legwinski ● ▲	Malbranque	Davis	Hayes ●63	Marlet ●31 63	Market ●31 63	Harley ▲	Market ▲31 63	—
23-02	H	Arsenal	1-3	1-4	9	U.D.Rennie	Van der Sar	Finnan	Goma	Melville	Brevett	Legwinski ●	Malbranque	Knight ▲	Hayes	Saha 10	Market 10	Harley ▲	Clark ▲▲	Boa Morte ▲
02-03	H	Liverpool	0-1	0-2	10	A.G.Wiley	Van der Sar	Finnan	Goma	Ouaddou	Brevett ●	Davis ●	Boa Morte ●	Davis	Saha	Saha	Market	Clark ▲▲	Hayes ▲	Collins ▲
06-03	A	Chelsea	1-2	2-3	11	P.Jones	Van der Sar	Finnan	Goma	Melville	Brevett	Boa Morte ●	Harley	Collins	Saha 19 73	Saha 19 73	Market 73	Hayes ▲	Hayes ▲	Goldbaek ▲
16-03	A	Everton	0-2	1-2	12	G.P.Barber	Van der Sar	Finnan	Goma ●	Ouaddou	Brevett ●	Legwinski ●	Boa Morte ▲	Davis	Malbranque ▲42	Malbranque ▲42	Hayes ▲52	Hayes ▲52	Hayes ▲52	Ouaddou ▲
24-03	H	Tottenham	0-0	0-0	14	P.A.Durkin	Van der Sar	Finnan	Goma	Melville	Brevett	Legwinski	Malbranque	Davis	Saha	Saha	Market	Brevett ▲	Brevett ▲	—
30-03	A	Southampton	1-1	1-1	13	J.T.Winter	Van der Sar	Finnan ●	Goma	Melville	Harley ●	Legwinski	Malbranque ●	Davis	Hayes ▲	Marlet 7	Hayes ▲	Hayes ▲	Hayes ▲	Saha ▲
01-04	H	West Ham Utd	0-1	1-1	15	M.R.Halsey	Van der Sar	Finnan	Goma	Melville	Brevett	Legwinski 7	Malbranque ▲	Knight ▲	Hayes ▲	Marlet 7	Market 7	Harley ▲	Market 7	Boa Morte ▲
08-04	A	Newcastle Utd	0-1	1-1	16	A.G.Wiley	Van der Sar	Finnan	Goma	Melville	Brevett	Legwinski	Malbranque 52	Davis	Saha 76	Saha ▲	Hayes	Market ▲	Market ▲	Harley ▲
20-04	A	Leeds Utd	0-1	1-1	14	R.Styles	Van der Sar	Finnan	Goma	Melville 72	Brevett	Legwinski ●	Malbranque ●76	Davis	Saha ▲52	Saha ▲52	Hayes 76	Goldbaek ▲	Goldbaek ▲	Ouaddou ▲
23-04	H	Bolton	1-0	3-0	11	P.A.Durkin	Van der Sar	Finnan	Goma	Melville	Brevett	Legwinski 76	Malbranque 42	Davis	Saha 52	Saha 76	Hayes 76	Goldbaek 42	Hayes 76	Stolcers ▲
27-04	H	Leicester City	0-0	0-1	11	D.Pugh	Van der Sar	Finnan	Goma	Melville	Brevett	Legwinski ● ▲	Malbranque ●	Davis	Hayes	Hayes	Market	Collins ▲	Collins ▲	Saha ▲
11-05	A	Blackburn	0-0	0-3	13	C.J.Foy	Taylor	Finnan	Ouaddou ▲	Melville	Harley ▲	Goldbaek ▲	Legwinski ▲	Davis	Saha	Saha	Market	Willock ▲	Willock ▲	Knight ▲

F.A. Barclaycard Premiership
Squad List

Position	Name	Appearances	Appearances as Substitute	Goals or Clean Sheets	Goal Assists	Yellow Cards	Red Cards
G	M.Taylor	1					
G	E.van der Sar	37		15		1	
D	R.Brevett	34	1		3	5	
D	S.Finnan	38			2	3	
D	A.Goma	32	1		1	7	
D	J.Harley	5	5				
D	Z.Knight	8	2				
D	A.Melville	35			2	3	
D	A.Ouaddou	4	4				
D	K.Symons	2	2			1	
M	L.Clark	5	4				
M	J.Collins	29	5		1		
M	S.Davis	25	5		2	4	
M	B.Goldbaek	8	5	1	1	1	
M	S.Legwinski	30	3	3	3	8	
M	E.Lewis	1					
M	S.Malbranque	33	4	8	8	3	
M	A.Stolcers		5				
M	C.Willock		2				
F	K.Betsy		1				
F	L.Boa Morte	15	8	1	1	6	2
F	B.Hayles	27	8	8	2	7	
F	S.Marlet	21	5	6	4	1	
F	L.Saha	28	8	8	5	4	

It was not a pleasant experience for Boa Morte who missed a penalty and saw red.

Fulham were not getting everything their own way but Tigana continued to insist he would play attractive football at all costs. Sometimes, as he was discovering, it was not always enough to secure valuable points, though Fulham kept to a respectable mid-table position up until Christmas.

While they were struggling to win games, Fulham were keeping clean sheets. The goalless draw at Liverpool in December was their eighth game without conceding, a better record than any of their rivals. Yet they struggled in attack.

Fulham did record a win, their only success in seven, when they beat Everton at home. It was an ugly game though: Fulham had Boa Morte sent off (later changed to Malbranque following a case of mistaken identity) and a brawl led to the club receiving a £30,000 fine and an official Football Association warning.

In a six-game spell between late November and Boxing Day, the Cottagers scored in only one game while suffering a one-sided 4-0 defeat at Tottenham.

Off the field, Fulham were continuing their plans to grow and announced that, for next season they would share with Queens Park Rangers at Loftus Road while Craven Cottage was undergoing a £70m refit.

For their first season in the F.A. Barclaycard Premiership, Fulham had been given dispensation to continue to use terracing, a throwback to the old days, and Craven Cottage offered a unique atmosphere to visiting fans. It did little, though, to enhance their prospects.

The goal drought was a major concern. Even when Fulham stole another valuable win, in early January at Derby, they had to rely on an Horacio Carbonari own goal for the points. Tigana tried to sign Andy Cole

Win Barclaycard Premiership tickets – 4thegame.com

F.A. Barclaycard Premiership

Top Goal Scorer

Barry Hayles

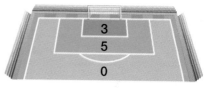

Total Premier League Goals Scored:	Percentage Of The Team's League Goals:
8	22%

Goals Scored From

3

5

0

Although Hayles finished with eight F.A. Barclaycard Premiership goals, level with Steed Malbranque and Luis Saha, he did so from fewer appearances. It was a far cry from the 90 Division One goals Fulham had scored a year earlier when the Cottagers were scoring for fun with Saha netting 27 and Luis Boa Morte and Hayles taking home 18 goals apiece. Hayles' total included a brace in the fiery 2-0 win over Everton and the striker can also boast the distinction of scoring the last goal at Craven Cottage – in the 3-0 win over Bolton – prior to the stadium's expensive refit.

"The manager said we must close down teams more and that players are switching off at crucial times. He wants the errors stamped out."

Barry Hayles

Goals Resulting From

Key

Open Play Corner Indirect Free Kick
Direct Free Kick Penalty

25%

50%

25%

	Right Foot	Left Foot	Header
Open Play	2	2	-
Set piece	1	1	2

Goal Assists

Total number of goal assists	2

Teams Scored Against

Against	Home	Away
Everton	2	0
Blackburn Rovers	1	0
Bolton Wanderers	1	0
Chelsea	1	0
Ipswich Town	1	0
Newcastle United	1	0
Sunderland	1	0
Total Goals Scored	8	0

The heart of the Barclaycard Premiership – 4thegame.com

It's a fact

Fulham suffered their worst sequence since April 1986 when they lost six successive League games between February and March.

> **"We're not going to be happy just sitting in mid-table, we really want to push for a European place so that we've got that to look forward to next season."**
>
> *Sean Davis*
> *(February 2002)*

and Norwegian star John Carew, but failed in both cases.

Marlet was failing to produce the goods. A hairline leg fracture had halted his season in October but he did score in the 3-2 home defeat by Manchester United in late December. Including the win over Derby, Fulham enjoyed back-to-back successes when Marlet, recalled to the French squad, and Saha scored in the 2-1 home win over Middlesbrough.

Fulham were suffering from the prolonged absence of midfielder Lee Clark, whose season effectively ended at Christmas. Add the injury to that of another key midfielder, Sean Davis, and perhaps their problems lay in the making, rather than the scoring, of goals.

In late January, Fulham played York in the F.A. Cup and made a generous £50,000 offer to boost the ailing club's financial plight. The gift was politely rejected and Fulham won 2-0. They then knocked Walsall out of the fifth round to give their fans a distraction from the less than satisfactory form in the League.

In Febuary, Tigana caused something of a shock by declaring, out of the blue, that he would quit if he became unhappy with life at Craven Cottage. Later that day

F.A. Barclaycard Premiership
Goals By Position

Key
Forward ■ Midfield ● League Position
Defence ■ Goalkeeper

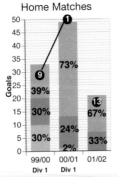

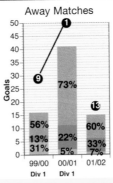

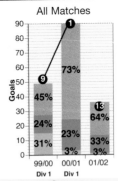

Chart Analysis

statistics powered by **SUPERBASE**™

Fulham managed considerably less goals than they had the previous season.

Even allowing for the eight less games they played in the F.A. Barclaycard Premiership, the 250% reduction in the number of goals scored was disappointing.

No goals were scored by defenders at home, as the rearguard contributed just a solitary away goal to the overall team total of 36.

Fulham were held to a goalless draw by Villa, their seventh so far. They recorded a win next time out, at home to Blackburn, and while the 2-0 victory seemed to carry little significance, their fans should have enjoyed it while they could because their team was about to embark on a worrying run that saw Fulham become one of the relegation candidates.

The Londoners set off on a run of six straight League defeats, their worst sequence since 1986, and one which was far removed from the successes of only a few months earlier. From mid-February to the end of March, Fulham failed to collect a single point.

Their only consolation was claiming a place in the F.A. Cup semi-final – against neighbours Chelsea – after winning 1-0 at West Bromwich Albion.

Another big name striker was linked with Fulham, Rangers' former Chelsea star Tore Andre Flo admitting he would consider a return to London, but that became sidelined as defeat followed defeat.

The run started at Middlesbrough where Fulham lost 2-1, but they felt hard done by after an incident in which Boro's Franck Queudrue, already booked, was lucky not to see red after fouling Hayles.

Fulham were furious and their anger contributed to the defeat. A 4-1 reverse at

F.A. Barclaycard Premiership
Team Performance Table

League Position	Team	Points won from a possible six	Percentage of points won at home	Percentage of points won away	Overall percentage of points won
1	Arsenal	0/6			
2	Liverpool	1/6			
3	Manchester Utd	0/6	27%	33%	30%
4	Newcastle Utd	4/6			
5	Leeds United	4/6			
6	Chelsea	1/6			
7	West Ham Utd	3/6			
8	Aston Villa	1/6	33%	20%	27%
9	Tottenham H	0/6			
10	Blackburn R	3/6			
11	Southampton	4/6			
12	Middlesbrough	3/6			
13	Fulham	44	83%	17%	50%
14	Charlton Athletic	2/6			
15	Everton	3/6			
16	Bolton W	4/6			
17	Sunderland	4/6			
18	Ipswich Town	1/6	60%	40%	50%
19	Derby County	4/6			
20	Leicester City	2/6			

The table shows how many points out of a possible six Fulham have taken off each of the teams in the four sections. The other columns show as a percentage how many points they have taken from those available.

Chart Analysis

statistics powered by  SUPERBASE™

Fulham did not fare badly against teams in the top five, taking just under a third of all points available from ten matches, including wins over Leeds and Newcastle United.

They collected less points against teams in the second sector than they did against those in the first.

The Cottagers performed best against teams in the bottom half of the table, although they did struggle on the road against teams in their own

sector, where they picked up just two out of a possible 12 points.

They showed their best form in home fixtures against teams in their own sector, where they picked up ten out of 12 points.

Fulham did not manage to take any points off three sides as well as failing to do the 'double' over any teams.

 Fixtures, results and match reports - 4thegame.com

Arsenal, a 2-0 home defeat by Liverpool and a 3-2 loss at Chelsea, where they succumbed to a late winner from Mikael Forssell, made for gloomy viewing.

They were not playing terribly badly, as witnessed both at Stamford Bridge and at Goodison Park, where they were unlucky to face Everton in their first game under David Moyes. Everton were pumped up for a win and despite a one-sided second half in Fulham's favour, they left with defeat number five. Number six arrived at home to Tottenham and Andy Melville, Fulham's Wales defender, admitted he was sick of hearing people say the team played well without getting their just rewards.

"Games are running out," admitted Melville, "and we need to get points before the F.A. Cup semi-final." Fulham finally halted the run, albeit in less than satisfactory fashion, with a 1-1 draw at Southampton. Marlet gave Fulham the lead but, after Rory Delap levelled, Tigana claimed his side needed six points from the next six games to be assured of F.A. Barclaycard Premiership survival.

The fear factor continued with a 1-0 home loss to West Ham on April Fool's Day but they stole a point at Newcastle, thanks to Saha's goal. A narrow 1-0 defeat in the F.A. Cup semi-final against Chelsea may have been disappointing, but their priorities were in the League and

It's a fact

Jean Tigana marked his 100th game in charge in all competitions when Fulham met Leicester City in April and drew 0-0.

"I work with my feelings all the time. If I am not happy, I will leave. I am happy here now but if one day I'm not happy, I'll take my bag and leave. The priority is the respect around me."

Jean Tigana
(February 2002)

F.A. Barclaycard Premiership
Goals By Time Period

Key: ■ Goals Scored □ Goals Conceded

Home Matches

Time of Goal (mins)	Goals Scored	Goals Conceded
0-15	3	
16-30	4	2
31-45	7	5
46-60	3	2
61-75	4	1
76-90	3	3

Away Matches

Time of Goal (mins)	Goals Scored	Goals Conceded
0-15	4	5
16-30	1	6
31-45	2	4
46-60	4	5
61-75	3	4
76-90	1	4

All Matches

Time of Goal (mins)	Goals Scored	Goals Conceded
0-15	4	8
16-30	5	8
31-45	9	9
46-60	7	7
61-75	7	5
76-90	4	7

Chart Analysis

statistics powered by ◆ SUPERBASE™

Overall, Fulham scored more goals than their opponents in only one time period, from 61-75 minutes. They made things hard for themselves at home, conceding three goals in the opening 15 minutes without reply.

Back in the top flight for the first time since 1968, the Cottagers failed to hit double figures in any of the time periods.

They also scored as many goals in the first half as they did in the second.

➡ **Win Barclaycard Premiership tickets - 4thegame.com**

F.A. Barclaycard Premiership
Goals Resulting From

Key ☐ Goals Scored ☐ Goals Conceded

	Six Yard Area				Inside Area				Outside Area				Total			
	Shots		Headers		Shots		Headers		Shots		Headers		Shots		Headers	
	Home	Away	Home	Away	Home	Away	Home	Away	Home	Away	Home	Away	Home	Away	Home	Away
Open Play	4	1	-	1	7	4	-	1	4	2	-	-	15	7	0	2
	-	6	1	-	8	16	1	-	2	3	-	-	10	25	2	0
Direct Free Kick									-	-			0	0		
									-	1			0	1		
Indirect Free Kick	-	-	1	-	1	-	2	-	-	-	-	-	1	0	3	0
	-	-	1	-	2	-	1	-	-	-	-	-	2	0	2	0
Penalty	-	-	-	-	-	1	-	-	-	-	-	-	0	1	0	0
	-	-	-	-	-	-	-	-	-	-	-	-	0	0	0	0
Corner	1	1	1	2	-	1	-	-	-	-	-	-	1	2	1	2
	-	1	-	-	-	-	-	-	-	-	-	-	0	1	0	0
Totals	5	2	2	3	8	6	2	1	4	2	0	0	17	10	4	4
	0	7	2	0	10	16	2	0	2	4	0	0	12	27	4	0

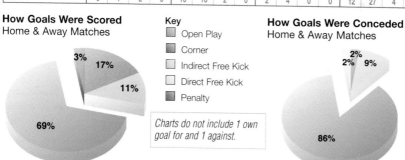

How Goals Were Scored
Home & Away Matches

3% 17% 11% 69%

Key
- ☐ Open Play
- ☐ Corner
- ☐ Indirect Free Kick
- ☐ Direct Free Kick
- ☐ Penalty

Charts do not include 1 own goal for and 1 against.

How Goals Were Conceded
Home & Away Matches

2% 2% 9% 86%

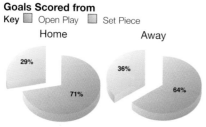

Goals Scored from
Key ☐ Open Play ☐ Set Piece

Home — 29% 71%

Away — 36% 64%

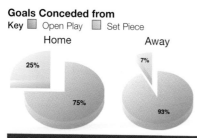

Goals Conceded from
Key ☐ Open Play ☐ Set Piece

Home — 25% 75%

Away — 7% 93%

Chart Analysis

While Fulham struggled from Open Play, their hard work on the training pitch paid off as they secured ten out of 36 goals scored from Corners and Indirect Free Kicks.

They also proved themselves adept at defending Set Pieces away from home, conceding just two out of 28 goals from dead ball situations.

Nearly 60% of their goals conceded were from Shots Inside Area.

BEST IN THE LEAGUE...
- **Most goals scored from Corners away**
- **Most goals scored from Indirect Free Kicks at home**

statistics powered by **SUPERBASE**™

 The heart of the Barclaycard Premiership – 4thegame.com

> "We knew our first season in the top flight would be tough. It was going to be a hard learning experience for the players and for the manager. So it has proved, but Jean is learning fast."
>
> *Chairman*
> *Mohamed Al Fayed*
> *(May 2002)*

It's a fact

The visit of Leicester in April was the final game at Craven Cottage before the proposed £70m refit of the famous old stadium, where they first played in 1896.

they proceeded to win their next two and confirm safety in some style.

Firstly, the Cottagers earned an unlikely win at Leeds thanks to Malbranque's lone goal. That was their first win in 10 F.A. Barclaycard Premiership games, and they followed it with a 3-0 win over Bolton.

It was Fulham's best win of the campaign and secured another season in the top flight, thanks to Bjarne Goldbaek's first goal of the season and late strikes from Marlet and Hayles.

The joy of safety was tempered by news that the club had suffered a British record loss of £24m. They then discovered they would have to leave the Cottage for two years, rather than one, following opposition by local residents.

The final game at the Cottage was also disappointing, with relegated Leicester forcing a goalless draw.

The season ended disappointingly with a 3-0 defeat at Blackburn though they enjoyed the compensation of qualifying for the Intertoto Cup, a possible back door route into Europe.

F.A. Barclaycard Premiership
Shot Efficiency

Key
■ Goals Scored ☐ Other Shots On Target

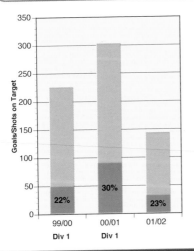

Season	Division	Shots Off Target	Shots On Target	Total Goals
1999 - 2000	1	n/a	224	49
2000 - 2001	1	n/a	301	90
2001 - 2002	P	194	142	32

Chart Analysis

Following promotion from Division One, Fulham managed less than half as many Shots On Target in the top flight.

Although the number of efforts on goal that were converted fell dramatically, the percentage was still above the level achieved two seasons ago.

statistics powered by **SUPERBASE**™

 All the latest news, views and opinion - 4thegame.com

F.A. Barclaycard Premiership

Team Discipline

Total Number Of Bookings

Total number of red cards	2
Total number of yellow cards	54

Referee Performance

Referee	Games Refereed	Red Cards	Yellow Cards
A.G.Wiley	4	-	8
G.P.Barber	2	-	7
P.Dowd	1	1	3

Type of Yellow Cards Received

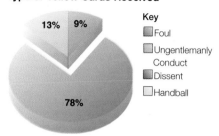

Key
☐ Foul
☐ Ungentlemanly Conduct
■ Dissent
☐ Handball

13% 9% 78%

Bookings by Position 1999/2000 - 2001/2002

Home Matches

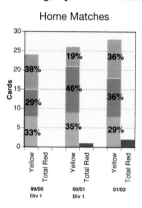

Away Matches

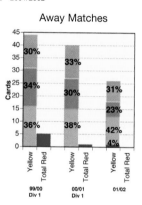

All Matches

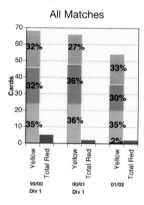

Chart Analysis

For the second season running, the number of cards picked up by Fulham players declined – although they did play eight less games as a result of gaining promotion from Division One.

The distribution of cautions throughout the team remained consistent with previous seasons, the one novelty being the yellow card picked up by Edwin van der Sar at Leeds towards the end of the campaign.

The split of Yellow Cards attributed to Fulham between games at Craven Cottage and on the road was fairly even, at 26 and 28 respectively.

Fulham's two Red Cards were both picked up at home by former Arsenal striker Luis Boa Morte.

> "We have the attitude to play well and try to respect the referee."
>
> *Assistant manager*
> *Christian Damiano*
> *(December 2001)*

statistics powered by **SUPERBASE**™

Ipswich Town

F.A. Barclaycard Premiership Final standing for the 2001-2002 season

Final Position		Games Played	Games Won	Games Drawn	Games Lost	Goals For	Goals Against	Total Points
17	Sunderland AFC	38	10	10	18	29	51	40
18	Ipswich Town	38	9	9	20	41	64	36
19	Derby County	38	8	6	24	33	63	30

"It's a difficult challenge for the club this season compared to the last couple. We almost did too well with our achievements."

George Burley (March 2002)

Club Honours and Records

Division 1 Champions: 1961-62

Division 2 Champions: 1960-61, 1967-68, 1991-92

Div 3 Champions: 1953-54, 1956-57

FA Cup Winners: 1978

UEFA Cup Winners: 1981

Texaco Cup Winners: 1973

Record victory:

7-0 v Portsmouth, Division 2, 11 November, 1964

Record defeat:

1-10 v Fulham, Division 1, 26 December, 1963

League goals in a season (team):

106, Division 3, 1955-56

League goals in a season (player):

41, Ted Phillips, Division 3, 1956-57

Career league goals:

203, Ray Crawford, 1958 to 1969

League appearances:

591, Mick Mills 1966 to 1982

Reported transfer fee paid: £4,000,000 to Wimbledon for Hermann Hreidarsson, August 2000

Reported transfer fee received: £6,500,000 from Newcastle United for Kieron Dyer, July 1999

AFTER finishing fifth and earning a place in the UEFA Cup in 2000-01, the only direction Ipswich could go was downwards but only after a roller coaster campaign at Portman Road.

The previous season's surprise package proved to be victims of their own success. After losing Richard Wright, their England goalkeeper, to Arsenal prior to the start of the campaign, a predictable yet nonetheless damaging transfer, they had to search for a replacement.

George Burley, the Manager of the Year, signed two – Norwich's promising Andy Marshall and, just before the start of the season, Sampdoria's Matteo Sereni. In addition, Nigerian star Finidi George arrived to boost Ipswich's midfield.

Jamie Scowcroft was another departure, for Leicester, but Burley added Sixto Peralta and Pablo Counago to his squad as Ipswich tried to consolidate their position knowing that whatever they achieved would only be a disappointment after the previous season's success.

Following an opening day loss at Sunderland, George struck twice on his home debut to hand Ipswich a 3-1 win over Derby. George was outstanding and, with Nigeria set to reach the World Cup finals, the former Real Mallorca star saw

 Win Barclaycard Premiership tickets - 4thegame.com

F.A. Barclaycard Premiership

Season Progression

Key
- ■ Win ■ Loss ■ Draw ❷ League Position
- ❷ Last Season's League Position

All Matches

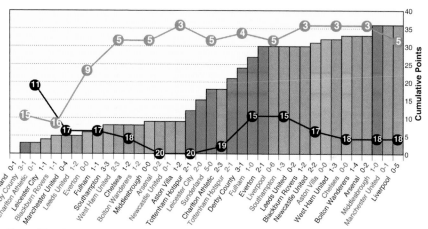

Home Matches

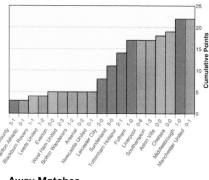

Away Matches

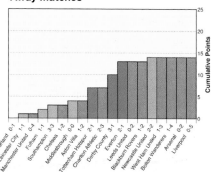

Chart Analysis

Following the highs of last season, when Ipswich qualified for the UEFA Cup after finishing fifth, the wheels came off for the Tractor Boys in 2001-02.

After losing at Sunderland on the opening day of the season, they beat Derby County 3-1 at home – their only win from the opening 17 matches – to leave them bottom of the pile come mid-December.

With relegation staring them in the face, Ipswich hit back with a stunning sequence of seven wins in eight outings to lift them clear of danger by the beginning of February.

After winning 2-1 at Everton on 2 February, their form nosedived again, prompted by a humiliating 6-0 defeat at home to Liverpool.

Just one win from their last 13 League matches – at home to Middlesbrough – saw them fall back into the bottom three where they stayed until the end of the season.

There was a remote chance that they could have stayed up had they beaten Liverpool on the last day of the season. Instead, Ipswich took another beating, losing 5-0 at Anfield.

statistics powered by ◆ **SUPERBASE**™

 The heart of the Barclaycard Premiership - 4thegame.com

> **"We have not played as well as we did last season but the form is coming back."**
>
> *George Burley*
> *(October 2001)*

this season as vital to his future plans. Certainly, Burley was delighted with the winger, saying: "His performance in that game was one of the best I've seen since I started watching football."

Ipswich also signed Danish defender Thomas Gaardsoe but the reasonable start was soon ruined. While Town were passing comfortably through the first two rounds of the UEFA Cup, with successes over Torpedo Moscow and Helsingborgs, they could not win in the F.A. Barclaycard Premiership. They lost at home to Charlton and went through September winning just two points from 12 thanks to draws against Leicester and Blackburn.

Titus Bramble, who had enjoyed such a good start to life in the top flight, appeared to have lost confidence and collected an Achilles injury in mid-September which ruled him out of five important League games.

Defeats against Manchester United and Leeds acted as a reminder to Ipswich as to how far they had slumped and in October matters progressed from bad to worse. Three draws, against Everton, Fulham and Southampton saw the Tractor Boys drop to 17th. More worryingly, in the 1-1 draw at Fulham, George lasted 12 minutes before suffering a depressed fracture of his cheekbone following a clash with defender Alain Goma.

It's a fact

Ipswich claimed their 49th Premier League win, against Derby in August. They had to wait until December, when they won 2-1 at Spurs, for their 50th.

F.A. Barclaycard Premiership
Half-Time/Full-Time Comparison

Key: ■ Win ■ Loss ■ Draw

Home				Away				Total			
Number of Home Half Time Wins	Full Time Result W	L	D	Number of Away Half Time Wins	Full Time Result W	L	D	Total number of Half Time Wins	Full Time Result W	L	D
6	4	1	1	2	1	-	1	8	5	1	2
Number of Home Half Time Losses	Full Time Result W	L	D	Number of Away Half Time Losses	Full Time Result W	L	D	Total number of Half Time Losses	Full Time Result W	L	D
6	-	6	-	9	-	7	2	15	-	13	2
Number of Home Half Time Draws	Full Time Result W	L	D	Number of Away Half Time Draws	Full Time Result W	L	D	Total number of Half Time Draws	Full Time Result W	L	D
7	2	2	3	8	2	4	2	15	4	6	5

Chart Analysis

statistics powered by ◆ SUPERBASE™

Although Ipswich won most of the games they were leading at half-time, they did conspire to lose one out of eight, at home to Leeds United.

They lost all six games at home in which they were trailing at the break, faring slightly better on the road where they managed to salvage a draw twice in the nine games in which they were behind at half-time.

They lost 40% of games in which they were level at the interval.

 All the latest news, views and opinion - 4thegame.com

F.A. Barclaycard Premiership Results Table

Key: 88 time of goal 88 time of assist ▲ player substituted ○ yellow card ● red card

DATE	H/A	OPPONENT	H/T	F/T	POS	REFEREE	TEAM											SUBSTITUTES USED		
18-08	A	Sunderland	0-1	0-1	17	G.Poll	Sereni	Makin ○	Bramble	McGreal ▲	Hreidarsson	Wright	Holland	Magilton ▲	Reuser	George	Stewart	Counago ▲	Clapham ▲	-
21-08	H	Derby County	1-0	3-1	5	E.K.Wolstenholme	Sereni	Makin	Bramble	Hreidarsson	Clapham ▲	George 14 76	Holland 14	Wright	Reuser 48 76	Naylor ▲48	Stewart ▲	Counago ▲	Wilnis ▲	Armstrong ▲
25-08	H	Charlton	0-0	0-1	11	S.W.Dunn	Sereni	Makin	Bramble ○	Hreidarsson	Clapham ▲	George	Holland	Wright ○	Reuser	Naylor ▲	Stewart ▲	Magilton ▲	Armstrong ▲	Counago ▲
08-09	A	Leicester City	1-0	1-1	12	B.Knight	Sereni ●	Makin ○	Bramble	McGreal	Hreidarsson	George ▲	Holland 13	Magilton ○	Wright	Reuser ○	Stewart ▲13	Armstrong ▲	Branagan ▲	-
16-09	H	Blackburn	1-0	1-1	12	G.Poll	Sereni	Makin	Bramble ○	McGreal	Hreidarsson ○	George ▲15	Holland	Magilton	Reuser ○ ▲	Armstrong ▲15	Stewart	Naylor ▲	Counago ▲	Wilnis ▲
22-09	A	Manchester Utd	0-2	0-4	17	N.S.Barry	Sereni	Wilnis ▲	Bramble	McGreal ○	Hreidarsson	Makin ▲	Holland	Magilton	George ▲	Armstrong	Stewart	Clapham ▲	Wright ▲	Reuser ▲
30-09	H	Leeds Utd	1-0	1-2	17	A.P.D'Urso	Sereni	Makin ▲	McGreal	Venus 22	Hreidarsson	George ▲	Holland	Magilton	Wright ▲	Armstrong	Stewart 22	Wilnis ▲	Counago ▲	Clapham ▲
13-10	H	Everton	0-0	0-0	16	C.R.Wilkes	Sereni	Makin ▲	McGreal	Venus	Hreidarsson	Wright ▲	Holland	Magilton	Reuser	Armstrong	Stewart	Wilnis ▲	George ▲	-
21-10	A	Fulham	0-1	1-1	17	M.A.Riley	Sereni	Wilnis ○ ▲	McGreal	Hreidarsson	Makin	Wright 55	Holland	Peralta ○ ▲55	Clapham	Armstrong ○	George ▲	Reuser ▲	Stewart ▲	Magilton ▲
24-10	A	Southampton	1-2	3-3	17	U.D.Rennie	Sereni	Makin ▲	McGreal	Venus 37 64 72	Hreidarsson	Wright	Holland	Peralta ○	Clapham	Armstrong ▲	Stewart 37 64 72	Naylor ▲	Wilnis ▲	-
28-10	H	West Ham Utd	0-1	2-3	17	S.W.Dunn	Sereni	Makin	Gaardsoe ○	Venus 63	Hreidarsson 63	Reuser	Holland 90	Wright ▲	Clapham ▲	Armstrong ▲	Stewart ○	Counago ▲	Magilton ▲	Peralta ▲90
04-11	A	Chelsea	0-1	1-2	18	R.Styles	Sereni	Makin	Bramble	Venus	Hreidarsson	Wright ○	Holland	Magilton	Clapham ▲	Naylor ○ ▲	Stewart 81 81	Reuser ▲	Counago ▲	-
18-11	H	Bolton	1-2	1-2	19	S.G.Bennett	Sereni	Makin ▲	Bramble	Venus	Hreidarsson	Peralta 45	Holland 45	Magilton ▲	Reuser	Bent D ▲	Counago	Le Pen ▲	Wright ▲	Naylor ▲
25-11	A	Middlesbrough	0-0	0-0	20	D.Pugh	Sereni	Makin	Bramble	Venus	Hreidarsson	Wright	Holland	Peralta ▲	Clapham	Armstrong ▲	Bent M ▲	Counago ▲	Naylor ○ ▲	Miller ▲
01-12	H	Arsenal	0-1	0-2	20	D.R.Elleray	Sereni	Makin ▲	Bramble	Venus ○	Hreidarsson	Wright	Holland	Peralta ▲	Clapham	Naylor ▲	Bent M	George ▲	Counago ▲	Gaardsoe ▲
09-12	H	Newcastle Utd	0-1	0-1	20	R.Styles	Sereni	Makin	McGreal ○	Venus	Hreidarsson ○	George ▲	Holland	Wright ▲	Clapham	Armstrong ▲	Bent M	Peralta ▲	Naylor ▲	Counago ○ ▲
17-12	A	Aston Villa	1-1	1-2	20	M.L.Dean	Sereni	Makin	McGreal	Venus	Hreidarsson	George ▲18	Holland	Magilton	Wright	Armstrong ▲	Naylor ○ 18	Bent M ▲	Clapham ▲	-
22-12	A	Tottenham	1-1	2-1	20	M.A.Riley	Sereni	Makin	McGreal ○ ▲40	Venus	Hreidarsson	George 40 88	Holland	Magilton ▲	Wright ○	Reuser	Bent M ▲	Armstrong ▲88	Naylor ▲	Bramble ▲
26-12	H	Leicester City	0-0	2-0	19	N.S.Barry	Sereni	Makin	Bramble	Venus	Hreidarsson	George ▲	Holland	Peralta ▲54	Reuser 48 54	Armstrong ▲	Bent M 48	Naylor ▲	Wright ▲	Magilton ▲
29-12	H	Sunderland	4-0	5-0	19	G.Poll	Sereni	Makin ○	Gaardsoe 26	Venus 26	Hreidarsson	George 16 31	Holland 31	Magilton	Reuser ▲	Armstrong ▲16 28	Bent M ○ ▲	Naylor ▲86	Wright ▲	Clapham ▲86
01-01	A	Charlton	2-2	2-3	19	U.D.Rennie	Sereni	Makin	Gaardsoe	Venus ○	Hreidarsson ○ 1	George	Holland	Magilton ▲5	Clapham ▲	Armstrong	Bent M 1 5	Reuser ▲	Peralta ▲	-
12-01	H	Tottenham	1-0	2-1	18	M.D.Messias	Marshall	Makin	McGreal 81	Venus 12 81	Hreidarsson	Wright	Holland	Magilton ▲	Reuser ▲	Armstrong ▲	Bent M 12	Stewart ▲	Peralta ▲	Clapham ▲
19-01	A	Derby County	0-0	3-1	17	P.A.Durkin	Marshall	Makin	McGreal	Venus	Hreidarsson ○	Wright 48	Holland	Peralta 67	Reuser ○ ▲87	Stewart ▲	Bent M ▲48 67	Armstrong ▲	Naylor ▲87	Clapham ▲
30-01	H	Fulham	1-0	1-0	15	A.G.Wiley	Marshall	Makin	McGreal ○	Venus	Hreidarsson	Wright ▲	Holland	Peralta	Clapham	Armstrong ▲10	Bent M 10	Stewart ▲	Reuser ▲	-
02-02	A	Everton	2-1	2-1	12	S.W.Dunn	Marshall	Makin	McGreal	Venus	Hreidarsson	Wright ▲	Holland 43	Peralta 10	Clapham 10 43	Armstrong ▲	Bent M	Stewart ▲	Magilton ▲	-
09-02	H	Liverpool	0-2	0-6	13	S.G.Bennett	Marshall	Makin	McGreal	Venus	Hreidarsson	Wright ▲	Holland	Peralta	Clapham	Armstrong ▲	Bent M	Magilton ▲	Stewart ▲	-
02-03	H	Southampton	0-0	1-3	15	M.R.Halsey	Marshall	Makin ▲	Bramble	Venus	Hreidarsson	George 82	Holland 82	Magilton	Reuser ▲	Stewart ▲	Bent M	Wright ▲	Counago ▲	Clapham ▲
06-03	A	Leeds Utd	0-0	0-2	16	D.J.Gallagher	Marshall ○	Wilnis ○	McGreal ○	Venus	Hreidarsson	George ▲	Holland	Magilton	Clapham	Stewart ▲	Armstrong ▲	Counago ▲	Bent M ▲	Miller ▲
13-03	A	Blackburn	0-2	1-2	17	P.Dowd	Sereni	Makin ○	McGreal ○	Venus 55	Hreidarsson	Wright	Holland	Magilton ▲	Clapham ▲	Stewart ▲55	Armstrong	Peralta ▲	Bent M ▲	George ▲
16-03	A	Newcastle Utd	0-0	2-2	17	M.A.Riley	Sereni	Makin	McGreal	Venus ○	Hreidarsson	Wright	Holland	Peralta ▲	Clapham	Stewart 50 63	Bent M ▲50 63	Armstrong ▲	Magilton ▲	-
23-03	H	Aston Villa	0-0	0-0	18	D.Pugh	Sereni	Makin ▲	McGreal	Venus	Hreidarsson	George ○ ▲	Holland	Wright	Clapham	Stewart ▲	Bent M	Magilton ▲	Armstrong ▲	Reuser ▲
30-03	A	West Ham Utd	0-1	1-3	18	A.G.Wiley	Sereni	Wilnis	McGreal	Venus	Hreidarsson	Wright ▲	Holland	Peralta ▲	Clapham	Stewart	Bent M ○ 70	Miller ○ ▲	George ▲70	-
01-04	H	Chelsea	0-0	0-0	18	E.K.Wolstenholme	Marshall	Wilnis	McGreal	Venus	Hreidarsson	George ▲	Holland	Miller	Peralta ▲	Armstrong ▲	Bent M	Stewart ▲	Clapham ▲	Bent D ▲
06-04	A	Bolton	0-4	1-4	18	J.T.Winter	Marshall	Wilnis	McGreal	Venus ▲	Hreidarsson	George ▲	Holland	Miller	Peralta ▲	Armstrong	Bent M	Bramble ▲	Stewart ▲90	Clapham ▲90
21-04	A	Arsenal	0-0	0-2	18	A.G.Wiley	Marshall	Bramble	McGreal	Hreidarsson	Clapham	George ▲	Holland	Miller	Reuser ▲	Stewart	Bent M ▲	Ambrose ▲	Armstrong ▲	Peralta ▲
24-04	H	Middlesbrough	0-0	1-0	18	A.P.D'Urso	Marshall	Bramble	McGreal	Venus ▲	Hreidarsson	Clapham 58	Holland	Peralta	Reuser	Stewart ▲	Bent M ▲	Armstrong ▲	Bent D ▲58	Wilnis ▲
27-04	H	Manchester Utd	0-1	0-1	18	R.Styles	Marshall	Bramble	McGreal ○	Hreidarsson ○	Clapham	George ▲	Holland	Miller	Reuser ▲	Peralta	Bent M ▲	Armstrong ▲	Bent D ▲	Wilnis ▲
11-05	A	Liverpool	0-2	0-5	18	S.W.Dunn	Marshall	Bramble	McGreal ▲	Venus	Hreidarsson	Clapham	Holland	Miller	Reuser	Bent D ▲	Bent M ▲	Armstrong ▲	Wilnis ▲	Stewart ▲

F.A. Barclaycard Premiership
Squad List

Position	Name	Appearances	Appearances as Substitute	Goals or Clean Sheets	Goal Assists	Yellow Cards	Red Cards
G	K.Branagan		1				
G	A.Marshall	13		3		1	
G	M.Sereni	25		5			1
D	T.Bramble	16	2			2	
D	J.Clapham	22	10	2	3		
D	T.Gaardsoe	3	1	1		1	
D	H.Hreidarsson	38		1	1	5	
D	C.Makin	30				4	
D	J.McGreal	27		1	1	7	
D	M.Venus	29		1	8	3	
D	F.Wilnis	6	8			2	
M	F.George	21	4	6	4	1	
M	M.Holland	38		3	4		
M	U.Le Pen		1				
M	J.Magilton	16	8		1	1	
M	T.Miller	5	3			1	
M	S.Peralta	16	6	3	3	2	
M	M.Reuser	18	6	1	4	3	
M	J.Wright	24	5	1	1	3	
F	D.Ambrose		1				
F	A.Armstrong	21	11	4	1	1	
F	D.Bent	2	3	1			
F	M.Bent	22	3	9	1	2	
F	P.Counago	1	12			1	
F	R.Naylor	5	9	1	3	3	
F	M.Stewart	20	8	6	5	1	

Marcus Stewart, who had scored 19 F.A. Barclaycard Premiership goals the previous season, was still scoring but not at such a prolific rate. His brace in the 3-3 draw at Southampton took his tally to four but bad luck befell him when, in November, he broke his jaw in a training ground incident, clashing with Peralta.

Prior to that, Ipswich lost 3-2 at home to West Ham and then went to Chelsea where they were beaten 2-1. A point was wrested off Middlesbrough, after which Ipswich added former Northern Ireland boss Bryan Hamilton to their coaching staff to assist Burley. December started with three successive defeats, sending Town to the foot of the table.

Typically, luck was to escape them again. Burley spent £1.4m on Frenchman Ulrich Le Pen who lasted just a few minutes before being carried off with a broken foot in the 2-1 home defeat by Bolton. Marcus Bent was signed from Blackburn for £3m in November and his presence signalled a slight improvement, though not immediately.

Ipswich beat Inter Milan at Portman Road but lost 4-1 in the return with Christian Vieri scoring a hat-trick. Back in the League, their form was poor and they were quickly reminded that no team at the bottom of the Premier League on Boxing Day had ever avoided relegation.

Chairman David Sheepshanks stood by his manager and insisted that even if the club were relegated, Burley would remain. Other clubs had reacted nervously through November and Dececmber, sacking managers left, right and centre, but Burley's position remained safe.

The response was fitting. Just before Christmas, Ipswich went to White Hart Lane and won 2-1. George was back and after he had levelled, Alun Armstrong, a late substitute, scored only his second

 Fixtures, results and match reports - 4thegame.com

F.A. Barclaycard Premiership
Top Goal Scorer

Marcus Bent

Total Premier League Goals Scored:	Percentage Of The Team's League Goals:
9	22%

Goals Scored From

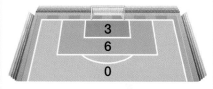

3
6
0

M arcus Bent arrived at the club in November 2001 after Marcus Stewart's failure to repeat his success of the previous season when he scored 19 goals to fire Ipswich into Europe. George Burley signed Bent from Blackburn where he had struggled to command a place in the first team. After taking time to settle in at Portman Road, Bent responded with six goals in as many games, his efforts coinciding with Ipswich's rejuvenation. Ultimately, it was not enough to stave off the threat of relegation. Towards the end of the campaign, Bent missed a costly penalty, in the goalless draw with Chelsea, but will still be satisfied with his return in his first season at Ipswich.

"At the age of 23 I feel Marcus has the potential to develop into one of the finest strikers in the F.A. Barclaycard Premiership."

George Burley

Goals Resulting From
Key

■ Open Play ■ Corner □ Indirect Free Kick
□ Direct Free Kick ■ Penalty

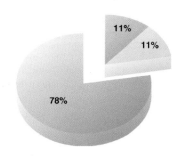

11%
11%
78%

Goal Assists

Total number of goal assists	1

Teams Scored Against

Against	Home	Away
Charlton Athletic	0	2
Newcastle United	0	2
Derby County	0	1
Fulham	1	0
Leicester City	1	0
Tottenham Hotspur	1	0
West Ham United	0	1
Total Goals Scored	**3**	**6**

	Right Foot	Left Foot	Header
Open Play	6	-	1
Set piece	-	-	2

 Win Barclaycard Premiership tickets - 4thegame.com

It's a fact

George Burley made 500 appearances as an Ipswich player and took charge for his 300th League game as manager in the 3-2 home defeat by West Ham.

"Things are beginning to work out here again. We've added experience at the back, we've got Marcus Stewart fit again and Marcus Bent has arrived from Blackburn and scored goals for us."

George Burley
(January 2002)

League goal of the season in the 88th minute.

It was a catalyst for better results and renewed hope. Leicester were the visitors to Portman Road next and Town won 2-0 before letting their previous frustrations out on Sunderland, who they beat 5-0 thanks to two more goals from Armstrong. It was a stunning recovery, halted only by a disappointment at Charlton, where Ipswich threw away a two-goal advantage to lose 3-2 on New Year's Day. The Tractor Boys had taken the lead after 53 seconds through Marcus Bent and, after the newcomer had scored again, Charlton were allowed back into the game.

If cynics thought that was the beginning of the end, Burley's men reckoned otherwise, as they bounced back to complete a swift 'double' over Spurs. Wins were coming thick and fast, thanks in the main to Bent. He scored six goals in six F.A. Barclaycard Premiership games to help Town to a run of seven wins out of eight. It was a stunning response to the fear of relegation with wins over Derby, Fulham and Everton. Given that the run was achieved without George, who was on international duty with Nigeria in the African Nations Cup in Mali, it was a remarkable show of resilience in adversity.

F.A. Barclaycard Premiership
Goals By Position

Key
Forward · Midfield · —❷— League Position
Defence · Goalkeeper

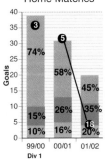

Home Matches

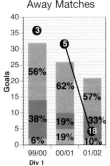

Away Matches

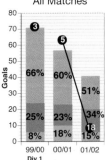

All Matches

Chart Analysis

statistics powered by SUPERBASE™

Ipswich scored 16 less goals than they managed the previous season.

While the contribution from forwards fell by nearly 10% as a share of the total, midfielders saw their percentage rise by a similar amount.

The Tractor Boys scored more goals on their travels than they did at home for the first time in the last three seasons.

 The heart of the Barclaycard Premiership - 4thegame.com

The good run continued into January when they moved up to 12th in the table after claiming their 1000th League win, a 2-1 success at Goodison Park. Suddenly, all thoughts of relegation were put on hold. However, if Town needed a reminder of how easy it is to lose concentration, it came on a defining day when Liverpool arrived in Suffolk.

Sereni, the subject of criticism from some quarters, lost his place in goal to Marshall. The former Norwich goalkeeper could have been forgiven for wishing he was back at Carrow Road as rampant Liverpool took control winning 6-0. Liverpool went top with two goals apiece from Emile Heskey and Michael Owen and, just as the win at Spurs had inspired Town, so this defeat acted as a catalyst to renewed fear.

It was the first of four successive losses, with the second a worrying 3-1 home reverse by Southampton. Leeds and Blackburn took advantage of Ipswich's lacking confidence and Sereni returned at Newcastle, where only a last minute penalty miss by Alan Shearer allowed Town a share of the spoils. When they forced only a goalless draw at home to Villa in their next outing, they were back in the relegation zone.

Time was running out and, after a 3-1 defeat at West Ham, Burley accepted the

F.A. Barclaycard Premiership
Team Performance Table

League Position	Team	Points won from a possible six	Percentage of points won at home	Percentage of points won away	Overall percentage of points won
1	Arsenal	0/6			
2	Liverpool	0/6			
3	Manchester Utd	0/6	0%	7%	3%
4	Newcastle Utd	1/6			
5	Leeds United	0/6			
6	Chelsea	1/6			
7	West Ham Utd	0/6			
8	Aston Villa	1/6	40%	20%	30%
9	Tottenham H	6/6			
10	Blackburn R	1/6			
11	Southampton	1/6			
12	Middlesbrough	4/6			
13	Fulham	4/6	47%	40%	43%
14	Charlton Athletic	0/6			
15	Everton	4/6			
16	Bolton W	0/6			
17	Sunderland	3/6			
18	**Ipswich Town**	36	75%	33%	54%
19	Derby County	6/6			
20	Leicester City	4/6			

The table shows how many points out of a possible six Ipswich Town have taken off each of the teams in the four sections. The other columns show as a percentage how many points they have taken from those available.

Chart Analysis

statistics powered by **SUPERBASE**™

Ipswich peformed very badly against teams in the top five of the table, taking just a solitary point – in a 2-2 draw at Newcastle – from a possible 30 points available.

Their form improved somewhat against teams in the second sector, where they also managed to do one of only two 'doubles', against Tottenham.

While they performed slightly better overall against teams in the third sector, they collected the largest share of points from their relegation rivals, where they picked up their second 'double', against Derby.

Overall, Ipswich failed to take any points off seven teams throughout the Premier League.

➡ **All the latest news, views and opinion – 4thegame.com**

remaining six games would show the team's real character. The way in which they folded, with little grit, suggested that, privately, Ipswich's players had accepted their fate, particularly with the prospect of playing Chelsea, Arsenal, Manchester United and Liverpool in the run-in.

They gained minimal comfort from a goalless draw with Chelsea even though Marcus Bent was frustratingly denied a winner when his penalty was saved by goalkeeper Carlo Cudicini. A 4-1 loss at rivals Bolton, for whom Fredi Bobic netted a first half hat-trick, left Ipswich on the brink. And at Highbury, despite performing well, they finally succumbed to two late goals from Freddie Ljungberg.

There was, however, a glimmer of hope when teenager Darren Bent, a product of the club's academy, came on as a substitute against Middlesbrough and within 25 seconds, and with his first touch, netted the winner. It meant they went into the following match with the unexpected opportunity to move out of the bottom three for the first time in more than a month – the only snag was that the next opponents were Manchester United.

To move out of the bottom three, they needed Sunderland to fail at Charlton on the afternoon of 27 April, and then to beat Manchester United in a game which kicked off at tea-time.

It's a fact

Ipswich suffered their longest sequence of successive League defeats, when they were beaten by Liverpool, Southampton, Leeds and Blackburn in February and March.

> "It was a game we had to win and, though everybody has written us off, we showed the courage and appetite. We have a mountain to climb, but we won't give up."
>
> *George Burley post Middlesbrough (April 2001)*

F.A. Barclaycard Premiership
Goals By Time Period

Key ▮ Goals Scored ▯ Goals Conceded

Home Matches

Time of Goal (mins)	Scored	Conceded
0-15	4	2
16-30	4	4
31-45	2	2
46-60	4	5
61-75	1	5
76-90	5	6

Away Matches

Time of Goal (mins)	Scored	Conceded
0-15	4	5
16-30	1	7
31-45	3	9
46-60	4	6
61-75	5	3
76-90	4	10

All Matches

Time of Goal (mins)	Scored	Conceded
0-15	8	7
16-30	5	11
31-45	5	11
46-60	8	11
61-75	6	8
76-90	9	16

Chart Analysis

statistics powered by ◆ SUPERBASE™

Overall, the only time Ipswich outscored their opponents was in the opening 15 minutes of matches. They then found themselves being outscored by more than two to one in the rest of the first half.

It was a similar story in the second half, especially in the last 15 minutes, when the Tractor Boys conceded most goals overall.

At home, Ipswich scored ten goals in each half.

➡ **Fixtures, results and match reports - 4thegame.com**

F.A. Barclaycard Premiership
Goals Resulting From

Key ☐ Goals Scored ☐ Goals Conceded

	Six Yard Area				Inside Area				Outside Area				Total			
	Shots		Headers		Shots		Headers		Shots		Headers		Shots		Headers	
	Home	Away	Home	Away	Home	Away	Home	Away	Home	Away	Home	Away	Home	Away	Home	Away
Open Play	1	-	1	1	7	9	-	-	2	4	-	-	10	13	1	1
	2	4	-	4	14	14	1	2	-	4	-	-	16	22	1	6
Direct Free Kick									-	-			0	0		
										1			0	1		
Indirect Free Kick	1	-	1	1	-	-	1	-	-	1	-	-	1	1	2	1
	-	-	-	-	-	3	-	-	1	-	-	-	1	3	0	0
Penalty	-	-	-	-	-	1	-	-	-	-	-	-	0	1	0	0
	1	-	-	-	1	3	-	-	-	-	-	-	2	3	0	0
Corner	2	1	1	2	-	-	3	1	-	-	-	-	2	1	4	3
	-	1	1	1	1	1	1	3	-	-	-	-	1	1	2	4
Totals	4	1	3	4	7	10	4	1	2	5	0	0	13	16	7	5
	3	4	1	5	16	21	2	5	1	5	0	0	20	30	3	10

How Goals Were Scored
Home & Away Matches

Key
- Open Play
- Corner
- Indirect Free Kick
- Direct Free Kick
- Penalty

Charts do not include 1 own goal against.

How Goals Were Conceded
Home & Away Matches

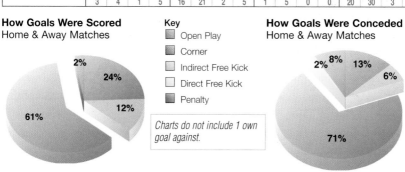

2% — 24% — 12% — 61%

2% — 8% — 13% — 6% — 71%

Goals Scored from
Key ☐ Open Play ☐ Set Piece

Home — 45% 55%   Away — 33% 67%

Goals Conceded from
Key ☐ Open Play ☐ Set Piece

Home — 26% 74%   Away — 30% 70%

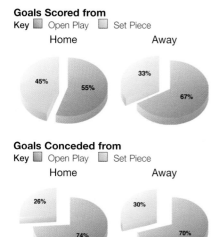

Chart Analysis

In what was a difficult season for them, Ipswich relied heavily on Set Pieces.

At home, nearly half their strikes came that way, including six goals from Corners. They also scored four from Corners away from home. However, these were balanced out by conceding eight goals from Corners.

Overall, they conceded over 40% of their goals from Shots Inside Area from Open Play.

BEST IN THE LEAGUE...
- **Most goals scored from Corners overall and at home**

WORST IN THE LEAGUE...
- **Most goals conceded from Open Play**

statistics powered by ◆ SUPERBASE™

➡ **Win Barclaycard Premiership tickets - 4thegame.com**

"After all the disappointments of the last few weeks this comes as a big lift to the club and a big lift for the fans too. The thrill won't make up for not being in the Premier League but it is still a big bonus."

Chairman David Sheepshanks after Ipswich were awarded a UEFA Cup place (May 2002)

It's a fact

Ipswich's 2-1 win at Everton in February was the 1,000th League win in the club's history.

Sunderland almost failed, drawing 2-2 at the Valley, and then Ipswich were denied a draw when Ruud van Nistelrooy won – and converted – a controversial penalty. The Dutchman won the kick when he fell under pressure from John McGreal and Titus Bramble.

So Ipswich's fate was to be determined on the final day of the season. They went to Liverpool, who needed a win to secure second place, requiring a win themselves to stave off the threat of relegation while hoping Sunderland would lose at home to already relegated Derby.

In the event, it was too much to expect. Town lost 5-0 at Anfield and must now hope their return to the top flight does not take as long as it did last time.

The Tractor Boys' disappointment at being relegated was tempered somewhat by the surprise news that they had been drawn to enter the 2002-03 UEFA Cup qualifying round via UEFA's Fair Play rankings. Ipswich had finished fourth in England's fair play competition behind Manchester United, Liverpool and Newcastle United, but all three of those clubs had already qualified for the Champions League. The Suffolk club become the first English club from outside the top division to compete in Europe since West Ham entered the Cup-Winners' Cup as F.A. Cup winners in 1980-81.

F.A. Barclaycard Premiership
Shot Efficiency

Key 🟥 Goals Scored ⬜ Other Shots On Target

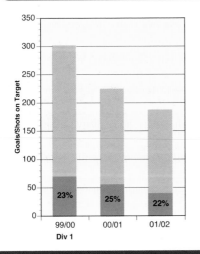

Season	Division	Shots Off Target	Shots On Target	Total Goals
1999 - 2000	1	n/a	303	71
2000 - 2001	P	n/a	226	57
2001 - 2002	P	201	189	41

Chart Analysis

Ipswich failed to capitalise on the fine form shown in their first season back in the top flight, and their performance in front of goal suffered accordingly.

Not only did they manage less Shots On Target, they also converted less of those into goals, as they dropped back to Division One.

statistics powered by **SUPERBASE** ™

➤ The heart of the Barclaycard Premiership - 4thegame.com

F.A. Barclaycard Premiership	Key
Team Discipline	▨ Forward ▦ Midfield ▨ Defence ▦ Goalkeeper

Total Number Of Bookings

Total number of red cards	1
Total number of yellow cards	44

Referee Performance

Referee	Games Refereed	Red Cards	Yellow Cards
R.Styles	3	-	7
B.Knight	1	1	3
M.A.Riley	3	-	6

Type of Yellow Cards Received

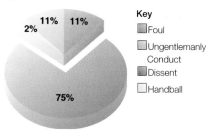

Key
- ▨ Foul
- ▨ Ungentlemanly Conduct
- ▨ Dissent
- ▨ Handball

2%, 11%, 11%, 75%

Bookings by Position 1999/2000 - 2001/2002

Home Matches

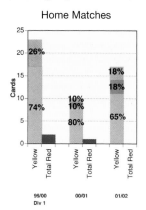

Away Matches

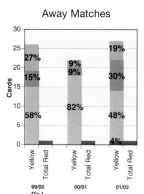

All Matches

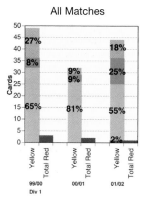

Chart Analysis

Despite finishing with one of the lowest Yellow Card hauls in the F.A. Barclaycard Premiership, Ipswich still registered a significant increase on the previous season, up from 32 to 44. This was not far off the 49 they collected in 1999-00 when they played eight more games, not including the play-offs, in Division One.

While the share of cards given to defenders fell sharply, the percentage attributed to forwards and midfielders doubled and nearly trebled respectively.

A quarter of their cautions were picked up for offences other than Fouls.

> "I won't bury my head in the sand and I won't hide. Too many of them were hiding. I won't have that. I won't hide so why should they?"
>
> *George Burley*
> *(November 2001)*

statistics powered by  SUPERBASE™

 All the latest news, views and opinion - 4thegame.com

F.A. Barclaycard Premiership

Final Premiership Table

Key: ☐ Champions League ☐ UEFA Cup ☐ Intertoto
☐ Relegated
P played, **HW** home win, **HD** home draw, **HL** home loss
HGF home goals for, **HGA** home goals against, **AW** away win
AD away draw, **AL** away loss, **AGF** away goals for
AGA away goals against, **PTS** points, **GD** goal difference.

	Team	P	HW	HD	HL	HGF	HGA	AW	AD	AL	AGF	AGA	PTS	GD
1	Arsenal	38	12	4	3	42	25	14	5	0	37	11	87	+43
2	Liverpool	38	12	5	2	33	14	12	3	4	34	16	80	+37
3	Manchester Utd	38	11	2	6	40	17	13	3	3	47	28	77	+42
4	Newcastle Utd	38	12	3	4	40	23	9	5	5	34	29	71	+22
5	Leeds Utd	38	9	6	4	31	21	9	6	4	22	16	66	+16
6	Chelsea	38	11	4	4	43	21	6	9	4	23	17	64	+28
7	West Ham Utd	38	12	4	3	32	14	3	4	12	16	43	53	-9
8	Aston Villa	38	8	7	4	22	17	4	7	8	24	30	50	-1
9	Tottenham H	38	10	4	5	32	24	4	4	11	17	29	50	-4
10	Blackburn R	38	8	6	5	33	20	4	4	11	22	31	46	+4
11	Southampton	38	7	5	7	23	22	5	4	10	23	32	45	-8
12	Middlesbrough	38	7	5	7	23	26	5	4	10	12	21	45	-12
13	Fulham	38	7	7	5	21	16	3	7	9	15	28	44	-8
14	Charlton Athletic	38	5	6	8	23	30	5	8	6	15	19	44	-11
15	Everton	38	8	4	7	26	23	3	6	10	19	34	43	-12
16	Bolton W	38	5	7	7	20	31	4	6	9	24	31	40	-18
17	Sunderland AFC	38	7	7	5	18	16	3	13	11	11	35	40	-22
18	Ipswich Town*	38	6	4	9	20	24	3	5	11	21	40	36	-23
19	Derby County	38	5	4	10	20	26	3	2	14	13	37	30	-30
20	Leicester City	38	3	7	9	15	34	2	6	11	15	30	28	-34

*Qualified for UEFA Cup via UEFA's Fair Play rankings

Average League Attendances

1	Manchester United	67,557
2	Newcastle United	51,372
3	Sunderland AFC	46,744
4	Liverpool	43,343
5	Leeds United	39,751
6	Chelsea	39,072
7	Arsenal	38,054
8	Aston Villa	35,011
9	Tottenham Hotspur	35,000
10	Everton	33,602
11	West Ham United	31,356
12	Southampton	30,632
13	Derby County	30,091
14	Middlesbrough	28,458
15	Blackburn Rovers	25,976
16	Bolton Wanderers	25,098
17	Ipswich Town	24,434
18	Charlton Athletic	24,096
19	Leicester City	19,835
20	Fulham	19,343
	Average League Attendance	34,441

While Manchester United may have come third in the League, they continued to attract the highest crowds in the F.A. Barclaycard Premiership by some margin. Newcastle were the only other team to average more than 50,000 spectators. Despite winning the Championship, Arsenal's average crowd attendance was only the seventh highest in the League. The Gunners won permission for a new stadium during the season and will hope to move to their new home by 2004-05. Fulham had the lowest crowd average in the top flight but they too will find their capacity swelled following a £70m refit at Craven Cottage which started following the end of the 2001-02 season.

➜ The heart of the Barclaycard Premiership – 4thegame.com

F.A. Barclaycard Premiership

Premiership Bookings Table

Key: M matches refereed, Y yellow cards, R red cards

Total Number of Yellow and Red Cards
1999-00 R=70 Y=1211 2000-01 R=62 Y=1176 2001-02 R=70 Y=1152

Referees (each with Y = yellow cards, R = red cards): A.G.Wiley, A.P.D'Urso, B.Knight, C.J.Foy, C.R.Wilkes, D.J.Gallagher, D.Pugh, D.R.Ellery, E.K.Wolstenholme, G.Barber, G.Poll, J.T.Winter, M.A.Riley, M.D.Messias, M.L.Dean, M.R.Halsey, N.S.Barry, P.A.Durkin, P.Dowd, P.Jones, R.Styles, S.G.Bennett, S.W.Dunn, U.D.Rennie

Season totals by club (M / Y / R)

Club	M	Y	R
Arsenal	38	71	6
Aston Villa	38	42	2
Blackburn Rovers	38	58	4
Bolton Wanderers	38	56	7
Charlton Athletic	38	63	3
Chelsea	38	69	3
Derby County	38	70	3
Everton	38	55	3
Fulham	38	54	2
Ipswich Town	38	44	1
Leeds United	38	69	5
Leicester City	38	75	5
Liverpool	38	41	3
Manchester United	38	54	1
Middlesbrough	38	52	7
Newcastle United	38	51	2
Southampton	38	36	5
Sunderland AFC	38	68	1
Tottenham Hotspur	38	58	4
West Ham United	38	66	3
Totals		**1152**	**70**

Referee totals (M / Y / R)

Referee	M	Y	R
A.G.Wiley	23	67	1
A.P.D'Urso	23	74	6
B.Knight	11	38	2
C.J.Foy	5	19	1
C.R.Wilkes	12	40	3
D.J.Gallagher	16	40	2
D.Pugh	10	35	0
D.R.Ellery	17	38	3
E.K.Wolstenholme	11	42	3
G.Barber	22	78	5
G.Poll	24	59	5
J.T.Winter	20	49	2
M.A.Riley	17	73	6
M.D.Messias	5	17	0
M.L.Dean	14	42	2
M.R.Halsey	21	64	2
N.S.Barry	17	43	4
P.A.Durkin	21	56	3
P.Dowd	5	21	2
P.Jones	14	39	1
R.Styles	18	67	1
S.G.Bennett	19	54	5
S.W.Dunn	19	55	3
U.D.Rennie	16	42	1
Totals		**1152**	**70**

F.A. Barclaycard Premiership

Player Performance

Top Goal Scorers

Pos	Player	Club	Goals
1	T.Henry	Arsenal	24
2	A.Shearer	Newcastle United	23
=	J.Hasselbaink	Chelsea	23
=	R.van Nistelrooy	Manchester United	23
5	M.Owen	Liverpool	19
6	O.Solskjaer	Manchester United	17
7	R.Fowler	Leeds United	15
8	E.Gudjohnsen	Chelsea	14
=	M.Pahars	Southampton	14
10	A.Cole	Blackburn Rovers	13

Most Goal Assists

Pos	Player	Club	Assists
1	L.Robert	Newcastle United	21
2	R.Giggs	Manchester United	18
3	R.Pires	Arsenal	16
4	N.Solano	Newcastle United	13
=	D.Bergkamp	Arsenal	13
6	E.Heskey	Liverpool	10
=	J.Hasselbaink	Chelsea	10

Most Booked Players

Pos	Player	Club	Y	R	SB	PTS
1	D.Mills	Leeds United	10	1	1	62
2	P.Ince	Middlesbrough	11	1	0	56
3	R.Savage	Leicester City	14	0	0	56
4	P.Vieira	Arsenal	10	0	1	50
5	S.Parker	Charlton Athletic	9	1	0	48
6	T.Repka	West Ham United	7	0	2	48
7	C.Short	Blackburn Rovers	3	2	1	46
8	L.Boa Morte	Fulham	6	1	1	46
9	M.Izzet	Leicester City	9	0	1	46
10	C.Bellamy	Newcastle United	8	1	0	44
=	F.Queudrue	Middlesbrough	8	1	0	44
12	P.Warhurst	Bolton Wanderers	7	1	0	40
13	R.Parlour	Arsenal	5	0	2	40
14	T.Gravesen	Everton	7	0	1	38
=	D.Matteo	Leeds United	7	0	1	38

R=Red Cards Y=Yellow Cards SB=Second Bookable Offence
PTS=Disciplinary Points
Positions based on F.A. Disciplinary Points:
Yellow Card=4 points, Second Bookable Offence=10 points and Red Card=12 points.

Arsenal's Thierry Henry soared to the top of the scoring charts after having netted 17 goals in each of his two previous seasons with the Gunners. He pipped Newcastle's Alan Shearer, Chelsea's Jimmy Floyd Hasselbaink and Manchester United's Ruud van Nistelrooy to the Golden Boot thanks to a brace on the last day of the season at home to Everton. Southampton's Marian Pahars was the highest placed scorer from a side in the bottom half of the table.

Another Frenchman topped the chart for Most Goal Assists. Newcastle's big-money summer signing Laurent Robert proved to be a sensational buy, his 21 assists helping the Toon to their best finish since finishing second in successive seasons from 1995 to 1997. Manchester United's Ryan Giggs came in second, while Arsenal's Robert Pires took third place. Both Newcastle and Arsenal had further representation in the top five with Solano and Bergkamp equal fourth.

Leeds United's Danny Mills rose to the top of the disciplinary charts after picking up two red cards to add to ten yellows. The players behind him comprise what some might term the 'usual suspects' except that is for Charlton's Scott Parker. Robbie Savage claimed third spot despite being the only person on the list not to see red by virtue of picking up the most yellow cards since Mark Hughes in 1998-99. Despite picking up one less red card than the previous season, Arsenal's Patrick Vieira rose to fourth after receiving twice as many yellow cards. Czech international Tomas Repka arrived at West Ham from Fiorentina in September with a reputation and did not disappoint, seeing red in two of his first three League outings.

 All the latest news, views and opinion - 4thegame.com

F.A. Barclaycard Premiership

Facts and Figures

Team Performance

Longest unbeaten streak:
Arsenal, 21 matches, 23/12/01 to 11/05/02
Longest run without winning:
Leicester City, 16, 08/12/01 to 30/03/02
Best Home Record:
Liverpool, W 12, D 5, L 2, Pts 41
Best Away Record:
Arsenal, W 14, D 5, L 0, Pts 47
Highest Percentage of Half-Time Deficits turned into Wins:
Arsenal, 67% (4 out of 6)

Bookings

Total Yellow Cards: 1,152
Average Yellow Cards per game: 3.03
Total Yellow Cards for Fouls: 893
Total Yellow Cards for Dissent: 129
Total Yellow Cards for Unsporting Behaviour: 122
Total Yellow Cards for Handball: 8
Most Yellow Cards: Leicester City, 75
Most Yellow Cards at home:
Derby County, 33
Most Yellow Cards away from home:
Leicester City, 45
Total Red Cards: 70
Average number of games between Red Cards: 5.43
Total Straight Red Cards: 44
Total Second Bookable Offences: 26
Most Red Cards: Bolton W, Middlesbrough, 7
Most Red Cards at home home:
Bolton Wanderers, 5
Most Red Cards away from home:
Arsenal, Leeds United, 4
Referee with the highest average of yellow cards per game: M.A.Riley, 4.29

Goals

Average Goals per game: 2.63
Most goals scored:
Manchester United, 87
Most Shots on Target:
Arsenal, 261
Highest Percentage of Shot Efficiency:
Manchester United, 87 goals from 256 attempts on target (34%)
Longest scoring streak:
Arsenal, 38 matches, 18/08/01 to 11/05/02
Most Goals scored by the defence:
Everton, 14 (out of 45)
Most Goals scored by the midfield:
Manchester United, 36 (out of 87)
Most Goals scored by the strikers:
Arsenal, 48 (out of 79)
Most goals in 0-15 minute time period:
Manchester United, 12
Most goals in 15-30 minute time period:
Arsenal, Leeds United, 12
Most goals in 30-45 minute time period:
Chelsea, Manchester United, 17
Most goals in 45-60 minute time period:
Manchester United, 16
Most goals in 60-75 minute time period:
Newcastle United, 17
Most goals in 75-90 minute time period:
Arsenal, Chelsea, 19
Time Period in which most goals scored:
76-90 minutes, 225 out of 1,001 (22%)
Time Period in which least goals scored:
16-30 minutes, 134 out of 1,001 (13%)
Most goals scored/conceded from Open Play:
Man Utd, 64 (out of 87)/Ipswich T, Leicester, 45 (out of 64)
Most goals scored/conceded from Corners:
Ipswich T, 10 (out of 41)/Southampton, 11 (out of 54)
Most goals scored/conceded from Indirect Free Kicks: Aston Villa, 7 (out of 46)/Chelsea, 7 (out of 38)
Most goals scored/conceded from Direct Free Kicks: Bolton W, 6 (out of 44)/Derby C, 4 (out of 63)
Most goals scored/conceded from Penalties:
Arsenal, 6 (out of 79)/Middlesbrough, 5 (out of 47)

 Fixtures, results and match reports – 4thegame.com

Leeds United

F.A. Barclaycard Premiership	Final standing for the 2001-2002 season							
Final Position		Games Played	Games Won	Games Drawn	Games Lost	Goals For	Goals Against	Total Points
4	Newcastle United	38	21	8	9	74	52	71
5	Leeds United	38	18	12	8	53	37	66
6	Chelsea	38	17	13	8	66	38	64

"It's been a difficult season from start to finish with too many things dominating off the field. We have been tested much more, but overall I think we have done well to qualify for the UEFA Cup."

David O'Leary (May 2002)

Club Honours and Records

Football League Champions: 1968-69, 1973-74, 1991-92

Division 2 Champions: 1923-24, 1963-64, 1989-90

FA Cup Winners: 1972

League Cup Winners: 1968

European Fairs Cup Winners: 1967-68, 1970-71

Record victory: 10-0 v Lyn, European Cup 1st Round, 1st Leg, 17 September, 1969

Record defeat:
1-8 v Stoke City, Division 1, 27 August, 1934

League goals in a season (team):
98, Division 2, 1927-28

League goals in a season (player):
42, John Charles, Division 2, 1953-54

Career league goals:
168, Peter Lorimer, 1965 to 1979 and 1983 to 1986

League appearances:
629, Jack Charlton, 1953 to 1973

Reported transfer fee paid: £18,000,000 to West Ham United for Rio Ferdinand, November 2000

Reported transfer fee received: £12,000,000 from Atletico Madrid for Jimmy Floyd Hasselbaink, August 1999

LEEDS began the season with Championship pretentions and finished grateful for a place in the UEFA Cup.

The Yorkshire Club had finished fourth in the F.A. Barclaycard Premiership the previous term and reached the semi-finals of the Champions League so optimism coming into the new campaign was high.

As a result of their good form, David O'Leary considered it unnecessary to make any summer alterations, other than to turn Robbie Keane's loan into a permanent move, at a cost of £11m from Inter Milan.

Even so, O'Leary made it clear he wanted to turn the success of the previous season into prizes, admitting he had addressed his players as to the importance of winning a trophy.

Off the field, Leeds chairman Peter Ridsdale had announced plans to investigate a move away from Elland Road. The proposals met with opposition from some fans, including threats to the chairman's family.

The campaign began encouragingly enough with a 2-0 Elland Road win over Southampton. It got better three days later when Leeds travelled to Highbury and despite the fact they finished with only nine men, O'Leary left his former club

 Fixtures, results and match reports - 4thegame.com

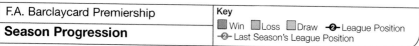

F.A. Barclaycard Premiership
Season Progression

Key
- Win
- Loss
- Draw
- League Position
- Last Season's League Position

All Matches

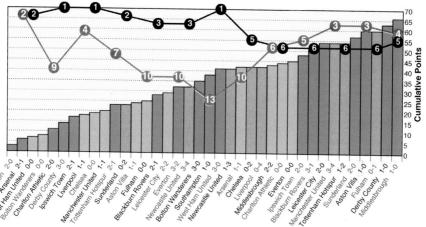

Home Matches

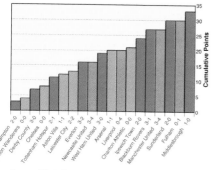

Away Matches

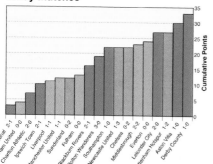

Chart Analysis

Leeds started the sesaon well, losing just once in their opening 17 fixtures to leave them third in the table.

They would have been far better placed if they had managed to convert any of the eight draws during that period into victories.

After losing to Newcastle just before Christmas, the Yorkshire club registered three straight wins to climb into first place on New Year's Day.

However, their Championship challenge came off the rails with a run of seven matches without a win.

By the time they returned to winning ways against Ipswich Town in early March, the damage had been done.

Despite picking up seven wins in their last ten matches, they were unable to finish any higher than fifth.

Although the season may be viewed with disappointment by Leeds fans, one encouraging sign was that they never suffered three defeats on the spin at any stage of the season.

statistics powered by **SUPERBASE**™

 Win Barclaycard Premiership tickets - 4thegame.com

> **"I want to build this stadium for nothing – and I'd be disappointed if there was not some left to throw into David's transfer pot."**
>
> *Chairman Peter Ridsdale on the new stadium (September 2001)*

with three points. There had been no love lost between the sides in the past and this was no exception.

Goals from Harte and Mark Viduka gave Leeds a 2-1 win but Lee Bowyer and Danny Mills were sent off after both picking up two yellow cards. To make matters worse, the pair were charged with misconduct for abusive language and later suffered further damaging punishment.

The prospect of a move to a new stadium received backing from shareholders and season ticket holders, hopeful that it would lead to a cash injection for players.

Not that Leeds seemed to need additional strength as they moved to the top of the F.A. Barclaycard Premiership in September after winning 2-0 at Charlton. O'Leary claimed his team could play better and refused to get excited, even though Leeds were to stay top until the end of October.

Ridsdale admitted he had rejected a £20m offer for Mark Viduka from Italy, while Dacourt was also interesting the Italians. Yet Leeds were determined, for now, to hold on to their key players.

Harry Kewell was another being admired from afar. He was key to Leeds' early season success, inspiring his side to a 3-0 win against Derby with two goals. The 2-1 win at Ipswich, thanks to a Mark Venus own goal, put them three

It's a fact

When Leeds beat Spurs 2-1 at Elland Road, extending their unbeaten start to 11 games, it represented their best start to a season since 1973-74.

F.A. Barclaycard Premiership
Half-Time/Full-Time Comparison

Key ■ Win ■ Loss ■ Draw

Home				Away				Total			
Number of Home Half Time Wins	Full Time Result W	L	D	Number of Away Half Time Wins	Full Time Result W	L	D	Total number of Half Time Wins	Full Time Result W	L	D
6	5	-	1	7	5	-	2	13	10	-	3
Number of Home Half Time Losses	Full Time Result W	L	D	Number of Away Half Time Losses	Full Time Result W	L	D	Total number of Half Time Losses	Full Time Result W	L	D
2	-	2	-	3	1	2	-	5	1	4	-
Number of Home Half Time Draws	Full Time Result W	L	D	Number of Away Half Time Draws	Full Time Result W	L	D	Total number of Half Time Draws	Full Time Result W	L	D
11	4	2	5	9	3	2	4	20	7	4	9

Chart Analysis

statistics powered by ● SUPERBASE™

Overall, Leeds did not lose any of the 13 games they were leading at half-time. However, they did drop points in three, most notably at home to relegated Leicester.

They failed to take points from only 20% of matches in which they were level at the break.

BEST IN THE LEAGUE...
- **Highest Percentage of half-time deficits converted into wins away**

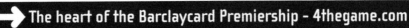

➤ The heart of the Barclaycard Premiership - 4thegame.com

F.A. Barclaycard Premiership Results Table

Key: 88 time of goal ● 88 time of goal ▲ 88 time of assist ▲ player substituted ● yellow card ● red card

DATE	H/A	OPPONENT	H/T	F/T	POS	REFEREE	TEAM											SUBSTITUTES USED		
18-08	H	Southampton	0-0	2-0	3	C.R.Wilkes	Martyn	Mills	Ferdinand 67	Matteo	Harte	Bowyer ●67	Batty ▲	Dacourt ●88	Kewell	Keane ▲	Viduka	Bakke ▲90	Smith ▲80	—
21-08	A	Arsenal	1-1	2-1	2	J.T.Winter	Martyn	Mills ●29	Ferdinand	Matteo	Harte 29	Bowyer ●	Bakke ◢	Dacourt ◢	Kewell ▲53	Smith ▲	Viduka 53	Batty ▲	Kelly ▲
25-08	A	West Ham Utd	0-0	0-0	2	P.A.Durkin	Martyn	Mills	Ferdinand	Matteo	Harte ▲	Bowyer	Batty	Dacourt	Kewell	Keane ◢	Viduka	Woodgate ▲	Maybury ◢ ▲
08-09	H	Bolton	0-0	0-0	3	S.G.Bennett	Martyn	Kelly	Ferdinand	Matteo	Harte	Wilcox ▲	Batty	Dacourt ●	Kewell	Keane	Viduka	Bakke ▲	—
16-09	A	Charlton	1-0	2-0	1	M.R.Halsey	Martyn	Mills 63	Ferdinand	Matteo	Harte 21	Bowyer	Batty 63	Dacourt ▲	Kewell	Keane ▲21	Viduka	Bakke ▲	McPhail ▲
23-09	H	Derby County	1-0	3-0	1	A.G.Wiley	Martyn	Mills	Ferdinand	Matteo ●	Harte 9	Bowyer 74 77	Batty	Dacourt ▲	Kewell 74 77	Keane	Viduka	Bakke ▲	—
30-09	A	Ipswich Town	0-1	2-1	1	A.P.D'Urso	Martyn	Mills	Ferdinand	Matteo ●	Harte	Bowyer 74 77	Batty	Bakke 9	Kewell 70 86	Keane 70	Viduka	Smith ▲	—
13-10	A	Liverpool	1-0	1-1	1	A.G.Wiley	Martyn	Mills	Ferdinand 27	Matteo	Harte	Bowyer	Batty	Dacourt	Kewell 27	Keane 70	Viduka	Batty ▲	—
21-10	H	Chelsea	0-0	0-0	1	P.A.Durkin	Martyn	Mills	Ferdinand	Matteo	Harte	Bowyer	Bakke ●	Dacourt ●	Kewell	Keane ▲	Viduka	Smith ▲	—
27-10	A	Manchester Utd	0-0	1-1	2	D.J.Gallagher	Martyn	Mills	Ferdinand	Matteo	Harte 77	Bowyer	Batty ◢	Dacourt ▲	Kewell ◢	Keane ▲	Viduka 77	Batty ▲	Smith ◢
04-11	H	Tottenham	0-0	2-1	1	S.G.Bennett	Martyn	Mills	Ferdinand	Matteo	Harte 61	Bowyer ▲	Bakke	Dacourt ▲	Kewell 61 82	Keane ◢	Viduka	Smith ▲	Johnson ◢ ▲
18-11	A	Sunderland	0-0	0-2	2	G.P.Barber	Martyn	Mills ●	Ferdinand	Matteo	Bakke	Batty	Dacourt ▲	Johnson	Keane ◢	Smith	Batty ▲	—
25-11	H	Aston Villa	1-1	1-1	2	N.S.Barry	Martyn	Mills ●	Ferdinand	Matteo	Harte	Bakke	Batty	Johnson ◢	Wilcox	Keane 17	Smith ● 17	—
02-12	A	Fulham	0-0	0-0	3	G.Poll	Martyn	Kelly	Ferdinand	Mills	Harte	Smith	Batty ◢	Johnson	Kewell ◢	Fowler	Viduka	Dacourt ▲	—
09-12	A	Blackburn	0-0	2-1	3	A.P.D'Urso	Martyn	Mills ◢	Ferdinand	Dudberry	Harte	Kelly 62	Batty	Dacourt ▲	Kewell 53 62	Fowler 53	Viduka	Wilcox ▲	—
16-12	H	Leicester City	1-0	2-2	4	R.Styles	Martyn	Mills 26	Ferdinand	Matteo	Harte	Kelly 59	Batty	Johnson ▲	Kewell 7	Fowler	Viduka 7 59	Bakke ◢ ▲	—
19-12	A	Everton	2-0	3-2	5	P.Jones	Martyn	Mills 26	Ferdinand	Matteo	Harte	Kelly 18	Batty ▲71	Johnson	Kewell	Fowler 26 71	Viduka ▲18	Keane ▲	—
22-12	H	Newcastle Utd	1-1	3-4	3	J.T.Winter	Martyn	Kelly ◢	Ferdinand	Mills	Harte 56	Bowyer 39 56	Batty ◢	Johnson 50	Kewell	Fowler 26 71	Viduka 39 50	Bakke ▲	—
26-12	A	Bolton	2-0	3-0	4	A.G.Wiley	Martyn	Kelly	Ferdinand	Woodgate	Matteo ▲	Smith 89	Batty 2	Bakke ▲	Smith	Fowler 2 16 89	Viduka 16	Harte ▲	Wilcox ◢
29-12	A	Southampton	0-0	1-0	3	M.R.Halsey	Martyn	Mills 3	Ferdinand	Woodgate	Harte	Kelly	Batty	Bowyer 88	Smith	Fowler ▲	Viduka 88	Harte ▲	Wilcox ▲
01-01	H	West Ham Utd	2-0	3-0	1	S.W.Dunn	Martyn	Mills ●7	Ferdinand	Woodgate	Harte	Kelly	Batty	Bowyer ●50	Smith ▲4	Fowler 50	Viduka 4 7	Wilcox ▲	—
12-01	A	Newcastle Utd	1-1	1-3	2	G.P.Barber	Martyn	Mills ●	Dudberry	Matteo	Harte	Kelly	Bowyer	Johnson ▲	Smith ▲1	Fowler ▲	Viduka 1	Wilcox ▲	—
20-01	H	Arsenal	1-1	1-1	3	M.R.Halsey	Martyn	Kelly	Ferdinand	Woodgate	Matteo	Bowyer	Batty	Johnson ●	Wilcox 6	Fowler 6	Viduka	Batty ▲	—
30-01	A	Chelsea	0-2	0-2	5	S.G.Bennett	Martyn	Kelly	Ferdinand	Woodgate ▲	Matteo	Bowyer	Batty	Johnson ◢	Wilcox ◢	Fowler ▲	Viduka	Harte ▲	Keane ▲
03-02	H	Liverpool	0-1	0-4	6	G.Poll	Martyn	Kelly	Ferdinand	Matteo	Harte	Bowyer	Batty ◢	Dacourt ▲	Kewell ◢	Fowler	Viduka	Keane ▲	Wilcox ◢
09-02	A	Middlesbrough	1-0	2-2	6	N.S.Barry	Martyn	Kelly	Ferdinand	Matteo	Harte 54	Bakke ●19	Batty ▲	Dacourt ▲	Kewell	Fowler 19 54	Viduka	Wilcox ▲	—
24-02	A	Charlton	0-0	0-0	5	M.L.Dean	Martyn	Kelly	Dudberry	Matteo	Harte	Keane	Bakke	Dacourt ▲	Kewell	Fowler	Viduka	Batty ▲	—
03-03	H	Everton	0-0	0-0	5	A.P.D'Urso	Martyn	Kelly	Ferdinand	Matteo ●	Harte	Smith	Batty ▲	Dacourt ▲	Kewell	Fowler	Viduka	—	—
06-03	H	Ipswich Town	0-0	2-0	5	D.J.Gallagher	Martyn	Kelly	Ferdinand	Matteo	Harte 77	Smith 77	Batty ◢	Bakke	Kewell	Fowler 46	Viduka 46	Keane ▲	—
17-03	A	Blackburn	2-0	3-1	6	G.Poll	Martyn	Mills ◢	Ferdinand	Woodgate	Harte	Smith ▲8	Batty ◢	Dacourt ◢	Kewell ▲71	Fowler 5 8	Viduka	Wilcox ▲	Bakke ▲71
23-03	A	Leicester City	2-0	2-0	4	S.W.Dunn	Martyn	Mills ●	Woodgate	Matteo	Harte	Smith	Batty ▲	Dacourt ▲	Kewell	Fowler 18 31	Viduka 18 31	Johnson ▲	—
30-03	H	Manchester Utd	1-3	3-4	5	D.R.Elleray	Martyn	Mills ●	Woodgate	Matteo	Harte 62	Smith	Batty ▲	Johnson ▲	Kewell	Fowler 62 80	Viduka 20	Bakke ▲	Bowyer▲20 80	Keane ▲
07-04	A	Sunderland	0-2	1-2	6	U.D.Rennie	Martyn	Mills	Woodgate	Matteo	Harte	Smith 8	Bowyer	Bakke	Bowyer	Fowler 52	Viduka 52	Keane ▲	—
13-04	A	Aston Villa	1-0	1-0	6	B.Knight	Martyn	Mills	Woodgate	Matteo	Harte	Smith	Bowyer	Bakke	Bowyer	Fowler 83	Viduka 83	Keane ▲83	—
20-04	H	Fulham	0-0	0-1	6	R.Styles	Martyn	Mills	Ferdinand	Matteo	Harte	Smith	Batty	Bakke	Keane 28	Keane 28	Viduka 28	—	—
27-04	A	Derby County	1-0	1-0	6	G.Poll	Martyn	Kelly	Ferdinand	Matteo	Harte	Bowyer 16	Johnson	Kewell ◢	Fowler	Smith 16	Keane ▲	Batty ◢	—
11-05	H	Middlesbrough	0-0	1-0	5	U.D.Rennie	Martyn ●	Kelly	Ferdinand	Matteo ●	Bowyer	Johnson	Johnson	Kewell ▲	Keane 63	Smith 63	Wilcox ▲	—

Leeds United

F.A. Barclaycard Premiership
Squad List

Position	Name	Appearances	Appearances as Substitute	Goals or Clean Sheets	Goal Assists	Yellow Cards	Red Cards
G	N.Martyn	38		18		1	
D	M.Duberry	3				1	
D	R.Ferdinand	31			2		
D	I.Harte	34	2	5		4	1
D	G.Kelly	19	1			3	2
D	D.Matteo	32				7	1
D	A.Maybury		1			1	
D	D.Mills	28		1	3	10	2
D	J.Woodgate	11	2			2	
M	E.Bakke	20	7	2	1	6	
M	D.Batty	30	6		3	8	
M	L.Bowyer	24	1	5	5	5	1
M	O.Dacourt	16	1			3	
M	S.Johnson	12	2		1	4	
M	H.Kewell	26	1	8	4	2	
M	S.McPhail		1				
M	J.Wilcox	4	9		1	3	
F	R.Fowler	22		12	6	1	
F	R.Keane	16	9	3	4	3	
F	A.Smith	19	4	4	6	6	1
F	M.Viduka	33		11	8	3	

points clear.

Off the field the re-trial of Lee Bowyer and Jonathan Woodgate over an alleged assault opened, while three draws halted the good run on the pitch. They came against Liverpool, Chelsea and Manchester United, timely reminders for the Yorkshiremen that they were not invincible, even though they might have been enjoying their best unbeaten start to a season since the days of Don Revie.

Leeds returned to the top after beating Spurs 2-1. Woodgate had not featured in the first team but Bowyer continued to play, only for his season to be interrupted by a hamstring injury collected in the Tottenham match. Seth Johnson, a £7m signing from Derby, made his debut and was seen as the perfect cover.

Leeds' good start finally ended at Sunderland, when they became the last F.A. Barclaycard Premiership team to lose their unbeaten status. The 2-0 defeat coincided with the absence of Australian pair Kewell and Viduka, called up for their country and missing for four games, including two in the League.

Meanwhile, the court case hogged the headlines, distracting Leeds from matters of a football nature although, to their credit, they persevered with two draws taking them into December.

O'Leary was linked with Leicester's Muzzy Izzet while he found himself the subject of speculation as Sir Alex Ferguson's successor at Old Trafford continued to be discussed. O'Leary insisted he was staying and demonstrated his determination to the cause by completing the season's most audacious transfer.

In November Leeds paid £11m for Robbie Fowler, ending his lifelong association with Liverpool. The news was met with shock in Merseyside but delight

F.A. Barclaycard Premiership

Top Goal Scorer

Robbie Fowler

Total Premier League Goals Scored:	Percentage Of The Team's League Goals:
12	23%

Goals Scored From

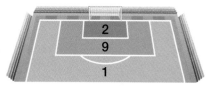

2
9
1

Despite arriving at Leeds with the season already well under way, Fowler still managed to finish top scorer for the Yorkshire club. The England striker had already scored a hat-trick for Liverpool – at Leicester – when David O'Leary paid £11m to pull off one of the shocks of the season. Fowler scored his first Leeds goals in the 3-2 win over Everton in December and then went on something of a spree, netting another hat-trick at Bolton – where he also missed a penalty – and a goal apiece against both West Ham and Arsenal, taking his tally to seven goals in six games. The player finished with 12 for Leeds, taking his League career total to 132.

> "This is a new chapter but one I am looking forward to. I am excited, not nervous."
> *Robbie Fowler*

Goals Resulting From
Key
■ Open Play ■ Corner □ Indirect Free Kick
□ Direct Free Kick ■ Penalty

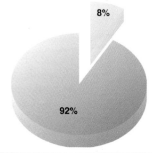

8%

92%

Goal Assists
Total number of goal assists	6

Teams Scored Against
Against	Home	Away
Bolton Wanderers	0	3
Blackburn Rovers	2	0
Everton	2	0
Arsenal	1	0
Ipswich Town	1	0
Leicester City	0	1
Middlesbrough	0	1
West Ham United	1	0
Total Goals Scored	**7**	**5**

	Right Foot	Left Foot	Header
Open Play	3	6	2
Set piece	-	-	1

> "Leeds are a great team and we feel we can go all the way. This side really suit the way I play."
>
> *Robbie Fowler*
> *(November 2001)*

in Yorkshire and the England star made a debut amid massive publicity in the goalless draw at Fulham.

With Viduka and Fowler in harness Leeds returned to winning ways with a 2-1 victory at Blackburn. Kewell scored both goals but injuries were beginning to mount up. Dacourt was ruled out for six weeks with a shoulder problem while Bowyer, Lucas Radebe and Michael Bridges were still absent.

The two-year legal ordeal facing Bowyer came to an end in mid-December when he was cleared of causing grievous bodily harm while Woodgate was convicted on the lesser charge of affray.

Leeds responded by fining Woodgate eight weeks' wages and Bowyer was fined four weeks'. Bowyer refused to accept internal disciplinary measures and was put on the transfer list, prompting enquiries from at least two F.A. Barclaycard Premiership rivals.

It was a distressing, not to mention distracting, period as Leeds were held to a 2-2 draw by struggling Leicester at Elland Road. Bowyer came off the transfer list after accepting his punishment and Leeds began to steady.

Against Newcastle, Bowyer returned but Leeds lost 4-3

F.A. Barclaycard Premiership
Goals By Position

Key: Forward ■ Midfield ●–❷ League Position ■ Defence ■ Goalkeeper

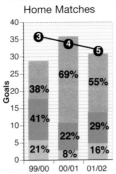

Home Matches

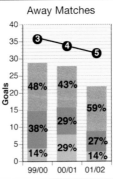

Away Matches

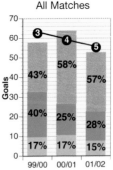

All Matches

Chart Analysis

statistics powered by **SUPERBASE**™

Leeds managed their fewest number of goals in the Premier League since 1996-7 when they finished 11th in George Graham's first season in charge.

The percentage contribution from defenders at home doubled while away from Elland Road it more than halved.

With the midfield unable to attain the levels of two seasons ago, it was left to the forwards to provide the lion's share of strikes.

in a remarkable game at Elland Road. Johnson and Kewell were the latest injury victims but that did not deter determined Leeds from returning to the top of the table thanks to wins over Bolton, Southampton and West Ham. The 3-0 victory over Bolton saw Fowler net a hat-trick – and miss a penalty – and the good run coincided with the news that O'Leary had committed his long-term future to the Elland Road club.

A shock 2-1 F.A. Cup defeat at Cardiff, where Smith was sent off for the second time this season, combined with crowd trouble in the stands to leave a nasty aftertaste. The red card meant Smith would be absent for four more games. Suspensions were to haunt Leeds' second half of the season.

Mills was sent off in the 3-1 defeat at Newcastle where Leeds also had six yellow cards and were fined. That Smith scored the season's quickest goal so far did little to lighten their load. Both Mills and Bowyer were later found guilty of misconduct at Highbury earlier in the season and were handed devastating bans totalling six games each. Bowyer's punishment included a charge from a game against Liverpool the previous season.

The 2-0 loss at Chelsea also brought more bad news as Woodgate and Johnson collected injuries and missed the next six

F.A. Barclaycard Premiership
Team Performance Table

League Position	Team	Points won from a possible six	Percentage of points won at home	Percentage of points won away	Overall percentage of points won
1	Arsenal	4/6			
2	Liverpool	1/6			
3	Manchester Ut	1/6	8%	42%	25%
4	Newcastle Utd	0/6			
5	**Leeds United**	**66**			
6	Chelsea	1/6			
7	West Ham Utd	4/6			
8	Aston Villa	4/6	73%	47%	60%
9	Tottenham H	3/6			
10	Blackburn R	6/6			
11	Southampton	6/6			
12	Middlesbrough	4/6			
13	Fulham	1/6	67%	60%	63%
14	Charlton Athletic	4/6			
15	Everton	4/6			
16	Bolton W	4/6			
17	Sunderland	3/6			
18	Ipswich Town	6/6	73%	80%	77%
19	Derby County	6/6			
20	Leicester City	4/6			

The table shows how many points out of a possible six Leeds United have taken off each of the teams in the four sections. The other columns show as a percentage how many points they have taken from those available.

Chart Analysis

statistics powered by **SUPERBASE**™

Leeds were let down by their home form against teams in their own sector, picking up just one point from a possible 12 thanks to a 1-1 draw with Arsenal in mid-January.

The Gunners were also the only team that Leeds managed to beat on their travels in the top five.

In both the second and the third sectors, Leeds performed better at home than they did away from Elland Road, although the pattern was reversed against teams in the bottom five.

Leeds managed to do the 'double' over four teams in the F.A. Barclaycard Premiership, while they were unable to take any points off just Newcastle.

The heart of the Barclaycard Premiership - 4thegame.com

weeks. Leeds were having to dip into their reserves and not surprisingly they faltered.

They entertained Liverpool in early February but, missing more than half a dozen key players, they slumped to a 4-0 defeat. It was their worst reverse at home for nearly two years and meant they dropped to sixth place in the process. Leeds went into a game at Middlesbrough without three banned players – Mills, Bowyer and Smith – but still earned a point from a 2-2 draw.

Defeat over two legs by PSV Eindhoven ended Leeds' UEFA Cup aspirations and goalless draws against Charlton and Everton were not surprising.

The frustrations of the season were spilling over to the fans with head coach Brian Kidd suffering abuse from Leeds followers at Goodison Park. The abuse even prompted chairman Ridsdale to walk round the touchline to speak with the fans. Later, Rio Ferdinand, Nigel Martyn and Alan Smith called a press conference to pledge their support for Kidd. The team responded by ending March with three wins, albeit against strugglers Ipswich, Blackburn and Leicester.

The run ended at home to Manchester United over Easter when the visitors led 4-1, eventually won 4-3 and left Leeds back in sixth spot.

It's a fact

Leeds only lost four away games, their fewest number of away defeats in the Premier League. They also conceded only 16 away goals, again a club record in the Premier League.

> "The fans have a right to be frustrated, but it's not right to accuse one coach. So we have decided to underline our support for Brian Kidd before the situation gets any worse."
>
> *Nigel Martyn*
> *(March 2002)*

F.A. Barclaycard Premiership
Goals By Time Period

Key
■ Goals Scored ■ Goals Conceded

Home Matches

Time of Goal (mins)

Period	Scored	Conceded
0-15	8	1
16-30	4	1
31-45	1	5
46-60	5	5
61-75	7	3
76-90	6	6

Goals

Away Matches

Time of Goal (mins)

Period	Scored	Conceded
0-15	2	2
16-30	8	2
31-45	1	3
46-60	4	4
61-75	3	1
76-90	4	4

Goals

All Matches

Time of Goal (mins)

Period	Scored	Conceded
0-15	10	3
16-30	12	3
31-45	2	8
46-60	9	9
61-75	10	4
76-90	10	10

Goals

Chart Analysis

statistics powered by ◆ SUPERBASE™

Although Leeds outscored their opponents by some margin in the opening half-hour of matches, they were let down in the last 15 minutes of the first half when they conceded four times as many goals as they scored.

After the break, they outscored opponents in only the 61-75 minute time period.

BEST IN THE LEAGUE...

• Joint most goals scored in 16-30 minutes

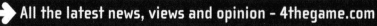
➡ All the latest news, views and opinion - 4thegame.com

Leeds United

F.A. Barclaycard Premiership

Goals Resulting From

	Six Yard Area				Inside Area				Outside Area				Total			
	Shots		Headers		Shots		Headers		Shots		Headers		Shots		Headers	
	Home	Away	Home	Away	Home	Away	Home	Away	Home	Away	Home	Away	Home	Away	Home	Away
Open Play	1	2	2	2	17	10	3	-	2	3	-	-	20	15	5	2
	2	2	1	1	9	4	1	3	2	2	-	-	13	8	2	4
Direct Free Kick									1	1			1	1		
									-	-			0	0		
Indirect Free Kick	-	-	1	1	-	-	-	-	-	-	-	-	0	0	1	1
	-	1	-	1	1	-	-	-	-	-	-	-	1	1	0	1
Penalty	-	-	-	-	1	-	-	-	-	-	-	-	1	0	0	0
	-	-	-	-	1	-	-	-	-	-	-	-	1	0	0	0
Corner	-	-	-	1	1	1	-	-	1	-	-	-	2	1	0	1
	1	-	-	1	1	-	-	1	-	-	-	-	2	0	1	1
Totals	1	2	3	4	19	11	3	0	4	4	0	0	24	17	6	4
	3	3	1	3	12	4	2	3	2	2	0	0	17	9	3	6

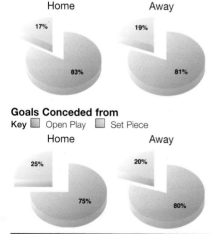

How Goals Were Scored
Home & Away Matches

2% 8% 4% 4%
82%

Key
- Open Play
- Corner
- Indirect Free Kick
- Direct Free Kick
- Penalty

Charts do not include 2 own goals for and 2 against.

How Goals Were Conceded
Home & Away Matches

3% 11% 9%
77%

Goals Scored from
Key ☐ Open Play ☐ Set Piece

Home
17%
83%

Away
19%
81%

Goals Conceded from
Key ☐ Open Play ☐ Set Piece

Home
25%
75%

Away
20%
80%

Chart Analysis

The Yorkshire club scored the majority of their goals from Open Play, with Shots Inside Area accounting for 27 out of 53 strikes.

Leeds' proportion of goals scored from Set Pieces was pretty low, with most success coming from Corners where they scored four. They managed the same number from Direct and Indirect Free Kicks combined.

While Leeds conceded nearly twice as many goals from Shots at home as they did away, the opposite was true with headers.

Although they didn't concede any goals from Direct Free Kicks, they did manager to score twice from those situations.

statistics powered by ◆ SUPERBASE™

➡ **Fixtures, results and match reports – 4thegame.com**

> **"This has been a disappointing season, there is no doubt about it, and when that happens at a big club like ours you can expect some players to come in and some to go out."**
>
> *David Batty*
> *(April 2002)*

It's a fact

Leeds started the season with a milestone; their 2-0 home win over Southampton was their 150th in the Premier League.

That disappointment was compounded by another loss, at Tottenham where Spurs won 2-1. It left Leeds in the worrying position of possibly having to rely on the much-maligned Intertoto Cup as their only hope of making it into Europe this season.

Successive victories improved Leeds' confidence if not their League position. They beat struggling Sunderland 2-0 at Elland Road but news that Woodgate would be out for the rest of the season, after a prank with a friend ended in the defender needing surgery on a broken jaw, only brought more bad news for the club.

Viduka scored his fourth goal in five games to earn Leeds three more points at Villa and the fact that Arsenal and Chelsea had qualified for the F.A. Cup final meant that Leeds were likely to earn a UEFA Cup spot after all for finishing in sixth.

It was just as well. Leeds lost 1-0 at home to Fulham with two games to go. They then went to Derby and, with an early goal from Bowyer, confirmed a top six finish.

Their form at the end of the season was promising, Smith's goal against Middlesbrough ensuring that Leeds finished fifth to guarantee their UEFA Cup spot and to end with four wins from five games.

F.A. Barclaycard Premiership
Shot Efficiency

Key
■ Goals Scored   □ Other Shots On Target

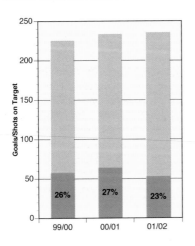

Season	Division	Shots Off Target	Shots On Target	Total Goals
1999 - 2000	P	n/a	225	58
2000 - 2001	P	n/a	233	64
2001 - 2002	P	214	235	53

Chart Analysis

As would be expected from one of the League's top sides, Shots On Target – up slightly on last year's figure – exceeded the number of Shots Off Target.

However, the conversion rate to goals dropped as Leeds struggled to match last year's goal total.

statistics powered by **◆ SUPERBASE**™

Leeds United

F.A. Barclaycard Premiership	Key
Team Discipline	■ Forward ■ Midfield ■ Defence ■ Goalkeeper

Total Number Of Bookings

Total number of red cards	5
Total number of yellow cards	69

Referee Performance

Referee	Games Refereed	Red Cards	Yellow Cards
G.P.Barber	2	1	9
A.P.D'Urso	3	1	7
J.T.Winter	2	2	5

Type of Yellow Cards Received

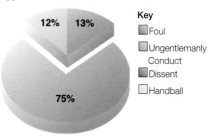

12%   13%

75%

Key
■ Foul
■ Ungentlemanly Conduct
■ Dissent
□ Handball

Bookings by Position 1999/2000 - 2001/2002

Home Matches

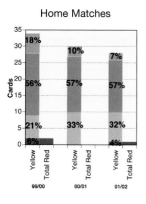

Away Matches

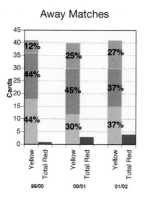

All Matches

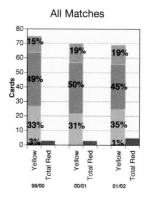

Chart Analysis

The number of overall cautions was in line with previous seasons, just one down on 2000-01. The percentage split throughout the team also remained consistent, with midfielders collecting the most, followed by defenders and forwards.

While the number of Yellow Cards picked up at home fell compared to last term by two, on the road it went up by one.

WORST IN THE LEAGUE...
• Joint most Red Cards away

> "If you take out Bowyer, Mills and Smith, then our disciplinary record compares favourably with other clubs who have cards spread evenly across the team."
>
> *David O'Leary*
> *(February 2002)*

statistics powered by  **SUPERBASE**™

 The heart of the Barclaycard Premiership - 4thegame.com

Leicester City

F.A. Barclaycard Premiership Final standing for the 2001-2002 season

Final Position		Games Played	Games Won	Games Drawn	Games Lost	Goals For	Goals Against	Total Points
18	Ipswich Town	38	9	9	20	41	64	36
19	Derby County	38	8	6	24	33	63	30
20	Leicester City	38	5	13	20	30	64	28

"I simply don't know what the comings and goings might be during the summer. All I can hope is there may be a surplus that I might be able to dip into for new signings."

Micky Adams (May 2002)

Club Honours and Records

Division 2 Champions: 1924-25, 1936-37, 1953-54, 1956-57, 1970-71, 1979-80

League Cup Winners: 1964, 1997, 2000

Record victory:

10-0 v Portsmouth, Division 1, 20 October, 1928

Record defeat:

0-12 v Nottingham Forest, Division 1, 21 April, 1909

League goals in a season (team):

109, Division 2, 1956-57

League goals in a season (player):

44, Arthur Rowley, Division 2, 1956-57

Career league goals:

259, Arthur Chandler, 1923 to 1935

League appearances:

528, Adam Black, 1920 to 1935

Reported transfer fee paid:

£5,000,000 to Wolves for Ade Akinbiyi, July 2000

Reported transfer fee received: £11,000,000 from Liverpool for Emile Heskey, March 2000

LEICESTER said farewell to Filbert Street in disappointing fashion. The season saw three managers at the old ground and, perhaps inevitably, relegation followed.

Leicester had finished the previous campaign in relegation form. Their good start had kept them in the top flight but nine defeats from their final ten games had the alarm bells ringing. Nevertheless, Peter Taylor continued with the club's blessing.

Taylor did relinquish his England Under-21 coaching duties to concentrate on his club responsibilities and spent more than £7m in the summer, with former England goalkeeper Ian Walker arriving from Spurs.

Dennis Wise ended his 11-year association with Chelsea when the 34-year-old arrived at Filbert Street, while Ipswich striker Jamie Scowcroft also signed. The Foxes failed with an audacious £1m offer for Coventry's John Hartson, who later joined former Leicester boss Martin O'Neill at Celtic. Steve Guppy also joined his old boss in Glasgow.

If optimism was low before the season's start, it was replaced by total pessimism after one week during which the Foxes played two, lost two, scored none and conceded nine.

 All the latest news, views and opinion – 4thegame.com

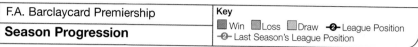

Leicester City

Key
Win ■ Loss ■ Draw ―②― League Position
―②― Last Season's League Position

All Matches

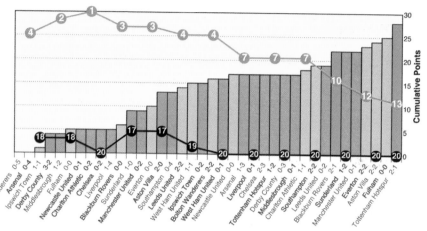

Home Matches

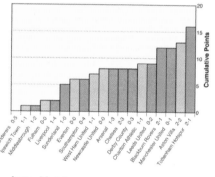

Away Matches

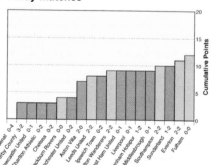

Chart Analysis

The Foxes began the season in disastrous fashion. They lost five out of their opening eight fixtures, including heavy defeats to Bolton and Arsenal, to leave them propping up the rest of the table.

A day after the 2-0 defeat at Charlton, Peter Taylor was axed and replaced by Dave Bassett.

Wins against Sunderland and Aston Villa in their next seven outings took them out of the relegation zone and seemed to offer hope of escape, but it was to prove a false dawn as a 4-0 defeat at home to Southampton sent them back to the bottom three where they stayed for the rest of the season.

That heavy defeat to Saints kicked off a 16-match run without winning which effectively condemned Leicester to Division One football.

When Micky Adams took sole control of the side for the last four games of the season, Leicester remained unbeaten although by then they were already down.

WORST IN THE LEAGUE...
• Longest run without winning

statistics powered by ◆ SUPERBASE™

"Obviously we have not started the way we wanted, but everyone within the squad is convinced that we can still finish in Europe."

Ian Walker
(August 2001)

It's a fact

Leicester's 2-1 defeat at Filbert Street by Middlesbrough in September was the club's 100th loss in the Premier League.

It was impossible to consider a worse start than the 5-0 home thrashing by F.A. Barclaycard Premiership newcomers Bolton. The booing started 40 minutes from the end and the thrashing was described by defender Frank Sinclair as a 'freak show'.

Two days after that loss, Darren Eadie was ruled out for the rest of the season while Gerry Taggart's fitness was also causing concern.

Next stop was Highbury where Leicester could not expect much return. They lost 4-0 and Wise suffered the ninth red card of his controversial career after clashing with Arsenal's Patrick Vieira.

Club chairman John Elsom insisted Taylor would be given a fair chance to turn City's fortunes around but luck was against them in the third game when, though they drew 1-1 against Ipswich, they had Lee Marshall sent off – a decision later overturned by referee Barry Knight – and Muzzy Izzet missed a penalty.

A 3-2 win at neighbours Derby, thanks to two goals from Dean Sturridge and a late penalty by Izzet, improved the flagging confidence even if the game finished controversially with a tunnel bust-up after Robbie Savage had won the late spot-kick.

It was to be Taylor's last win. September brought

F.A. Barclaycard Premiership
Half-Time/Full-Time Comparison

Key: ■ Win ■ Loss ■ Draw

Home				Away				Total			
Number of Home Half Time Wins	Full Time Result W	L	D	Number of Away Half Time Wins	Full Time Result W	L	D	Total number of Half Time Wins	Full Time Result W	L	D
4	1	2	1	4	1	-	3	8	2	2	4
Number of Home Half Time Losses	Full Time Result W	L	D	Number of Away Half Time Losses	Full Time Result W	L	D	Total number of Half Time Losses	Full Time Result W	L	D
7	-	5	2	10	-	9	1	17	-	14	3
Number of Home Half Time Draws	Full Time Result W	L	D	Number of Away Half Time Draws	Full Time Result W	L	D	Total number of Half Time Draws	Full Time Result W	L	D
8	2	2	4	5	1	2	2	13	3	4	6

Chart Analysis

statistics powered by ◆ SUPERBASE™

Leicester managed just five wins all season. Most of them – three – came, surprisingly, when they were level at the interval.

They squandered half-time leads on six out of eight occasions, including losing two out of the four games they were in front in at home.

Overall, they lost 14 out of 17 games in which they went into the break behind.

F.A. Barclaycard Premiership Results Table

Key: 88 time of goal · 88 time of assist · ▲ player substituted · player substituted · yellow card · ● red card

DATE	H/A	OPPONENT	H/T	F/T	POS	REFEREE	TEAM											SUBSTITUTES USED		
18-08	H	Bolton	0-4	0-5	20	R.Styles	Flowers	Rowett ▲	Impey	Sinclair	Elliott	Davidson	Savage	Wise	Akinbiyi	Sturridge ▲	Izzet ▲	Gunnlaugsson ▲	Lewis ▲	Marshall ▲
25-08	A	Arsenal	0-2	0-4	20	A.P.D'Urso	Flowers	Rowett ●	Impey	Sinclair	Lewis	Stewart	Savage	Wise ●	Akinbiyi	Scowcroft ▲	Izzet ▲	Marshall ▲	Delaney ▲	Jones ▲
08-09	A	Ipswich Town	1-1	1-1	18	B.Knight	Walker	Marshall ●	Impey	Sinclair	Elliott	Davidson	Savage	Jones	Akinbiyi	Scowcroft	Izzet 90	Stewart ▲	Sturridge ▲90	-
15-09	A	Derby County	1-1	3-2	17	G.P.Barber	Walker	Sinclair	Marshall	Davidson	Elliott	Stewart 30	Savage 90	Jones	Akinbiyi 65	Sturridge ▲30 65	Izzet 90	Benjamin ▲	Oakes ▲	-
17-09	H	Middlesbrough	1-0	1-2	18	N.S.Barry	Walker	Sinclair ▲	Marshall	Davidson	Elliott	Stewart ▲	Savage 90	Wise	Akinbiyi ▲9	Sturridge	Izzet	Jones ▲9	Benjamin ▲	Impey ▲
22-09	H	Fulham	0-0	0-0	18	E.K.Wolstenholme	Walker	Marshall	Sinclair	Davidson	Elliott	Stewart ▲	Savage	Wise	Scowcroft	Sturridge	Izzet	Rowett ▲	Impey ▲	-
26-09	A	Newcastle Utd	0-1	0-1	19	D.Pugh	Walker	Rowett ▲	Marshall	Lewis	Elliott	Impey	Savage	Wise	Scowcroft ▲	Benjamin ▲	Jones ▲	Sinclair ▲	Akinbiyi ▲	
29-09	A	Charlton	0-2	0-2	20	M.L.Dean	Walker	Sinclair ▲	Marshall	Lewis	Heath	Davidson	Savage	Wise	Scowcroft	Benjamin	Izzet ▲	Wise ▲	Benjamin ▲▲	Impey ▲
13-10	A	Chelsea	0-2	0-2	20	J.T.Winter	Walker	Sinclair ▲	Marshall	Davidson	Elliott	Rowett ●	Savage	Jones	Akinbiyi	Sturridge	Izzet	Gunnlaugsson ▲	Impey ▲	Lewis ▲
20-10	H	Liverpool	0-3	1-4	20	M.R.Halsey	Walker	Marshall	Sinclair	Davidson 58	Elliott	Savage	Jones ▲	Wise 58	Benjamin	Sturridge ▲	Impey ▲	Piper ▲	
29-10	A	Blackburn	0-0	0-0	20	R.Styles	Walker	Sinclair	Marshall	Davidson	Elliott	Sinclair	Izzet	Wise	Benjamin	Akinbiyi	Scowcroft ▲	Piper ▲	
03-11	H	Sunderland	0-1	1-0	17	S.W.Dunn	Walker	Marshall	Sinclair	Davidson	Elliott 61	Sinclair	Izzet	Wise	Akinbiyi 61	Benjamin ▲	Impey ▲	Scowcroft ▲	
24-11	A	Manchester Utd	0-1	0-2	18	A.P.D'Urso	Walker	Sinclair	Marshall	Davidson ▲	Elliott	Impey	Izzet	Wise	Akinbiyi	Benjamin ▲	Rogers ▲	Scowcroft ▲	
24-11	H	Everton	0-0	0-0	19	U.D.Rennie	Walker	Sinclair	Marshall	Davidson	Elliott	Savage	Izzet	Wise ●	Scowcroft	Benjamin	Rogers ▲	Benjamin ▲	
01-12	A	Aston Villa	1-0	2-0	17	S.G.Bennett	Walker	Marshall	Sinclair	Davidson	Elliott 12	Rogers ▲	Savage	Wise ●	Akinbiyi ▲12	Scowcroft 52	Benjamin ▲	Stewart ▲	
08-12	H	Southampton	0-1	0-4	19	G.Poll	Walker	Marshall ▲	Sinclair	Heath	Davidson	Impey	Savage	Wise	Akinbiyi ▲12	Scowcroft 88	Deane ▲	Oakes ▲	Izzet ▲
16-12	A	Leeds United	0-1	2-2	18	R.Styles	Walker	Marshall	Sinclair	Davidson 78	Elliott	Impey ▲	Izzet 88	Oakes ▲	Deane 78	Scowcroft	Akinbiyi ▲	Wise ▲	
22-12	H	West Ham Utd	1-1	1-1	19	E.K.Wolstenholme	Walker	Marshall	Sinclair	Stewart	Elliott ● ●	Savage ●	Izzet 43	Oakes ▲	Deane ▲	Scowcroft 43	Akinbiyi ▲	Rogers ▲	Wise ▲
26-12	A	Ipswich Town	1-1	1-1	20	N.S.Barry	Walker	Marshall	Rogers ▲	Elliott	Rogers ▲	Savage	Wise ▲22	Deane 27	Stewart ▲	Akinbiyi ▲	Impey ▲	Davidson ▲
29-12	H	West Ham Utd	2-1	2-2	20	M.A.Riley	Walker	Marshall	Sinclair	Elliott	Davidson	Rogers ▲27	Savage ▲	Wise	Deane 27	Akinbiyi ▲	Jones ▲	Izzet ▲●	Impey ▲
12-01	A	Newcastle Utd	0-1	0-1	20	D.J.Gallagher	Walker	Impey	Laursen	Laursen	Scowcroft	Savage	Wise	Deane	Akinbiyi ▲	Stewart ▲	Marshall ▲	
19-01	H	Newcastle Utd	0-0	0-0	20	A.G.Wiley	Walker ▲	Sinclair	Laursen	Davidson	Savage	Izzet	Oakes ▲	Akinbiyi	Scowcroft	Flowers ▲	Stewart ▲	
23-01	A	Arsenal	0-2	1-3	20	D.R.Elleray	Flowers	Laursen	Elliott	Davidson ▲	Impey 68	Savage	Oakes ▲	Izzet 68	Scowcroft ●	Benjamin ▲	Jones ▲	Akinbiyi ▲
30-01	A	Liverpool	0-0	0-1	20	B.Knight	Walker	Laursen	Elliott	Stewart ▲	Izzet	Oakes ▲	Piper	Scowcroft ●	Benjamin ▲	Marshall ▲	Rogers ▲
02-02	H	Chelsea	1-0	2-3	20	G.P.Barber	Walker	Sinclair	Elliott	Davidson ▲	Impey ▲	Jones ▲	Izzet	Oakes 24 68	Piper	Scowcroft 24 68	Marshall ▲	Benjamin ▲	
09-02	A	Tottenham	0-1	1-2	20	M.A.Riley	Walker	Sinclair	Elliott	Stewart	Laursen	Oakes 79	Savage	Oakes 79	Davidson 79	Piper	Scowcroft	
23-02	H	Derby County	0-0	0-3	20	E.K.Wolstenholme	Walker	Sinclair	Laursen	Davidson	Impey ▲	Savage	Izzet ●	Piper	Akinbiyi	Scowcroft	Marshall ▲	Deane ▲
02-03	A	Middlesbrough	0-1	0-1	20	E.K.Wolstenholme	Walker	Sinclair	Elliott ●	Davidson ●	Marshall	Savage	Izzet 68	Piper	Dickov ▲	Deane ▲	Jones ▲	Oakes ▲
09-03	A	Charlton	1-1	1-1	20	G.R.Wilkes	Walker	Sinclair	Laursen	Delaney	Scowcroft ▲20	Savage	Izzet	Piper 20	Dickov ▲	Deane ▲	Oakes ▲	Ashton ▲
16-03	H	Southampton	2-2	2-2	20	M.L.Dean	Walker	Marshall	Laursen	Piper	Delaney	Savage	Izzet 23	Deane ▲21 23	Dickov ▲21	Reeves ▲	Heath ▲	
23-03	H	Leeds Utd	0-2	0-2	20	S.W.Dunn	Walker	Marshall ▲	Elliott	Ashton	Piper	Savage	Izzet	Deane ▲	Dickov ▲21	Oakes ▲	Wright ▲	Sinclair ▲
30-03	H	Blackburn	1-0	2-1	20	G.P.Barber	Walker	Marshall ▲	Elliott	Ashton ▲	Piper ▲	Savage 46	Oakes ▲	Deane 8	Dickov 8 46	Reeves ▲	Rowett ▲	
01-04	A	Sunderland	1-2	1-2	20	N.S.Barry	Walker	Marshall	Elliott 8	Rowett	Reeves ▲	Savage	Oakes ▲	Izzet ▲	Dickov ▲8	Ashton ▲	Piper ▲	Stevenson ▲
06-04	H	Manchester Utd	0-0	0-1	20	A.P.D'Urso	Walker	Sinclair	Elliott ●	Davidson ●	Piper	Marshall	Deane	Dickov ▲	Ashton ▲	Jones ▲	Reeves ▲	-
13-04	A	Everton	2-0	2-2	20	U.D.Rennie	Walker	Rowett	Heath	Davidson	Piper	Savage 18	Marshall ●	Deane ▲18 27	Dickov	Ashton ▲	Stevenson ▲	Reeves ▲
20-04	H	Aston Villa	1-2	2-2	20	G.Poll	Walker	Rowett ▲	Sinclair ▲24	Davidson ▲24	Marshall	Savage 67	Izzet ●24	Deane ▲18 27	Dickov	Oakes ▲	Stevenson ▲67	Ashton ▲
27-04	A	Fulham	0-0	0-0	20	G.Pugh	Walker	Rowett ●	Sinclair	Elliott	Rogers	Marshall	Savage	Piper	Dickov ▲	Davidson ▲	Stevenson ▲	Oakes ▲
11-05	H	Tottenham	0-0	2-1	20	D.R.Elleray	Walker	Ashton ▲	Sinclair	Elliott 71	Rogers	Impey	Marshall 60	Izzet ▲	Dickov ▲60	Davidson ▲	Williamson ▲	Taggart ▲	Stevenson ▲

F.A. Barclaycard Premiership
Squad List

Position	Name	Appearances	Appearances as Substitute	Goals or Clean Sheets	Goal Assists	Yellow Cards	Red Cards
G	T.Flowers	3	1				
G	I.Walker	35		7			
D	C.Davidson	29	1			4	3
D	D.Delaney	2	1				1
D	M.Elliott	31			4	4	1
D	M.Heath	3	2				
D	J.Laursen	10				1	
D	L.Marshall	29	6		2	3	1
D	A.Rogers	9	4		1	1	
D	G.Rowett	9	2			3	
D	F.Sinclair	33	2		1	8	
D	G.Taggart		1				
D	T.Williamson		1				
M	J.Ashton	3	4				
M	A.Impey	20	7		1	3	
M	M.Izzet	29	2	4	3	9	1
M	M.Jones	6	4	1			
M	J.Lewis	4	2				1
M	S.Oakes	16	5	1	2	2	
M	M.Reeves	1	4			1	
M	R.Savage	35			4	14	
M	J.Stevenson		6	1			
M	J.Stewart	9	3		1	2	
M	D.Wise	15	2	1	1	6	1
F	A.Akinbiyi	16	5	2	1	3	
F	T.Benjamin	4	7			2	
F	B.Deane	13	2	6	1	2	
F	P.Dickov	11	1	4	1	4	
F	A.Gunnlaugsson		2				
F	M.Piper	14	2	1	1		
F	J.Scowcroft	21	3	5	1	3	
F	D.Sturridge	8	1	3			
F	T.Wright		1				

nothing but problems and the heat was back on Taylor when Middlesbrough won 2-1 at Filbert Street. After a goalless draw at Fulham, they lost again, at Newcastle and Charlton, where another player, Junior Lewis, was wrongly sent off, with the decision later overturned.

All of this combined to cost Taylor his job. On the last day of September, the former Gillingham boss was sacked after just 15 months following a sequence of 18 games in which Leicester had won once and lost 14 times.

Former West Ham manager Harry Redknapp was the first to be linked with the vacancy as caretaker Garry Parker presided over the damaging 6-0 Worthington Cup defeat by Leeds.

Redknapp ruled himself out of the job so Leicester, surprisingly, turned to the experienced Dave Bassett, with Brighton manager Micky Adams as his assistant.

The day after the appointments, Leicester announced losses of £5.8m for the previous financial year and, on the pitch, Bassett failed to make an immediate improvement with a 2-0 defeat at Chelsea – leaving City without a goal for 530 minutes – followed by a 4-1 home thrashing by Liverpool.

Taylor joined Brighton as Adams' replacement while Bassett threatened his players with changes. Sturridge left for Wolves and, for a short spell, results improved even if goals were at a premium. After Wise scored against Liverpool, Leicester managed just one more in the next four matches, but defensively they were improving. Two goalless draws, at Blackburn and against Everton, and a 1-0 victory over Sunderland lifted spirits and lifted the Foxes to 17th place.

Izzet asked for a move after being linked with several clubs but Ade Akinbiyi hit back at his growing army of critics by

 The heart of the Barclaycard Premiership – 4thegame.com

F.A. Barclaycard Premiership

Top Goal Scorer — **Brian Deane**

Total Premier League Goals Scored:	Percentage Of The Team's League Goals:
6	**20%**

Goals Scored From

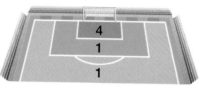

4
1
1

G oals were hard to come by at Leicester as the Foxes paid the price for the lack of a regular scorer. Ever since Emile Heskey left Filbert Street for Liverpool in March 2000, Leicester have struggled in front of goal. Ade Akinbiyi and Trevor Benjamin both stuttered, while new signing Jamie Scowcroft was bugged by injuries. Deane arrived in December from Middlesbrough, for whom he had scored once, and on his full debut for Dave Bassett scored in the 2-2 draw against one of his former clubs Leeds. His tally, though, was the lowest from the top Leicester scorer for 24 years since Geoff Salmons and Roger Davies managed four apiece in 1977-78.

"This is a big chance for me to restart my career and show people what I can do."

Brian Deane

Goals Resulting From
Key
◻ Open Play ◻ Corner ◻ Indirect Free Kick
◻ Direct Free Kick ◼ Penalty

100%

Goal Assists

Total number of goal assists	1

Teams Scored Against

Against	Home	Away
Everton	0	2
Southampton	0	2
Bolton Wanderers	0	1
Leeds United	0	1
Total Goals Scored	**0**	**6**

	Right Foot	Left Foot	Header
Open Play	3	1	2
Set piece	-	-	-

It's a fact

Leicester's draw against Southampton in March took their Premier League points' tally to 300.

> **"I don't criticise players unnecessarily but I don't see why I should sit here and defend the indefensible. If I was a young manager, I might have beaten half the team up tonight – with a baseball bat."**
>
> *Dave Bassett after losing to Ipswich on Boxing Day (December 2001)*

scoring the winner against Sunderland in early November. Injuries continued to ruin Bassett's planning, so he signed up Nottingham Forest defender Alan Rogers for just £50,000, with another £50,000 pledged if relegation was avoided.

After losing at Old Trafford and drawing at home to Everton, again without scoring, they claimed another rare win, beating Aston Villa 2-0 at Villa Park with another goal from Akinbiyi, and Scowcroft adding a second to justify Bassett's decision to recall him.

Bassett also took Middlesbrough's Brian Deane for a nominal fee to boost their attacking options. Yet a 4-0 home defeat by Southampton highlighted the problems Bassett had inherited. Confirmation that Gary Rowett was out for at least three months and Taggart would probably miss the rest of the season only made matters worse.

The 2-0 Boxing Day defeat at Ipswich infuriated Bassett. Afterwards, he launched a scathing attack on his players.

Leicester were back at the bottom of the F.A. Barclaycard Premiership, a position they occupied throughout the rest of the season. Bassett remained

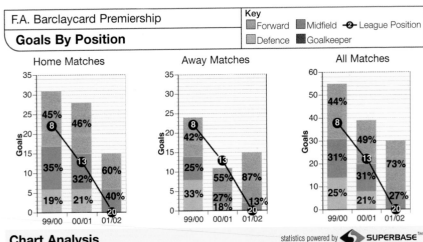

F.A. Barclaycard Premiership
Goals By Position

Key — Forward, Midfield, Defence, Goalkeeper, League Position

Home Matches / Away Matches / All Matches

Chart Analysis

statistics powered by **SUPERBASE**™

Leicester managed just 30 goals, split evenly between home and away, their lowest ever total in seven seasons in the Premier League, and nearly half as many as two seasons ago when they finished in the top half of the table.

While they managed to up their final tally of away strikes by four goals compared to last season, there was a sharp fall at home. It was particularly disappointing that no goals at all were scored by defenders all season.

 Fixtures, results and match reports – 4thegame.com

determined and signed Danish international Jacob Laursen. Leicester had 16 points and Bassett set a target of a further 24 from 18 games to take the tally up to 40.

It was hard, though, to see where those points would come from. A 1-0 loss at West Ham was followed by a goalless draw against Newcastle and then a 3-1 home defeat by Arsenal when Leicester played the final half-hour with ten men, not for disciplinary reasons, but because Sinclair was injured after all three substitutes had been used at the interval.

Further bad news was to come on the injury front when Wise discovered in January that he needed a thigh operation, ruling him out for the rest of the campaign. Deane, too, was out for a month with a torn calf muscle.

The loss against Arsenal was the first of six successive defeats as Leicester's future was effectively determined by February. When Leicester lost 1-0 at Middlesbrough, thanks to a solitary Sinclair own goal, the writing was on the wall.

Bassett was furious with Mauricio Taricco during the 2-1 defeat at White Hart Lane, accusing the Argentine of feigning injury when he clutched his face with both hands as if he had been butted. "That man is a disgrace to the game," claimed Bassett.

With relegation a certainty, Leicester

F.A. Barclaycard Premiership
Team Performance Table

League Position	Team	Points won from a possible six	Percentage of points won at home	Percentage of points won away	Overall percentage of points won
1	Arsenal	0/6			
2	Liverpool	0/6			
3	Manchester Utd	0/6	7%	7%	7%
4	Newcastle Utd	1/6			
5	Leeds United	1/6			
6	Chelsea	0/6			
7	West Ham Utd	1/6			
8	Aston Villa	4/6	53%	27%	40%
9	Tottenham H	3/6			
10	Blackburn R	4/6			
11	Southampton	1/6			
12	Middlesbrough	0/6			
13	Fulham	2/6	20%	20%	20%
14	Charlton Athletic	1/6			
15	Everton	2/6			
16	Bolton W	1/6			
17	Sunderland	3/6			
18	Ipswich Town	1/6	33%	33%	33%
19	Derby County	3/6			
20	**Leicester City**	28			

The table shows how many points out of a possible six Leicester City have taken off each of the teams in the four sections. The other columns show as a percentage how many points they have taken from those available.

Chart Analysis

statistics powered by **SUPERBASE**™

Leicester performed identically both at home and away against teams in all but the second sector.

Against the top five teams, they managed to take a solitary point off Newcastle and Leeds, collecting not a single point from their six matches against Arsenal, Liverpool and Manchester United.

They also failed to take any points off Chelsea and Middlesbrough, and did not register any 'doubles' themselves all season.

The most points they took off any team was four, against both Aston Villa and Blackburn from the second sector.

had to plan for the future and gave Middlesbrough permission to talk to Izzet with a view to a possible £6m transfer. However, the Turkish international turned his back on the move.

Adams hinted that he wanted the manager's job at Leicester and that he would move if not promoted. Paul Dickov, the Manchester City striker, arrived in late February after the departure of Akinbiyi, to Crystal Palace.

After the defeat by Boro, draws against Charlton and Southampton were followed by a 2-0 home defeat by Leeds. Victory over Blackburn with two Dickov goals at the end of March did little to lift the air of depression hanging over Filbert Street.

They started April with a 2-1 defeat at Sunderland and, a day later, announced that the new £35m stadium nearing completion little more than a long free kick away from Filbert Street was to be named the 'the Walkers Bowl', not as some had suggested, in honour of the goalkeeper, but in a £1.5m deal with major sponsors Walkers.

Then came more major news for Foxes fans. Leicester confirmed that assistant boss Micky Adams was to become the club's new manager. On the same day they also announced that Martin George would replace John Elsom as chairman.

It's a fact

Leicester went 16 League games without a win between 1 December and 23 March. It was their worst sequence without a victory in the Premier League.

"I would like to say how appreciative I am of the maturity of Dave Bassett for allowing the succession to take place, and I look forward to Micky Adams bringing back success to this club."
Chairman John Elsom (April 2002)

F.A. Barclaycard Premiership
Goals By Time Period

Key ■ Goals Scored ■ Goals Conceded

Home Matches

Time of Goal (mins)	Scored	Conceded
0-15	2	5
16-30	3	3
31-45	1	8
46-60	3	3
61-75	5	6
76-90	1	9

Away Matches

Time of Goal (mins)	Scored	Conceded
0-15	2	4
16-30	7	6
31-45	6	
46-60	1	6
61-75	1	2
76-90	4	6

All Matches

Time of Goal (mins)	Scored	Conceded
0-15	4	9
16-30	10	9
31-45	1	14
46-60	4	9
61-75	6	8
76-90	5	15

Chart Analysis

statistics powered by **SUPERBASE**™

Leicester scored a third of all their goals between 16-30 minutes. It was the only time that they outscored their opponents during the matches they played.

At other times, they really struggled, especially at the end of both halves, when they were comfortably outscored both home and away. They seemed to crumble at home towards the end of matches, managing to reply just once to nine goals conceded.

The heart of the Barclaycard Premiership - 4thegame.com

F.A. Barclaycard Premiership
Goals Resulting From

Key
☐ Goals Scored ☐ Goals Conceded

	Six Yard Area				Inside Area				Outside Area				Total			
	Shots		Headers		Shots		Headers		Shots		Headers		Shots		Headers	
	Home	Away	Home	Away	Home	Away	Home	Away	Home	Away	Home	Away	**Home**	**Away**	**Home**	**Away**
Open Play	1	4	1	1	4	3	2	1	-	1	-	-	**5**	**8**	**3**	**2**
	1	4	1	3	15	8	3	5	4	1	-	-	20	13	4	8
Direct Free Kick									-	-			**0**	**0**		
									3	1			3	1		
Indirect Free Kick	-	1	-	-	1	-	-	-	-	1	-	-	**1**	**2**	**0**	**0**
	-	1	2	-	1	1	-	-	-	1	-	-	1	3	2	0
Penalty	-	-	-	-	1	1	-	-	-	-	-	-	**1**	**1**	**0**	**0**
	-	-	-	-	2	3	-	-	-	-	-	-	2	3	0	0
Corner	-	-	1	1	2	-	2	-	-	-	-	-	**2**	**0**	**3**	**1**
	1	-	-	-	-	-	-	1	-	-	-	-	1	0	1	1
Totals	1	5	2	2	8	4	4	1	0	2	0	0	**9**	**11**	**6**	**3**
	2	5	4	3	19	12	3	6	6	3	0	0	27	20	7	9

How Goals Were Scored
Home & Away Matches

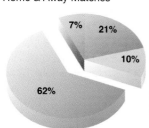
7% 21% 10% 62%

Key
■ Open Play
■ Corner
☐ Indirect Free Kick
☐ Direct Free Kick
■ Penalty

Charts do not include 1 own goal for and 1 against.

How Goals Were Conceded
Home & Away Matches

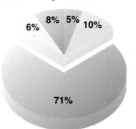
6% 8% 5% 10% 71%

Goals Scored from
Key ☐ Open Play ☐ Set Piece

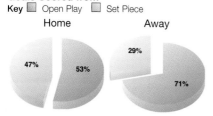

Home
47% 53%

Away
29% 71%

Goals Conceded from
Key ☐ Open Play ☐ Set Piece

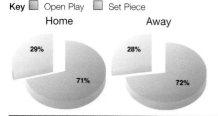

Home
29% 71%

Away
28% 72%

Chart Analysis

Leicester relied heavily on Set Pieces overall and especially at home, where they notched 7 out of 15 goals from dead ball situations.

They succumbed most frequently at Filbert Street to Shots Inside Area.

The proportion of goals conceded from Open Play and Set Pieces remained pretty consistent both home and away.

WORST IN THE LEAGUE...
• **Most goals conceded from Open Play overall and at home**

statistics powered by SUPERBASE™

All the latest news, views and opinion – 4thegame.com

> "The Walkers Bowl is one of the best state-of-the-art stadia in the country and a flagship development, not just for the club but the community and city of Leicester as a whole."
>
> *Chief executive Steve Kind*
> *(April 2002)*

Adams replaced Dave Bassett, who would take up a new role as director of football, after the next game – against Manchester United.

Leicester faced United at Filbert Street knowing a defeat would confirm the inevitable and it eventually came when Ole Gunnar Solskjaer netted the game's only goal.

Leicester's next game was, perhaps, painful. Former boss Martin O'Neill brought his new Scottish champions, Celtic, to Filbert Street to face a Leicester side led by Adams for the first time.

After their fate was determined, Leicester under Adams enjoyed successive League draws, at Everton and at home to Villa.

The general dislike of the name for the new stadium forced a change; fan power dictated that 'the Walkers Bowl' would be changed, not too radically, to 'the Walkers Stadium'.

The penultimate fixture saw Leicester hold Fulham to a goalless draw at Craven Cottage, where Savage collected his 14th caution of the season.

At least Leicester finished with a win, the first under Adams. Tottenham were the last visitors to Filbert Street but Matthew Piper offered hope for the future with the winner.

F.A. Barclaycard Premiership
Shot Efficiency

Key
■ Goals Scored ☐ Other Shots On Target

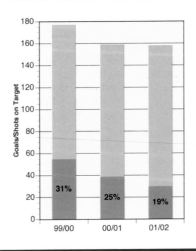

Season	Division	Shots Off Target	Shots On Target	Total Goals
1999 - 2000	P	n/a	177	55
2000 - 2001	P	n/a	159	39
2001 - 2002	P	140	158	30

Chart Analysis

The percentage of Shots On Target converted to goals by Leicester City fell by 6% for the second season running to just 19%, the second worst in the F.A. Barclaycard Premiership.

Their final goal total of 30 was their lowest ever in seven seasons in the Premier League.

statistics powered by **◆ SUPERBASE™**

 Fixtures, results and match reports – 4thegame.com

F.A. Barclaycard Premiership	Key
Team Discipline	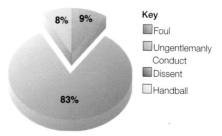 Forward ■ Midfield / □ Defence ■ Goalkeeper

Total Number Of Bookings

Total number of red cards	5
Total number of yellow cards	75

Referee Performance

Referee	Games Refereed	Red Cards	Yellow Cards
E.K.Wolstenholme	3	1	8
A.P.D'Urso	4	1	7
R.Styles	3	-	9

Type of Yellow Cards Received

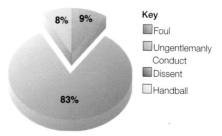

8% 9% 83%

Key
- □ Foul
- □ Ungentlemanly Conduct
- ■ Dissent
- □ Handball

Bookings by Position 1999/2000 - 2001/2002

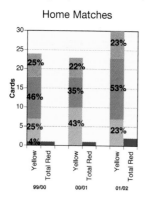

Home Matches

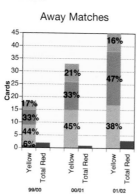

Away Matches

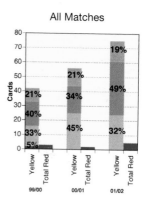

All Matches

Chart Analysis

Not only did Leicester top the pile when it came to cautions, they also clocked a club record number of Yellow Cards in their seven seasons in the Premier League.

While the number of bookings increased both home and away, midfielders claimed the lion's share of all cautions, taking over from the defence as the main offenders.

Red Cards also rose to their highest level since 1994-95 when the Foxes were also relegated from the top flight.

WORST IN THE LEAGUE...
- **Most Yellow Cards overall and away**

> "There wasn't much more we could have done. The players realise they have made individual errors."
> *Dave Bassett*
> *(April 2002)*

statistics powered by ◆ SUPERBASE™

→ **Win Barclaycard Premiership tickets - 4thegame.com**

Liverpool

F.A. Barclaycard Premiership Final standing for the 2001-2002 season

Final Position		Games Played	Games Won	Games Drawn	Games Lost	Goals For	Goals Against	Total Points
1	Arsenal	38	26	9	3	79	36	87
2	Liverpool	38	24	8	6	67	30	80
3	Manchester United	38	24	5	9	87	45	77

"When you take into account the trials and tribulations of this club, losing Babbel, Berger and Barmby, and then my illness, I think that in adversity our performances have been remarkable."

Gerard Houllier (May 2002)

Club Honours and Records

Football League Champions: 1900-01, 1905-06, 1921-22, 1922-23, 1946-47, 1963-64, 1965-66, 1972-73, 1975-76, 1976-77, 1978-79, 1979-80, 1981-82, 1982-83, 1983-84, 1985-86, 1987-88, 1989-90
Division 2 Champions:
1893-94, 1895-96, 1904-05, 1961-62
FA Cup Winners:
1965, 1974, 1986, 1989, 1992, 2001
League Cup Winners:
1981, 1982, 1983, 1984, 1995, 2001
League Super Cup Winners: 1986
European Cup Winners:
1976-77, 1977-78, 1980-81, 1983-84
UEFA Cup Winners: 1972-73, 1975-76, 2000-01
European Super Cup Winners: 1977, 2001
Record Victory: 11-0 v Stromsgodset Drammen, European Cup Winners' Cup 1st Round, 1st Leg, 17 September, 1974
Record defeat: 1-9 v Birmingham City, Division 2, 11 December, 1954
League goals in a season (team):
106, Division 2, 1895-96
League goals in a season (player):
41, Roger Hunt, Division 2, 1961-62
Career league goals:
245, Roger Hunt, 1959 to 1969
League appearances:
640, Ian Callaghan, 1960 to 1978
Reported transfer fee paid: £11,000,000 to Leicester City for Emile Heskey, March 2000
Reported transfer fee received: £11,000,000 from Leeds United for Robbie Fowler, November 2001

LIVERPOOL endured a traumatic season to finish second, securing automatic entry into the Champions League.

Having won the treble of F.A. Cup, Worthington Cup and UEFA Cup the previous season, Liverpool wanted more of the same. Success in the F.A. Barclaycard Premiership and the Champions League would allow Gerard Houllier's team to be spoken of in the same breath as the great teams of Bill Shankly and Bob Paisley.

In the summer, Robbie Fowler, Steven Gerrard, Jamie Carragher and Dietmar Hamann all signed new contracts as optimism grew ahead of the new campaign.

Christian Ziege, a bit-part player the previous season, was sold to Tottenham while Norwegian youngster John Arne Riise, wanted by Fulham, was signed from Monaco. The August signing of Polish international Jerzy Dudek, courted by Arsenal, cast doubts over the future of Sander Westerveld, who had played in all but two of Liverpool's 63 games the previous season. In addition England's promising Under-21 goalkeeper Chris Kirkland was signed from Coventry.

If Westerveld needed any indication of

The heart of the Barclaycard Premiership - 4thegame.com

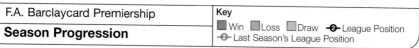

Liverpool

F.A. Barclaycard Premiership

Season Progression

Key: ■ Win ■ Loss □ Draw –②– League Position –②– Last Season's League Position

All Matches

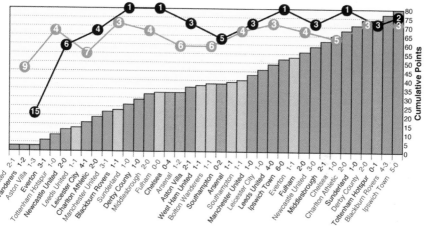

Home Matches

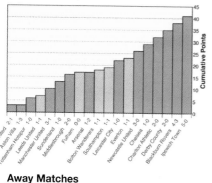

Away Matches

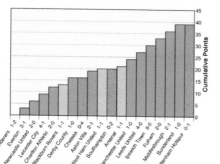

Chart Analysis

After two defeats in the first three games, Liverpool embarked on a 12-match unbeaten run, comprising nine victories, to head the F.A. Barclaycard Premiership in mid-December.

The last of those games, a 0-0 Anfield draw against Fulham, was also the first in a dire run in which just eight points and one win were collected in nine matches.

There followed a sensational sequence as Liverpool battled for the title, dropping just two points in 12 games and winning seven on the bounce before defeat at Tottenham Hotspur took the pressure off table-toppers Arsenal.

Wins over Blackburn and Ipswich at the end of the season ensured second place and automatic qualification for the Champions League group stages.

BEST IN THE LEAGUE...
- **Most points won at home**

statistics powered by **SUPERBASE**™

→ **All the latest news, views and opinion - 4thegame.com**

> "At 3-0 up we did take our foot off the pedal and maybe we should not have. Bayern are a great side and they looked like they might get back into it. But our defence played great and kept them at bay."
>
> *Emile Heskey after the Super Cup Final (August 2001)*

It's a fact

When Liverpool beat Manchester United home and away, they became the only team to achieve a Premier League 'double' twice over the Red Devils.

his standing, he received it even before the arrival of Dudek and Kirkland with Pegguy Arphexad starting against FC Haka of Finland in the qualifying stages of the Champions League. Westerveld played in the Charity Shield win over Manchester United but Arphexad was back for the start of the League campaign, against West Ham United.

Houllier admitted that the main target was the F.A. Barclaycard Premiership but not everything was sweetness and light in the Anfield camp. Fowler had been dropped from the Charity Shield squad following a training ground incident involving assistant manager Phil Thompson. It was the first sign that Fowler's lifelong association with Liverpool might be coming to an end though he did return after a two-game absence.

A 2-1 opening day win over West Ham, with a brace from Michael Owen, was not hugely impressive. With Fowler dropped and Emile Heskey suffering from flu, Jari Litmanen partnered Owen, who scored to take his latest sequence to 15 goals in ten games.

Liverpool made it five trophies in 2001 by beating Bayern Munich 3-2 in the Super Cup in Monaco but they fell to earth with a bump when they lost 2-1 at Bolton. Dudek arrived in time for his debut against Aston Villa at

F.A. Barclaycard Premiership
Half-Time/Full-Time Comparison

Key: ■ Win ■ Loss ■ Draw

Home				Away				Total			
Number of Home Half Time Wins	Full Time Result W	L	D	Number of Away Half Time Wins	Full Time Result W	L	D	Total number of Half Time Wins	Full Time Result W	L	D
9	8	-	1	10	9	-	1	19	17	-	2
Number of Home Half Time Losses	Full Time Result W	L	D	Number of Away Half Time Losses	Full Time Result W	L	D	Total number of Half Time Losses	Full Time Result W	L	D
3	-	2	1	4	-	3	1	7	-	5	2
Number of Home Half Time Draws	Full Time Result W	L	D	Number of Away Half Time Draws	Full Time Result W	L	D	Total number of Half Time Draws	Full Time Result W	L	D
7	4	-	3	5	3	1	1	12	7	1	4

Chart Analysis

statistics powered by ◆ SUPERBASE™

As the second best team in the League, Liverpool were predictably consistent throughout the matches they played.

They won 17 out of 19 games they were leading at half-time, and lost just once out of the 12 occasions when they were on level terms at the break.

On the down side, in the seven games they were losing at the interval, they went on to collect two solitary points.

 Fixtures, results and match reports – 4thegame.com

DATE	H/A	OPPONENT	H/T	F/T	POS	REFEREE	TEAM											SUBSTITUTES USED		
18-08	H	West Ham Utd	1:1	2:1	6	J.T.Winter	Arphexad	Babbel	Henchoz	Hyypia	Carragher	Biscan	McAllister 19	Hamann 78	Murphy ▲	Litmanen	Owen 19.78	Redknapp ▲	Riise ▲	Barmby ▲
27-08	A	Bolton	0:1	1:2	12	G.Poll	Westerveld	Babbel ▲	Henchoz ○	Hyypia	Carragher	Gerrard	McAllister 66	Hamann	Murphy	Fowler ▲	Owen	Redknapp ▲	Riise ▲66	Barmby ▲
08-09	H	Aston Villa	1:1	1:3	15	A.P.D'Urso	Dudek	Carragher ○	Henchoz ▲	Hyypia	Riise ▲	Gerrard ●46	McAllister 46	Hamann	Heskey	Fowler	Owen ▲	Owen ▲	Murphy ▲	Vignal ●
15-09	A	Everton	2:1	3:1	8	P.A.Durkin	Dudek	Carragher	Henchoz	Hyypia	Vignal	Gerrard 12	McAllister	Hamann	Murphy ▲	Heskey 30	Owen 30	McAllister ▲	Smicer ▲	-
22-09	H	Tottenham	0:0	1:0	5	D.J.Gallagher	Dudek	Carragher	Henchoz ○	Hyypia	Vignal ○	Barmby	Biscan	Hamann	Riise 52	Litmanen 57	Fowler ▲	Heskey ▲	Owen ▲	McAllister ▲
30-09	A	Newcastle Utd	1:0	2:0	6	G.P.Barber	Dudek	Carragher ○	Henchoz ○	Hyypia	Vignal	Murphy .86	Biscan	Hamann	Riise 57	Heskey	Fowler .86	Heskey ▲	Owen ▲	McAllister ▲
13-10	H	Leeds Utd	1:1	1:1	6	A.G.Wiley	Dudek	Carragher ○	Henchoz	Hyypia	Riise	Smicer	McAllister	Hamann	Murphy ▲69	Heskey	Fowler 69	Redknapp ▲	Litmanen ▲	Barmby ▲
20-10	A	Leicester City	3:0	4:1	4	M.R.Halsey	Dudek	Wright	Carragher	Hyypia 11	Riise 4	Gerrard ▲	McAllister 11	Hamann	Murphy ▲69	Heskey ▲	Fowler 4 43 90	Heskey ▲	Smicer ▲90	Berger ▲
27-10	A	Charlton	2:0	2:0	4	P.Jones	Dudek	Wright ●14	Henchoz	Carragher	Riise	Gerrard	Redknapp ○▲	Hamann 43	Murphy	Litmanen ▲	Owen ▲43	Berger ▲	Fowler ▲	Heskey ▲
04-11	H	Manchester Utd	2:0	3:1	2	G.Poll	Dudek	Carragher	Henchoz	Hyypia	Riise 39	Smicer ▲	Gerrard	Hamann 39	Murphy	Heskey 32 51	Owen ▲32 51	Fowler ▲	Berger ▲	-
17-11	A	Blackburn	1:0	1:1	1	M.A.Riley	Dudek	Carragher	Henchoz	Hyypia	Riise	Gerrard 30	McAllister	Hamann	Berger ▲	Fowler	Owen ▲30	Murphy ▲	Heskey ▲	-
25-11	H	Sunderland	1:0	1:0	1	S.G.Bennett	Dudek	Carragher	Henchoz	Hyypia	Riise	Smicer ▲	Gerrard 30	Hamann ●	Murphy	Fowler ▲	Owen ○6	Fowler ▲	McAllister ▲	Wright ▲
01-12	A	Derby County	1:0	1:0	1	G.P.Barber	Dudek	Carragher	Henchoz	Hyypia	Riise	Murphy	Gerrard	Hamann ▲21	Berger ▲6	Fowler	Owen ○6	Murphy ▲	McAllister ▲	Litmanen ▲
08-12	H	Middlesbrough	2:0	2:0	1	D.J.Gallagher	Dudek	Carragher	Henchoz	Hyypia	Riise	Murphy	McAllister	Hamann	Berger 27 45	Litmanen 45	Owen ▲27	Heskey ▲		
12-12	H	Fulham	0:0	0:0	1	J.T.Winter	Dudek	Carragher	Henchoz	Hyypia	Riise	Murphy ▲	Gerrard ▲	Hamann	McAllister	Heskey	Owen	Litmanen ▲	Biscan ▲	
16-12	A	Chelsea	0:2	0:4	3	M.R.Halsey	Dudek	Carragher ▲	Henchoz	Hyypia	Riise	Gerrard	Biscan ▲	Hamann	Murphy ○	Heskey	Owen	Litmanen ▲	Wright ▲	
23-12	H	Arsenal	0:1	1:2	3	P.A.Durkin	Dudek	Carragher	Henchoz ○	Hyypia	Riise	Murphy	Gerrard	Hamann	Heskey	Berger ▲	Owen 55	Litmanen ▲55	Smicer ▲	
26-12	A	Aston Villa	1:1	2:1	3	A.P.D'Urso	Dudek	Carragher	Henchoz ○	Hyypia	Riise	Smicer ▲73	Gerrard	Hamann	Berger ▲73	Heskey	Owen	Litmanen ▲9	McAllister ▲	Anelka ▲
29-12	A	West Ham Utd	0:1	1:1	4	R.Styles	Dudek	Carragher	Henchoz ▲	Hyypia	Riise	Smicer ▲	McAllister ▲	Hamann	Murphy ▲	Berger	Owen 88	Heskey ▲88	Gerrard ▲	Litmanen ▲
01-01	H	Bolton	0:0	1:1	4	C.R.Wilkes	Wright	Wright ▲	Henchoz	Hyypia	Riise	Smicer ▲	Gerrard 50	Hamann	Murphy ▲	Anelka	Owen 50	Litmanen ▲	Heskey ▲	Anelka ▲
09-01	A	Southampton	0:0	2:0	5	G.Poll	Dudek	Wright ▲	Henchoz	Hyypia	Carragher ○	Smicer ▲	Gerrard	Hamann	Murphy ▲	Anelka ▲	Owen 50	Berger ▲	Heskey ▲	Riise ▲
13-01	A	Arsenal	0:1	1:1	5	S.W.Dunn	Dudek	Carragher	Henchoz	Hyypia	Riise 68	Murphy ▲	Gerrard 68	Hamann	Anelka ▲	Berger	Owen	McAllister ▲	Heskey ▲	
19-01	H	Southampton	1:0	1:1	5	N.S.Barry	Dudek	Carragher	Henchoz ○	Hyypia	Riise	Murphy 8	Gerrard	Hamann 8	Berger ▲	Heskey	Owen 8	McAllister ▲	Smicer ▲	Anelka ▲
22-01	A	Manchester Utd	0:0	1:0	3	G.P.Barber	Dudek	Wright ○	Henchoz	Hyypia	Carragher ○	Murphy ▲85	Gerrard	Hamann	Anelka ▲85	Riise	Owen ●85	Anelka ▲	Berger ▲	
30-01	H	Leicester City	0:0	1:0	4	B.Knight	Dudek	Wright	Henchoz	Hyypia	Carragher ○	Smicer ○	McAllister	Hamann 57	Heskey	Riise	Anelka ▲61	McAllister ▲	Riise ▲	
03-02	A	Leeds Utd	1:0	4:0	3	G.Poll	Dudek	Wright ▲	Henchoz	Hyypia	Carragher	Murphy 17	Gerrard ▲61	Hamann	Heskey 61 63 90	Riise	Owen 90	Anelka ▲61	Heskey ▲63 90	
09-02	H	Ipswich Town	6:0	6:0	3	S.G.Bennett	Dudek ▲	Xavier 16	Henchoz	Hyypia	Wright	Murphy 52	Gerrard ▲16 43 62	Hamann	Riise 43 71 90	Riise	Owen 62 71	Anelka ▲90	Arphexad ▲	
23-02	H	Everton	0:0	1:0	3	D.R.Elleray	Dudek	Xavier 90	Henchoz	Hyypia	Wright	Murphy 72	McAllister	Hamann	Riise	Anelka 72	Owen	Smicer ▲	Heskey ▲	
02-03	A	Fulham	1:0	2:0	3	A.G.Wiley	Dudek	Xavier 90	Henchoz	Hyypia	Wright ▲	Smicer ▲	Murphy ▲	Hamann	Riise	Heskey	Anelka 13	Litmanen ▲90	Barmby ▲	
06-03	A	Newcastle Utd	1:0	1:0	3	J.T.Winter	Dudek	Xavier	Henchoz ○	Hyypia	Riise	Smicer ▲75	Murphy ○	Hamann 75	Heskey 53	Riise	Anelka 32	Owen ▲	Litmanen ▲	Barmby ▲
16-03	A	Middlesbrough	1:0	2:1	3	A.P.D'Urso	Dudek ○	Xavier ▲	Henchoz ○	Carragher	Hyypia	Smicer ▲33	Murphy ▲33	Hamann	Murphy 32 53	Riise 84	Heskey 33 84	Anelka ▲	Gerrard ▲	
24-03	H	Chelsea	0:0	1:0	3	M.R.Halsey	Dudek	Xavier ▲	Henchoz	Hyypia	Carragher ○	Murphy	Gerrard	Hamann	Berger ▲	Riise	Anelka	Litmanen ▲90	Smicer ▲90	Owen ▲90
30-03	H	Charlton	2:0	2:0	3	D.J.Gallagher	Dudek	Xavier ▲	Henchoz	Hyypia	Riise	Murphy 23	Gerrard	Hamann	Berger	Heskey	Anelka	Smicer ▲23 36	McAllister ▲	Litmanen ▲
13-04	A	Sunderland	0:0	1:0	3	D.J.Gallagher	Dudek	Xavier ▲	Henchoz	Hyypia	Carragher 55	Gerrard ○55	Litmanen ▲	Hamann	Riise	Anelka	Owen 55	Berger ▲	Heskey ▲	Murphy ▲
20-04	H	Derby County	1:0	2:0	3	M.A.Riley	Dudek	Carragher	Henchoz	Hyypia	Riise	Smicer ▲15	Gerrard ○	Hamann	Murphy ▲	Anelka	Owen 15 89	Heskey ▲89	Berger ▲	Berger ▲
27-04	A	Tottenham	0:1	0:1	3	P.Jones	Dudek	Xavier ▲	Henchoz	Hyypia 53	Carragher	Smicer ▲	Murphy ▲	Hamann	Murphy 87	Anelka	Owen ○	Anelka ▲39	Litmanen ▲	Berger ▲
08-05	H	Blackburn	2:1	4:3	3	A.G.Wiley	Dudek	Carragher 87	Henchoz	Hyypia	Riise 24 39	Murphy 24 53	Gerrard ▲	Hamann	Heskey 87	Riise 13 35	Anelka 39	Smicer ▲	Xavier ▲	Berger ▲
11-05	H	Ipswich Town	2:0	5:0	2	S.W.Dunn	Dudek	Xavier 13	Henchoz	Hyypia	Carragher 46	Murphy ▲57	Gerrard ▲	Hamann	Riise 13 35	Heskey	Owen 46 88	McAllister ▲	Smicer ▲35 57	Anelka ▲88

F.A. Barclaycard Premiership
Squad List

Position	Name	Appearances	Appearances as Substitute	Goals or Clean Sheets	Goal Assists	Yellow Cards	Red Cards
G	P.Arphexad	1	1				
G	J.Dudek	35		18			
G	C.Kirkland	1					
G	S.Westerveld	1					
D	M.Babbel	2					
D	J.Carragher	33				2	7
D	S.Henchoz	37					4
D	S.Hyypia	37		3			3
D	J.Riise	34	4	7	4	1	
D	G.Vignal	3	1			2	
D	S.Wright	10	2		1	2	1
D	A.Xavier	9	1	1	2	1	
M	N.Barmby	2	4			1	
M	P.Berger	12	9	1	3		
M	I.Biscan	4	1				
M	S.Gerrard	26	2	3	8	5	1
M	D.Hamann	31		1	6	2	1
M	G.McAllister	14	11		4		
M	D.Murphy	31	5	6	8	4	
M	J.Redknapp	2	2	1		1	
M	V.Smicer	13	9	4	5	2	
F	N.Anelka	13	7	4	2		
F	R.Fowler	8	2	3	2	2	
F	E.Heskey	26	9	9	10	3	
F	J.Litmanen	8	13	4	1		
F	M.Owen	25	4	19	3	1	

Anfield – but they lost again, the visitors winning 3-1 while Gerrard was sent off.

Liverpool dropped to tenth despite a 3-1 derby win over Everton in September where Nick Barmby was dropped for his own safety amid fears he could be a target for abuse from fans of his former club.

Owen committed himself to Liverpool for five more years and fortunes improved on the field with wins over Spurs and Newcastle. The fact that the holders were dispatched from the Worthington Cup by little Grimsby at Anfield did not seen to worry the club excessively. Yet events during the 1-1 draw with Leeds on 13 October were to prove a defining moment in Liverpool's season.

During the second half of the 1-1 draw, Houllier was rushed to the Royal Liverpool Hospital after complaining of chest pains. He was transferred to a heart and lung unit and overnight underwent an 11-hour open-heart operation which saved his life.

Liverpool immediately insisted that Houllier would not be replaced, even though he was told he would have to rest for a minimum of three months. Thompson was put in charge and, after winning in Kiev in the Champions League, the players responded to the worrying incident by beating Leicester 4-1.

Houllier was discharged from hospital in early November and, after beating Charlton, Liverpool faced Manchester United at Anfield in November and won 3-1 to take the leadership of the F.A. Barclaycard Premiership for the first time since September 1998.

Owen shone again, scoring twice to take his tally for club and country to 23 goals in just 21 competitive games. Riise was also coming of age, scoring a spectacular free kick as Liverpool rose to the challenge of wresting the title off United.

The Reds drew with Blackburn and

 Win Barclaycard Premiership tickets – 4thegame.com

F.A. Barclaycard Premiership
Top Goal Scorer

Michael Owen

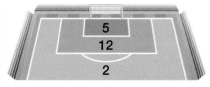

Total Premier League Goals Scored:	Percentage Of The Team's League Goals:
19	28%

Goals Scored From

5
12
2

O wen was again in a class of his own at Anfield, notching his best F.A. Barclaycard Premiership haul with 19 goals, the perfect way to cap a season in which the international front his goals had propelled England to the World Cup finals. Add two more in the F.A. Cup and six in Europe and it was another fruitful season for the striker, who struck his 100th goal in 183 games in the 1-1 December draw at West Ham. Owen was particularly prolific in the first half of the season, when he scored 23 goals in 21 games for Liverpool and England. He was named European Footballer of the Year in December – the first Englishman to receive the honour in 22 years since Kevin Keegan in 1979.

"It would be great to be among the goals all the time but I know that is not possible. I will hit a lean patch sooner or later and when I do, I'll start getting some stick."
Michael Owen

Goals Resulting From
Key
- Open Play
- Corner
- Indirect Free Kick
- Direct Free Kick
- Penalty

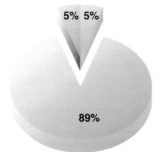

5% 5%

89%

	Right Foot	Left Foot	Header
Open Play	13	1	3
Set piece	1	1	-

Goal Assists

Total number of goal assists	3

Teams Scored Against

Against	Home	Away
Derby County	2	1
Ipswich Town	1	2
West Ham United	2	1
Charlton Athletic	1	1
Manchester United	2	0
Blackburn Rovers	0	1
Everton	0	1
Leeds United	0	1
Middlesbrough	1	0
Southampton	1	0
Sunderland	0	1
Total Goals Scored	**10**	**9**

➡ The heart of the Barclaycard Premiership - 4thegame.com

"Marco van Basten won it three times, Michel Platini as well...add my name to those of Franz Beckenbauer, Johann Cruyff, Rivaldo, Bobby Charlton, Kevin Keegan – I am extremely proud.."

Michael Owen on being named European Footballer Of The Year (December 2001)

were given a lesson by Barcelona in Europe, losing 3-1 at Anfield. Fowler finally left, joining Leeds for £11m.

Three straight League wins maintained Liverpool's position at the top before they suffered their worst reverse, a 4-0 December drubbing at Chelsea, their heaviest defeat for nine years. Owen was missing with a hamstring problem but that was no excuse. A 2-1 home defeat by ten man Arsenal two days before Christmas allowed the Gunners to leapfrog over Liverpool into second place. It also set the alarm bells ringing at Anfield.

With Fowler departed, Liverpool made a shock swoop for former Arsenal star Nicolas Anelka, unwanted by Paris St-Germain and signed on loan to the end of the season.

The pressure, however, was on Thompson. With Houllier still recovering at home, Liverpool dropped valuable points at the turn of the year. A draw at West Ham was followed by another stalemate, against Bolton, and a shock defeat at Southampton where Owen was again absent. Sami Hyypia, again outstanding in defence, had conceded a penalty as the Saints marched to a 2-0 win. From being 11 points ahead of United a month earlier, Liverpool had slipped to a point adrift of the Champions

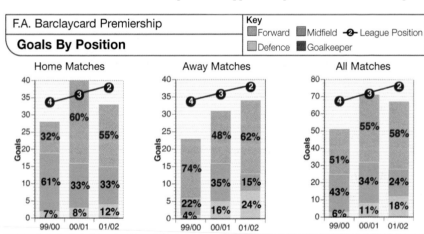

F.A. Barclaycard Premiership
Goals By Position

Key
Forward   Midfield   League Position
Defence   Goalkeeper

Chart Analysis

statistics powered by **SUPERBASE**™

Despite scoring four less goals overall compared to last season, Liverpool managed to finish one place higher in the table.

For the first time ever in their Premier League history, the Reds scored more goals on the road than they did at Anfield.

Overall, the number of goals attributed to forwards and defenders rose, while the share from midfield dropped by 10%.

 All the latest news, views and opinion – 4thegame.com

with just over half the season played.

Liverpool drew Arsenal in the F.A. Cup but had to meet the Gunners in the League beforehand and drew 1-1 at Highbury. Another draw, at home to Southampton, left the Reds anchored in fifth place but, after exiting the F.A. Cup at Highbury, fortunes began to improve. Carragher had foolishly been dismissed during the Cup tie after throwing a coin back into the crowd. He went on to miss four games but Abel Xavier crossed the city to sign for Liverpool to add his weight to the squad.

Heskey had struggled in attack – he last scored in November – but he followed the winner against Leicester at the end of January with four goals in two games as the Reds returned to winning ways.

Houllier was back at training, offering a timely boost, and the Reds hit ten goals in seven days, beginning with a stunning 4-0 February win over Leeds at Elland Road. Inspired by a virtuoso performance from Gerrard, an own goal by Rio Ferdinand, and the latest from Owen, they secured a remarkable win. Ipswich were the next to suffer, losing 6-0 to the travelling Reds.

That win took Liverpool back to the top of the F.A. Barclaycard Premiership but with Carragher suspended, Gerrard injured and Heskey rested, the Reds were held to a 1-1 draw against Everton.

March wins over Fulham, Newcastle

F.A. Barclaycard Premiership
Team Performance Table

League Position	Team	Points won from a possible six	Percentage of points won at home	Percentage of points won away	Overall percentage of points won
1	Arsenal	1/6			
2	Liverpool	80			
3	Manchester Utd	6/6	58%	83%	71%
4	Newcastle Utd	6/6			
5	Leeds United	4/6			
6	Chelsea	3/6			
7	West Ham Utd	4/6			
8	Aston Villa	3/6	80%	33%	57%
9	Tottenham H	3/6			
10	Blackburn R	4/6			
11	Southampton	1/6			
12	Middlesbrough	6/6			
13	Fulham	4/6	60%	80%	70%
14	Charlton Athletic	6/6			
15	Everton	4/6			
16	Bolton W	1/6			
17	Sunderland	6/6			
18	Ipswich Town	6/6	87%	80%	83%
19	Derby County	6/6			
20	Leicester City	6/6			

The table shows how many points out of a possible six Liverpool have taken off each of the teams in the four sections. The other columns show as a percentage how many points they have taken from those available.

Chart Analysis

statistics powered by  SUPERBASE™

Liverpool performed strongly throughout the League. Against teams in their own sector, they collected 17 points out of 24 overall, including ten out of 12 away from home.

Conversely their form away from Anfield dipped considerably against teams in the second sector.

It then picked up again against teams in the third sector, where they picked up three extra points on their travels compared to games at Anfield.

As expected they won the greatest number of points in games against teams in the bottom five, where they registered half of their eight 'doubles'.

Liverpool managed to take points off every team in the Premier League at some point in the season.

➡ Fixtures, results and match reports - 4thegame.com

and Middlesbrough were followed by a 1-0 win over Chelsea, Vladimir Smicer netting the winner, and Liverpool were top again. All this achieved without Owen, who had suffered his hamstring problem again.

Away from the League, Liverpool played Roma at home needing a win to qualify for the quarter-finals of the Champions League. Houllier surprised everybody by taking his place on the bench and a 2-0 win secured their progress. Thompson described the occasion as one of Liverpool's greatest nights.

At the end of March, with the finishing post in sight, Liverpool beat Charlton with another goal from Smicer, while Owen returned with his 23rd club goal of the season, and 15th of the League campaign, to keep the Reds ahead of Arsenal and Manchester United.

Liverpool's European dream ended when, in successive games, they won 1-0 at home to Bayer Leverkusen but lost 4-2 in Germany. There were fears that Owen had broken his foot in the BayArena, but X-rays confirmed only bruising, allowing both Houllier and Sven-Goran Eriksson a collective sigh of relief.

On the League front Liverpool remained firmly attached to the coat-tails of leaders Arsenal. Owen proved his fitness with the winner at Sunderland and then scored

It's a fact

Liverpool set a club record of seven straight Premier League wins when they beat Derby 2-0 at home in April.

"There's no shock Emile is back scoring goals. Every striker has a run without goals. It's how you come out of them that counts and Emile has certainly done that well."

Michael Owen on Emile Heskey (February 2002)

F.A. Barclaycard Premiership
Goals By Time Period

Key
■ Goals Scored   ■ Goals Conceded

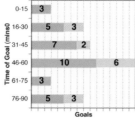

Home Matches

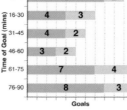

Away Matches

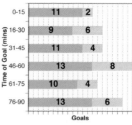

All Matches

Chart Analysis

statistics powered by **SUPERBASE**™

Overall, Liverpool consistently outscored opponents throughout their games. They were particularly strong in the opening 15 minutes, scoring 11 and conceding just two, both away from home.

They finished strongly too, scoring over twice as many goals in the final half-hour at home and away than they conceded.

At home, Liverpool did not concede any goals during 0-15 and 61-75 minutes.

 Win Barclaycard Premiership tickets – 4thegame.com

Liverpool

F.A. Barclaycard Premiership
Goals Resulting From

	Six Yard Area				Inside Area				Outside Area				Total			
	Shots		Headers		Shots		Headers		Shots		Headers		Shots		Headers	
	Home	Away	Home	Away	Home	Away	Home	Away	Home	Away	Home	Away	Home	Away	Home	Away
Open Play	2	2	2	1	18	19	1	1	4	4	-	-	24	25	3	2
	3	2	-	1	5	6	1	1	-	2	-	-	8	10	1	2
Direct Free Kick									-	-			0	0		
									-	-			0	0		
Indirect Free Kick	-	-	1	1	-	-	2	-	1	-	-	-	1	0	3	1
	-	-	-	-	1	-	1	-	-	-	-	-	1	0	1	0
Penalty	-	-	-	-	-	1	-	-	-	-	-	-	0	1	0	0
	-	-	-	-	2	1	-	-	-	-	-	-	2	1	0	0
Corner	1	2	1	-	-	1	-	1	-	-	-	-	1	3	1	1
	-	-	-	-	1	1	-	1	-	-	-	-	1	1	0	1
Totals	3	4	4	2	18	21	3	2	5	4	0	0	26	29	7	4
	3	2	0	1	9	8	2	2	0	2	0	0	12	12	2	3

How Goals Were Scored
Home & Away Matches

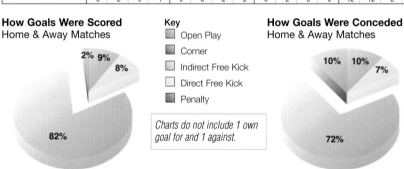

Key
- ☐ Open Play
- ☐ Corner
- ☐ Indirect Free Kick
- ☐ Direct Free Kick
- ☐ Penalty

2% 9% 8% 82%

How Goals Were Conceded
Home & Away Matches

10% 10% 7% 72%

Charts do not include 1 own goal for and 1 against.

Goals Scored from
Key ☐ Open Play ☐ Set Piece

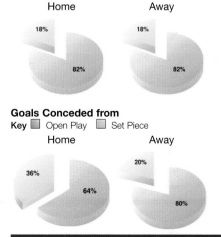

Home — 18% / 82% Away — 18% / 82%

Goals Conceded from
Key ☐ Open Play ☐ Set Piece

Home — 36% / 64% Away — 20% / 80%

Chart Analysis

Liverpool's consistency extended to their scoring feats at home and away.

Not only did they score an identical number of goals from both Open Play and Set Pieces at home and away, they scored over 50% of their goals overall from Shots Inside Area from Open Play.

The Reds conceded nearly twice as many goals from Set Pieces at home as they did away.

However, they did score over twice as many goals from Headers overall as they conceded.

statistics powered by SUPERBASE™

→ **The heart of the Barclaycard Premiership – 4thegame.com**

> "'Moving from Anfield is not a decision that has been taken lightly. We have had to look at what is in the best interests of the club in the future. We must keep up with the game's other leading clubs."
>
> *Chief executive*
> *Rick Parry*
> *(May 2002)*

It's a fact

Michael Owen scored his 100th goal for Liverpool in 183 games in the 1-1 draw at West Ham in January. He had been on 99 for three weeks.

both goals in the 2-0 win over Derby, taking his tally to four goals in three games.

The long-serving Jamie Redknapp severed his Anfield ties with a free transfer to Tottenham in mid-April but England striker Emile Heskey claimed he wanted to finish his career at Anfield and was linked with a new £10m contract.

Next stop for Liverpool was White Hart Lane, a ground where they had lost on their previous three visits. A win was vital but Spurs' Gus Poyet scored the game's only goal, leaving Liverpool two points behind Manchester United and four behind leaders Arsenal who had a game in hand.

In their penultimate game, Liverpool won 4-3 in a thriller with Blackburn while Arsenal were winning the title at Old Trafford. That meant that a win in the final game, at home to Ipswich would guarantee second spot.

A 5-0 thrashing duly brought the season to a satisfying end with Riise scoring two more sensational goals and Owen claiming his 19th of the season in the League.

In the week following the end of the season, Liverpool announced plans to leave their Anfield home and move into a new state of the art stadium in Stanley Park – just 300 yards away from the site of the world-famous ground.

F.A. Barclaycard Premiership
Shot Efficiency

Key ■ Goals Scored ■ Other Shots On Target

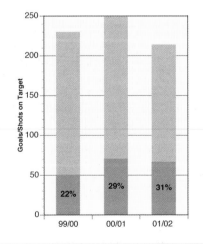

Season	Division	Shots Off Target	Shots On Target	Total Goals
1999 - 2000	P	n/a	230	51
2000 - 2001	P	n/a	249	71
2001 - 2002	P	200	214	67

Chart Analysis

Although Liverpool managed the least Shots On Target in their ten years in the Premier League, they also finished with their highest ever percentage converted into goals.

In a season which saw them hit the target more often than not, they hit 7% more Shots On Target than Off.

statistics powered by ● SUPERBASE™

 All the latest news, views and opinion - 4thegame.com

Liverpool

Key
■ Forward ■ Midfield
□ Defence ■ Goalkeeper

Total Number Of Bookings

Total number of red cards	3
Total number of yellow cards	41

Referee Performance

Referee	Games Refereed	Red Cards	Yellow Cards
A.P.D'Urso	3	1	5
G.P.Barber	3	-	8
M.R.Halsey	3	-	6

Type of Yellow Cards Received

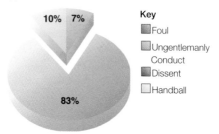

10% 7% 83%

Key
■ Foul
□ Ungentlemanly Conduct
■ Dissent
□ Handball

Bookings by Position 1999/2000 - 2001/2002

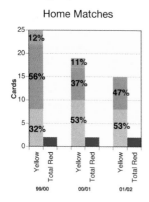

Home Matches

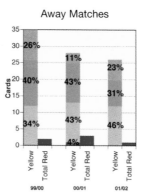

Away Matches

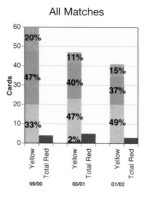

All Matches

Chart Analysis

Liverpool saw the number of cards decline on all fronts as they registered their lowest final tally of bookings and Red Cards since 1995-96 and 1998-99 respectively.

The contribution from forwards was non-existent at Anfield with the front men focused on scoring goals. That left the midfielders and defenders to share the cautions fairly evenly between them.

Although Liverpool's matches were refereed by 17 different officials, four of those did not hand out any cards in the five matches they officiated at.

"This season has told me a lot in terms of the mental strength my players possess. It tells me they can deal with what the future will bring, when they try to take the next step, the one that is the most exciting to play for."

Gerard Houllier
(April 2002)

statistics powered by SUPERBASE™

Manchester United

Final Position		Games Played	Games Won	Games Drawn	Games Lost	Goals For	Goals Against	Total Points
	F.A. Barclaycard Premiership Final standing for the 2001-2002 season							
2	Liverpool	38	24	8	6	67	30	80
3	Manchester United	38	24	5	9	87	45	77
4	Newcastle United	38	21	8	9	74	52	71

> "I think some people react to adversity. I have always done that and we will be ready for next season."
>
> *Sir Alex Ferguson (May 2002)*

Club Honours and Records

Premier League Champions: 1992-93, 1993-94, 1995-96, 1996-97, 1998-99, 1999-00, 2000-01

Football League Champions: 1907-08, 1910-11, 1951-52, 1955-56, 1956-57, 1964-65, 1966-67

Division 2 Champions: 1935-36, 1974-75

FA Cup Winners: 1909, 1948, 1963, 1977, 1983, 1985, 1990, 1994, 1996, 1999

League Cup Winners: 1992

European Cup Winners: 1967-68, 1998-99

European Cup Winners' Cup Winners: 1990-91

European Super Cup Winners: 1991

Inter-Continental Cup: 1999

Record victory:
10-0 v RSC Anderlecht, European Cup Preliminary Round, 2nd Leg, 26 September, 1956

Record defeat:
0-7 v Blackburn Rovers, Division 1, 10 April, 1926

League goals in a season (team):
103, Division 1, 1956-57 and 1958-59

League goals in a season (player):
32, Dennis Viollet, 1959-60

Career league goals:
199, Bobby Charlton, 1956-73

League appearances:
606, Bobby Charlton, 1956-73

Reported transfer fee paid: £28,100,000 to Lazio for Juan Sebastian Veron, July 2001

Reported transfer fee received: £16,600,000 from Lazio for Jaap Stam, August 2001

MANCHESTER United suffered a traumatic season in 2001-02. What began so promisingly ended with third place and having to enter pre-qualification for the Champions League.

In the summer of 2001, confusion reigned over the future of Sir Alex Ferguson. During June, the board announced it would enter into negotiations with the manager to agree a remuneration package which would 'enhance the terms of his current contract with Manchester United'.

On the pitch, United seemed better prepared than ever before. The seven-times winners of the Premier League were seeking their fourth successive title, something that had never been achieved before in top flight football.

Ruud van Nistelrooy's £19m transfer from PSV Eindhoven, put on ice after the Dutchman suffered a serious knee injury, was back on again, and he was soon joined by Juan Sebastian Veron. Lazio's Argentine international arrived at Old Trafford for a British record £28.1m. A day later United announced that Ferguson was staying and would take up an ambassadorial role. Ferguson, who lost his assistant Steve McClaren to Middlesbrough before the start of the

manutd.com Official Manchester United Website

Manchester United

Key
■ Win ■ Loss ■ Draw −❷− League Position
−❷− Last Season's League Position

All Matches

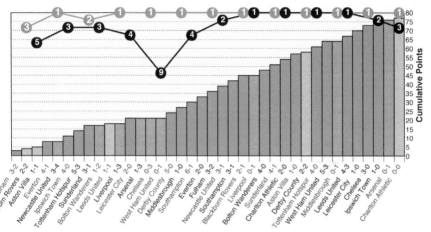

Home Matches

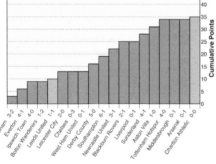

Away Matches

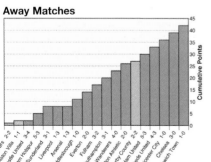

Chart Analysis

After picking up 17 points in their opening eight fixtures, United produced the worst run in their Premier League history to tumble to ninth following five defeats in the next seven games.

The home loss to West Ham United was number six of the season, the third in a row and the first time that the club had lost two consecutive home games in the Premier League.

They bounced back in some style, winning 12 out of the next 13 to soar from ninth in the table to top.

Although their form remained good in the run-in, an unexpected defeat at home to Middlesbrough cost them dear. They relinquished the title to Arsenal on the penultimate day of the season, their sixth home defeat of and their ninth overall, their highest tally ever in the Premier League.

BEST IN THE LEAGUE...
• **Joint longest scoring streak away from Home**

statistics powered by ◆ SUPERBASE™

> **"It is the nature of the team at the moment that there is a casualness about our defending."**
>
> *Sit Alex Ferguson*
> *(August 2001)*

season, said: "When you've been at the club as long as I have it gets in your blood." Meanwhile, Bayern Munich's Ottmar Hitzfeld and Martin O'Neill of Celtic were being tipped as potential successors.

Having won the previous season's title with a month to spare, United approached the season's curtain raiser, the Charity Shield, with some confidence. Van Nistelrooy got off the mark in Cardiff, but United lost 2-1 to Liverpool.

The Red Devils started the F.A. Barclaycard Premiership campaign with a 3-2 win over newly-promoted Fulham but Ferguson was not impressed, lambasting his defence for the way Louis Saha was able to score twice.

In their next game, United drew 2-2 at Blackburn where David Beckham scored an own goal as well as scoring at the right end. By conceding four in their opening two games, United had suffered their worst defensive start to a season for six years. The reckless act of Fabien Barthez dribbling out of his area was not the last time the goalkeeper's antics gave his side problems.

Absent from that game was Jaap Stam, sold to Lazio for £16.6m. It was a move which surprised many observers although shortly afterwards Laurent Blanc arrived on a free transfer from Inter Milan.

September produced goals galore, but not all of them at

It's a fact

When United lost 2-1 at home to Bolton, it was the first time in their Premier League history that they had lost after taking the lead at Old Trafford.

F.A. Barclaycard Premiership
Half-Time/Full-Time Comparison

Key: ■ Win ■ Loss ■ Draw

Home				Away				Total			
Number of Home Half Time Wins	Full Time Result W	L	D	Number of Away Half Time Wins	Full Time Result W	L	D	Total number of Half Time Wins	Full Time Result W	L	D
9	9	-	-	10	8	1	1	19	17	1	1
Number of Home Half Time Losses	Full Time Result W	L	D	Number of Away Half Time Losses	Full Time Result W	L	D	Total number of Half Time Losses	Full Time Result W	L	D
2	-	2	-	4	1	2	1	6	1	4	1
Number of Home Half Time Draws	Full Time Result W	L	D	Number of Away Half Time Draws	Full Time Result W	L	D	Total number of Half Time Draws	Full Time Result W	L	D
8	2	4	2	5	4	-	1	13	6	4	3

Chart Analysis

statistics powered by ◆ SUPERBASE™

Manchester United were unstoppable at home whenever they went into the break holding an advantage. Equally, the two games they were losing at half-time at Old Trafford ended in defeat for the Reds.

Although they only managed to convert one half-time defeat into a win, it came in memorable fashion; down 3-0 at Tottenham when the players went in for the break, the game finished 5-3 to United.

---

manutd.com Official Manchester United Website

F.A. Barclaycard Premiership — Results Table

DATE	H/A	OPPONENT	H/T	F/T	POS	REFEREE	TEAM										SUBSTITUTES USED			
19-08	A	Fulham	1-1	3-2	4	P.Jones	Barthez	Irwin ▲	Neville G	Stam	Silvestre 53	Beckham 35	Neville P ▲	Veron ▲	Giggs 35	Scholes	v. N'rooy ▲51 53	Cole ▲51	Brown ▲	Chadwick ▲
22-08	A	Blackburn	1-0	2-2	3	A.G.Wiley	Barthez	Irwin ▲	Johnsen	Brown	Silvestre	Beckham 78	Keane	Veron 20	Giggs 20	Scholes ▲	van Nistelrooy ▲	Neville G ▲	Yorke ▲78	Cole ▲
26-08	A	Aston Villa	0-1	1-1	5	G.P.Barber	Carroll	Neville G ▲	Johnsen	Brown	Silvestre ▲	Beckham ▲	Keane	Veron 21	Giggs 90	Scholes ▲	van Nistelrooy ▲	Cole ▲	Solskjær ▲	Neville P ▲
08-09	H	Everton	2-0	4-1	2	D.J.Gallagher	Barthez	Neville G ▲	Blanc	Brown	Neville P	Chadwick ▲40	Keane 21	Veron 64	Fortune 46	Cole 40	Yorke ▲	van Nistelrooy ▲	Silvestre ▲	Beckham ▲90
15-09	A	Newcastle Utd	1-2	3-4	4	S.G.Bennett	Barthez	Neville G ▲'62	Blanc	Brown	Neville P	Beckham	Keane ●	Veron 64	Giggs 62	Cole ▲29	v. N'rooy 29 64	Scholes ▲		
22-09	H	Ipswich Town	2-0	4-0	3	N.S.Barry	Barthez	Neville P	May	Johnsen 13	Silvestre	Chadwick ▲	Scholes	Butt	Fortune	Cole 20 89 90	Cole 20 89.90	Veron ▲	Scholes ▲89	
29-09	A	Tottenham	0-3	5-3	2	J.T.Winter	Barthez	Neville G 46	Blanc 58	Johnsen	Irwin ▲	Beckham '58 87	Scholes ▲	Veron 76	Fortune	Cole 46	van Nistelrooy 72	Silvestre ▲76 87	Solskjær ▲76 87	
13-10	A	Sunderland	1-0	3-1	3	G.Poll	Carroll	Neville G	Blanc ▲	Brown	Silvestre	Chadwick 34 66	Butt	Scholes ▲	Giggs ▲59	Cole 66 59	Solskjær ▲	Yorke ▲	Stewart ▲	Neville P ▲
20-10	H	Bolton	1-1	1-2	3	G.P.Barber	Barthez	Neville P	May ▲	Brown	Silvestre	Scholes ▲	Butt	Veron 25	Yorke ▲	Cole 25	Solskjær ▲	Chadwick ▲	Neville G ▲	Giggs ▲
27-10	H	Leeds Utd	0-2	1-1	5	D.J.Gallagher	Barthez	Neville P	Blanc	Brown	Silvestre	Beckham ▲50	Butt ● ▲	Veron	Giggs 89	Scholes ●	van Nistelrooy	Solskjær ▲89	Yorke ▲	·
04-11	A	Liverpool	0-2	1-3	6	G.Poll	Barthez	Irwin ▲50	Blanc	Brown	Silvestre	Beckham ▲-50	Butt ◄ ▲	Veron	Fortune	Yorke ▲	van Nistelrooy	Solskjær ▲	Scholes ▲	Yorke ▲
17-11	H	Leicester City	1-0	2-0	4	A.P.D'Urso	Barthez	Neville G ▲49	Blanc	Irwin ▲	Silvestre ▲14	Beckham 20	Scholes	Veron ▲	Giggs ●	Yorke 49	van Nistelrooy ▲'20	Fortune ▲	Silvestre ▲	·
25-11	A	Arsenal	0-1	1-3	6	P.Jones	Barthez	Neville G	Blanc ▲	Brown	Silvestre ▲14	Beckham	Keane	Veron ▲	Fortune	Scholes 14	van Nistelrooy ▲	Neville P ▲	Yorke ▲	Solskjær ▲
01-12	H	Chelsea	0-1	0-3	7	A.G.Wiley	Barthez	Brown	Blanc	Keane	Silvestre	Beckham ▲	Scholes ●	Veron	Fortune ▲	Cole ▲	Cole ▲	Solskjær ▲	Chadwick ▲	Neville G ▲
08-12	H	West Ham Utd	0-0	0-1	9	P.A.Durkin	Barthez	Neville P	Blanc	O'Shea	Silvestre	Chadwick ▲	Keane ●	Butt ▲	Scholes	Solskjær	Solskjær ▲	Yorke ▲	Cole ▲	Beckham ▲
12-12	H	Derby County	2-0	5-0	5	M.R.Halsey	Barthez ▲	Neville G	Blanc	Silvestre 6	Veron	Veron 10 63	Keane 10 63	Butt ▲	Scholes 89	Solskjær 6 10 58 89	Solskjær 6 10 58 89	v. N'rooy ▲56 63	Carroll ▲	Silvestre ▲
15-12	A	Middlesbrough	0-0	1-0	5	D.R.Elleray	Barthez ▲	Neville G	Blanc	Silvestre	Veron	Keane ▲	Keane ▲	Veron ▲	Scholes	Solskjær	Solskjær ▲41	Giggs ▲75	Neville P ▲	·
22-12	H	Southampton	3-0	6-1	4	S.W.Dunn	Carroll	Neville P 78	O'Shea ▲	Blanc	Veron	Keane ▲34 72	Veron	Scholes 89	Solskjær	Solskjær ▲41	Solskjær ▲41	Wallwork ▲	Giggs ▲72 78	Beckham ▲
26-12	A	Everton	0-0	2-0	5	U.D.Rennie	Barthez ▲	Neville G	Blanc	Veron	Butt 41	Butt ▲	Butt	Scholes ●1 54	Giggs 5 45 47	Solskjær	Giggs 5 45 47	van Nistelrooy 85	Beckham ▲78	·
30-12	A	Fulham	2-1	3-2	5	D.J.Gallagher	Barthez	Neville G ●	Blanc	Veron	Butt	Beckham 45	Butt	Scholes	Scholes 50 62	Solskjær ●'450	Giggs 5 45 47	van Nistelrooy ▲24	Beckham ▲	·
02-01	H	Newcastle Utd	1-0	3-1	7	P.Jones	Barthez	Neville P ▲	Blanc ▲	Veron	Butt	Beckham ▲	Butt	Scholes 50 62	Solskjær 50 62	Solskjær ●'450	van Nistelrooy 45 63	Irwin ▲	Yorke ▲	·
13-01	A	Southampton	2-1	3-1	1	S.G.Bennett	Barthez	Neville P ▲	Blanc ●	Silvestre ▲	Veron	Beckham ▲45	Keane 62	Scholes 24	Scholes 9.45	Solskjær 63	van Nistelrooy 45	Giggs ▲81	Beckham ▲	Butt ▲
19-01	H	Blackburn	1-0	2-1	1	U.D.Rennie	Barthez	Neville G ●	Blanc 45	Silvestre	Veron ●	Beckham	Keane 81	Veron	Scholes	Solskjær	van Nistelrooy	Giggs ▲	Irwin ▲	Butt ▲
22-01	H	Liverpool	0-0	0-1	1	G.P.Barber	Barthez	Neville P	Blanc	Silvestre	Veron	Beckham ▲	Keane	Butt	Scholes	Giggs	van Nistelrooy	Solskjær ▲		
29-01	A	Bolton	2-0	4-0	1	A.P.D'Urso	Barthez	Neville P	Blanc ▲	Silvestre	Veron ▲	Beckham 39 64	Keane ▲	Scholes	Giggs 15 84	Solskjær ▲15 39 64	Solskjær ▲15.39 64	van Nistelrooy 84	Fortune ▲	O'Shea ▲
02-02	H	Sunderland	4-1	4-1	1	R.Styles	Barthez	Neville P 6	Blanc ◄	Silvestre	Beckham 25 28	Beckham 25 28	Scholes	Giggs ▲25 44	Giggs 6	Solskjær 6	Solskjær 6	van N'rooy 28 44	Butt ▲	O'Shea ▲
10-02	A	Charlton	1-0	2-0	1	A.G.Wiley	Barthez	Neville P 6	Blanc ◄	Silvestre	Beckham	Keane 33	Keane 33	Veron	Giggs ▲74	Solskjær ▲74	Solskjær ▲33 74	van Nistelrooy ▲	Fortune ▲	Veron ▲
23-02	H	Aston Villa	0-0	1-0	1	J.T.Winter	Barthez	Irwin ▲	Blanc	Johnsen	Beckham	Keane	Keane	Butt	Veron	Solskjær	van Nistelrooy 50	Johnsen ▲	Fortune ▲	·
03-03	A	Derby County	1-1	2-2	1	S.W.Dunn	Barthez	Neville G	Johnsen	Silvestre	Beckham	Scholes 41	Veron 60	Veron ▲	Scholes 41	Fortune	Solskjær	Johnsen ▲	O'Shea ▲	·
06-03	H	Tottenham	2-0	4-0	1	M.A.Riley	Barthez	Neville G	Blanc ▲	Silvestre	Beckham 15 64	Keane ▲76	Veron ▲	Giggs ▲41	Scholes ●43	van N'rooy 15 43 64 76	van N'rooy 15 43 64 76	Butt ▲	O'Shea ▲	Fortune ▲
16-03	A	West Ham Utd	2-2	5-3	1	M.R.Halsey	Barthez	Johnsen	Blanc	Silvestre	Beckham 16 21 88	Keane	Butt 21	Scholes ▲43	Scholes 16 54 88	Solskjær ▲54 63	van Nistelrooy ▲63	Fortune ▲	Butt ▲	Fortune ▲
30-03	A	Middlesbrough	0-1	0-1	1	S.G.Bennett	Barthez	Johnsen	Blanc ●	Silvestre	Beckham ● '55	Veron ▲	Keane 81	Fortune ▲	Giggs	Solskjær	Solskjær	Scholes ▲	Fortune ▲	Neville P ▲
30-03	H	Leeds Utd	3-1	4-3	1	D.R.Elleray	Barthez	Johnsen	Blanc	Silvestre 8	Beckham ● '55	Butt	Butt	Scholes ● : 8.37	Scholes ▲37 39 55	Solskjær ▲37 39 55	van Nistelrooy ▲39 55	Scholes ▲	Fortune ▲	Giggs ▲
06-04	H	Leicester City	0-0	1-0	1	Carroll	Carroll	Neville P ▲	Blanc	Silvestre	Neville P ●'61	Scholes	Keane	Fortune ▲	Fortune	Solskjær 61	Brown ▲	Butt ▲	Veron ▲	·
20-04	H	Chelsea	2-0	3-0	1	A.P.D'Urso	Barthez	Irwin ▲	O'Shea	Johnsen	Solskjær '41 96	Scholes 15	Scholes 15	Veron	Giggs ▲41	Fortune	van Nistelrooy 41	Fortune ▲	Neville P ▲	Giggs ▲
27-04	A	Ipswich Town	1-0	1-0	2	R.Styles	Carroll	Neville P ●	Blanc	Chadwick ▲	Beckham ▲	Keane	Keane	Butt	Giggs	Fortian	van Nistelrooy 45 45	Silvestre ▲	Scholes ▲	Solskjær ▲
05-05	H	Arsenal	0-0	0-1	2	P.A.Durkin	Barthez ▲	Neville P ●	Blanc	Silvestre ▲	Veron ▲	Veron ▲	Scholes	Giggs	Solskjær	Fortian	Solskjær ▲	van Nistelrooy ▲	Fortune ▲	·
11-05	H	Charlton	0-0	0-3	3	G.Poll	Barthez ▲	Neville P ●	Brown	Irwin ▲	Stewart ▲	Keane	Keane	Scholes	Fortune	Fortian	Giggs ▲	van Nistelrooy ▲	O'Shea ▲	Van der Gouw ▲

F.A. Barclaycard Premiership
Squad List

Position	Name	Appearances	Appearances as Substitute	Goals or Clean Sheets	Goal Assists	Yellow Cards	Red Cards
G	F.Barthez	32		9		1	
G	R.Carroll	6	1	4			
G	R.v der Gouw		1				
D	L.Blanc	29		1	1	4	
D	W.Brown	15	2				
D	D.Irwin	10	2		1	3	
D	R.Johnsen	9	1	1			
D	D.May	2					
D	G.Neville	31	3		3	4	
D	P.Neville	21	7	2	1	4	
D	J.O'Shea	4	5			1	
D	M.Silvestre	31	4		6	3	
D	J.Stam	1					
D	R.Wallwork		1				
M	D.Beckham	23	5	11	8	6	
M	N.Butt	20	5	1	1	5	
M	L.Chadwick	5	3		3		
M	Q.Fortune	8	6	1			
M	R.Giggs	18	7	7	18	1	
M	R.Keane	28		3	6	4	1
M	P.Scholes	30	5	8	9	9	
M	M.Stewart	2	1				
M	J.Veron	24	2	5	1	3	
F	A.Cole	7	4	4	6		
F	D.Forlan	6	7				
F	O.Solskjaer	23	7	17	9	3	
F	R.v Nistelrooy	29	3	23	8	3	
F	D.Yorke	4	6	1	2		

the right end for United. They beat Everton 4-1 but lost in a seven-goal thriller at St James' Park where Newcastle won 4-3 but only after United had come back from 3-1 down to level.

After beating Ipswich 4-0, United again showed their ability to bounce back, this time at White Hart Lane. Despite trailing 3-0 at half-time, goals from five different players, including Blanc, secured an unlikely win and served as a reminder that United were far from out of the title race.

Rumours abounded about the identity of Ferguson's successor. Holland manager Louis van Gaal claimed he had been approached while even England coach Sven-Goran Eriksson was linked.

As winter beckoned, United slipped down the table. A 1-1 draw against Leeds was followed by a 3-1 loss at Liverpool; that the win took Liverpool to the top for the first time in three years was not lost on United. November finished badly, with another loss against Championship rivals, this time at Highbury, where, once again, Barthez was exposed.

When United followed the London defeat with a 3-0 home loss against Chelsea, the Old Trafford alarm bells were ringing louder than ever before in recent seasons.

The Theatre Of Dreams, ordinarily a fortress, was losing its intimidating tag, witnessed by another home defeat a week later. This time, it was West Ham who took a 1-0 victory as United slumped to ninth place.

Missing from the game were Veron, Giggs, van Nistelrooy and Blanc, while Beckham was on the bench, but excuses were thin on the ground.

Going into December, United needed a miracle and they almost achieved it, winning their next eight games to lead the F.A. Barclaycard Premiership for the first

F.A. Barclaycard Premiership
Top Goal Scorer

Ruud van Nistelrooy

Total Premier League Goals Scored:	Percentage Of The Team's League Goals:
23	**26%**

Goals Scored From

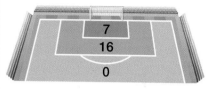

7
16
0

A year after his dream move to Old Trafford had collapsed because of serious injury, van Nistelrooy completed his transfer from PSV Eindhoven and made the 2001-02 season one to remember. His outstanding contribution saw the Dutchman, named as the PFA's Player of the Year, bag a record Premier League final tally for United while it was the best finishing total outright since Brian McClair returned 24 in the 1987-88 season. After opening his account with a goal in the Charity Shield, he began his League career with a brace against Fulham. During the course of the season, he set a Premier League record of scoring in eight consecutive games.

"His temperament is just fantastic, that's why Ruud is just sheer class. He is an incredible player."

Sir Alex Ferguson

Goal Assists

Total number of goal assists	8

Goals Resulting From
Key
- ■ Open Play   ■ Corner   □ Indirect Free Kick
- □ Direct Free Kick   ■ Penalty

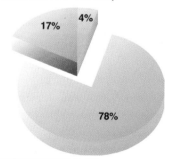

4%
17%
78%

Teams Scored Against

Against	Home	Away
Southampton	3	1
Fulham	2	1
Tottenham Hotspur	2	1
Newcastle United	1	1
Sunderland	2	0
Aston Villa	1	0
Blackburn Rovers	1	0
Bolton Wanderers	0	1
Chelsea	0	1
Derby County	1	0
Everton	0	1
Ipswich Town	0	1
Leicester City	1	0
Middlesbrough	0	1
Total Goals Scored	**14**	**9**

	Right Foot	Left Foot	Header
Open Play	13	2	3
Set piece	4	1	-

It's a fact

When Alan Shearer scored for Newcastle at Old Trafford on New Year's Day, it was the 32nd goal to be conceded by United – equalling the number of goals conceded over the whole of the previous season.

"It's a marvellous achievement to score in eight games in a row. He's in great form. I always feel if he gets a chance he will score."

Sir Alex Ferguson on Ruud van Nistelrooy (January 2002)

time in January.

Normal service was resumed against Derby. Ferguson's men were rampant, winning 5-0 against Colin Todd's team, a victory that included two goals from Ole Gunnar Solskjaer, who was beginning to find his scoring boots alongside van Nistelrooy. When United won 1-0 at Middlesbrough in mid-December, it was the first clean sheet they had claimed on their travels.

Van Nistelrooy scored his first hat-trick, in the 6-1 thrashing of Southampton, then, following the 3-2 Boxing Day success at Fulham, Andy Cole's time at Old Trafford came to an end when the England striker joined Blackburn.

United entered 2002 with renewed optimism. The winning run continued on New Year's Day when Paul Scholes netted twice in the 3-1 win over Newcastle.

United staged another comeback, in the F.A. Cup at Villa, before beating Southampton and Blackburn, thus extending their run of successive F.A. Barclaycard Premiership wins to eight.

The 2-1 win over Blackburn was memorable for two other reasons: it was the first time in 76 League games that

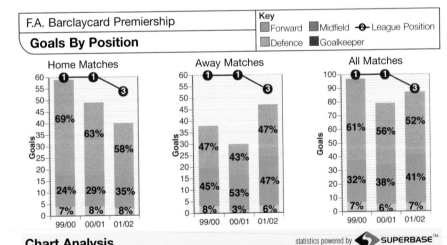

Chart Analysis

statistics powered by SUPERBASE™

United's finishing total of 87 goals was the second highest in their Premier League history. For the second successive season, the overall contribution from strikers fell, while that of the midfield rose.

BEST IN THE LEAGUE...
- **Most goals scored overall and away**
- **Most goals scored by midfield overall and away**

United were unchanged; and, in scoring for the eighth successive League game, van Nistelrooy set a new Premier League record.

United were showing interest in adding another striker to their squad. At the end of January, they moved for Uruguayan forward Diego Forlan, paying Independiente £6.9m for the player.

Prior to the signing, United's great run came to an end. Liverpool, one of their key rivals, were the culprits in a match that only served to highlight what a sensational title race was unfolding.

The Merseysiders won with a late goal from Danny Murphy to hand United their seventh defeat of the season. Ferguson's face was a picture of despondency as he considered it may have been one defeat too many. In addition, United soon left the F.A. Cup, at Middlesbrough, but they refused to give up in the League and beat Bolton 4-0, Solsjkaer claiming United's second hat-trick of the season.

In February, with the club's title hopes still alive, Ferguson announced he was to stay put at Old Trafford. He eventually signed a new contract at the end of a month in which United won all four League games.

Soon afterwards, Roy Keane agreed a new four-year deal and United qualified for the quarter-finals of the Champions

F.A. Barclaycard Premiership
Team Performance Table

League Position	Team	Points won from a possible six	Percentage of points won at home	Percentage of points won away	Overall percentage of points won
1	Arsenal	0/6			
2	Liverpool	0/6			
3	**Manchester Utd**	**77**	33%	25%	29%
4	Newcastle Utd	3/6			
5	Leeds United	4/6			
6	Chelsea	3/6			
7	West Ham Utd	3/6			
8	Aston Villa	4/6	60%	73%	67%
9	Tottenham H	6/6			
10	Blackburn R	4/6			
11	Southampton	6/6			
12	Middlesbrough	3/6			
13	Fulham	6/6	67%	100%	83%
14	Charlton Athletic	4/6			
15	Everton	6/6			
16	Bolton W	3/6			
17	Sunderland	6/6			
18	Ipswich Town	6/6	80%	87%	83%
19	Derby County	4/6			
20	Leicester City	6/6			

The table shows how many points out of a possible six Manchester United have taken off each of the teams in the four sections. The other columns show as a percentage how many points they have taken from those available.

Chart Analysis

statistics powered by SUPERBASE™

Manchester United failed to take enough points off the teams in their own sector while continuing to dispose of teams in the lower reaches of the League.

Despite doing the 'double' over seven teams, United were unable to take any points off the top two teams. They also drew with Leeds as they managed to take only a third of the points available from the home matches against teams in their own sector.

Their form throughout the rest of the table was pretty impressive.

Interestingly, they performed better in all three sectors away from home than they did at Old Trafford. In fact, their record travelling to teams in the third sector was perfect with five wins out of five.

manutd.com Official Manchester United Website

League. What had epitomised United's season was a determination never to believe they could lose. It was on display again at Upton Park, where West Ham led twice before United won 5-3. Beckham scored twice while off the pitch negotiations continued over a new contract for the England captain.

With Keane and Solskjaer absent, United stumbled at home again. McClaren, having knocked his old club out of the F.A. Cup, led Middlesbrough to a narrow win at Old Trafford – United's fifth home loss. Interestingly, three of the five had followed Champions League ties.

Still, United bounced back. At Elland Road towards the end of March, they raced to a 4-1 lead, eventually leaving with a 4-3 victory to stay in the hunt for the title.

In Europe, they beat Deportivo La Coruna 2-0 in Spain, while back in England they sent Leicester down with a 1-0 win at Filbert Street, before progressing to the Champions League semi-finals by winning 3-2 at home to La Coruna.

The win came at a cost – the nation was stunned when Beckham, injured a week earlier by Diego Tristan, hobbled off after a horrendous challenge by Argentine Pedro Duscher, one of two La Coruna players later sent off.

United admitted a day later that Beckham would be out

It's a fact

Ruud van Nistelrooy set a new Premier League record when he scored in his eighth consecutive League game, at home to Blackburn in January.

"I've always said I enjoy it. I know the pressure of the situation at this club. In the main though, I've had 15-and-a-half years which I've enjoyed."

Sir Alex Ferguson
(February 2002)

F.A. Barclaycard Premiership
Goals By Time Period

Key ■ Goals Scored ■ Goals Conceded

Home Matches

Time of Goal (mins)	Goals Scored	Goals Conceded
0-15	6	4
16-30	7	
31-45	7	1
46-60	8	4
61-75	4	4
76-90	8	4

Away Matches

Time of Goal (mins)	Goals Scored	Goals Conceded
0-15	6	6
16-30	4	3
31-45	10	5
46-60	8	4
61-75	10	2
76-90	9	8

All Matches

Time of Goal (mins)	Goals Scored	Goals Conceded
0-15	12	10
16-30	11	3
31-45	17	6
46-60	16	8
61-75	14	6
76-90	17	12

Chart Analysis

statistics powered by ◆ SUPERBASE™

United scored most goals in the last 15 minutes of each half. However, they did concede more towards the end of the game than they did approaching half-time. They were particularly strong in the first half at home, where they scored 20 and conceded just five goals.

BEST IN THE LEAGUE...
• Most goals scored 0-15, 31-45 (joint) and 46-60 minutes

Manchester United

F.A. Barclaycard Premiership
Goals Resulting From

Key ☐ Goals Scored ☐ Goals Conceded

	Six Yard Area				Inside Area				Outside Area				Total			
	Shots		Headers		Shots		Headers		Shots		Headers		Shots		Headers	
	Home	Away	Home	Away	Home	Away	Home	Away	Home	Away	Home	Away	Home	Away	Home	Away
Open Play	4	6	1	-	20	22	3	3	2	3	-	-	26	31	4	3
	2	3	1	3	9	9	1	2	3	3	-	-	14	15	2	5
Direct Free Kick									3	2	-	-	3	2		
									-	2			0	2		
Indirect Free Kick	1	-	-	2	-	1	-	-	-	2	-	-	1	3	0	2
	-	-	-	-	-	-	-	1	-	1	-	-	0	1	0	1
Penalty	-	1	-	-	3	1	-	-	-	-	-	-	3	2	0	0
	-	-	-	-	-	-	-	-	-	-	-	-	0	0	0	0
Corner	1	-	-	-	1	-	1	2	-	-	-	-	2	0	1	2
	-	-	1	1	-	1	-	-	-	-	-	-	0	1	1	1
Totals	6	7	1	2	24	24	4	5	5	7	0	0	35	38	5	7
	2	3	2	4	9	10	1	3	3	6	0	0	14	19	3	7

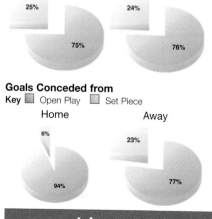

How Goals Were Scored
Home & Away Matches

6% 6% 6% 7%
75%

Key
- ☐ Open Play
- ☐ Corner
- ☐ Indirect Free Kick
- ☐ Direct Free Kick
- ☐ Penalty

Charts do not include 2 own goals for and 2 against.

How Goals Were Conceded
Home & Away Matches

5% 7% 5%
84%

Goals Scored from
Key ☐ Open Play ☐ Set Piece

Home — 25% / 75%
Away — 24% / 76%

Goals Conceded from
Key ☐ Open Play ☐ Set Piece

Home — 6% / 94%
Away — 23% / 77%

Chart Analysis

While the distribution of goals scored from Open Play and Set Pieces remained consistent both home and away, it was a completely different story with the goals conceded. At home, in particular, they were practically impenetrable from Set Pieces, conceding just one out of 17 in this fashion.

BEST IN THE LEAGUE…
- Most goals scored from Open Play overall and away
- Joint most goals scored from Direct Free Kicks at home

WORST IN THE LEAGUE…
- Most goals conceded from Direct Free Kicks away

statistics powered by ◆ SUPERBASE™

manutd.com Official Manchester United Website

> **"The club has bent over backwards to be fair in their dealings with me and I always knew that Manchester United were the only club I ever wanted to play for."**
>
> *David Beckham*
> *(May 2002)*

It's a fact

When United were beaten by Chelsea and West Ham, it was the first time they had lost consecutive games at Old Trafford in the Premier League.

for at least six weeks after breaking the second metatarsal bone in his left foot. They also lost Johnsen for the rest of the season, but the hunt for the title continued.

United confounded their critics by winning 3-0 at Chelsea and, after a 2-2 Champions League semi-final draw against Bayer Leverkusen, they were less convincing at Ipswich where they scraped a 1-0 win by virtue of a controversial penalty.

They relinquished the title to Arsenal at Old Trafford where a Sylvain Wiltord goal earned the Gunners the Championship and the coveted Double. It meant that United went into the final game, against Charlton, needing to win and for Liverpool to either lose or draw to Ipswich for them to finish second.

In the event, Liverpool won 5-0, United drew 0-0 and their disappointment was complete. Denis Irwin announced he was leaving, while Ronny Johnsen's career at Old Trafford was also over. The season did, however, end with some good news as Beckham signed a new five-year contract ending nearly a year of speculation surrounding his future.

F.A. Barclaycard Premiership **Shot Efficiency**	Key ■ Goals Scored ■ Other Shots On Target

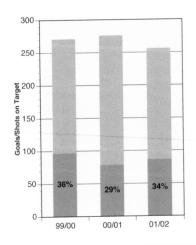

Season	Division	Shots Off Target	Shots On Target	Total Goals
1999 - 2000	P	n/a	271	97
2000 - 2001	P	n/a	276	79
2001 - 2002	P	266	256	87

Chart Analysis

United finished with the best goal conversion rate from Shots On Target. They improved 5% on last season, notching eight more goals from less Shots On Target.

BEST IN THE LEAGUE...
• **Highest percentage of Shot Efficiency**

statistics powered by  SUPERBASE™

---

manutd.com Official Manchester United Website

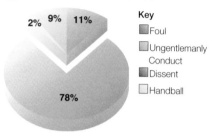

F.A. Barclaycard Premiership

Team Discipline

Key
- Forward
- Defence
- Midfield
- Goalkeeper

Total Number Of Bookings

Total number of red cards	1
Total number of yellow cards	54

Referee Performance

Referee	Games Refereed	Red Cards	Yellow Cards
S.G.Bennett	3	1	6
P.A.Durkin	2	-	9
D.R.Elleray	2	-	5

Type of Yellow Cards Received

2% 9% 11% 78%

Key
- Foul
- Ungentlemanly Conduct
- Dissent
- Handball

Bookings by Position 1999/2000 - 2001/2002

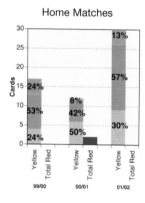

Home Matches

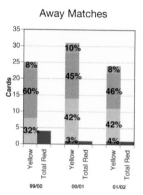

Away Matches

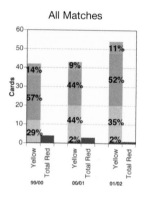

All Matches

Chart Analysis

United collected over 50 Yellow Cards for the first time since 1998-99, although their Red Card tally fell to its lowest since 1997-98.

In a season which saw midfielders pick up over half of all cautions, the team suffered most at home where they saw a 250% increase in the number of Yellow Cards collected compared to the previous season.

The booking for the goalkeeper was picked up by Fabien Barthez in the 3-1 defeat at Highbury in November.

"He gets three games for that red card, and you see some things that go on in the game of football. It makes it all so stupid."
Sir Alex Ferguson on Roy Keane's dismissal at Newcastle (September 2001)

statistics powered by **SUPERBASE**™

Middlesbrough

F.A. Barclaycard Premiership Final standing for the 2001-2002 season								
Final Position		Games Played	Games Won	Games Drawn	Games Lost	Goals For	Goals Against	Total Points
11	Southampton	38	12	9	17	46	54	45
12	Middlesbrough	38	12	9	17	35	47	45
13	Fulham	38	10	14	14	36	44	44

"There have been times this season when we have had to win ugly, but there were also times when we played some exciting and flowing football."

Steve McLaren (May 2002)

Club Honours and Records

Division 1 Champions: 1994-95

Division 2 Champions: 1926-27, 1928-29, 1973-74

Amateur Cup Winners: 1895, 1898

Anglo-Scottish Cup Winners: 1976

Record victory: 9-0 v Brighton & Hove Albion, Division 2, 23 August, 1958

Record defeat: 0-9 v Blackburn Rovers, Division 2, 6 November, 1954

League goals in a season (team): 122, Division 2, 1926-27

League goals in a season (player): 59, George Camsell, Division 2, 1926-27

Career league goals: 326, George Camsell, 1925 to 1939

League appearances: 563, Tim Williamson, 1902 to 1923

Reported transfer fee paid: £8,000,000 to Aston Villa for Ugo Ehiogu, October 2000

Reported transfer fee received: £12,000,000 from Atletico Madrid for Juninho, July 1997

STEVE McClaren decided to leave Old Trafford, and the security his place alongside Sir Alex Ferguson afforded, to take charge at Middlesbrough. Ultimately, there were few complaints as Boro reached an F.A. Cup semi-final and finished 12th in the League.

With Terry Venables leaving after securing Middlesbrough's F.A. Barclaycard Premiership status and with Bryan Robson having resigned, the club turned to McClaren, who signed a five-year contract. He was given permission to rejoin England coach Sven-Goran Eriksson's back room staff but his chief aim was to improve the fortunes of a team that had fought to retain their F.A. Barclaycard Premiership status.

McClaren completed the signing of Slovakian striker Szilard Nemeth, a deal already agreed before his arrival. He then turned to Aston Villa's Gareth Southgate, who somewhat surprisingly agreed a £6.5m switch to the North East. Next up, he returned to Old Trafford to sign United pair Mark Wilson and Jonathan Greening for a combined fee of £4m.

Some feared that McClaren's lack of managerial experience could work against Boro. The 4-0 opening day thrashing by Arsenal, in which they finished with ten

 Fixtures, results and match reports - 4thegame.com

F.A. Barclaycard Premiership

Season Progression

Key
■ Win ■ Loss □ Draw —❷— League Position
—❷— Last Season's League Position

All Matches

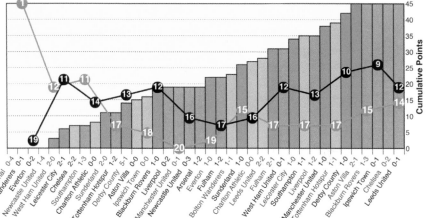

Home Matches

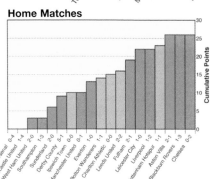

Away Matches

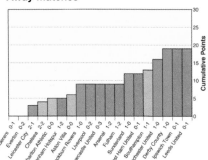

Chart Analysis

An inauspicious start saw Steve McClaren begin his managerial reign at Middlesbrough with four straight defeats.

The new boss broke his duck with a 2-0 home win over West Ham and followed that two days later with a 2-1 victory at Leicester to lift them to 11th by mid-September.

A poor run in December of four defeats in five saw them slip to just above the relegation zone.

However, they rallied to pick up three wins both home and away after the turn of the year, including two wins on the spin at the start of the April, to see them safe.

Up to ninth place and through to the semi-finals of the F.A. Cup, defeat in the latter to Arsenal prompted a run of four straight losses in the former but by then their top flight status was assured.

statistics powered by ◆ SUPERBASE™

➜ **Win Barclaycard Premiership tickets – 4thegame.com**

> **"I've always stated that our performances have been better than our results, and it's only a matter of time until we turn it around and we get what we deserve."**
>
> *Steve McClaren*
> *(September 2001)*

It's a fact

Four successive defeats, by Arsenal, Bolton, Everton and Newcastle, represented Boro's worst ever start to a season.

men after the dismissal of Ugo Ehiogu, offered worrying portents.

McClaren insisted there was no need to panic, although losing the previous season's top scorer Alen Boksic with a calf injury for five games after the Arsenal defeat did little to improve confidence. Two more defeats, at Bolton and Everton, were followed by a fourth straight loss, at home to near neighbours Newcastle. In addition to losing 4-1 and dropping to the foot of the F.A. Barclaycard Premiership, a second Boro man saw red as keeper Mark Schwarzer received his marching orders.

McClaren's first win as a manager finally arrived, in mid-September when Boro beat West Ham 2-0 with goals from Brian Deane and Allan Johnston, who had signed in the summer from Rangers. Two days later, at Filbert Street, Middlesbrough won again, beating Leicester 2-1 with Greening opening his goalscoring account.

Off the pitch, Boro were finding the transfer market was a minefield. Their problems started when their signing of South African striker Benni McCarthy, from Celta Vigo, fell through after his work permit was rejected.

With Boksic back, they stole a 2-2 draw at Chelsea and McClaren said: "It shows what a bit of belief, hard work and character can do."

F.A. Barclaycard Premiership
Half-Time/Full-Time Comparison

Key: ■ Win ■ Loss ■ Draw

Home				Away				Total			
Number of Home Half Time Wins	W	L	D	Number of Away Half Time Wins	W	L	D	Total number of Half Time Wins	W	L	D
6	5	-	1	6	4	2	-	12	9	2	1
Number of Home Half Time Losses	W	L	D	Number of Away Half Time Losses	W	L	D	Total number of Half Time Losses	W	L	D
6	-	4	2	8	1	5	2	14	1	9	4
Number of Home Half Time Draws	W	L	D	Number of Away Half Time Draws	W	L	D	Total number of Half Time Draws	W	L	D
7	2	3	2	5	-	3	2	12	2	6	4

Chart Analysis

statistics powered by ◆ SUPERBASE™

The fact that Middlesbrough went into the break at least a goal behind on 14 occasions affected their ability to finish higher in the table. From these games, they managed to collect just seven points.

Boro had a poor return from games in which they were level at the interval, losing six out of 12 overall, and failing to win any out of five on their travels.

The heart of the Barclaycard Premiership - 4thegame.com

F.A. Barclaycard Premiership Results Table

Key: ○○ time of goal ○○ time of assist ▲ player substituted ○ yellow card ● red card

DATE	H/A	OPPONENT	H/T	F/T	POS	REFEREE	TEAM										SUBSTITUTES USED		
18-08	A	Arsenal	0-1	0-4	19	G.P.Barber	Schwarzer	Fleming	Southgate	Ehiogu ●	Cooper	Greening	Mustoe ▲	Ince ○	Windass	Job	Boksic	Wilson ▲	Ricard ▲	-
21-08	H	Bolton	0-1	0-1	20	S.W.Dunn	Schwarzer	Fleming	Southgate	Ehiogu	Cooper	Greening	Mustoe ▲	Ince	Deane	Job	Ricard ▲	Okon ▲	Windass ▲	-
25-08	A	Everton	0-1	0-2	19	U.D.Rennie	Schwarzer	Fleming	Southgate	Ehiogu	Vickers ▲	Cooper	Okon ▲	Ince	Greening	Job	Ricard ▲	Windass ▲	Nemeth ▲	Mustoe ▲
08-09	H	Newcastle Utd	1-1	1-4	20	G.Poll	Schwarzer ●	Fleming	Southgate	Vickers	Cooper 3	Greening	Mustoe ▲	Ince ○3	Deane	Windass ▲	Ricard ▲	Job ▲	Crossley ▲	-
15-09	H	West Ham Utd	2-0	2-0	19	M.A.Riley	Schwarzer	Fleming	Southgate	Ehiogu	Cooper ▲41	Greening ○	Mustoe ▲	Ince 31	Johnston ▲41	Deane 31	Windass ▲	Gavin ▲	Wilson ▲	-
17-09	A	Leicester City	2-1	2-1	11	N.S.Barry	Schwarzer	Fleming	Southgate	Ehiogu	Cooper	Greening 88	Mustoe ▲	Ince 85	Johnston ▲	Deane	Windass ▲	Nemeth ▲	Wilson ▲	Marinelli ▲
23-09	H	Chelsea	2-2	2-2	12	R.Styles	Fleming ▲	Southgate	Gavin	Ehiogu	Cooper	Greening	Mustoe ▲	Ince	Johnston ▲	Deane	Boksic 90	Wilson ▲	Marinelli ▲	Stockdale ▲61
29-09	H	Southampton	0-0	1-3	14	A.G.Wiley	Schwarzer	Fleming	Southgate	Ehiogu	Cooper	Greening	Mustoe ▲	Wilson	Johnston ▲	Deane ▲	Boksic 75	Okon ▲	Nemeth ▲75	Marinelli ▲
13-10	A	Charlton	0-0	0-0	14	D.R.Elleray	Crossley	Stockdale	Southgate	Ehiogu	Gavin ▲	Queudrue	Wilson ○	Ince	Greening	Nemeth ▲	Boksic ▲	Mustoe ▲	Windass ▲	Marinelli ▲
22-10	H	Sunderland	2-0	2-0	13	M.R.Halsey	Schwarzer	Stockdale	Southgate	Ehiogu	Queudrue ○2	Greening	Mustoe ●	Ince	Marinelli ▲20	Nemeth ▲20	Boksic ▲20	Johnston ▲	Windass ▲	Wilson ▲
27-10	H	Tottenham	1-0	1-2	14	M.L.Dean	Schwarzer	Stockdale ▲	Southgate	Ehiogu	Queudrue	Greening	Mustoe ▲	Ince 9	Marinelli ▲2	Nemeth ▲	Boksic 9	Johnston ▲	Windass ▲	Cooper ▲
03-11	A	Derby County	0-0	5-1	13	N.S.Barry	Schwarzer	Stockdale	Southgate	Ehiogu	Queudrue 60	Greening ▲57	Wilson	Ince 9	Marinelli 49 57 82	Nemeth ▲49	Boksic ▲60	Johnston ▲	Deane ▲	Windass ▲
17-11	A	Aston Villa	0-0	0-0	13	P.Jones	Crossley	Stockdale	Southgate	Ehiogu	Queudrue ▲	Greening	Marinelli ▲	Marinelli ●	Johnston ▲	Nemeth ▲	Boksic ▲	Stamp ▲	Cooper ○▲	Windass ▲
25-11	H	Ipswich Town	0-0	0-0	14	D.Pugh	Crossley	Stockdale	Southgate	Ehiogu	Queudrue	Greening	Mustoe ▲	Marinelli ▲	Johnston ▲	Nemeth ▲	Boksic	Wilson ▲	Hudson ▲	Windass ▲
01-12	A	Blackburn	1-0	1-1	12	B.Knight	Crossley ○	Cooper ○	Southgate	Ehiogu	Queudrue ▲	Greening 44	Mustoe ▲	Ince	Johnston ▲	Nemeth ▲	Boksic ▲44	Wilson ▲	Windass ▲	Gavin ▲
08-12	A	Liverpool	0-2	0-2	15	D.J.Gallagher	Crossley ▲	Stockdale	Southgate	Ehiogu ○	Queudrue ▲	Greening	Mustoe ▲	Ince	Marinelli	Nemeth ▲	Boksic	Beresford ▲	Wilson ▲	Ricard ▲
15-12	H	Manchester Utd	0-1	0-3	16	D.R.Elleray	Crossley	Stockdale	Southgate	Ehiogu ○	Queudrue ●	Greening	Mustoe ▲	Ince ○	Ricard ▲	Ricard ▲	Boksic	Campbell ▲	-	Ricard ▲
26-12	A	Newcastle Utd	1-0	1-3	16	M.R.Halsey	Crossley	Stockdale	Southgate	Ehiogu ○	Queudrue	Greening	Mustoe ▲	Ince	Marinelli ▲	Whelan ▲	Boksic	Campbell ▲	Okon ▲	Ricard ▲
29-12	A	Arsenal	1-0	1-2	16	A.P.D'Urso	Crossley	Stockdale	Southgate	Ehiogu ▲	Queudrue	Greening ▲	Mustoe	Ince	Marinelli ▲	Whelan ▲21	Ricard	Cooper ▲	Campbell ▲	Johnston ▲
01-01	H	Everton	0-0	1-0	16	R.Styles	Crossley	Stockdale	Southgate	Festa 50	Queudrue ▲50	Greening ▲	Mustoe ▲	Ince	Marinelli ▲	Whelan ▲	Ricard	Gavin ○▲	Boksic ▲	Stamp ▲
12-01	A	Fulham	1-2	1-2	17	M.L.Dean	Crossley	Stockdale	Southgate	Ehiogu	Cooper 8	Greening ▲	Mustoe ▲	Ince	Marinelli ▲8	Whelan	Ricard ▲	Stamp ▲	Windass ▲	Nemeth ▲
19-01	H	Bolton	1-0	1-1	18	G.Poll	Crossley	Festa ●	Southgate	Ehiogu ▲	Queudrue ▲	Greening	Marinelli ○	Ince	Johnston 38	Whelan 38	Nemeth ▲	Campbell ▲	Cooper ▲	Windass ▲
29-01	A	Sunderland	1-0	1-0	14	P.A.Durkin	Crossley	Stockdale	Southgate	Ehiogu ●	Gavin	Queudrue	Marinelli ▲	Ince	Greening	Whelan ▲14	Boksic	Mustoe ▲14	Campbell ▲	Gordon ▲
03-02	H	Charlton	0-0	0-0	16	M.A.Riley	Crossley	Stockdale ▲	Southgate	Festa ●	Gavin	Queudrue	Stamp ▲14	Ince	Greening	Whelan	Windass ▲	Campbell ○▲	Marinelli ▲	-
09-02	H	Leeds Utd	0-1	2-2	16	N.S.Barry	Gavin ▲	Crossley	Southgate	Ehiogu ○	Festa	Queudrue	Stamp ▲	Ince ○50	Greening ▲	Whelan	Boksic ▲9	Boksic ▲	Windass ▲88	Mustoe ▲
19-02	A	Fulham	1-0	1-1	11	D.J.Gallagher	Crossley	Stockdale ○	Southgate	Ehiogu ▲	Queudrue ▲	Greening	Mustoe ▲	Ince	Carbone ▲26	Boksic 26 78	Carbone 88	Nemeth ▲78	Murphy ▲	Windass ▲88
23-02	A	West Ham Utd	0-0	0-1	12	C.J.Foy	Schwarzer	Stockdale	Southgate	Ehiogu ●	Queudrue	Greening ▲	Mustoe ○▲	Ince	Carbone ▲36	Boksic	Mustoe ▲	Boksic ▲	Murphy ▲	Nemeth ▲
02-03	H	Leicester City	1-0	1-0	12	E.K.Wolstenholme	Schwarzer	Stockdale	Southgate	Ehiogu ▲	Queudrue	Greening ▲	Mustoe ▲	Ince	Carbone	Boksic	Carbone 38 64	Murphy ▲	Windass ▲	Nemeth ▲
06-03	A	Southampton	0-1	1-1	13	U.D.Rennie	Schwarzer	Festa ●	Southgate	Ehiogu	Queudrue	Greening	Mustoe ▲	Wilkshire	Carbone 56	Whelan 56	Carbone	Stockdale ▲	Windass ▲	-
16-03	H	Liverpool	0-1	1-2	13	A.P.D'Urso	Schwarzer	Festa	Southgate 89	Ehiogu	Queudrue ▲	Festa	Mustoe ▲	Wilkshire ○	Wilkshire	Carbone	Boksic	Gavin ▲	Marinelli ▲89	Nemeth ▲
23-03	A	Manchester Utd	1-0	1-0	10	S.G.Bennett	Schwarzer	Stockdale ▲	Southgate	Ehiogu	Queudrue 69	Greening ▲	Mustoe ▲	Ince ○	Carbone 9	Whelan	Boksic ▲9	Wilkshire ▲	Windass ▲	-
30-03	H	Tottenham	1-1	1-1	11	P.Dowd	Crossley	Stockdale	Southgate	Ehiogu	Queudrue 69	Greening	Mustoe ▲	Wilkshire	Carbone	Whelan	Boksic 69	Windass ▲	Murphy ▲	-
01-04	H	Derby County	1-0	1-0	10	P.A.Durkin	Schwarzer	Stockdale	Southgate	Ehiogu	Queudrue 38	Greening	Mustoe 12	Ince	Wilkshire	Carbone	Carbone	-	-	-
06-04	A	Aston Villa	1-0	2-1	9	G.P.Barber	Schwarzer	Stockdale ▲	Southgate	Ehiogu 64	Queudrue ▲	Wilkshire	Mustoe ▲	Greening	Johnston ▲	Whelan ▲	Carbone 38 64	Windass ▲	-	-
20-04	A	Blackburn	0-1	1-3	9	N.S.Barry	Schwarzer	Festa ○	Southgate	Festa	Queudrue ▲	Wilkshire ▲	Mustoe ○▲	Wilkshire	Johnston ▲	Windass	Carbone ▲90	Marinelli ▲	Murphy ▲	Debeve ▲
24-04	A	Ipswich Town	0-0	0-1	12	A.P.D'Urso	Schwarzer	Stockdale ▲	Southgate	Cooper	Queudrue	Downing	Debeve ▲	Downing	Johnston ▲	Nemeth ▲	Carbone	Marinelli ▲	Hudson ▲	Nemeth ▲
27-04	H	Chelsea	0-2	0-2	10	B.Knight	Schwarzer	Stockdale	Cooper	Ehiogu ○	Queudrue ▲	Greening	Mustoe ▲	Windass ▲	Windass ▲	Whelan ○	Carbone 69	Nemeth ▲	Debeve ▲	Downing ▲
11-05	A	Leeds United	0-0	0-1	12	U.D.Rennie	Schwarzer	Stockdale	Southgate	Ehiogu	Cooper ▲	Greening	Mustoe ▲	Ince	Downing ▲	Nemeth	Nemeth ▲	Debeve ▲	Murphy ▲	Windass ▲

F.A. Barclaycard Premiership
Squad List

Position	Name	Appearances	Appearances as Substitute	Goals or Clean Sheets	Goal Assists	Yellow Cards	Red Cards
G	M.Beresford		1				
G	M.Crossley	17	1	8			
G	M.Schwarzer	21		4			1
D	C.Cooper	14	4	2	1	3	
D	U.Ehiogu	29		1		2	2
D	G.Festa	8		1		1	2
D	C.Fleming	8					
D	J.Gavin	5	4			2	
D	D.Gordon		1				
D	D.Murphy		5				
D	F.Queudrue	28		2	3	8	1
D	G.Southgate	37		1			
D	R.Stockdale	26	2	1		2	
D	S.Vickers	2					
M	M.Debeve	1	3				
M	S.Downing	2	1				
M	J.Greening	36		1	2	4	
M	M.Hudson		2				
M	P.Ince	31		2	3	11	1
M	A.Johnston	13	4	1		1	
M	C.Marinelli	12	8	2	4	2	
M	R.Mustoe	31	5	2	1	2	
M	P.Okon	1	3				
M	P.Stamp	3	3		1		
M	L.Wilkshire	6	1			1	
M	M.Wilson	2	8			1	
F	A.Boksic	20	2	8	2	2	
F	A.Campbell		4			1	
F	B.Carbone	13		1	5	1	
F	B.Deane	6	1	1		1	
F	J.Job	3	1			1	
F	S.Nemeth	11	10	3	2		
F	H.Ricard	6	3			2	
F	N.Whelan	18	1	4		2	
F	D.Windass	8	19	1		2	

A 3-1 home defeat by Southampton and a goalless draw at Charlton – where Boro squandered 14 goal-scoring chances – halted the good run and though they savoured a 2-0 victory over rivals Sunderland, Boro finished with ten men again, captain Paul Ince seeing red in the club's 1,000th home League win.

McClaren saw the need to boost his defence and signed French defender Franck Queudrue on loan for the rest of the season from Lens. The month of October began with signs of an improvement, Middlesbrough beating Derby 5-1 at the Riverside, where Carlos Marinelli, in only his third start, scored twice while Boksic netted his fifth goal in six games. The Croatian later claimed he wanted to finish his career with the club.

Players left as McClaren looked to clear the decks in an effort to persuade chairman Steve Gibson to give him funds to buy. Steve Vickers joined Birmingham, Curtis Fleming moved to Crystal Palace and Brian Deane signed for Leicester, while Dean Windass and Dean Gordon left for loan spells at Sheffield Wednesday and Cardiff City respectively.

Boro lost Schwarzer when he underwent a hernia operation in November, and Wales international Mark Crossley took over in goal. Schwarzer's absence coincided with another dreadful sequence. In December, Boro lost four F.A. Barclaycard Premiership games in succession. Given the opposition was Liverpool, Manchester United, Newcastle and Arsenal, McClaren could be forgiven for cursing his luck, both with the sequence of fixtures and the results.

A win over Everton on New Year's Day did little to paper over the cracks of a poor run which many believed was down to poor defending. McClaren dropped Colin Cooper but the defender refused to be a

F.A. Barclaycard Premiership
Top Goal Scorer

Alen Boksic

Total Premier League Goals Scored:	Percentage Of The Team's League Goals:
8	23%

Goals Scored From

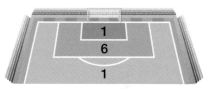

1
6
1

The Croatian striker returned four fewer goals than he had the previous season following his move from Lazio in the summer of 2000. With the World Cup finals in mind, Boksic offered some consistency in front of goal to finish as Middlesbrough's top scorer for the second season in succession. In the previous campaign, he had scored only three of his 12 at home; this time he netted four at the Riverside and four on his travels. Disappointingly, his total was the lowest by a Boro top scorer since the seven claimed by Nick Barmby in the 1995-96 season.

"The F.A. Barclaycard Premiership is so beautiful and fascinating because of the tradition of English football. Over the last few years the Championship has improved very much."

Alen Boksic

Goals Resulting From
Key
■ Open Play ■ Corner □ Indirect Free Kick
□ Direct Free Kick ■ Penalty

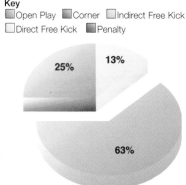

13%
25%
63%

Goal Assists

Total number of goal assists	2

Teams Scored Against

Against	Home	Away
Blackburn Rovers	0	1
Chelsea	0	1
Derby County	1	0
Fulham	1	0
Manchester United	0	1
Southampton	1	0
Sunderland	1	0
Tottenham Hotspur	0	1
Total Goals Scored	**4**	**4**

	Right Foot	Left Foot	Header
Open Play	4	-	1
Set piece	2	1	-

➤ **Fixtures, results and match reports - 4thegame.com**

> "We have to be big enough to deal with our fans' reaction. They are going to be on edge and that will transmit to the players."
>
> *Gareth Southgate*
> *(January 2002)*

substitute and later held clear-the-air talks with his manager.

McClaren admitted making a tentative enquiry for Manchester United's Dwight Yorke and that more players would have to leave before newcomers could be signed.

The club made another move to strengthen their squad when Diego Forlan, the Uruguayan striker based in Argentina, flew in for talks. He returned to South America having signed for Manchester United and McClaren could be forgiven for cursing his former club, even if he was to gain hasty revenge.

While the team's problems were beginning to get to the fans, things began to look up in the New Year. Form improved in the League and the F.A. Cup offered some welcome respite, with victories over Wimbledon and the sweetness of a 2-0 fourth round triumph over Manchester United at the Riverside.

That game highlighted the problems McClaren had encountered in finding a settled side. The partnership of Noel Whelan and Windass was the 12th different strike partnership used by the manager. Not that it hindered Boro, with Whelan and Andy Campbell scoring in front a

F.A. Barclaycard Premiership
Goals By Position

Key
Forward Midfield —②— League Position
Defence Goalkeeper

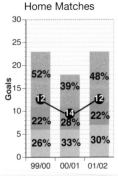

Home Matches

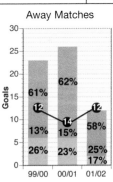

Away Matches

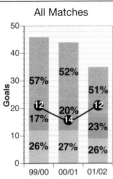

All Matches

Chart Analysis

statistics powered by **SUPERBASE**™

Although Middlesbrough scored nine less goals overall compared to last season, they finished two places higher in the table in the same position as they had two seasons earlier when they scored 11 goals more.

Alarmingly, the number of goals scored on the road more than halved.

BEST IN THE LEAGUE...
• **Most goals scored by defenders at home**

 Win Barclaycard Premiership tickets – 4thegame.com

disappointingly low 17,624 crowd.

Tragedy struck Cooper when his two-year-old son died and he was withdrawn from the squad to face Sunderland. His teammates, shocked by the news, rallied to win 1-0 at the Stadium of Light, although Gianluca Festa was sent off.

Benito Carbone arrived on loan from Bradford City after originally rejecting the move, as McClaren finally increased his squad. After two draws in early February, and another F.A. Cup win, over Blackburn, spirits were rising.

Boro even had to strenuously deny that McClaren was returning to Old Trafford as successor to former mentor Sir Alex Ferguson. Clearly his stock was rising.

After enquiring in vain about Celtic's John Hartson, they agreed a £6m deal for Leicester's Muzzy Izzet, but the Turkish international eventually rejected the move to further frustrate McClaren in the transfer market.

Despite the set-backs off the field, McClaren was finally proving his managerial worth, with Boro easing up the table whilst relishing a sixth round F.A. Cup tie against Everton. Wins over Fulham and Leicester saw Boro move up to 12th place before they won 3-0 against Everton to book a semi-final spot.

Goals were not forthcoming but nor were Boro conceding either. After the 2-1

F.A. Barclaycard Premiership
Team Performance Table

League Position	Team	Points won from a possible six	Percentage of points won at home	Percentage of points won away	Overall percentage of points won
1	Arsenal	0/6			
2	Liverpool	0/6			
3	Manchester Utd	3/6	7%	20%	13%
4	Newcastle Utd	0/6			
5	Leeds United	1/6			
6	Chelsea	1/6			
7	West Ham Utd	3/6			
8	Aston Villa	4/6	47%	33%	40%
9	Tottenham H	1/6			
10	Blackburn R	3/6			
11	Southampton	1/6			
12	**Middlesbrough**	**45**			
13	Fulham	3/6	58%	17%	38%
14	Charlton Athletic	2/6			
15	Everton	3/6			
16	Bolton W	1/6			
17	Sunderland	6/6			
18	Ipswich Town	1/6	73%	60%	67%
19	Derby County	6/6			
20	Leicester City	6/6			

The table shows how many points out of a possible six Middlesbrough have taken off each of the teams in the four sections. The other columns show as a percentage how many points they have taken from those available.

Chart Analysis

statistics powered by SUPERBASE™

Middlesbrough really struggled against teams in the top five, failing to take any points from Arsenal, Liverpool and Newcastle United.

However, they did manage to take points off all the other teams in the table.

In addition, the one win they did register against top five opposition was memorable enough, 1-0 at Old Trafford on Steve McClaren's return.

Overall, they fared similarly against teams in the second and their own sector, although they did fail to win any of the matches against the teams around them away from home.

Middlesbrough did the 'double' over three teams, all of which finished in the bottom five of the table.

The heart of the Barclaycard Premiership - 4thegame.com

> **"Each game is significant but the big result for us came in the League match at Old Trafford. It gave us belief in what we are doing and knowing that we are going in the right direction."**
>
> Steve McLaren (April 2002)

home defeat by Liverpool, McClaren returned to Old Trafford and engineered yet another success over United which went some way to assuring his new club's top flight status while putting a spoke in his former club's title aspirations.

It came at the end of March when, despite the continued absence of Cooper, Boro stole a win thanks to a goal from Boksic, who was beginning to hone his talents ahead of the World Cup finals. Some delightful individual performances from players such as Carbone and Ince took Boro into the top half of the table for the first time.

They consolidated their position – with an eye on their semi-final against Arsenal – when they were held to a 1-1 draw by Tottenham. In front of the home fans, Queudrue enhanced his growing reputation with his second goal for the club.

McClaren helped point one of his former clubs closer to relegation when Boro started April with a 1-0 win at Derby thanks to Robbie Mustoe's second goal of the season. The win also effectively secured Boro's safety.

Another impressive victory, at home to Villa, took Boro to ninth place and more than vindicated the decision to appoint McClaren. Indeed, after the same number of games a year earlier, they were 17th.

F.A. Barclaycard Premiership
Goals By Time Period

Key: ■ Goals Scored   ■ Goals Conceded

Home Matches

Time of Goal (mins)	Goals Scored	Goals Conceded
0-15	3	
16-30	2	1
31-45	4	7
46-60	5	4
61-75	4	6
76-90	5	8

Away Matches

Time of Goal (mins)	Goals Scored	Goals Conceded
0-15	5	2
16-30	1	3
31-45	1	6
46-60	1	5
61-75	1	2
76-90	3	3

All Matches

Time of Goal (mins)	Goals Scored	Goals Conceded
0-15	8	2
16-30	3	4
31-45	5	13
46-60	6	9
61-75	5	8
76-90	8	11

Chart Analysis

statistics powered by ◆ SUPERBASE™

Middlesbrough were hard to break down in the first 15 minutes, conceding no goals at home and just two on their travels.

They seemed to struggle after that, particularly at the end of each half, when they conceded 24 out of 47 goals.

Away from home, Middlesbrough only managed to score more than once in the opening and closing 15 minutes of matches.

 All the latest news, views and opinion - 4thegame.com

F.A. Barclaycard Premiership
Goals Resulting From

Key ☐ Goals Scored ☐ Goals Conceded

	Six Yard Area				Inside Area				Outside Area				Total			
	Shots		Headers		Shots		Headers		Shots		Headers		Shots		Headers	
	Home	Away	Home	Away	Home	Away	Home	Away	Home	Away	Home	Away	Home	Away	Home	Away
Open Play	1	1	1	-	6	7	2	-	3	-	-	-	10	8	3	0
	6	3	-	1	8	7	-	-	2	4	-	-	16	14	0	1
Direct Free Kick									1	-			1	0		
									1	-			1	0		
Indirect Free Kick	-	-	-	1	1	1	1	-	1	-	-	-	2	1	1	1
	-	-	1	1	1	-	1	-	-	-	-	-	1	0	2	1
Penalty	-	-	-	-	1	1	-	-	-	-	-	-	1	1	0	0
	-	-	-	-	4	1	-	-	-	-	-	-	4	1	0	0
Corner	1	-	3	-	-	1	-	-	-	-	-	-	1	1	3	0
	-	1	1	1	-	1	1	1	-	-	-	-	0	2	2	2
Totals	2	1	4	1	8	10	3	0	5	0	0	0	15	11	7	1
	6	4	2	3	13	9	2	1	3	4	0	0	22	17	4	4

How Goals Were Scored
Home & Away Matches

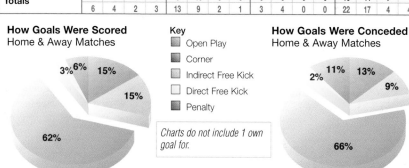

3% 6% 15%
15%
62%

Key
- Open Play
- Corner
- Indirect Free Kick
- Direct Free Kick
- Penalty

Charts do not include 1 own goal for.

How Goals Were Conceded
Home & Away Matches

2% 11% 13%
9%
66%

Goals Scored from
Key ☐ Open Play ☐ Set Piece

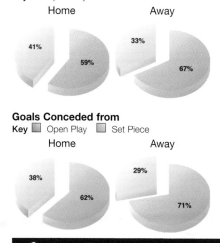

Home
41%
59%

Away
33%
67%

Goals Conceded from
Key ☐ Open Play ☐ Set Piece

Home
38%
62%

Away
29%
71%

Chart Analysis

Middlesbrough scored a larger proportion of goals from Set Pieces at home than they did away. Overall, they scored five goals each from Corners and Indirect Free Kicks.

However, they did let in five goals from Penalties, contributing to the fact that they conceded three more goals from Set Pieces than they scored.

WORST IN THE LEAGUE...
- **Most goals conceded from Penalties overall and at home**

statistics powered by SUPERBASE™

→ **Fixtures, results and match reports - 4thegame.com**

However, the win came at a cost. Whelan was injured in the early stages and the torn hamstring he suffered meant the striker would miss the F.A. Cup semi-final against Arsenal at old Trafford.

Also absent was Ince, who was suspended, but Boro fought Arsenal all the way and only an unfortunate own goal by Gianluca Festa prevented his side from reaching the final. Perhaps the fact that Boro were safe and with little else to play for explained their next two results.

They entertained Blackburn at the Riverside but lost 3-1 after Queudrue was sent off.

Injuries were affecting Boro as well; when they visited Ipswich, they were missing nine first team players. Cooper returned after a three-month absence and a debut was handed to teenager Stuart Downing.

In the event, Ipswich's need was greater and the team fighting for their F.A. Barclaycard Premiership existence stole a narrow 1-0 win. Boro suffered a third successive defeat at home to Chelsea.

Boro finished with a fifth successive defeat, at Elland Road, and for the third game they failed to score. Clearly, more will be expected now McClaren has settled in at the Riverside.

It's a fact

The 1-0 home defeat by Manchester United in November was Boro's 100th loss in the Premier League.

F.A. Barclaycard Premiership	Key
Shot Efficiency	▣ Goals Scored □ Other Shots On Target

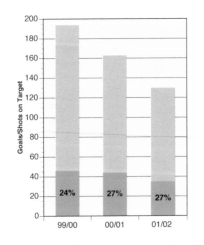

Season	Division	Shots Off Target	Shots On Target	Total Goals
1999 - 2000	P	n/a	194	46
2000 - 2001	P	n/a	163	44
2001 - 2002	P	179	130	35

Chart Analysis

Boro finished with just 130 Shots On Target, their lowest ever total in seven seasons in the Premier League.

Nevertheless, they still managed the same efficiency rate as the previous season in notching 35 goals.

➤ **Win Barclaycard Premiership tickets – 4thegame.com**

F.A. Barclaycard Premiership	Key
Team Discipline	☐ Forward ▨ Midfield ☐ Defence ■ Goalkeeper

Total Number Of Bookings

Total number of red cards	7
Total number of yellow cards	52

Referee Performance

Referee	Games Refereed	Red Cards	Yellow Cards
N.S.Barry	4	1	5
A.P.D'Urso	3	-	6
C.J.Foy	1	1	4

Type of Yellow Cards Received

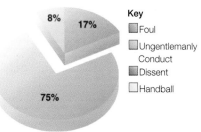

Key
- ▨ Foul
- ☐ Ungentlemanly Conduct
- ■ Dissent
- ☐ Handball

8% 17% 75%

Bookings by Position 1999/2000 - 2001/2002

Home Matches	Away Matches	All Matches

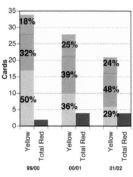 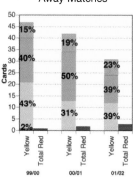 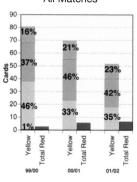

Chart Analysis

While Yellow Cards decreased for the second year running, Red Cards went up in the same period to reach their highest number in Middlesbrough's seven seasons in the Premier League. The same pattern can be seen in the home and away charts.

All seven Red Cards handed out to Middlesbrough players came from different officials.

WORST IN THE LEAGUE...
- Joint most red cards overall

"I don't think anybody is completely satisfied and I've never known a manager yet who's completely happy with the way things are going. You look at the top clubs throughout the world and they're forever searching to get better."
Steve McLaren
(January 2002)

statistics powered by  SUPERBASE™

 The heart of the Barclaycard Premiership – 4thegame.com

Newcastle United

F.A. Barclaycard Premiership Final standing for the 2001-2002 season							
Final Position		Games Played	Games Won	Games Drawn	Games Lost	Goals For	Goals Against	Total Points
3	Manchester United	38	24	5	9	87	45	77
4	Newcastle United	38	21	8	9	74	52	71
5	Leeds United	38	18	12	8	53	37	66

"I had to prove that I could still do it after my injury, but more than anything else, I am delighted at the way things have gone for the team this season. I would say we have been magnificent as a team."

Alan Shearer (May 2002)

Club Honours and Records

Football League Champions:
1904-05, 1906-07, 1908-09, 1926-27

Division 1 Champions: 1992-93

Division 2 Champions: 1964-65

FA Cup Winners:
1910, 1924, 1932, 1951, 1952, 1955

Texaco Cup Winners: 1974, 1975

European Fairs Cup Winners: 1968-69

Anglo-Italian Cup Winners: 1972-73

Record victory:
13-0 v Newport County, Division 2, 5 October, 1946

Record defeat:
0-9 v Burton Wanderers, Division 2, 15 April, 1895

League goals in a season (team):
98, Division 1, 1951-52

League goals in a season (player):
36, Hughie Gallacher, Division 1, 1926-27

Career league goals:
178, Jackie Milburn, 1946 to 1957

League appearances:
432, Jim Lawrence, 1904 to 1922

Reported transfer fee paid: £15,000,000 to Blackburn Rovers for Alan Shearer, July 1996

Reported transfer fee received: £8,000,000 from Liverpool for Dietmar Hamann, July 1999

BOBBY Robson, the elder statesman of English football, saw Newcastle United qualify for the Champions League. It was a fitting reward for a sometimes difficult season but one in which former England skipper Alan Shearer was once again outstanding

Having taken Newcastle to 11th, their best top flight finish for three years, Robson entered the 2001-02 campaign full of optimism. At times he clashed with the local media but generally he had the backing of the majority of the Toon Army.

In the summer he made what proved to be some inspired signings. In came Welsh striker Craig Bellamy – from Coventry for £6m – while Frenchman Laurent Robert followed for £10.5m from Paris St-Germain. In addition, he signed Bolton defender Robbie Elliott on a free transfer.

Although no senior stars left, there was pressure on Robson after Leeds became linked with a bid for the brilliant Kieron Dyer. The manager put a £25m tag on the player in an attempt to ward off potential buyers. The bad news came before the season's start when Dyer, after two operations on his shins, was ruled out for the early part of the campaign.

The Magpies were gifted a goal on the opening day of the F.A. Barclaycard

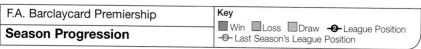

Newcastle United

F.A. Barclaycard Premiership
Season Progression

Key
■ Win ■ Loss ■ Draw ➋ League Position
➋ Last Season's League Position

All Matches

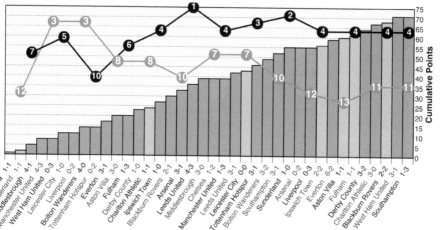

Home Matches

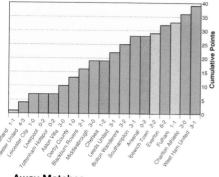

Away Matches

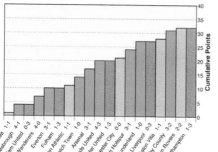

Chart Analysis

Following a mixed start which saw Newcastle pick up 14 points from a possible 27, the Magpies' form picked up to propel them upwards in the table.

They won eight out of the next ten matches – including a run of five wins on the spin – to put them top of the tree come Boxing Day.

Newcastle recovered from back-to-back defeats around the turn of the year to Chelsea and Manchester United to post a run of five wins in six to leave them second come the end of February.

They slipped up again at the start of March, losing to Championship rivals Arsenal and Liverpool, in what proved to be fatal blows to their title ambitions.

With four wins and four draws from their last nine outings, Newcastle comfortably secured fourth spot and a place in the qualifiers for the Champions League.

statistics powered by ◆ SUPERBASE™

➜ **Fixtures, results and match reports – 4thegame.com**

> **"It's bigger than Manchester United, it's bigger than Arsenal, it's bigger than Liverpool. Here at St James' Park, that match is bigger than anything."**
>
> *Bobby Robson on Newcastle v Sunderland (August 2001)*

It's a fact

Newcastle finally won a game in London, at the 30th attempt, when they beat Arsenal 3-1 at Highbury in December, ending a capital drought going back more than four years.

Premiership when Chelsea keeper Ed de Goey blundered to let Clarence Acuna steal a 1-1 draw.

They reached the final of the Intertoto Cup – and UEFA Cup qualification – but European dreams vanished when they were held to a 4-4 home draw by the Frenchmen of Troyes and went out on the away goals rule.

Back to the League and a 1-1 draw at home to local rivals Sunderland was followed by a reminder that Alan Shearer was back to his best with a brace in the 4-1 win at Middlesbrough. Welsh midfielder Gary Speed was missing and was absent for four games with a hamstring problem.

Robson signed Robert's former Paris St-Germain teammate Sylvain Distin to bolster the defence and their enigmatic start followed the upwards curve when Manchester United visited St James' Park.

Newcastle won 4-3, the visitors had Roy Keane sent off and Robson was fourth in the F.A. Barclaycard Premiership. Newcastle travelled to London, where they had forgotten to win, and duly returned with a 3-0 defeat by West Ham United.

Dyer was still missing and Carl Cort was waiting for his first appearance of the season as September continued to provide unpredictable results. A 1-0 win over Leicester courtesy of Nolberto Solano's first goal of the season was

F.A. Barclaycard Premiership
Half-Time/Full-Time Comparison

Key: ■ Win ☐ Loss ■ Draw

Home				Away				Total			
Number of Home Half Time Wins	Full Time Result W	L	D	Number of Away Half Time Wins	Full Time Result W	L	D	Total number of Half Time Wins	Full Time Result W	L	D
8	7	-	1	3	3	-	-	11	10	-	1
Number of Home Half Time Losses	Full Time Result W	L	D	Number of Away Half Time Losses	Full Time Result W	L	D	Total number of Half Time Losses	Full Time Result W	L	D
5	1	4	-	9	2	5	2	14	3	9	2
Number of Home Half Time Draws	Full Time Result W	L	D	Number of Away Half Time Draws	Full Time Result W	L	D	Total number of Half Time Draws	Full Time Result W	L	D
6	4	-	2	7	4	-	3	13	8	-	5

Chart Analysis

statistics powered by **SUPERBASE**™

Newcastle did not lose any of the 24 matches in which they were either winning or on level terms at half-time. As well as holding on to their lead in ten out of 11 games, they converted 62% of their draws into wins.

Although they were behind in 14 games at the interval, they managed to turn three of those into wins – more than any other team in the F.A. Barclaycard Premiership.

Win Barclaycard Premiership tickets - 4thegame.com

F.A. Barclaycard Premiership Results Table

Key: 88 time of goal   88 time of assist   ▲ player substituted   ▲ player substituted   ◯ yellow card   ● red card

DATE	H/A	OPPONENT	H/T	F/T	POS	REFEREE	TEAM										SUBSTITUTES USED		
19-08	A	Chelsea	0-1	1-1	10	A.P.D'Urso	Given	Barton	Hughes	Elliott	Dabizas	Bassedas ▲	Lee	Acuna ▲77	Robert 77	Ameobi	Bellamy	Lua Lua ▲	Griffin ▲	O'Brien ▲
26-08	A	Sunderland	1-1	1-1	14	M.A.Riley	Given	Barton ▲	Hughes	Elliott	Dabizas	Solano	Lee	Acuna ▲	Robert ◯43	Ameobi ▲	Bellamy 43	Acuna ▲	O'Brien ▲	Shearer ▲
08-09	H	Middlesbrough	1-1	4-1	7	G.Poll	Given	Barton ▲	Hughes	Elliott	Dabizas 60	Solano	Lee	Acuna	Robert 34 60 62 77	Shearer ▲34 77	Bellamy ▲	Ameobi ▲	O'Brien ▲	Lua Lua ▲
15-09	A	Manchester Utd	2-1	4-3	3	S.G.Bennett	Given	Griffin	O'Brien	Elliott ◯	Dabizas 52	Solano ▲	Lee ▲34	Acuna	Robert 5 52	Shearer 5 82	Bellamy	Barton ▲	Distin ▲	Ameobi ▲
23-09	H	West Ham Utd	0-1	0-3	8	P.Jones	Given	Barton ▲	O'Brien	Elliott	Dabizas	Solano 33	Lee	Acuna	Robert	Shearer	Bellamy	Distin ▲	Ameobi ▲	
26-09	A	Leicester City	1-0	1-0	5	D.Pugh	Given	Griffin	O'Brien	Elliott	Dabizas ◯	Solano	Lee	Acuna ◯	Robert	Shearer	Bellamy ◯	Ameobi ▲		
30-09	A	Liverpool	0-1	0-2	8	G.P.Barber	Given	Griffin	O'Brien	Elliott	Dabizas ▲	Solano	Lee	Acuna ▲	Robert	Shearer	Bellamy ◯	Speed ▲	Ameobi ▲	
13-10	H	Bolton	4-0	4-0	4	M.A.Riley	Given	Hughes	O'Brien	Elliott	Dabizas ▲	Solano 42	Lee	Speed ▲	Robert 60 72	Shearer 42 72 85	Bellamy ▲65	Acuna ▲	Distin ▲	Ameobi ▲
21-10	H	Tottenham	0-2	0-2	4	A.G.Wiley	Given	Hughes ▲	O'Brien	Distin	Dabizas	Solano	Lee	Speed 20	Robert ▲	Shearer	Bellamy ▲	Acuna ▲	Lua Lua ▲	Ameobi ▲
27-10	A	Everton	1-3	1-3	6	J.T.Winter	Given	Hughes	O'Brien	Elliott 37	Dabizas	Solano	Lee 50 82	Speed	Robert 85	Shearer 48	Bellamy 18 48	Lua Lua ▲	Bernard ▲	
03-11	H	Aston Villa	1-0	3-0	3	C.R.Wilkes	Given	Hughes 66	O'Brien	Elliott	Dabizas	Solano	Lee ▲	Speed	Robert	Shearer 50	Bellamy 37 82	Bernard ▲	Distin ▲	
17-11	H	Fulham	0-2	1-3	6	E.K.Wolstenholme	Given	Hughes	O'Brien	Elliott	Dabizas ▲	Solano 66	Lee ▲	Speed	Robert ▲	Shearer 29	Bellamy	Ameobi ▲	Distin ▲	Lua Lua ▲
24-11	H	Derby County	1-0	1-0	3	R.Styles	Given	Hughes	O'Brien	Elliott	Dabizas	Solano	Lee	Speed	Robert ▲29	Shearer	Bellamy	Lua Lua ▲		
01-12	A	Charlton	0-0	1-1	4	A.P.D'Urso	Given	Hughes	O'Brien	Elliott	Dabizas	Solano	Lee	Speed 73	Robert ▲	Shearer ●	Bellamy ▲	Lua Lua ▲	Ameobi ▲	
09-12	A	Ipswich Town	1-0	1-0	4	R.Styles	Given	Hughes	O'Brien	Elliott	Dabizas	Solano 20	Lee	Speed 20	Robert ▲	Shearer	Bellamy ▲	Dyer ▲	Bernard ▲	
15-12	H	Blackburn	2-1	2-1	3	S.W.Dunn	Given	Hughes	O'Brien	Distin	Dabizas	Solano 66	Lee	Speed 70	Bernard 66	Shearer	Ameobi ▲	Acuna ▲	Lua Lua ▲	
18-12	A	Arsenal	0-1	3-1	4	G.Poll	Given	Hughes	O'Brien	Elliott ▲	Dabizas ▲	Dyer ▲	Lee	Speed	Bernard	Shearer 85	Bellamy ●	Robert ▲85 90	Distin ▲	Lua Lua ▲60 90
22-12	A	Leeds United	1-1	4-3	1	J.T.Winter	Given	Hughes	O'Brien	Elliott 58	Dabizas ▲	Solano 89	Dyer 38 58 89	Speed 70	Robert ▲	Shearer 70	Bellamy ▲38	Distin ▲	Lua Lua ▲	Bernard ▲
26-12	H	Middlesbrough	1-0	3-0	1	M.R.Halsey	Given	Hughes	O'Brien	Distin	Dabizas ▲	Solano ▲58	Dyer ▲37	Speed 28 58	Robert ▲	Shearer 28	Bellamy 82	Lua Lua ▲	Lee ▲	Bernard ▲82
29-12	H	Chelsea	1-2	1-2	2	S.G.Bennett	Given	Hughes	O'Brien	Distin	Dabizas	Solano ▲37	Lee	Speed	Robert ▲	Shearer 37	Bellamy	Bernard ▲	Lua Lua ▲	Ameobi ▲
12-01	A	Manchester Utd	1-3	1-3	4	P.Jones	Given	Hughes	Distin	Elliott 69	Dabizas ▲	Dyer 59 97	Lee	Speed	Dyer	Shearer 69	Bellamy ▲59 87	Bernard ▲	Ameobi ▲	
19-01	H	Leicester City	0-0	0-0	4	G.P.Barber	Given	Hughes	O'Brien	Elliott	Dabizas	Solano 43	Dyer	Speed	Robert ●	Shearer	Bellamy	Cort ▲	Distin ▲	
30-01	A	Tottenham	3-1	3-1	3	M.L.Dean	Given	Hughes 78	O'Brien	Distin	Dabizas	Solano	McClen ▲	Acuna 67	Solano	Shearer 69	Bellamy 69 78	Robert ▲67		
02-02	H	Bolton	2-2	3-2	2	D.R.Elleray	Given	Hughes 43 79	O'Brien	Distin ▲	Dabizas	Solano 22	McClen ▲	Speed	Robert	Shearer 22 43	Bellamy 79	Acuna ▲	Jenas ▲	
09-02	H	Southampton	3-1	3-1	2	B.Knight	Given	Hughes	O'Brien	Distin ▲	Dabizas 64	Solano 29	McClen	Speed 24	Robert 24	Shearer 29 45	Bellamy 45	Jenas ▲	Elliott ▲	
24-02	A	Sunderland	0-0	2-1	2	N.S.Barry	Given	Hughes	O'Brien	Distin	Dabizas 64	Solano	Jenas	Speed	Dyer	Shearer 64	Bellamy ▲	Cort ▲		
02-03	A	Arsenal	0-2	0-3	4	A.G.Wiley	Given	Hughes	Distin	Elliott 69	Dabizas	Solano	Jenas	Speed	Robert	Shearer	Ameobi ▲	Cort ▲	Lua Lua ▲	Bernard ▲
06-03	A	Liverpool	0-2	0-3	4	J.T.Winter	Given	Hughes	O'Brien	Distin 46	Dabizas ▲	Solano 60	Jenas ▲60	Acuna	Robert 60 87	Shearer 87	Cort ▲	Ameobi ▲	Lua Lua ▲	Dyer ▲
16-03	H	Ipswich Town	0-0	1-0	4	M.A.Riley	Given	Hughes	O'Brien	Elliott ▲	Dabizas	Solano 71 73	Jenas 73	Speed	Robert ▲13 15 59	Shearer 13 15 59	Cort ▲15	Lua Lua ▲88	Acuna ▲	Bernard ▲88
29-03	H	Everton	1-1	6-2	4	G.Poll	Given	O'Brien 59	O'Brien	Distin	Dabizas	Solano	Dyer ▲71	Jenas 73	Robert ▲3	Shearer 13	Cort ▲	Acuna ▲	Bernard ▲	
05-04	A	Aston Villa	1-1	1-1	4	S.W.Dunn	Given	Hughes	O'Brien ▲	Elliott	Distin ▲	Solano	Dyer	Speed 3	Robert ▲	Shearer 3	Cort ▲	Acuna ▲	Dabizas ▲	Bellamy ▲
08-04	A	Fulham	1-0	1-1	4	A.G.Wiley	Given	Hughes ▲	O'Brien ▲	Elliott	Distin	Solano	Dyer 21	Speed	Robert ▲21	Shearer	Cort ▲	Jenas ▲	Lua Lua ▲90	Bernard ▲
13-04	H	Derby County	0-0	3-2	4	R.Styles	Given	Hughes ▲	O'Brien ▲	Distin	Dabizas	Solano 76 90	Dyer 73 76	Speed	Robert 73	Shearer 89	Cort ▲	Jenas ▲	Lua Lua ▲90	Bernard ▲
20-04	H	Charlton	1-0	3-0	4	M.L.Dean	Given	Hughes	O'Brien ▲	Elliott 46	Distin	Solano 22	Dyer	Speed 22 89	Robert	Shearer 89	Lua Lua 46	Jenas ▲	Dabizas ▲	Bernard ▲
23-04	A	Blackburn	2-2	2-2	4	U.D.Rennie	Given	Distin ▲	Distin	Elliott ▲	Dabizas	Solano 63	Dyer	Speed	Robert 71	Shearer 63 71	Lua Lua ▲	Bernard ▲	Jenas ▲	Acuna ▲88
27-04	H	West Ham Utd	1-1	3-1	4	P.A.Durkin	Given	Hughes	O'Brien ▲	Distin ▲	Dabizas	Solano 65	Dyer ▲	Speed	Robert 41 53 65	Shearer 41	Lua Lua ▲53	Bellamy ▲	Jenas ▲	Bernard ▲88
11-05	A	Southampton	0-2	1-3	4	A.P.D'Urso	Given	Hughes	Distin	Bernard	Dabizas	Solano	Dyer ▲	Speed	Robert 54	Shearer 54	Lua Lua	Jenas ▲	Distin ◯	Cort ▲

F.A. Barclaycard Premiership

Squad List

Position	Name	Appearances	Appearances as Substitute	Goals or Clean Sheets	Goal Assists	Yellow Cards	Red Cards
G	S.Given	38		9		2	
D	W.Barton	4	1			1	
D	O.Bernard	4	12	3		1	
D	N.Dabizas	33	2	3		6	
D	S.Distin	20	8			4	
D	R.Elliott	26	1	1	4	4	
D	A.Griffin	3	1				
D	A.Hughes	34			4	1	
D	A.O'Brien	31	3	2		3	
M	C.Acuna	10	6	3		3	
M	C.Bassedas	1	1				
M	K.Dyer	15	3	3	6		
M	J.Jenas	6	6		1		
M	R.Lee	15	1	1	2	3	
M	J.McClen	3					
M	L.Robert	34	2	8	21	7	
M	N.Solano	37		7	13	3	
M	G.Speed	28	1	5	5	3	
F	F.Ameobi	4	11				
F	C.Bellamy	26	1	9	5	8	1
F	C.Cort	6	2	1			
F	L.Lua Lua	4	16	3	3		
F	A.Shearer	36	1	23	6	2	1

followed by a home defeat by Liverpool before they won 4-0 at Bolton.

That victory saw Bellamy score for only the second time in the League, though he had netted four Worthington Cup goals already by that stage. Wins against Everton and Aston Villa included more goals from Bellamy, who claimed he wanted to spend the rest of his career on Tyneside.

However, Newcastle were struggling to find consistency, as witnessed by the 3-1 reverse at Fulham. The London jinx, which now extended to 27 games without a win in the capital, struck again. The hoodoo was present again on the opening day of December. Not only did the Magpies draw at Charlton, they had Shearer sent off for only the second time in his career for allegedly elbowing Jon Fortune.

Shearer protested his innocence and almost immediately the card was rescinded, leaving the striker free to play without suspension. A 1-0 Worthington Cup defeat at Chelsea was followed by four straight wins that saw Newcastle rise to the top the table.

After beating Blackburn, Newcastle returned to London, and finally broke their capital jinx at the 30th attempt. The match, however, was not for the faint-hearted. Referee Graham Poll sent off Arsenal's Ray Parlour and Newcastle's Bellamy – another red card later rescinded – and, after trailing to Robert Pires' early goal, United levelled through Andy O'Brien on the hour mark.

Alan Shearer converted an 86th minute penalty and Robert completed the win. Astonishing scenes followed, with Arsenal's Thierry Henry launching a verbal attack at the referee. Newcastle were just relieved to end their barren spell in the capital, while moving into top spot, a position they retained thanks to another prolific display, the 4-3 win at Leeds.

Despite trailing 3-1 at one stage, a last

The heart of the Barclaycard Premiership – 4thegame.com

F.A. Barclaycard Premiership

Top Goal Scorer

Alan Shearer

Total Premier League Goals Scored:	Percentage Of The Team's League Goals:
23	**31%**

Goals Scored From

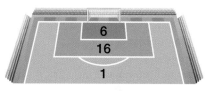

6
16
1

S hearer's decision to retire from international football continued to reap benefits for Newcastle. The striker made up for the disappointment of his injury-ravaged season in 2000-01 by returning to decisive goalscoring form and breaking a number of records in the process. He became only the ninth player to score 100 Newcastle goals and also broke the 200 Premier League goal barrier – in the 3-0 home win over Charlton. Shearer, who also scored four cup goals, might have celebrated more – he had one goal taken away by the awards panel and missed two penalties.

> "I'm sure there'll come a time when the goals aren't flowing and when that happens, I'll have to deal with it."
> *Alan Shearer*

Goal Assists

Total number of goal assists	6

Teams Scored Against

Against	Home	Away
Bolton Wanderers	2	1
Middlesbrough	1	2
Southampton	2	1
Aston Villa	1	1
Blackburn Rovers	0	2
Arsenal	0	1
Charlton Athletic	1	0
Chelsea	1	0
Derby County	1	0
Everton	1	0
Ipswich Town	1	0
Leeds United	0	1
Manchester United	0	1
Tottenham Hotspur	0	1
West Ham United	1	0
Total Goals Scored	**12**	**11**

Goals Resulting From

Key

■ Open Play ■ Corner ☐ Indirect Free Kick
☐ Direct Free Kick ■ Penalty

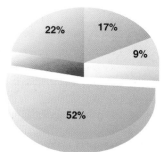

22%   17%
9%
52%

	Right Foot	Left Foot	Header
Open Play	8	1	3
Set piece	8	-	3

> "It takes a brilliant team to win the title, but we're only on the verge of that. We've had a lot of luck at the moment – whether that can remain with us until the end of the season I don't know."
>
> *Bobby Robson*
> *(December 2001)*

minute winner from Solano confirmed Newcastle as realistic Championship contenders in what was becoming the closest ever Premier League title race.

Boxing Day brought another win, 3-0 at home to Middlesbrough in the 100th Tyne-Tees derby, as Newcastle returned to the top spot having relinquished it earlier in the day after Arsenal had beaten Chelsea.

It was Chelsea in turn who ruined the Magpies' Christmas celebrations by winning 2-1 at St James' Park. Incredibly, it was the first time for 20 months in the Premier League that Shearer had scored and Newcastle had not gone on to win. Not surprisingly, Robson was named F.A. Barclaycard Premiership manager of the month while at large there were increasing calls for him to be knighted in the Queen's New Year's Day honours' list.

The honour escaped Robson, Arsenal were back on top and Newcastle lost again, this time at Old Trafford, where Shearer scored in his 500th career start.

The title race refused to give any clues to the future winners and Newcastle surged back to the top. After a Michael Duberry own goal, the men of the moment, Dyer and Bellamy, secured Newcastle's lead again.

F.A. Barclaycard Premiership	Key
Goals By Position	▩ Forward ▦ Midfield ➋ League Position ▢ Defence ▪ Goalkeeper

Home Matches

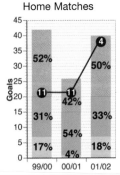

Away Matches

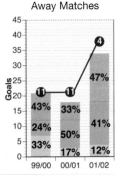

All Matches

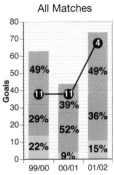

Chart Analysis

statistics powered by ◆ SUPERBASE™

Although Newcastle finished with their highest overall goal tally since their debut Premier League season in 1993-94, they did so by scoring two less at home than they had a couple of seasons ago.

Away from St James' Park, Newcastle netted 34 times, their highest ever in the Premier League and equal to the total they achieved in 1992-93 when they stormed to the Division One title, eight points clear of West Ham.

 Fixtures, results and match reports – 4thegame.com

A goalless draw at struggling Leicester was followed by the news that Speed was out with a broken toe but, more worryingly, Dyer had aggravated a foot problem in training and was to miss the next six League games.

London suddenly offered no fear for the Geordies, who won 3-1 at Spurs before beating Bolton and Southampton. The 3-1 win over the Saints, in which Shearer also hit the woodwork three times, was particularly memorable for Roberts' 33 metre, 76mph free kick goal.

Kevin Keegan made an emotional return with Manchester City in the F.A. Cup but left a loser as Solano scored the goal that took United into the quarter-finals. Another League win, over Sunderland at the end of February, kept them clinging to the coat-tails of leaders Manchester United. Robson was named manager of the month, again, for the club's perfect record in February.

Nottingham Forest's highly rated midfielder Jermaine Jenas arrived for £5m and soon settled, while stalwarts Robert Lee and Warren Barton left St James' Park for Derby. More bad news on the injury front was to follow as Bellamy, so influential alongside Shearer, was ruled out for the immediate future with a knee injury.

The Welshman's absence coincided with a dip in fortunes as United lost their

F.A. Barclaycard Premiership
Team Performance Table

League Position	Team	Points won from a possible six	Percentage of points won at home	Percentage of points won away	Overall percentage of points won
1	Arsenal	3/6			
2	Liverpool	0/6			
3	Manchester Utd	3/6	50%	50%	50%
4	**Newcastle Utd**	**71**			
5	Leeds United	6/6			
6	Chelsea	1/6			
7	West Ham Utd	3/6			
8	Aston Villa	4/6	60%	40%	50%
9	Tottenham H	3/6			
10	Blackburn R	4/6			
11	Southampton	3/6			
12	Middlesbrough	6/6			
13	Fulham	1/6	87%	47%	67%
14	Charlton Athletic	4/6			
15	Everton	6/6			
16	Bolton W	6/6			
17	Sunderland	4/6			
18	Ipswich Town	4/6	73%	87%	80%
19	Derby County	6/6			
20	Leicester City	4/6			

The table shows how many points out of a possible six Newcastle United have taken off each of the teams in the four sections. The other columns show as a percentage how many points they have taken from those available.

Chart Analysis

statistics powered by  SUPERBASE™

The Magpies took half of the points available in matches against teams in the top half of the table.

While they failed to take any points off Liverpool in the top five, they did do the 'double' over Leeds.

At St James' Park, they enjoyed most success against teams in the third sector, picking up 13 out of a possible 15 points.

As expected, they performed best overall against teams in the bottom five of the table, winning seven and drawing three of these ten matches.

Newcastle managed to do the 'double' over five teams, although none of those was against sides in the second sector.

→ **Win Barclaycard Premiership tickets - 4thegame.com**

grip on the title chase. Arsenal, unbeaten on their travels, left St James' Park with a 2-0 win, and then another of their title challengers, Liverpool beat the Toon 3-0.

March also saw United's Cup aspirations ended by the Gunners. After a 1-1 home draw, they lost 3-0 in the replay at Highbury. In between, they were held to a 2-2 home draw by Ipswich, Shearer missing a penalty, leaving them in fourth spot.

They ended March with a Good Friday bang. Everton, buoyant under new boss David Moyes, were hammered 6-2, with a brace from Solano and further goals by Olivier Bernard, Shearer, O'Brien and Cort's first League strike for ten months.

Shearer moved a step closer to a remarkable milestone with his 199th Premier League goal in the 1-1 draw against Aston Villa, for whom Peter Crouch scored his first goal. Another draw followed, against Fulham, in which Dyer dropped another hint to Sven-Goran Eriksson with a goal and a fine performance.

Newcastle were now comfortably fourth and the Champions League was beckoning. They went to Derby, who were fighting for their F.A. Barclaycard Premiership lives, and a thrilling, sometimes controversial affair, ended with a 3-2 win for the Toon Army.

It's a fact

Newcastle won 12 home games, their best return for five years.

> "You can't live with him. People can't catch him, he's alert, he's bright, he has got fantastic ability, he runs with the ball and not only that he just plays the right pass at the right time."
>
> *Bobby Robson on Kieron Dyer (March 2002)*

F.A. Barclaycard Premiership

Goals By Time Period

Key
■ Goals Scored ■ Goals Conceded

Home Matches

Time of Goal (mins)	Goals Scored	Goals Conceded
0-15	3	5
16-30	7	4
31-45	9	8
46-60	8	1
61-75	5	3
76-90	8	2

Away Matches

Time of Goal (mins)	Goals Scored	Goals Conceded
0-15	1	2
16-30	2	10
31-45	3	2
46-60	6	8
61-75	12	4
76-90	10	3

All Matches

Time of Goal (mins)	Goals Scored	Goals Conceded
0-15	4	7
16-30	9	14
31-45	12	10
46-60	14	9
61-75	17	7
76-90	18	5

Chart Analysis

statistics powered by ◆ SUPERBASE™

Overall, Newcastle grew in confidence as their matches wore on, scoring progressively more goals as time elapsed. The same pattern can be seen in reverse when looking at goals conceded from 16 minutes onwards. In the last 15 minutes, Newcastle outscored their opponents by nearly four to one.

BEST IN THE LEAGUE...
• Most goals in 61-75 minutes

➤ The heart of the Barclaycard Premiership – 4thegame.com

Newcastle United

F.A. Barclaycard Premiership
Goals Resulting From

	Six Yard Area				Inside Area				Outside Area				Total			
	Shots		Headers		Shots		Headers		Shots		Headers		Shots		Headers	
	Home	Away	Home	Away	Home	Away	Home	Away	Home	Away	Home	Away	Home	Away	Home	Away
Open Play	1	7	1	-	17	11	3	4	4	-	-	-	22	18	4	4
	3	3	1	1	10	13	2	1	3	2	-	-	16	18	3	2
Direct Free Kick									3	2	-	-	3	2		
									-	-	-	-	0	0		
Indirect Free Kick	-	-	1	2	1	1	-	-	-	-	-	-	1	1	1	2
	-	-	-	-	-	-	1	1	-	-	-	1	0	1	1	1
Penalty	-	-	-	-	2	3	-	-	-	-	-	-	2	3	0	0
	-	-	-	-	-	1	-	-	-	-	-	-	0	1	0	0
Corner	1	2	1	2	1	-	2	-	-	-	-	-	2	2	3	2
	1	-	-	2	-	1	-	1	1	2	-	-	2	3	0	3
Totals	2	9	3	4	21	15	5	4	7	2	0	0	30	26	8	8
	4	3	1	3	10	15	3	3	4	5	0	0	18	23	4	6

How Goals Were Scored
Home & Away Matches

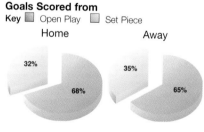

7% 7% 13%
7%
67%

Key
- ■ Open Play
- ■ Corner
- ☐ Indirect Free Kick
- ☐ Direct Free Kick
- ■ Penalty

Charts do not include 2 own goals for and 1 against.

How Goals Were Conceded
Home & Away Matches

2% 16%
6%
76%

Goals Scored from
Key ■ Open Play ■ Set Piece

Home	Away

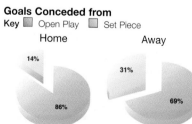

Home: 32% / 68%
Away: 35% / 65%

Goals Conceded from
Key ■ Open Play ■ Set Piece

Home | Away

Home: 14% / 86%
Away: 31% / 69%

Chart Analysis

Newcastle scored well from Set Pieces, racking up a third of their overall strikes in this manner.

They were helped by five Penalties converted compared to just the one conceded.

In fact, they conceded very few goals from Set Pieces at home – just three out of 23 – where they were most susceptible to Shots Inside Area from Open Play.

BEST IN THE LEAGUE...
- **Joint most goals scored from Direct Free Kicks at home**

statistics powered by ◆ SUPERBASE™

→ All the latest news, views and opinion – 4thegame.com

> **"I could never have imagined I would score 200 goals in the Premier League and the reaction those fans gave me in the last few minutes will live with me forever."**
>
> *Alan Shearer*
> *(April 2002)*

Two of Newcastle's goals looked offside and Derby boss John Gregory was so incensed that he was sent off for his protestations. Derby led 2-0 but, for the ninth time in the campaign, Newcastle came from behind to win.

Laurent Robert replied with a free kick before Dyer levelled with the first controversial goal. Gary Speed struck a post and substitute Jermaine Jenas hit the crossbar before Solano served up the opportunity for another substitute, Lomano Lua Lua, to complete the remarkable transformation in injury time.

During the match Shearer suffered a broken nose in a bizarre accident when he clashed with former teammate and best friend Rob Lee. The striker recovered for the next outing at home to Charlton. Not only did Newcastle win 3-0 but Shearer claimed his 200th Premier League goal. A 2-2 draw at Blackburn, with Shearer scoring twice more, confirmed fourth place and started massive celebrations among the travelling fans.

United said goodbye to their fans with a 3-1 win over West Ham. Shearer scored again and Lua Lua netted his third goal in four games. The season ended disappointingly with a 3-1 defeat at Southampton, Shearer netting again against one of his former clubs.

It's a fact

When Newcastle lost 2-1 at home to Chelsea, it was the first time for 20 months that they had not won when Alan Shearer had scored.

F.A. Barclaycard Premiership	Key
Shot Efficiency	■ Goals Scored ■ Other Shots On Target

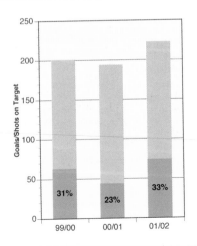

Season	Division	Shots Off Target	Shots On Target	Total Goals
1999 - 2000	P	n/a	201	63
2000 - 2001	P	n/a	194	44
2001 - 2002	P	230	223	74

Chart Analysis

The percentage of Shots On Target converted to goals by Newcastle Utd rose by an incredible 10% compared to last season.

Their 33% efficiency rate was their best ever in nine years in the Premier League as they notched 30 more goals than they had in the previous campaign.

statistics powered by **SUPERBASE**™

➡ **Fixtures, results and match reports – 4thegame.com**

Newcastle United

F.A. Barclaycard Premiership

Team Discipline

Key
■ Forward ■ Midfield
□ Defence ■ Goalkeeper

Total Number Of Bookings

Total number of red cards	2
Total number of yellow cards	51

Referee Performance

Referee	Games Refereed	Red Cards	Yellow Cards
A.P.D'Urso	3	1	7
G.Poll	3	1	6
E.K.Wolstenholme	1	-	6

Type of Yellow Cards Received

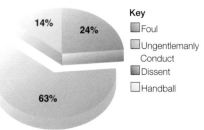

Key
□ Foul
□ Ungentlemanly Conduct
■ Dissent
□ Handball

14% 24% 63%

Bookings by Position 1999/2000 - 2001/2002

Home Matches

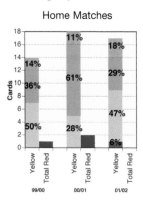

Away Matches

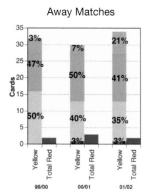

All Matches

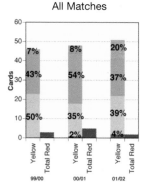

Chart Analysis

A drop in bookings at home compared to last season did not quite compensate for a rise away from St James' Park, as Newcastle clocked up three more cautions overall.

However, they did manage to collect their least amount of Red Cards since 1996-97 – and in fact, both the reds picked up in 2001-02 were later rescinded.

While the cards attributed to midfielders dropped, the share of those picked up by forwards more than doubled.

Of the Yellow Cards handed out to the team overall, nearly a quarter were for Dissent.

> "Injuries are a fact of life and you can't ask players to go around trying to protect themselves. That's not how it works. They have to go into tackles wholly committed."
>
> *Bobby Robson*
> *(April 2002)*

statistics powered by ◆ SUPERBASE™

➤ **Win Barclaycard Premiership tickets - 4thegame.com**

Southampton

F.A. Barclaycard Premiership Final standing for the 2001-2002 season

Final Position		Games Played	Games Won	Games Drawn	Games Lost	Goals For	Goals Against	Total Points
10	Blackburn Rovers	38	12	10	16	55	51	46
11	Southampton	38	12	9	17	46	54	45
12	Middlesbrough	38	12	9	17	35	47	45

"The first priority was to avoid relegation. We had a chance to move on and finish in the top half of the table but we had a bit of a wobble and we'll be looking to improve on that next season."

Gordon Strachan (May 2002)

Club Honours and Records

Division 3 Champions: 1921-22 (South), 1959-60

FA Cup Winners: 1976

Record victory: 9-3 v Wolverhampton Wanderers, Division 2, 18 September, 1965

Record defeat:

0-8 v Tottenham Hotspur, Division 2, 28 March, 1936

0-8 v Everton, Division 1, 20 November, 1971

League goals in a season (team):

112, Division 3 (South), 1957-58

League goals in a season (player):

39, Derek Reeves, Division 3, 1959-60

Career league goals:

185, Mike Channon, 1966 to 1977 and 1979 to 1982

League appearances:

713, Terry Paine, 1956 to 1974

Reported transfer fee paid: £4,000,000 to Derby County for Rory Delap, July 2001

Reported transfer fee received: £8,100,000 from Tottenham for Dean Richards, September 2001

NEW stadium, new manager, refreshed hope. Southampton moved into the St Mary's Stadium and following Gordon Strachan's arrival in October, they turned relegation fears around to finish safe.

Saints kicked off the campaign with Stuart Gray at the helm, his appointment having been made permanent after he had stepped in as caretaker the previous season following Glenn Hoddle's departure to Spurs.

Southampton had been linked with George Graham, Bruce Rioch, Harry Redknapp and Steve McClaren. After the latter chose to stay in the north, Gray was given the job full-time at the end of June.

Hassan Kachloul, whose contract had expired, left for Aston Villa, but Saints signed Derby's Rory Delap, who agreed a club record £4m move, and Swedish international Anders Svensson.

Southampton were also linked with a move for German striker Oliver Bierhoff while Tottenham were rebuffed in attempts to sign Dean Richards, put off by a £10m price tag.

The new stadium was unveiled in a friendly against the Spaniards of Espanyol but it finished with a 4-3 loss and the pristine arena, while regularly filled, was to prove a stone around the Saints' necks.

F.A. Barclaycard Premiership

Season Progression

All Matches

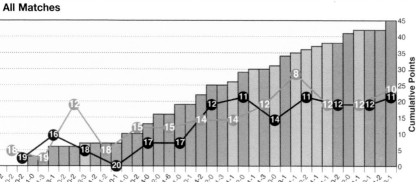

Home Matches

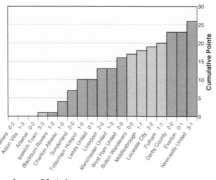

Away Matches

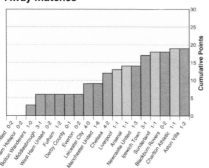

Chart Analysis

Southampton got off to a terrible start, losing their first three games 2-0 each time.

Although they produced two wins in their next five outings, it was not enough to spare new manager Stuart Gray the sack.

Former Coventry boss Gordon Strachan was appointed in his place and the fiery Scot quickly set about his task.

Although Saints lost three out of their next four, they followed that with a run of six wins in their next nine games, finishing with consecutive victories over Chelsea and Liverpool at the start of January, to climb to 12th in the table.

From that point, the eight draws that Southampton picked up were in marked contrast to the solitary one gained in the first half of the season at home to Ipswich in Strachan's first game in charge.

However, the points they collected were enough to see them finish safely in 11th, nine points clear of relegation.

> "The players work terrifically hard on a daily basis and it is that which has been one of the main characteristics of this football club for many years. It is an advantage and can get us out of corners."
>
> *Coach Mick Wadsworth (September 2002)*

It's a fact

When 31,198 spectators crammed into the St Mary's Stadium to see the 1-0 win over Charlton, it was the biggest home crowd to see the Saints for 32 years.

After an opening day loss at Leeds where Claus Lundekvam was sent off, they started F.A. Barclaycard Premiership life at St Mary's with a 2-0 home defeat by Chelsea. A third loss, at Spurs, saw Saints in 19th place.

Having missed Jason Dodd early on, things began to look up when they were awarded £1m in compensation from Spurs after the loss of their manager. On the pitch, September improved with their first win, at Bolton, where Marian Pahars struck his first goal of the season. More money from White Hart Lane followed when Richards finally rejoined Hoddle. The fee was £8.1m but the move only went ahead after Richards agreed to forsake more than £1m as part of his contract agreement.

The departure was a blow to Saints, who lost 3-1 at home to Aston Villa in a game which saw both sides lose a player. While St Mary's was proving something of a jinx, Saints won again on their travels at Middlesbrough.

Gray's position was beginning to look uncomfortable and successive defeats by Arsenal and at West Ham spelt the end for the likeable manager. He was sacked and, almost immediately, replaced by former Coventry boss Gordon Strachan.

Some fans were unhappy that the man who had taken Coventry down had been given the task of rescuing

---

F.A. Barclaycard Premiership	Key
Half-Time/Full-Time Comparison	■ Win ■ Loss ■ Draw

Home				Away				Total			
Number of Home Half Time Wins	Full Time Result W	L	D	Number of Away Half Time Wins	Full Time Result W	L	D	Total number of Half Time Wins	Full Time Result W	L	D
6	4	-	2	1	1	-	-	7	5	-	2
Number of Home Half Time Losses	Full Time Result W	L	D	Number of Away Half Time Losses	Full Time Result W	L	D	Total number of Half Time Losses	Full Time Result W	L	D
6	-	5	1	10	1	6	3	16	1	11	4
Number of Home Half Time Draws	Full Time Result W	L	D	Number of Away Half Time Draws	Full Time Result W	L	D	Total number of Half Time Draws	Full Time Result W	L	D
7	3	2	2	8	3	4	1	15	6	6	3

Chart Analysis

statistics powered by ◆ SUPERBASE™

Though they didn't lose any of the seven games they were winning at half-time, Southampton struggled to get their noses in front away from home.

Yet they battled hard, and even though they were down in ten games on their travels, they did manage to take points away from four of those fixtures, including beating Chelsea 4-2 on New Year's Day after being 2-1 down at the break.

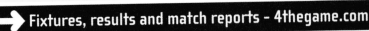

➡ Fixtures, results and match reports - 4thegame.com

F.A. Barclaycard Premiership Results Table

Key: 00 time of goal   00 time of booking   ● player substituted   ▲ player substitute   ○ player sent off

DATE	H/A	OPPONENT	H/T	F/T	POS	REFEREE	Team (XI)	Substitutes Used
18-08	A	Leeds Utd	0-0	0-2	18	C.R.Wilkes	Jones, Delap, Richards, Lundekvam●, Bridge, Marsden▲, Oakley, Svensson, Davies, Rosler▲, Pahars▲	Beattie▲, Tessem▲, Benali▲
25-08	H	Chelsea	0-1	0-2	18	D.R.Elleray	Jones, Delap, Richards, Lundekvam, Bridge, Marsden▲, Oakley, Svensson, Davies, Rosler▲, Pahars▲	Beattie▲, Tessem▲, Ripley▲
09-09	A	Tottenham	0-0	1-0	19	A.G.Wiley	Jones, Delap, Richards, Lundekvam, Bridge, Tessem▲, Oakley, Svensson, Davies, Rosler, Pahars▲	Beattie▲, Murray▲, Draper▲
15-09	A	Bolton	0-0	1-0	18	D.Pugh	Jones, El-Khalej▲, Williams, Lundekvam, Bridge 77, Delap, Oakley, Svensson, Tessem▲, Beattie, Davies	Pahars▲77, Le Tissier▲
24-09	A	Aston Villa	1-2	1-3	20	S.W.Dunn	Jones, Delap●, El-Khalej, Lundekvam, Bridge●, Tessem▲, Oakley, Svensson, Davies, Beattie 45, Pahars▲45	Le Tissier▲, McDonald▲, Benali▲
29-09	H	Middlesbrough	0-0	3-1	16	A.G.Wiley	Jones, El-Khalej, Monk●, Lundekvam, Bridge 67, Marsden●, Marsden, Svensson, Davies, Beattie 67 85, Pahars▲72 72	McDonald▲, Ripley▲, Benali▲
13-10	H	Arsenal	0-0	0-2	17	G.P.Barber	Jones, Dodd, El-Khalej, Lundekvam, Bridge, Marsden▲, Oakley, Svensson, Davies, Beattie, Pahars▲85	Ripley▲, McDonald▲
20-10	A	West Ham Utd	0-0	0-2	19	N.S.Barry	Jones, Dodd, El-Khalej, Lundekvam, Bridge, Marsden, Draper, Svensson, Davies, Beattie, Pahars▲	Dodd▲, Ripley▲
24-10	H	Ipswich Town	2-1	3-3	18	U.D.Rennie	Jones, Delap, Williams, Lundekvam, Bridge, Ripley▲, Oakley, Tessem●, Marsden 51, Beattie, Pahars▲	Ripley▲
27-10	A	Fulham	1-2	1-2	18	A.P.D'Urso	Jones, Dodd, Williams, Lundekvam, Bridge, Delap, Oakley, Svensson, Tessem▲, Beattie●13 22, Pahars 13 22 51	Davies▲, Petrescu▲
03-11	H	Blackburn	1-1	1-2	19	A.G.Wiley	Jones, Dodd, Williams, El-Khalej, Bridge, Telfer, Oakley, Svensson, Marsden, Beattie▲32, Pahars	Tessem▲, Williams▲, Rosler▲
17-11	A	Derby County	0-1	0-1	17	P.A.Durkin	Jones, Dodd, Williams, Lundekvam, Bridge, Telfer, Oakley, Svensson, Marsden, Beattie 35, Pahars 35	Delap▲, Petrescu▲
24-11	H	Charlton	0-0	0-2	17	D.J.Gallagher	Jones, Dodd, Williams, Lundekvam, Bridge, Telfer, Oakley, Svensson, Marsden, Beattie▲, Pahars	Le Tissier▲, Davies▲
02-12	A	Everton	0-0	0-2	18	J.T.Winter	Jones, Dodd, Williams, Lundekvam, Bridge, Telfer, Oakley, Svensson, Marsden, Beattie 58, Pahars▲68	Davies▲
08-12	A	Leicester City	1-0	4-0	17	G.Poll	Jones, Dodd 89, Williams, Lundekvam, Bridge, Telfer 74, Oakley, Svensson 12 74, Marsden, Beattie, Pahars	Davies▲
15-12	H	Sunderland	1-0	2-0	17	D.Pugh	Jones, Dodd, Williams, Lundekvam, Bridge, Telfer, Oakley, Svensson 67, Marsden▲42, Beattie 63, Pahars	Davies▲
22-12	A	Manchester Utd	0-3	1-6	15	S.W.Dunn	Jones, Dodd, Williams, Lundekvam, Bridge, Telfer 55, Marsden, Svensson, Marsden, Beattie, Pahars	Delap▲
26-12	H	Tottenham	0-0	0-1	17	P.Jones	Jones, Dodd 56, Williams 56, Lundekvam, Bridge, Telfer, Delap, Svensson, Davies, Beattie▲, Pahars▲55 73	Fernandes▲
29-12	H	Leeds Utd	0-0	0-1	17	M.R.Halsey	Jones, Dodd, Williams 55, Lundekvam, Bridge, Telfer▲, Delap▲, Svensson, Marsden, Beattie, Pahars	Ormerod▲
01-01	H	Chelsea	1-2	2-4	12	G.Poll	Jones, Dodd, Williams, Lundekvam, Bridge, Telfer, Delap, Svensson, Marsden, Beattie, Pahars▲71	Ormerod▲
09-01	H	Liverpool	1-0	1-1	12	E.K.Wolstenholme	Jones, Dodd 3, Williams, Lundekvam, Bridge, Telfer, Delap, Svensson, Marsden 63, Beattie, Delgado▲	Ormerod▲
13-01	H	Manchester Utd	1-2	1-3	15	S.G.Bennett	Jones, Dodd, Williams, Lundekvam, Bridge, Telfer, Marsden, Svensson, Fernandes▲, Beattie 7 73, Le Tissier▲	Le Tissier▲
19-01	A	Liverpool	1-0	1-2	14	N.S.Barry	Jones, Dodd, Williams, Lundekvam, Bridge, Telfer, Marsden, Svensson, Fernandes▲, Beattie 63, Pahars	Tessem▲
30-01	H	West Ham Utd	1-0	2-0	11	P.Dowd	Jones, Dodd, Williams, Lundekvam, Bridge, Telfer, Oakley, Svensson 64, Fernandes▲43 64, Beattie▲3, Pahars	Davies▲43 64, Blackis▲
02-02	A	Arsenal	0-1	1-1	13	C.R.Wilkes	Jones, Dodd, Williams, Lundekvam, Bridge, Telfer, Oakley, Svensson 79, Marsden, Davies 46, Pahars	Fernandes▲79, Tessem▲, Le Tissier
09-02	H	Newcastle Utd	1-3	3-1	14	B.Knight	Jones, Dodd, Williams, Lundekvam, Bridge, Telfer, Oakley, Svensson 39, Marsden, Davies▲43, Pahars 39	Tessem▲
23-02	A	Bolton	0-0	0-1	11	E.K.Wolstenholme	Jones, Delap 52 88, Williams, Lundekvam, Bridge, Delap●, Marsden, Svensson, Fernandes▲, Davies, Pahars	Delap▲
02-03	H	Ipswich Town	0-0	3-1	11	M.R.Halsey	Jones, Delap, Williams, Lundekvam, Bridge, Telfer, Oakley 52 61, Svensson, Marsden 88, Davies, Ormerod▲61	Telfer▲
06-03	A	Middlesbrough	1-0	1-1	12	U.D.Rennie	Jones, Delap, Williams, Lundekvam, Bridge, Telfer, Oakley, Svensson, Marsden, Tessem, Ormerod 38	Ormerod▲
16-03	H	Leicester City	1-2	2-2	11	M.L.Dean	Jones, Telfer, Williams, Lundekvam, Bridge, Marsden▲, Oakley, Svensson 28, Davies, Davies, Pahars 28 86	Beattie▲86, Fernandes▲
23-03	A	Sunderland	0-1	1-1	11	M.D.Messias	Jones, Telfer, Williams, Lundekvam, Bridge, Marsden, Oakley, Svensson 87, Delap 21, Davies, Pahars	Tessem▲87
30-03	H	Fulham	1-1	2-2	11	J.T.Winter	Jones, Dodd 21, Williams, Lundekvam, Bridge, Telfer, Oakley, Svensson 21, Delap, Ormerod, Ormerod	Ormerod▲
01-04	A	Blackburn	0-2	1-2	11	C.R.Wilkes	Jones, Telfer, Williams 86, Lundekvam, Bridge, Telfer, Oakley, Delap, Fernandes, Ormerod, Pahars	Fernandes▲
06-04	A	Derby County	1-0	2-0	11	S.G.Bennett	Jones, Dodd 29, Williams, El-Khalej 86, Bridge, Telfer, Oakley 29, Delap 54, Marsden, Beattie, Pahars▲54	Tessem▲, Pahars▲54
13-04	H	Charlton	0-1	1-1	11	P.Dowd	Jones, Dodd, Williams, Lundekvam, Bridge, Telfer, Oakley, Svensson, Delap, Beattie, Pahars▲	Tessem▲, Ormerod▲
20-04	H	Everton	0-1	1-1	11	M.R.Halsey	Jones, Dodd, Williams, Lundekvam, Bridge, Telfer, Delap, Svensson, Tessem, Beattie, Pahars●	Ormerod▲, Fernandes▲
27-04	A	Aston Villa	0-2	1-2	12	D.R.Elleray	Moss, Dodd, Williams●, Lundekvam, Bridge, Telfer 90, Delap, Svensson, Fernandes, Beattie 52, Ormerod▲52	Davies▲, Tessem▲
11-05	H	Newcastle Utd	2-0	3-1	11	A.P.D'Urso	Moss, Dodd, El-Khalej●, Lundekvam, Bridge, Telfer, Delap, Svensson 16, Ormerod▲22, Beattie 22 90, Pahars▲16	Monk▲, Tessem▲, Fernandes▲

Southampton

F.A. Barclaycard Premiership
Squad List

Position	Name	Appearances	Appearances as Substitute	Goals or Clean Sheets	Goal Assists	Yellow Cards	Red Cards
G	P.Jones	36		9			
G	N.Moss	2					
D	F.Benali		3				
D	W.Bridge	38			2		
D	J.Dodd	26	3		4	3	
D	T.El-Khalej	12	1		2	2	1
D	C.Lundekvam	34				2	1
D	G.Monk	1	1			1	
D	D.Richards	4					
D	P.Williams	27	1			2	5
M	I.Bleidelis		1				
M	R.Delap	24	4	2	2	3	2
M	M.Draper	1	1			1	
M	F.Fernandes	6	5	1	1		
M	M.Le Tissier		4			1	
M	C.Marsden	27	1	3	1	4	1
M	P.Murray		1				
M	M.Oakley	26	1	1	3	1	
M	D.Petrescu		2				
M	S.Ripley	1	4		1		
M	A.Svensson	33	1	4	6		
M	P.Telfer	27	1	1	2	1	
M	J.Tessem	7	15	2		2	
F	J.Beattie	24	4	12	6	3	
F	K.Davies	18	5	2		5	
F	A.Delgado		1				
F	S.McDonald		2				
F	B.Ormerod	8	10	1	3		
F	M.Pahars	33	3	14	9	2	
F	U.Rosler	3	1				

Southampton's worrying position but Strachan defended his record and promised he would keep his new team up.

The early signs were far from encouraging. Saints forced a 3-1 lead at home against Ipswich, only to be held to a 3-3 draw. They followed that with three straight defeats, by Fulham, Blackburn and Derby, as they slumped to the foot of the F.A. Barclaycard Premiership.

Strachan wasted little time in adding to his squad, which was still without Matt Le Tissier. He returned to Coventry to sign defender Paul Williams and midfielder Paul Telfer.

Saints had shown battling qualities under Strachan and they finally got that elusive first home win – but not before a Pagan priestess had been brought in to perform a ritual dance outside the stadium, built, as it was, on an ancient burial ground.

Pahars, with his seventh goal of the season, confirmed Southampton's first ever F.A. Barclaycard Premiership win at St Mary's in late November and, within minutes of the final whistle where players and fans alike celebrated as if a cup had been won, T-shirts were on sale proclaiming the legend: "1st Win: I was there!"

Strachan signed Ecuadorian pair Agustin Delgado and Kleber Chala, though they were to feature rarely as Saints tried to move out of the danger zone.

In December, the manager made another signing in Blackpool striker Brett Ormerod and he sat on the bench as Southampton raced to their best away win for nearly 17 years with a 4-0 thrashing of Leicester at Filbert Street.

After Saints won at home again, against Sunderland, Strachan admitted bringing in a sports psychologist to help his players, They may well have required an extra

F.A. Barclaycard Premiership

Top Goal Scorer

Marian Pahars

Total Premier League Goals Scored:	Percentage Of The Team's League Goals:
14	30%

Goals Scored From

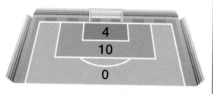

4
10
0

P ahars scored more F.A. Barclaycard Premiership goals than any other Saints striker since Matt Le Tissier finished as leading marksman with 19 in the 1994-95 season. With Le Tissier having announced his retirement in March 2002, Pahars is all set to replace Le God in the fans' affections. Signed from Skonto Riga in February 1999, the Latvian international quickly endeared himself with the South Coast fans after scoring a brace against Everton on the last day of the season to keep the Saints up. Following this latest haul, his League tally rises to 39. Pahars enjoyed a better first half of the season, with nine coming in a 14-game spell.

"Perhaps the manager felt we were lacking a little bit of fitness when he came in. But I am scoring goals because I feel much fitter and I think it has affected everyone."

Marian Pahars

Goals Resulting From
Key
■ Open Play ■ Corner □ Indirect Free Kick
□ Direct Free Kick ■ Penalty

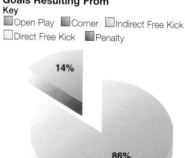

14%

86%

	Right Foot	Left Foot	Header
Open Play	6	2	4
Set piece	2	-	-

Goal Assists

Total number of goal assists	9

Teams Scored Against

Against	Home	Away
Leicester City	2	1
Aston Villa	1	0
Blackburn Rovers	1	0
Bolton Wanderers	0	1
Charlton Athletic	1	0
Chelsea	0	1
Derby County	1	0
Ipswich Town	1	0
Manchester United	0	1
Middlesbrough	0	1
Newcastle United	0	1
Sunderland	1	0
Total Goals Scored	8	6

The heart of the Barclaycard Premiership – 4thegame.com

> **"We're in good form and I can't disguise the fact I'm very happy. I'm proud of my players and they deserve a pat on the back."**
>
> *Gordon Strachan (January 2002)*

session after the next game, the 6-1 humiliation at Old Trafford.

Still, Saints were showing signs of improvement, with Williams proving a rock in defence in place of Richards. How satisfying then, when Spurs – along with Hoddle and Richards – came back to Southampton on Boxing Day for the first time and left St Mary's with a 1-0 defeat. This time James Beattie grabbed the winner.

After a disappointing home defeat by Leeds, they eked out a famous win at Chelsea, followed by confirmation that the St Mary's jinx was over as they beat Liverpool at their new home.

The 4-2 New Year's Day win at Stamford Bridge was particularly impressive. Just seven minutes had gone when Beattie converted a 35 yard free kick and, though Chelsea took the lead, further goals from Pahars, Chris Marsden and another from Beattie secured a memorable and invaluable win.

Another arrival, Rennes winger Fabrice Fernandes, boosted the squad further and he was on the bench as Saints beat Liverpool 2-0. The win, thanks to a penalty from Beattie and an own goal by Liverpool's John Arne

F.A. Barclaycard Premiership
Goals By Position

Key: Forward · Midfield · League Position · Defence · Goalkeeper

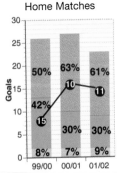

Home Matches

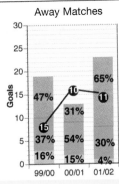

Away Matches

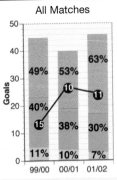

All Matches

Chart Analysis

statistics powered by **SUPERBASE**™

Southampton scored their most goals overall since 1997-98 despite registering their lowest tally at home since 1995-96.

Goals were evenly split between home and away – although the 23 scored on their travels was the highest for seven years.

The distribution of goals was heavily weighted towards the strikers with defenders contributing just three out of 46.

All the latest news, views and opinion – 4thegame.com

Riise, took Strachan's men to the heady heights of 12th place.

Next on the agenda was the visit of Manchester United. The Saints' PA announcer set the tone when he paused as he read out the teams and said 'oh dear' before listing the presence of Ruud van Nistelrooy. Though Beattie put Southampton ahead within three minutes with his 12th goal, the Dutchman responded five minutes later.

Beattie hobbled off soon after with an ankle ligament injury that was to rule him out for nearly three months, and later goals from David Beckham and Ole Gunnar Solskjaer halted Saints' run. F.A. Cup defeat at Division One strugglers Rotherham was followed by a 1-1 draw at Liverpool.

A win over West Ham was followed by a spirited draw at Arsenal, taking Saints to eighth. It also brought the comical sight of substitute Le Tissier being booked as he warmed up on the touchline!

While Pahars continued his habit of scoring against Newcastle with his fifth goal in four games against the Magpies, he couldn't prevent a 3-1 defeat at St James' Park. After that, Saints proceeded to set off on a run of six games without losing to make certain of their safety.

One player responsible for the improvement was left back Wayne Bridge,

F.A. Barclaycard Premiership
Team Performance Table

League Position	Team	Points won from a possible six	Percentage of points won at home	Percentage of points won away	Overall percentage of points won
1	Arsenal	1/6			
2	Liverpool	4/6			
3	Manchester Utd	0/6	40%	13%	27%
4	Newcastle Utd	3/6			
5	Leeds United	0/6			
6	Chelsea	3/6			
7	West Ham Utd	3/6			
8	Aston Villa	0/6	40%	20%	30%
9	Tottenham H	3/6			
10	Blackburn R	0/6			
11	**Southampton**	45			
12	Middlesbrough	4/6			
13	Fulham	1/6	42%	33%	38%
14	Charlton Athletic	4/6			
15	Everton	0/6			
16	Bolton W	4/6			
17	Sunderland	4/6			
18	Ipswich Town	4/6	60%	67%	63%
19	Derby County	3/6			
20	Leicester City	4/6			

The table shows how many points out of a possible six Southampton have taken off each of the teams in the four sections. The other columns show as a percentage how many points they have taken from those available.

Chart Analysis

statistics powered by  SUPERBASE™

While Southampton performed pretty well at home to teams in the top five, they were let down by their form away from home.

This carried over against teams in the second sector, where they picked up the same amount of points at home and did slightly better on their travels.

Although they did slightly better overall against teams in their own sector, they collected most points from fixtures against teams in the bottom five.

Southampton failed to take points off five teams in the F.A. Barclaycard Premiership, and did not manage to do the 'double' over any.

➡ Fixtures, results and match reports – 4thegame.com

whose continued development was rewarded with his first senior England cap in February.

Delap suffered his second red card in the 0-0 draw against Bolton and, after a 3-1 win at Ipswich, three draws maintained Southampton's unbeaten sequence. Perhaps the players were being helped by their fans. A scientific survey, using the latest sound equipment revealed that Southampton fans were the most tuneful.

Strachan was clearly enjoying life and even talked about the possibility of European football coming to St Mary's as the progression continued.

There was some sad, if not totally unpredictable, news as after 16 years at Southampton, Le Tissier announced he would retire at the end of the season. It had been a tough campaign for the crowd favourite, forced to sit on the sidelines by a succession of niggling injuries. The man nicknamed 'Le God' had scored 209 goals in 462 appearances and the announcement brought to an end the career of one of the most talented players ever to wear the red and white of Southampton.

Four successive draws followed before they lost 2-0 to Blackburn on 1 April. Strachan was typically frank. He claimed to be 'very disappointed', adding: "We did some nice things, but this competition isn't about being nice."

It's a fact

Saints set a club record with five away wins. That included a 4-0 win at Leicester in December, their best away win for nearly 17 years.

> "They supported us in their numbers even at the start of the season when we weren't doing so well at the new stadium and it's a big lift knowing you have around 30,000 people cheering for you each home game."
>
> *Rory Delap (March 2002)*

F.A. Barclaycard Premiership
Goals By Time Period

Key
■ Goals Scored ■ Goals Conceded

Home Matches

Time of Goal (mins)	Goals Scored	Goals Conceded
0-15	2	5
16-30	6	2
31-45	5	5
46-60	4	2
61-75	4	4
76-90	2	4

Away Matches

Time of Goal (mins)	Goals Scored	Goals Conceded
0-15	2	3
16-30	8	
31-45	2	7
46-60	5	3
61-75	7	4
76-90	7	7

All Matches

Time of Goal (mins)	Goals Scored	Goals Conceded
0-15	4	8
16-30	6	10
31-45	7	12
46-60	9	5
61-75	11	8
76-90	9	11

Chart Analysis

statistics powered by ◆ SUPERBASE™

Southampton were outscored by nearly two to one in the first half of matches. They seemed to rally after the restart, when they scored more goals overall than their opponents from 46-60 and 61-75 minutes.

However, they did concede twice as many goals as they scored in the last 15 minutes of matches at home.

Away from St Mary's, they scored only four goals in the first half all season.

Win Barclaycard Premiership tickets – 4thegame.com

F.A. Barclaycard Premiership
Goals Resulting From

Key
☐ Goals Scored ☐ Goals Conceded

	Six Yard Area				Inside Area				Outside Area				Total			
	Shots		Headers		Shots		Headers		Shots		Headers		Shots		Headers	
	Home	Away	Home	Away	Home	Away	Home	Away	Home	Away	Home	Away	Home	Away	Home	Away
Open Play	1	4	3	-	6	12	3	-	-	-	-	-	7	16	6	0
	2	3	3	2	10	10	-	2	3	4	-	-	15	17	3	4
Direct Free Kick									1	1			1	1		
									1	1			1	1		
Indirect Free Kick	-	-	1	-	-	-	1	2	1	1	-	-	1	1	2	2
	-	-	-	-	-	-	-	-	-	-	-	-	0	0	0	0
Penalty	-	-	-	-	3	1	-	-	-	-	-	-	3	1	0	0
	-	-	-	-	-	2	-	-	-	-	-	-	0	2	0	0
Corner	-	-	-	-	-	-	1	1	-	-	-	-	0	0	1	1
	1	4	2	1	-	2	-	1	-	-	-	-	1	6	2	2
Totals	1	4	4	0	9	13	5	3	2	2	0	0	12	19	9	3
	3	7	5	3	10	14	0	3	4	5	0	0	17	26	5	6

How Goals Were Scored
Home & Away Matches

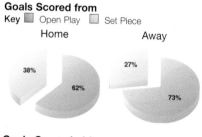

5% 9% 5% 14%
67%

Key
■ Open Play
■ Corner
☐ Indirect Free Kick
☐ Direct Free Kick
■ Penalty

Charts do not include 3 own goals for.

How Goals Were Conceded
Home & Away Matches

4% 4%
4% 20%
72%

Goals Scored from
Key ■ Open Play ☐ Set Piece

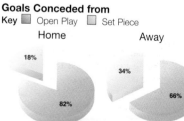

Home
38% 62%

Away
27% 73%

Goals Conceded from
Key ■ Open Play ☐ Set Piece

Home
18% 82%

Away
34% 66%

Chart Analysis

Southampton scored a high proportion of goals from Set Pieces at their new stadium.

Overall, they scored nearly as many goals from Indirect Free Kicks alone as they did from all the other Set Pieces put together.

They also benefited from three own goals and scored four Penalties.

In terms of goals conceded, the Saints shipped a fifth of their goals from Corners.

BEST IN THE LEAGUE...
- Most goals scored from Penalties at home
- Most goals conceded from Corners overall and away

statistics powered by ◆ SUPERBASE™

> "Even if the club offered me a contract for sentimental reasons I could not take money under false pretences. If I thought I could play on at my best that would be different – but my body is not so much giving me hints as screaming at me."
>
> *Matt Le Tissier*
> *(March 2002)*

It's a fact

Jo Tessem claimed Southampton's 450th goal in the Premier League when he headed the equaliser at Arsenal in February.

A 2-0 home win over Derby kept Saints in 11th place and after a 1-1 draw at Charlton, the club's 99th in the Premier League, Southampton suffered a disappointing home defeat. Everton, another club to change managers during the course of the season, won 1-0 with a goal by Steve Watson in a dire affair and then Saints lost 2-1 at Villa.

Le Tissier, meanwhile, revealed he could still be playing on the South Coast – with Jewson Wessex League club Eastleigh. The Saints legend said he would consider playing games for Eastleigh after receiving an approach from the club's assistant manager David Hughes – a former Southampton teammate.

The season ended with a home win. Svensson, soon to join Sweden's World Cup party, claimed the first goal in a 3-1 win over Newcastle and, after a Beattie penalty, Tessem claimed the 1,001st and final goal of the 2001-02 F.A. Barclaycard Premiership season.

F.A. Barclaycard Premiership
Shot Efficiency

Key ■ Goals Scored ■ Other Shots On Target

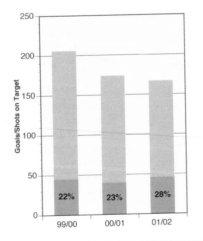

Season	Division	Shots Off Target	Shots On Target	Total Goals
1999 - 2000	P	n/a	206	45
2000 - 2001	P	n/a	174	40
2001 - 2002	P	179	167	46

Chart Analysis

Southampton's ability to convert 28% of their Shots On Target into goals earned them their highest end of season tally since they notched 50 in the 1997-98 season.

They managed this despite registering less Shots On Target than in both the previous seasons.

statistics powered by **◆ SUPERBASE**™

> **All the latest news, views and opinion - 4thegame.com**

F.A. Barclaycard Premiership	
Team Discipline	

Total Number Of Bookings

Total number of red cards	5
Total number of yellow cards	36

Referee Performance

Referee	Games Refereed	Red Cards	Yellow Cards
C.R.Wilkes	3	1	6
A.P.D'Urso	2	1	2
S.W.Dunn	2	1	1

Type of Yellow Cards Received

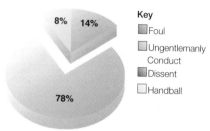

Key
- 🟦 Foul
- ⬜ Ungentlemanly Conduct
- ⬛ Dissent
- ⬜ Handball

8% · 14% · 78%

Bookings by Position 1999/2000 - 2001/2002

Home Matches
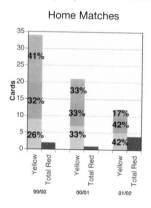

Away Matches
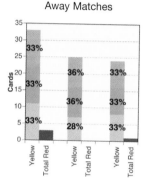

All Matches
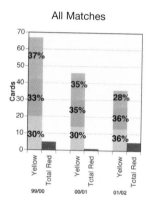

Chart Analysis

The number of Yellow Cards picked up by Southampton players fell to its lowest level ever in the Premier League. It was also the least amount collected by any club in the top flight in the 2001-02 season.

Away from home, not only did they pick up twice as many bookings as they did at home, those Yellow Cards were equally distributed throughout the outfield positions.

However, while the number of cautions declined, the five Red Cards collected during the course of the season equalled the number picked up two years ago.

BEST IN THE LEAGUE...
- **Least amount of Yellow Cards**

statistics powered by SUPERBASE™

> "I used someone with stress management myself years ago, when I was a player at Manchester United and Leeds. I will do anything that is legal to make players feel better about themselves."
>
> *Gordon Strachan on his decision to bring in a sports psychologist (December 2001)*

➡ Fixtures, results and match reports - 4thegame.com

Sunderland AFC

F.A. Barclaycard Premiership Final standing for the 2001-2002 season								
Final Position		Games Played	Games Won	Games Drawn	Games Lost	Goals For	Goals Against	Total Points
16	Bolton Wanderers	38	9	13	16	44	62	40
17	Sunderland AFC	38	10	10	18	29	51	40
18	Ipswich Town	38	9	9	20	41	64	36

"This season, the highlights have been few and far between. We've had too many disappointments but determination and togetherness in the face of adversity eventually brings reward."

Sunderland AFC Club Statement (May 2002)

Club Honours and Records

Football League Champions: 1891-92, 1892-93, 1894-95, 1901-02, 1912-13, 1935-36

Division 1 Champions: 1995-96, 1998-99

Division 2 Champions: 1975-76

Division 3 Champions: 1987-88

FA Cup Winners: 1937, 1973

Record victory:
11-1 v Fairfield, FA Cup 1st Round, 2 February, 1895

Record defeat:
0-8 v Sheffield Wednesday, Division 1, 26 December, 1911, 0-8 v West Ham United, Division 1, 19 October, 1968, 0-8 v Watford, Division 1, 25 September, 1982

League goals in a season (team):
109, Division 1, 1935-36

League goals in a season (player):
43, Dave Halliday, Division 1, 1928-29

Career league goals:
209, Charlie Buchan, 1911 to 1925

League appearances:
537, Jim Montgomery, 1962 to 1977

Reported transfer fee paid: £4,500,000 to Chelsea for Emerson Thome, September 2000, £4,500,000 to Rangers for Claudio Reyna, December 2001

Reported transfer fee received: £5,100,000 from West Ham United for Don Hutchison, August 2001

AFTER finishing seventh in successive seasons the Black Cats found little luck and had to wait until the final game of the campaign to secure their F.A. Barclaycard Premiership status.

Reid signed Bordeaux's Lilian Laslandes, Argentinian teenager Nicolas Medina, 19-year-old Frenchman David Bellion, and Grasshopper Zurich defender Bernt Haas. After finishing seventh, optimism was high but, at times throughout the 2001-02 season, the manager of the Black Cats must have wondered if he had run one over.

At the start of the campaign, Reid had to contend with interest in Don Hutchison from West Ham and Rangers: the Scottish midfielder eventually moved to London for £5m soon after.

If Reid was looking for indicators for the coming season, he could have spotted one when Emerson Thome his Brazilian defender was sent off in a pre-season friendly against NAC Breda in Holland and missed three important F.A. Barclaycard Premiership games.

Nevertheless, Sunderland started promisingly with a 1-0 win over Ipswich thanks to a Kevin Phillips penalty. Although Thome began his ban three games later in the 1-0 home win over

F.A. Barclaycard Premiership	Key
Season Progression	■ Win ■ Loss ■ Draw ➋ League Position ➋ Last Season's League Position

All Matches

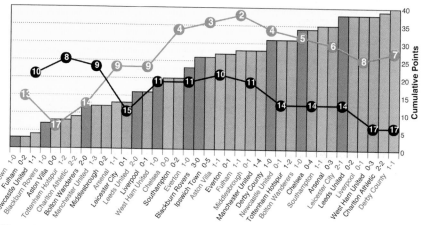

Home Matches

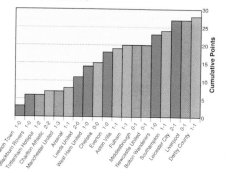

Away Matches

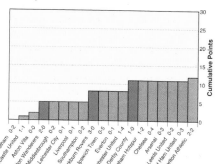

Chart Analysis

Sunderland were inconsistent in the first half of the season, managing to string together consecutive wins on just one occasion.

This left them stuck in mid-table at the halfway mark with 26 points from 19 games.

They kicked off the second half of their campaign with a 5-0 defeat at Ipswich Town four days after Christmas.

Although they followed that with a 1-1 draw at home to Aston Villa, their form in general declined as they battled to stave off the threat of relegation.

Three wins and three draws in their next 16 games kept them floating above the drop-zone.

Sunderland then secured their F.A. Barclaycard Premiership status by drawing 1-1 at home to Derby on the last day of the season.

statistics powered by ◆ SUPERBASE™

> "The record didn't strike me when the ball hit the back of the net. It would have been nice to reach the 100 at home but I'll take it anywhere. I'll just head for another record now."
>
> *Kevin Phillips*
> *(September 2001)*

It's a fact

When Stefan Schwarz scored for the Black Cats against Arsenal in late October, he became the first Sunderland midfielder to claim a goal.

Blackburn, September saw Sunderland rise to fifth spot. Reid showed an interest in West Ham winger Trevor Sinclair while Alex Rae left for Wolves.

Defender George McCartney was rewarded for his rapid improvement by earning his first senior cap for Northern Ireland but Reid had a goalkeeping problem to contend with. Thomas Sorensen broke his nose while on international duty with Denmark and missed three League games before returning for the win over Bolton in which he saved a penalty.

Phillips was scoring with a pleasing frequency – he had six goals by the time he netted in the victory over Bolton and brought up 100 League goals for Sunderland in 147 games. The England man, playing for a place in the World Cup finals, was on target again when Sunderland entertained Manchester United although the visitors won 3-1.

October turned into a poor month for the Black Cats. After the United defeat, they lost 2-0 at Middlesbrough in the Tees-Wear derby when two unlikely errors by Sorensen proved costly. They then held on for a 1-1 draw at home to Arsenal courtesy of a ballooned penalty miss by the Gunners' Patrick Vieira. Stefan Schwarz's goal in that game at the end of October was the first Sunderland goal

F.A. Barclaycard Premiership
Half time - Full time Comparative Chart

Key: ■ Win □ Loss ▨ Draw

Home				Away				Total			
	Full Time Result				Full Time Result				Full Time Result		
Number of Home Half Time Wins	W	L	D	Number of Away Half Time Wins	W	L	D	Total number of Half Time Wins	W	L	D
4	3	-	1	2	1	-	1	6	4	-	2
Number of Home Half Time Losses	W	L	D	Number of Away Half Time Losses	W	L	D	Total number of Half Time Losses	W	L	D
6	-	3	3	10	-	10	-	16	-	13	3
Number of Home Half Time Draws	W	L	D	Number of Away Half Time Draws	W	L	D	Total number of Half Time Draws	W	L	D
9	4	2	3	7	2	3	2	16	6	5	5

Chart Analysis

statistics powered by **SUPERBASE**™

Sunderland managed to hold on to points in 11 out of 16 games they were drawing at half-time, including six wins.

At home, they held on to their lead in three out of four games, and managed to battle back in three out of the six they were losing at the break to salvage a point.

Away from home, the Black Cats lost ten out of ten games they were losing at the interval.

Barclaycard Premiership Results Table

Key: ● = time of goal ▲ = time of substitution ... player substituted ...

DATE	H/A	OPPONENT	H/T	F/T	POS	REFEREE	TEAM											SUBSTITUTES USED		
18-08	H	Ipswich Town	1-0	1-0	7	G.Poll	Sorensen	Haas	Craddock	Thorne	Gray	Arca	McCann	Schwarz 37	Kilbane 37	Laslandes	Quinn	Phillips 37	Laslandes ▲	Rae ▲	Quinn ▲
22-08	A	Fulham	0-0	0-2	12	B.Knight	Sorensen	Haas	Craddock	McCartney	Gray	Hutchison	McCann	Schwarz ▲	Kilbane	Quinn		Phillips	Laslandes ▲	Bellion ▲	Quinn ▲
26-08	A	Newcastle Utd	1-1	1-1	10	M.A.Riley	Sorensen	Haas	Craddock	Thorne	Gray	Hutchison	McCann	Schwarz ▲34	Kilbane	Quinn		Phillips 34	Arca ▲	Rae ▲	Bellion ▲
08-09	H	Blackburn	0-0	1-0	6	M.L.Dean	Sorensen	Haas	Craddock	McCartney	Gray	Rae ▲	McCann	Schwarz 80	Arca	Laslandes		Phillips	Laslandes ▲	Quinn ▲80	
16-09	A	Aston Villa	0-0	0-0	7	U.D.Rennie	Macho	Haas	Craddock	McCartney	Gray	Arca	McCann	Schwarz	Kilbane	Quinn		Phillips	Laslandes ▲		
19-09	H	Tottenham	0-1	1-2	8	P.A.Durkin	Macho	Haas	Craddock	McCartney ▲	Gray	Arca	McCann	Schwarz	Kilbane	Quinn 79		Phillips 79	Williams ▲	Laslandes ▲	
22-09	H	Charlton	0-1	2-2	7	A.P.D'Urso	Macho	Haas	Williams	Williams	Gray	Arca	McCann 76	Laslandes	Kilbane	Quinn 74 76		Phillips 74			
29-09	A	Bolton	0-0	2-0	5	D.R.Elleray	Sorensen	Williams	Craddock 82	Varga	Gray	Arca 82	McCann	Schwarz 77	Kilbane 77	Quinn		Phillips 77			
13-10	H	Manchester Utd	0-1	1-3	9	G.Poll	Sorensen	Williams	Craddock	Varga	Gray	Arca	Thirlwell	Schwarz 82	Kilbane ▲	Quinn		Phillips 82	Bellion ▲		
20-10	A	Middlesbrough	0-2	0-2	12	M.R.Halsey	Sorensen	Haas	Craddock	Varga	Gray	McAteer	McCann	Schwarz ▲	Arca	Quinn		Phillips	Laslandes ▲	Bellion ▲	
27-10	H	Arsenal	0-2	0-3	12	M.A.Riley	Sorensen	Haas ▲	Craddock ●	Varga	Varga ▲	Gray	McCann	Schwarz 54	Arca	Quinn		Phillips	Williams ▲	Quinn ▲	
03-11	A	Leeds United	0-0	0-1	15	S.W.Dunn	Sorensen	Haas	Craddock ●	Thorne	Varga ▲	Gray	McCann	Schwarz 54	Arca	Quinn		Phillips	McCartney ▲	Quinn ▲	
18-11	H	Leeds United	0-0	2-0	13	G.P.Barber	Sorensen	Williams	Craddock	Thorne	Gray	McAteer ▲47	McCann	Thirlwell	Arca 47	Quinn ▲55		Phillips 55	Laslandes ▲	McCartney ▲	Butler ●
25-11	A	Liverpool	0-1	0-1	13	S.G.Bennett	Sorensen	Williams ▲	Craddock	Thorne	Gray	McAteer ●	McCann	Thirlwell ▲	Arca ▲	Quinn		Phillips	McCartney ▲	Laslandes ▲	
01-12	H	West Ham Utd	0-0	0-0	11	P.Jones	Sorensen	Williams	Craddock	Thorne	Gray	McAteer ▲	McCann	Thirlwell ●	Arca 85	Quinn		Phillips 85	Laslandes ▲	Butler ▲	
09-12	A	Chelsea	0-1	0-2	13	D.Pugh	McCartney	Williams	Craddock	Williams	Gray	Arca ▲	McCann	Thirlwell	Kilbane	Laslandes ▲		Phillips	Quinn ▲	Laslandes ▲	
15-12	A	Southampton	0-1	0-2	13	N.S.Barry	Sorensen	Haas	Craddock	Thorne	Gray	McAteer ▲76	McCann	Reyna	Kilbane	Quinn		Phillips	Quinn ▲	Laslandes ▲	
22-12	H	Everton	0-0	1-0	11	B.Knight	Sorensen	Haas	Williams 17	Craddock	Gray	McAteer	McCann	Reyna 76	Arca	Quinn ▲		Phillips	Kyle ▲		
26-12	A	Blackburn	2-0	3-0	9	C.R.Wilkes	Sorensen	Haas ▲	Williams 17	Thorne	Gray ▲	McAteer	McCann	Reyna	Arca ▲32	Quinn ▲17 32		Phillips 88	Kyle ▲88	Kilbane ▲88	McCartney ▲
29-12	H	Ipswich Town	0-4	0-5	10	G.Poll	Sorensen	Haas	Williams	Thorne 86	Gray ▲	McAteer	McCann	Reyna	Arca	Quinn ▲		Phillips 88	Kyle ▲	Kilbane ▲	McCartney ▲
01-01	H	Aston Villa	0-1	1-1	11	M.A.Riley	Sorensen	Haas	Craddock	Varga	Gray	Arca ▲	McCann	Reyna ▲	Arca 86	Quinn		Phillips	Thirlwell ▲	Kilbane ▲	
12-01	A	Everton	0-1	0-1	12	D.R.Elleray	Sorensen	Haas	Craddock	Varga	Gray	Arca ▲	McCann	McAteer	Thirlwell	Kilbane		Phillips	Quinn ▲	Bellion ▲	
19-01	H	Fulham	0-1	1-1	11	P.Jones	Sorensen	Haas	Craddock	Varga	Gray	McAteer ●	McCann ▲	Schwarz ●66	Kilbane	Quinn		Phillips 66	Williams ▲	Quinn ▲	
29-01	H	Middlesbrough	0-1	1-1	11	P.A.Durkin	Sorensen	Haas ▲	Craddock	Varga ▲	Gray	McAteer ▲	Reyna	Schwarz	Kilbane	Quinn		Phillips	Arca ▲	Quinn ▲	Bellion ▲
02-02	A	Manchester Utd	1-4	1-4	15	R.Styles	Macho	Haas ▲	Craddock	Varga ▲	Gray	McAteer ▲12	McCann	Reyna	Williams	Kilbane		Phillips 12	Quinn ▲	Arca ▲	McCartney ▲
09-02	A	Derby County	0-0	0-1	14	G.Poll	Sorensen	Craddock	Craddock	Bjorklund	Gray 80	McAteer	McCann	Reyna	Arca ▲	Quinn ▲80		Phillips	Kyle ▲	Bellion ▲	Williams ▲
24-02	H	Newcastle Utd	0-0	0-1	14	G.P.Barber	Sorensen	Haas	Craddock	Bjorklund	Gray ●	McCartney	Reyna	Schwarz ▲	Kilbane	Quinn ▲		Phillips	Mboma ▲	Butler ▲	
02-03	A	Tottenham	1-1	1-2	14	R.Styles	Sorensen	Haas ▲45	Craddock ▲	Bjorklund ▲	McCartney	McCartney	McCann	McAteer	Arca ▲	Mboma ▲45		Phillips	Williams ▲	Schwarz ▲	Quinn ▲
05-03	H	Bolton	1-0	1-0	13	G.Poll	Sorensen	Haas	Craddock	Williams	McCartney	Gray	McCann	Schwarz ●	McAteer 42	Mboma ▲		Phillips ▲42	Quinn ▲		
16-03	A	Chelsea	0-1	0-4	14	B.Knight	Sorensen	Williams	Craddock	McCartney	Gray	Thirlwell ▲	McCann	Schwarz ▲	Gray	Kilbane ▲		Mboma	Bellion ▲	Quinn ▲	Butler ▲
22-03	H	Southampton	0-3	0-3	16	M.D.Messias	Sorensen	Williams	Craddock	McCartney	Gray	McAteer 62	McCann ●	Reyna	Mboma ▲	Mboma ▲		Phillips 62	Bjorklund ▲	Kyle ▲	Quinn ▲
30-03	A	Arsenal	0-3	0-3	16	P.A.Durkin	Sorensen	Williams	Craddock	Bjorklund	Gray ▲	McAteer ▲	McCann	Reyna	McAteer ▲	Mboma ▲		Phillips 62	Butler ▲	Thirlwell ▲	Quinn ▲
01-04	H	Leicester City	2-1	2-1	14	N.S.Barry	Sorensen	Williams ●	Bjorklund	Gray ●	Gray ●	McCartney	McCann ●	Reyna ▲3 18	Kilbane ●	Quinn 3		Phillips 18	Thirlwell ▲	Bellion ▲	Quinn ▲
07-04	A	Leeds Utd	0-1	0-2	15	P.Jones	Sorensen	Williams ▲	Craddock	Bjorklund ▲	McCartney	Gray	McCann	Reyna	McAteer	Quinn		Phillips	Bellion ▲	Thirlwell ▲	Mboma ▲
13-04	H	Liverpool	0-0	0-1	15	D.J.Gallagher	Sorensen	Williams	Craddock ▲	Bjorklund	McCartney	Gray	McCann	Reyna ●	Thirlwell	Quinn		Phillips ▲42	Kyle ▲		
20-04	A	West Ham Utd	0-3	0-3	17	S.G.Bennett	Sorensen	Williams	Craddock ●	Bjorklund	McCartney	Thirlwell ▲	McCann	Reyna	Thirlwell	Quinn		Mboma	Bellion ▲	Quinn ▲	Butler ▲
27-04	H	Charlton	2-1	2-2	17	E.K.Wolstenholme	Sorensen	Williams	Craddock	McCartney	McCartney	Kilbane 2 10	McCann 2 10	Butler	Kilbane ▲	Quinn ●		Phillips ▲10	Kyle ▲	McCartney ▲	Butler ▲
11-05	H	Derby County	1-1	1-1	17	A.G.Wiley	Sorensen	Williams	Craddock	Bjorklund	Gray ▲	Kilbane	Butler	Reyna	Kilbane	Quinn ▲		Phillips 17	Mboma ▲	Mboma ▲	

F.A. Barclaycard Premiership

Squad List

Position	Name	Appearances	Appearances as Substitute	Goals or Clean Sheets	Goal Assists	Yellow Cards	Red Cards
G	J.Macho	4		1			
G	T.Sorensen	34		10			
D	J.Bjorklund	11	1			2	
D	J.Craddock	30		1		3	
D	M.Gray	35			1	1	
D	B.Haas	27			1	7	
D	G.McCartney	12	6			3	
D	E.Thome	12		1		3	
D	S.Varga	9				1	
D	D.Williams	23	5		1	3	
M	J.Arca	20	2	1	4	3	
M	T.Butler	2	5			1	
M	D.Hutchison	2					
M	K.Kilbane	24	4	2	2	3	
M	J.McAteer	26		2	5	8	
M	G.McCann	29			1	9	
M	A.Rae	1	2				
M	C.Reyna	17		3		2	1
M	S.Schwarz	18	2	1	4	7	
M	P.Thirlwell	11	3			2	
F	D.Bellion		9				
F	K.Kyle		6			1	
F	L.Laslandes	5	7			1	
F	P.Mboma	5	4	1		2	
F	K.Phillips	37		11	5	3	
F	N.Quinn	24	14	6	3	3	

to be scored by a midfielder.

Reid added Blackburn's Jason McAteer to his squad in mid-October but Sunderland fared little better in November, with a defeat at Leicester and Liverpool either side of an important 2-0 home win over Leeds. Quinn was outstanding without scoring as Sunderland won with goals from Julio Arca and Phillips. The defeat prevented Leeds from returning to the top of the table.

It was achieved without the influential Jody Craddock, who gashed a shin at Leicester and was to feature in only one of the next nine League outings.

Sunderland started the final month of 2001 encouragingly; another Phillips goal earned the points against West Ham, taking Reid's team to 11th. They failed to add another win in their next game after Phillips had a penalty saved by the visitors' Carlo Cudicini.

Although Rangers' USA star Claudio Reyna arrived in time to make his debut at Southampton, Saints won 2-0 and Reid read the riot act to his players. They responded with their first back-to-back wins, at home to Everton, thanks to Reyna's first goal, and at Blackburn, where Quinn scored a brace in the 3-0 victory.

Sunderland rose briefly to ninth before a 5-0 loss at Ipswich at the end of the year followed by a 1-1 draw at home to Villa on New Year's Day – where another penalty miss by Phillips was to prove costly – saw them slump again. In the New Year, they suffered an F.A. Cup exit at the hands of Division One West Bromwich Albion followed by a 1-0 defeat at Everton.

The 2-1 home defeat against Albion was particularly damaging and Sunderland were booed off the pitch. Reid could offer no excuses for such a poor display.

Sunderland's poor form was compounded by the goalscoring drought

F.A. Barclaycard Premiership

Top Goal Scorer

Kevin Phillips

Total Premier League Goals Scored:	Percentage Of The Team's League Goals:
11	**38%**

Goals Scored From

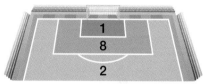

1
8
2

Kevin Phillips suffered his worst goalscoring season for Sunderland who, as a team, finished with the lowest goal total in the F.A. Barclaycard Premiership. In his fifth term with the Black Cats, Phillips crept into double figures only in late April. His season mirrored the problems his team suffered throughout a disappointing campaign in which they found scoring a chore from all areas. Phillips also missed three penalties, including two in the League. When he netted early in the 2-2 draw at Charlton in April, it ended a goal drought lasting 10 games, his longest spell without scoring since he arrived at Sunderland in 1997.

"Kevin Phillips is still getting chances and I know he'll get goals for us. As long as he gets there and keeps having chances, he will score goals."

Peter Reid

Goals Resulting From

Key
- Open Play
- Corner
- Indirect Free Kick
- Direct Free Kick
- Penalty

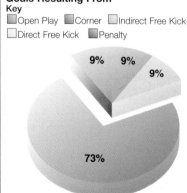

9% 9% 9%
73%

	Right Foot	Left Foot	Header
Open Play	7	-	1
Set piece	2	-	1

Goal Assists

Total number of goal assists	5

Teams Scored Against

Against	Home	Away
Manchester United	1	1
Bolton Wanderers	0	1
Charlton Athletic	0	1
Derby County	1	0
Fulham	1	0
Ipswich Town	1	0
Leeds United	1	0
Newcastle United	0	1
Tottenham Hotspur	1	0
West Ham United	1	0
Total Goals Scored	**7**	**4**

"The big difference between us this season and last season is that we haven't been scoring goals. You've got to score goals from every section of the team. We aren't and the figures are there for all to see."

*Peter Reid
(April 2002)*

suffered by top scorer Phillips, who was finding life particularly difficult. When he netted an outstanding equaliser in the 1-1 draw with Fulham it was his first goal for 702 minutes.

Fulham were superior but Phillips' goal took some of the pressure off Reid, who was forced to put a £10m price tag on Sorensen following speculation that the highly-rated goalkeeper was wanted by Aston Villa.

Reid made another signing in February with Venezia's Swedish defender Joachim Bjorklund arriving for £1.5m. After another defeat, against Middlesbrough, the pressure mounted again on Reid. Of the adverse reaction from the crowd, the manager admitted: "It is not nice and I can't say I didn't hear it."

Sunderland then visited Old Trafford, Phillips scored his 12th goal, Bjorklund made his debut – and the Black Cats lost 4-1.

Laslandes, a disappointment since his arrival, was loaned out to FC Cologne as Sunderland attempted to pull away from what was beginning to look like a relegation battle. Goals were not forthcoming. Indeed, Quinn's strike at Derby to secure three important points against

F.A. Barclaycard Premiership
Goals By Position

Key: Forward, Midfield, League Position, Defence, Goalkeeper

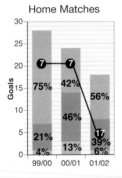
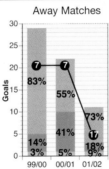
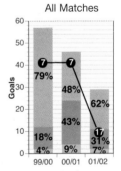

Chart Analysis

statistics powered by SUPERBASE™

Sunderland scored just over half as many goals as they had managed two seasons previously and their position in the table suffered accordingly.

While the contribution from strikers increased compared to last season in terms of percentage share of the teams goals, it declined in real terms as they registered 18 strikes compared to 22 the previous term.

relegation rivals was one of only four in seven games. It was also Sunderland's first League win in seven.

Reid, whose squad was one of the smallest in the top flight, failed to sign Dwight Yorke from Manchester United but made an exciting addition to the squad in February when Cameroon international striker Patrick Mboma arrived from Parma on loan until the end of the season.

Former African player of the year Mboma, fresh from helping his country win the African Nations Cup, made his debut in the derby against Newcastle at the Stadium of Light as a half-time substitute. He could not prevent the Magpies from stealing a 1-0 win after Newcastle goalkeeper Shay Given had pulled off a series of outstanding saves.

Midfielder Gavin McCann was missing with knee ligament damage and another loss, in early March at Tottenham, was followed by a 1-0 win over Bolton thanks to McAteer's first goal for the club. Whenever things were looking up, results went against the Black Cats. Sunderland went to London and lost 4-0 at Chelsea and then faced another huge test against Southampton at home.

A win was needed and Sunderland were leading through McAteer's second goal in successive appearances but Jo Tessem's late equaliser was not the best way for

F.A. Barclaycard Premiership
Team Performance Table

League Position	Team	Points won from a possible six	Percentage of points won at home	Percentage of points won away	Overall percentage of points won
1	Arsenal	1/6			
2	Liverpool	0/6			
3	Manchester Utd	0/6	27%	7%	17%
4	Newcastle Utd	1/6			
5	Leeds United	3/6			
6	Chelsea	1/6			
7	West Ham Utd	3/6			
8	Aston Villa	2/6	53%	27%	40%
9	Tottenham H	0/6			
10	Blackburn R	6/6			
11	Southampton	1/6			
12	Middlesbrough	0/6			
13	Fulham	1/6	40%	7%	23%
14	Charlton Athletic	2/6			
15	Everton	3/6			
16	Bolton W	6/6			
17	**Sunderland**	**40**			
18	Ipswich Town	3/6	83%	50%	67%
19	Derby County	4/6			
20	Leicester City	3/6			

The table shows how many points out of a possible six Sunderland have taken off each of the teams in the four sections. The other columns show as a percentage how many points they have taken from those available.

Chart Analysis

statistics powered by **SUPERBASE**™

Sunderland struggled most away to teams in the top sector and the third sector, picking up two points from a possible 30.

They performed well at home to teams in the second sector, picking up over half of the available points thanks in chief to wins over West Ham and Blackburn.

Surprisingly, their form tailed off against teams in the third sector.

However, they reserved their best performances for teams in their own sector, winning a succession of six-pointers to hoist themselves clear of relegation.

Sunderland managed to do the 'double' twice, against newly-promoted Blackburn and Bolton, and failed to take any points off four teams.

safc.com Sunderland AFC Official Website

Peter Reid to celebrate his forthcoming seventh anniversary as Sunderland manager.

When Reid had arrived on Wearside, Sunderland were struggling to stay in Division One; now, seven years on, and Reid admitted: "It is déjà vu. I feel I'm in the same situation as when I first came here. Then I had seven games to beat the drop as I have now."

The first of those seven games was at Highbury. With Arsenal in rampant form, the Gunners scored three goals in the opening half-hour and Sunderland were left in 16th place, just three points above the drop-zone. "We're in a dogfight now," admitted Reid. "We're down there because we've not played well enough. It's in our hands."

April started with a win, with American international skipper Claudio Reyna scoring twice in the 2-1 win over Leicester. It was not enjoyable to watch but that wasn't the point; a win was all that mattered.

After the Leicester success, Sunderland went to Leeds and, under the watchful eye of Sven-Goran Eriksson, the home side won 2-0. The fixture list was not being kind to Sunderland. Next up came Liverpool at home and another defeat followed, with Reyna sent off to boot.

Sunderland could have won but for second half misses from Quinn, who was denied a goal by Liverpool

It's a fact

When Kevin Phillips scored for Sunderland at home to Fulham in January, it was his first F.A. Barclaycard Premiership goal for 702 minutes.

"I am enjoying my time with Sunderland very much. It's exciting to be playing in the Premiership, and I know I want to stay here."

Patrick Mboma
(April 2002)

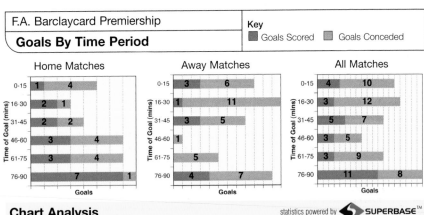

F.A. Barclaycard Premiership
Goals By Time Period

Key: ■ Goals Scored ■ Goals Conceded

Chart Analysis

statistics powered by ◆ SUPERBASE™

Sunderland scored more than twice as many goals in the last 15 minutes of matches than they did in any other time period.

They were vulnerable both home and away in the opening half-hour, conceding 22 goals and scoring just seven.

The only times Sunderland outscored their their opponents were between 16-30 and 75-90 minutes at the Stadium of Light.

Sunderland AFC

F.A. Barclaycard Premiership

Goals Resulting From

	Six Yard Area				Inside Area				Outside Area				Total			
	Shots		Headers		Shots		Headers		Shots		Headers		Shots		Headers	
	Home	Away	Home	Away	Home	Away	Home	Away	Home	Away	Home	Away	Home	Away	Home	Away
Open Play	3	2	1	-	5	2	1	1	4	1	-	-	12	5	2	1
	-	1	2	2	5	16	1	1	3	4	-	-	8	21	3	3
Direct Free Kick									1	-			1	0		
									-	1			0	1		
Indirect Free Kick	-	-	-	-	-	-	2	3	-	-	-	-	0	0	2	3
	1	1	1	1	-	-	1	1	-	-	-	-	1	1	2	2
Penalty	-	-	-	-	1	-	-	-	-	-	-	-	1	0	0	0
	-	-	-	-	-	1	-	-	-	-	-	-	0	1	0	0
Corner	-	1	-	-	-	1	-	-	-	-	-	-	0	2	0	0
	-	1	-	1	-	1	1	1	-	-	-	-	0	2	1	2
Totals	3	3	1	0	6	3	3	4	5	1	0	0	14	7	4	4
	1	3	3	4	5	18	3	3	3	5	0	0	9	26	6	7

How Goals Were Scored
Home & Away Matches

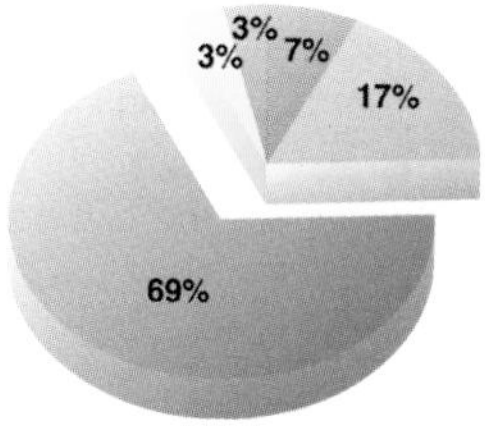

3% 3% 7%
17%
69%

Key
■ Open Play
■ Corner
■ Indirect Free Kick
☐ Direct Free Kick
■ Penalty

Charts do not include 3 own goals against.

How Goals Were Conceded
Home & Away Matches

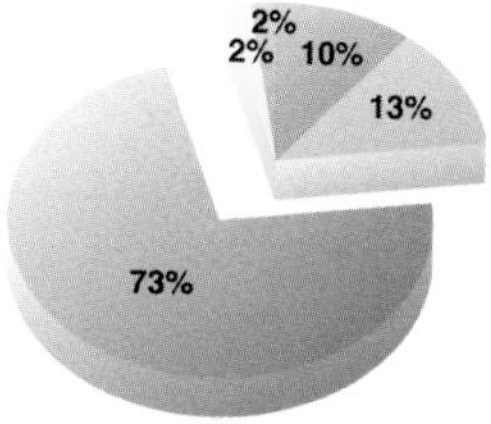

2% 2% 10%
13%
73%

Goals Scored from
Key ■ Open Play ■ Set Piece

Home
22%
78%

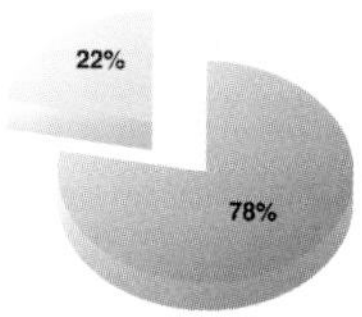

Away
45% 55%

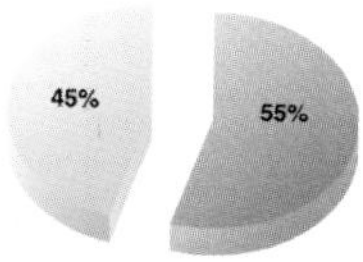

Goals Conceded from
Key ■ Open Play ■ Set Piece

Home
27%
73%

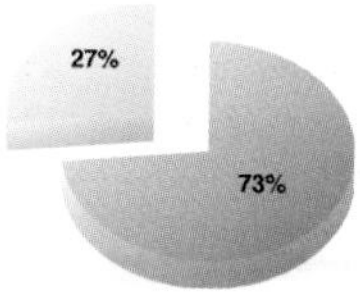

Away
27%
73%

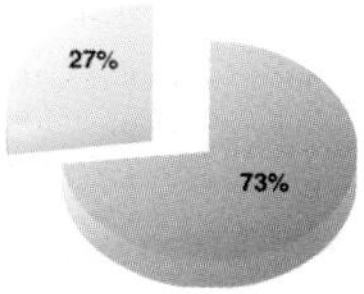

Chart Analysis

Sunderland relied heavily on Set Pieces away from home, scoring five out of 11 from Corners and Indirect Free Kicks.

At home, where they scored nearly twice as many goals, the spread was less even, with most success coming from Shots from Open Play, where they registered 12 out of 18 goals.

They conceded an identical proportion of goals from Set Pieces and Open Play at home and away.

statistics powered by ◆ SUPERBASE™

> **"I had a feeling we'd do it. I'm not ecstatic about the season, I'm not saying I'm doing cartwheels, but certainly I was confident going into this game."**
>
> *Peter Reid after clinching safety at home to Derby on the last day of the season (May 2002)*

It's a fact

Sunderland set two club records with their away form. Their three wins and 11 goals on the road was their lowest return in four Premier League campaigns.

goalkeeper Jerzy Dudek's brilliant acrobatic save and his own off-target header.

Reid wanted one more win to secure safety but his side was now 17th and offered an abject display at West Ham, losing 3-0 – their fifth successive defeat in London.

All eyes were now on Ipswich. But Reid warned: "It's not in Ipswich's hands. It is in ours. We must get back on the training ground and then go out and produce a good performance against Charlton." So Sunderland travelled to the capital on the back of a run of one win in seven F.A. Barclaycard Premiership games.

They couldn't afford to lose at Charlton and when Jason Euell scored after 66 seconds, the future looked bleak. But Sunderland hit back almost immediately withTommy Butler, making his full debut, helping Kilbane equalise. Then Sunderland were ahead after just 11 minutes when Phillips scored his first goal for nearly three months. A win would have left Sunderland safe but an 82nd minute Charlton equaliser from Kevin Lisbie ruined everything.

The final day of the season was fraught with nerves. Ipswich had the chance to survive and send Sunderland down. Instead the Tractor Boys lost 5-0 at Liverpool and so Sunderland's 1-1 draw with Derby was academic.

F.A. Barclaycard Premiership	Key
Shot Efficiency	■ Goals Scored ■ Other Shots On Target

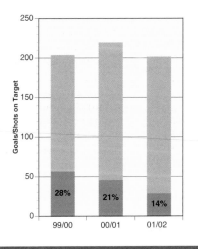

Season	Division	Shots Off Target	Shots On Target	Total Goals
1999 - 2000	P	n/a	204	57
2000 - 2001	P	n/a	220	46
2001 - 2002	P	224	202	29

Chart Analysis

Sunderland converted the least amount of Shots On Target into goals in the top flight as they registered their lowest goal total in their four seasons in the Premier League.

In percentage terms, they converted half the amount of Shots On Target as they did two seasons ago.

statistics powered by  **SUPERBASE**™

---

safc.com Sunderland AFC Official Website

F.A. Barclaycard Premiership	Key
Team Discipline	☐ Forward ■ Midfield ☐ Defence ■ Goalkeeper

Total Number Of Bookings

Total number of red cards	1
Total number of yellow cards	68

Referee Performance

Referee	Games Refereed	Red Cards	Yellow Cards
P.Jones	3	-	7
M.A.Riley	3	-	6
B.Knight	3	-	5

Type of Yellow Cards Received

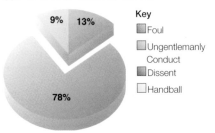

Key
- ☐ Foul
- ☐ Ungentlemanly Conduct
- ■ Dissent
- ☐ Handball

9% 13% 78%

Bookings by Position 1999/2000 - 2001/2002

Home Matches

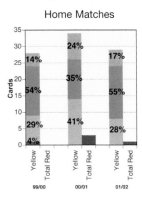

Away Matches

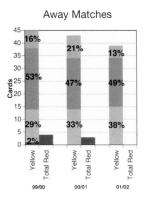

All Matches

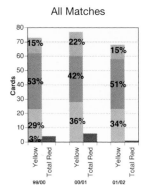

Chart Analysis

As the overall number of bookings fell to its lowest level since Sunderland's return to the top flight, so the Black Cats saw a sharp decline in the number of Red Cards picked up, down to one from six last season.

Midfielders accounted for just over half of all cautions as both forwards and defenders saw their share of bookings decline.

The one Red Card they did pick up was shown to Claudio Reyna in the 1-0 home defeat to Liverpool. D.J.Gallagher, the referee responsible, did not hand out any other cards to Sunderland players during the match.

> "It has been a fantastic seven years. This is a fantastic club to manage and the only disappointment about the anniversary is the season we have had."
>
> *Peter Reid (March 2002)*

statistics powered by  SUPERBASE™

Tottenham Hotspur

F.A. Barclaycard Premiership Final standing for the 2001-2002 season

Final Position		Games Played	Games Won	Games Drawn	Games Lost	Goals For	Goals Against	Total Points
8	Aston Villa	38	12	14	12	46	47	50
9	Tottenham Hotspur	38	14	8	16	49	53	50
10	Blackburn Rovers	38	12	10	16	55	51	46

> **"Things have got to change next season if we are to get success and things will change. There is a lot of hard work to be done."**
>
> *Glenn Hoddle (May 2002)*

Club Honours and Records

Football League Champions: 1950-51, 1960-61

Division 2 Champions: 1919-20, 1949-50

FA Cup Winners:

1901, 1921, 1961, 1962, 1967, 1981, 1982, 1991

League Cup Winners: 1971, 1973, 1999

European Cup Winners' Cup Winners: 1962-63

UEFA Cup Winners: 1971-72, 1983-84

Record victory: 13-2 v Crewe Alexandra, FA Cup 4th Round (replay), 3 February, 1960

Record defeat:

0-8 v Cologne, UEFA Intertoto Cup, 22 July, 1995

League goals in a season (team):

115, Division 1, 1960-61

League goals in a season (player):

37, Jimmy Greaves, Division 1, 1962-63

Career league goals:

220, Jimmy Greaves, 1961 to 1970

League appearances:

655, Steve Perryman, 1969 to 1986

Reported transfer fee paid: £11,000,000 to Dynamo Kiev for Sergei Rebrov, July 2000

Reported transfer fee received: £5,500,000 from Lazio for Paul Gascoigne, July 1991

IT was difficult to know whether Spurs fans were satisfied with the season. Tottenham got to the Worthington Cup final, but lost to Blackburn and missed out on Europe. However, they did finish ninth, their best position for six years.

Hoddle had won three and lost three of his first seven League games in charge after replacing George Graham in March of 2001. Following a busy summer in which he made some promising signings, Tottenham's most popular manager of recent times had good reason to begin the season in optimistic mood.

The departure of Sol Campbell was inevitable. His subsequent move to Arsenal was hard to take for most Spurs fans and the response to his North London defection was predictably hostile.

Netherthless, Hoddle appeased the fans by persuading a former Tottenham favourite back to White Hart Lane when he signed Footballer of the Year Teddy Sheringham, the previous season's top scorer at Manchester United. After four years at Old Trafford, Sheringham at the age of 35 had returned.

He was Hoddle's first signing after agreeing a two-year contract. Next to arrive was Liverpool wing back Christian Ziege followed by another veteran,

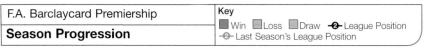

Tottenham Hotspur

F.A. Barclaycard Premiership
Season Progression

All Matches

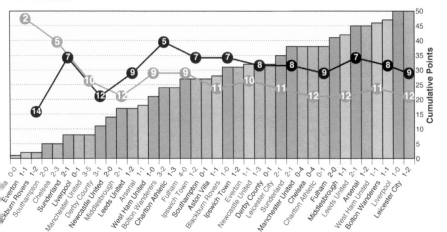

Home Matches

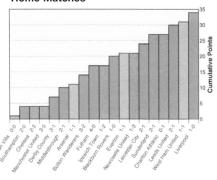

Away Matches

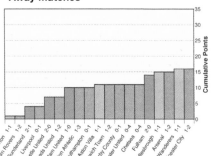

Chart Analysis

Tottenham had a shaky start to the season, winning just twice in their opening eight matches. The last game in that sequence, at home to Manchester United, saw Spurs lose 5-3 after leading 3-0 at the interval.

The result spurred the Londoners on as they registered six wins in the next nine to push themselves up to seventh in the table by mid-December.

However, they only managed one win in the next eight to leave them adrift of the top six at the start of February.

Back-to-back wins against Leicester and Sunderland offered some hope of a charge for Europe but in the event it failed to materialise.

Although Spurs struggled away from home, where they won just four and lost 11 out of 19 matches, they still managed to finish three places higher than the previous season.

 Win Barclaycard Premiership tickets – 4thegame.com

> **"I personally am not happy when I hear the abuse that Sol is getting. Yes, we were disappointed at the time but that is now history. Although I was surprised at that decision it was his free choice."**
>
> *Glenn Hoddle on*
> *Sol Campbell*
> *(August 2001)*

It's a fact

When Spurs beat Leicester at White Hart Lane in February, they took their Premier League points' haul to 501.

Chelsea midfielder Gus Poyet.

In addition, Hoddle signed promising Red Star Belgrade defender Goran Bunjevcevic, while United States international goalkeeper Kasey Keller arrived as cover for Neil Sullivan following the sale of Ian Walker to Leicester. Spurs lost another defender when Luke Young joined Charlton but the emergence of Ledley King and Anthony Gardner persuaded Hoddle that he had sufficient back-up in defence.

Injuries, a problem that always seems to rear its head at Spurs, troubled the club again. Indeed, they began the season without long-term absentees Stephen Carr, Tim Sherwood, Ben Thatcher, Gardner, Willem Korsten and Chris Armstrong, while Sheringham and Oyvind Leonhardsen were unavailable for the opening game at home to Aston Villa.

The match was a dour affair, which produced no goals; the only excitement came when former Spurs favourite David Ginola made a late entrance for the visitors.

Sheringham returned but another draw followed in controversial circumstances when Spurs were held to a 1-1 stalemate at Everton. They were reduced to nine men for the last 25 minutes after referee David Elleray dismissed Gary Doherty and Poyet. Doherty was sent off after

---

F.A. Barclaycard Premiership
Half-Time/Full-Time Comparison

Key: ■ Win ☐ Loss ■ Draw

Home				Away				Total			
Number of Home Half Time Wins	Full Time Result W	L	D	Number of Away Half Time Wins	Full Time Result W	L	D	Total number of Half Time Wins	Full Time Result W	L	D
8	6	2	-	7	3	-	4	15	9	2	4
Number of Home Half Time Losses	Full Time Result W	L	D	Number of Away Half Time Losses	Full Time Result W	L	D	Total number of Half Time Losses	Full Time Result W	L	D
3	2	1	-	7	-	7	-	10	2	8	-
Number of Home Half Time Draws	Full Time Result W	L	D	Number of Away Half Time Draws	Full Time Result W	L	D	Total number of Half Time Draws	Full Time Result W	L	D
8	2	2	4	5	1	4	-	13	3	6	4

Chart Analysis

statistics powered by **SUPERBASE**™

Tottenham conspired to lose two out of eight games they were leading at home at half-time.

Otherwise, they proved resilient at White Hart Lane, converting two out of three losses into wins, and taking points from six out of eight fixtures in which they were on level terms.

Away from home, they lost seven out of seven matches in which they were behind at the interval.

 The heart of the Barclaycard Premiership - 4thegame.com

T.A. Barclaycard Premiership Results Table

DATE	H/A	OPPONENT	F/T	POS	REFEREE	TEAM											SUBSTITUTES USED		
18.08	H	Aston Villa	0-0	0-0	9	Sullivan	Taricco △	King	Doherty ○	Bunjevcevic	Ziege ○	Freund ▲	Clemence	Poyet	Ferdinand	Rebrov	Iversen ▲	Perry △	Anderton ▲
20.08	A	Everton	1-0	1-1	9	Sullivan	Taricco	King	Doherty ●	Bunjevcevic	Ziege	Freund ▲	Anderton 45	Poyet ●	Iversen 45	Sheringham	Clemence ▲	Davies ▲	·
25.08	A	Blackburn	0-1	1-2	14	Sullivan	Taricco △	King	Doherty	Perry	Ziege 89	Clemence ◄	Anderton ▲	Poyet	Iversen	Sheringham 89	Davies ▲	Retrov ▲	Freund ▲
09.09	H	Southampton	0-0	2-0	11	Sullivan	Taricco	King	Doherty	Bunjevcevic	Ziege 76	Freund	Anderton ▲	Davies 76 87	Ferdinand	Sheringham 87	Leonhardsen ▲	·	·
16.09	A	Chelsea	2-1	2-3	11	Sullivan	Taricco	King	Perry	Bunjevcevic	Ziege	Freund	Anderton △	Davies 66	Ferdinand ● 89	Sheringham 66 89	Rebrov ●	Thelwell ▲	·
19.09	H	Sunderland	1-0	2-1	7	Sullivan	Taricco	King	Perry 26	Ziege 26	Davies 51	Freund	Anderton △	Poyet	Ferdinand	Sheringham 51	Rebrov ▲	Leonhardsen ▲	·
22.09	A	Liverpool	0-0	0-1	10	Sullivan	Taricco	King	Perry	Ziege	Davies	Freund	Anderton	Poyet	Ferdinand	Sheringham	Rebrov ▲	·	·
29.09	H	Manchester Utd	3-0	3-5	13	Sullivan	Taricco	King	Richards 15	Perry	Ziege 15 45	Freund ●	Anderton ▲	Poyet ● 25 45	Ferdinand 25 45	Sheringham	Rebrov ▲	Davies ▲	·
15.10	A	Derby County	2-1	3-1	12	Sullivan	Taricco	King	Richards	Perry	Ziege 10 41	Freund	Anderton	Poyet 90	Ferdinand 10	Sheringham 41	Rebrov ▲	·	·
21.10	H	Newcastle Utd	2-0	2-1	7	Sullivan	Taricco △	King	Richards	Perry	Ziege	Freund	Anderton a 8 20	Poyet 20	Ferdinand a 8 20	Sheringham 58	Sherwood △	Davies ▲	·
27.10	A	Middlesbrough	0-1	2-1	7	Sullivan	Taricco ▲ 58	King	Richards	Perry	Ziege	Freund	Anderton	Poyet 61	Ferdinand 61	Sheringham 58	Thatcher ▲	Davies ▲	Retrov ▲
04.11	A	Leeds Utd	0-0	1-2	9	Sullivan	Taricco	King	Richards	Perry	Ziege ▲ 52	Freund △	Anderton	Poyet ▲ 52	Ferdinand	Sheringham	Davies ▲	Retrov ▲	·
17.11	H	Arsenal	0-0	1-1	9	Sullivan	Taricco	King	Richards	Perry	Ziege	Freund	Anderton	Poyet 90	Ferdinand	Sheringham	Retrov ▲ 90	Davies △	·
24.11	A	West Ham Utd	1-0	1-0	6	Sullivan	Davies	King	Richards	Perry ▲	Ziege	Freund	Anderton	Poyet ▲ 49	Ferdinand 49	Sheringham	Leonhardsen △	Retrov ▲ 90	·
08.12	A	Bolton	0-2	1-3	5	Sullivan	Davies 71	King	Richards	Perry ▲	Ziege 96	Freund	Bunjevcevic △	Poyet 85	Ferdinand ▲ 20 40 71	Sheringham 86	Bunjevcevic ▲ 48	Ferdinand 47 48	Leonhardsen ▲
15.12	H	Fulham	2-0	4-0	6	Sullivan	Davies 71	King	Richards	Perry ▲	Taricco	Freund	Anderton	Poyet	Rebrov	Sherwood	Sherwood ▲	Iversen △	·
22.12	H	Ipswich Town	1-1	1-2	7	Sullivan	Taricco	King	Richards 44	Perry ▲	Ziege	Freund	Anderton 44	Davies △ 11	Rebrov ▲ 11	Sheringham 77	Gardner ▲	Poyet ▲ 77	·
26.12	A	Southampton	0-0	0-1	7	Sullivan	Taricco	King	Richards	Gardner △	Ziege	Freund	Anderton	Poyet ▲	Ferdinand ▲	Sheringham	Gardner ▲	Davies ▲	Sherwood ▲
29.12	A	Aston Villa	1-0	1-1	7	Keller	Taricco	King	Richards 44	Perry	Ziege ▲ 39	Freund	Anderton	Poyet 58	Ferdinand	Sheringham	Sherwood ▲ 39	Davies ▲	Gardner ▲
12.01	H	Ipswich Town	0-1	1-2	8	Sullivan	Taricco	King	Richards	Perry	Ziege ▲ 39	Sherwood	Anderton	Poyet 58	Ferdinand ▲	Rebrov 58	Iversen ▲	Etherington ▲	Davies △
19.01	H	Everton	1-1	1-1	8	Sullivan	Davies	Gardner	Richards 16	Perry	Taricco △	Sherwood	Anderton	Leonhardsen ▲	Ferdinand ▲ 5	Sheringham	Retrov ▲	Etherington ▲	·
30.01	H	Newcastle Utd	1-0	1-3	8	Sullivan	Davies ▲	King	Richards	Perry	Taricco △	Sherwood	Anderton	Poyet ▲	Ferdinand 16	Sheringham	Leonhardsen ▲	Etherington ▲	Anderton ▲
02.02	A	Derby County	0-1	0-1	8	Sullivan	Taricco	King	Richards	Perry ▲	Thatcher ●	Sherwood	Anderton	Iversen	Leonhardsen ○	Sheringham 81	Etherington ▲ 30	Poyet ▲	Thelwell ▲
09.02	H	Leicester City	0-1	0-1	8	Keller	Davies ▲	Gardner	Richards	Thatcher	Taricco	Sherwood	Anderton 44	Iversen 36	Etherington ○ 10	Sheringham 53	Clemence ○	Retrov ▲	Etherington ▲
02.03	H	Sunderland	1-1	2-1	8	Keller	Taricco △	Gardner	Richards	Thatcher	Anderton	Sherwood	Leonhardsen ○	Iversen	Etherington ▲	Sheringham 81	Poyet ▲	Retrov ▲	Clemence ▲
06.03	A	Manchester Utd	0-2	0-4	8	Sullivan	Davies ○	King	Richards	Thatcher	Sherwood	Sherwood	Anderton 36 61	Iversen	Ferdinand ▲ 63	Retrov ▲	Davies ▲	Retrov ▲ △	Anderton ▲
13.03	A	Chelsea	0-1	0-4	9	Keller	Davies	Gardner	Perry	Thatcher	Anderton	Sherwood	Etherington 32	Poyet 8	Sheringham 53	Doherty ▲	Retrov ▲	Iversen ▲ 53	Etherington ▲
18.03	H	Charlton	0-0	0-1	9	Keller	King	Perry	Richards	Ziege	Anderton	Sherwood	Ziege 28 31	Iversen	Sheringham 28 31	Perry ●	Iversen ▲	Gardner ▲	Ferdinand ▲
24.03	A	Fulham	2-0	2-0	9	Sullivan	King	Anderton ▲	Perry	Thatcher	Poyet	Anderton	Iversen 31	Poyet 31	Sheringham 28 31	Retrov ▲	Davies ▲	Sheringham △	Perry ▲
30.03	H	Middlesbrough	0-1	1-2	8	Keller	Gardner	Richards 16	Thatcher ▲ 10	Anderton △	Poyet △ 31	Sherwood	Etherington 32	Etherington ▲	Retrov ▲ 30	Sheringham	Sheringham △	·	·
01.04	H	Leeds Utd	2-0	2-1	7	Keller	Gardner	Perry	Thatcher ●	Anderton 30	Davies 30	Sherwood	Etherington ●	Iversen 10	Sheringham a 30	Retrov ▲	Retrov ▲	Clemence ▲	·
06.04	A	Arsenal	0-1	1-2	8	Keller	King △	Gardner	Richards	Perry	Anderton ▲ 31	Sherwood	Anderton	Poyet ▲ 31	Sheringham 81	Retrov ▲	Davies ▲	Retrov ▲	Etherington ▲
13.04	H	West Ham Utd	0-0	1-1	8	Keller	Davies	Gardner	Perry	Thatcher	Anderton	Sherwood	Iversen	Poyet	Sheringham 53	Doherty ▲	Davies ▲	Iversen ▲ 53	·
20.04	H	Bolton	1-0	1-1	8	Keller	Davies	Gardner	Perry ●	Thatcher	Anderton	Sherwood	Iversen ▲ 8	Poyet 8	Sheringham 53	Doherty ▲	Retrov ▲ △	Doherty ▲	·
27.04	H	Liverpool	1-0	1-2	9	Keller	Davies 41	Gardner	Perry ○	Taricco	Anderton	Clemence	Iversen ▲ 8	Poyet 41	Sheringham	Retrov ▲	Sheringham ▲	·	·
11.05	A	Leicester City	0-0	1-2	9	Keller	Davies △	Gardner	Thatcher	Anderton	Anderton	Clemence ▲ 53	Iversen	Poyet	Sheringham 53	Doherty ▲	Etherington ▲	·	·

F.A. Barclaycard Premiership

Squad List

Position	Name	Appearances	Appearances as Substitute	Goals or Clean Sheets	Goal Assists	Yellow Cards	Red Cards
G	K.Keller	9		2			
G	N.Sullivan	29		6			
D	G.Bunjevcevic	5	1		1		
D	G.Doherty	4	3			1	1
D	A.Gardner	11	4			3	
D	L.King	32					
D	C.Perry	30	3			9	
D	D.Richards	24		2	1	3	
D	M.Taricco	30			2	4	1
D	B.Thatcher	11	1		1	3	
D	A.Thelwell		2				
D	C.Ziege	27		5	9	6	
M	D.Anderton	33	2	3	6	1	
M	S.Clemence	4	2		1	1	
M	S.Davies	22	9	4	5		
M	M.Etherington	3	8		1	1	
M	S.Freund	19	1			6	
M	O.Leonhardsen	2	5		1		
M	G.Poyet	32	2	10	6	6	1
M	T.Sherwood	15	4			5	
F	L.Ferdinand	22	3	9	3	4	
F	S.Iversen	12	6	4	3	1	
F	S.Rebrov	9	21	1	3		
F	T.Sheringham	33	1	10	3	4	1

conceding a penalty but the red card was later rescinded.

Tottenham agreed to pay Southampton £1m compensation for Hoddle – and then beat them 2-0 at White Hart Lane with Ziege and Simon Davies scoring the goals.

Chelsea were the next visitors and, given their shocking record against their London neighbours, they shouldn't have expected anything more than a 3-2 defeat. Despite Sheringham opening his account with two goals, Spurs' inability to beat Chelsea at home since 1987 seemed to act as a mental block.

Spurs asked a sports psychologist to exorcise the demons but Chelsea, who had Frank Lampard sent off, won thanks to Marcel Desailly's last-gasp goal. Another blow came when Bunjevcevic fractured his cheekbone, soon after Doherty had ruptured knee ligaments.

Ziege was proving that he was an able goalscorer. When he netted at Sunderland in the 2-1 win, it was his third goal in four League games, while Sheringham hit the winner with his third in two games.

After the 1-0 defeat at Liverpool, Spurs and Sheringham faced Manchester United at White Hart Lane. They gave a debut to Southampton's Dean Richards who had finally been given the green light to join his former manager at a cost of £8.1m at the end of September.

Richards opened the scoring as Spurs raced into a remarkable 3-0 first half lead and United's early-season problems were exposed again. A remarkable comeback highlighted Spurs' own defensive shortcomings since the departure of Campbell. King, Chris Perry and Richards at the heart of Spurs' back three were powerless as United went on a goal rampage, netting five times.

If Spurs were shell-shocked in defeat, the psychologist obviously knew his job.

➡ All the latest news, views and opinion – 4thegame.com

F.A. Barclaycard Premiership
Top Goal Scorer

Gustavo Poyet

Total Premier League Goals Scored:	Percentage Of The Team's League Goals:
10	20%

Goals Scored From

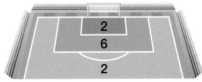

2
6
2

Despite the return of Teddy Sheringham alongide fellow veteran Les Ferdinand, Gus Poyet had a typically inspired season in front of goal. Signed from Chelsea in the summer of 2001, the Uruguyan midfielder arrived with a goalscoring pedigree, having notched 36 League goals in four seasons with the Blues. Although he took until October to net his first League goal in a white shirt, he went on to score regularly throughout the campaign. By the time he struck the winner against Liverpool in late April, he was able to celebrate his 14th goal, including four in cup games. Although Sheringham finished with the same amount of goals, he made one more start.

> "I said to the boys, to everybody, even to my family, that I'm very critical of myself when I miss a chance."
>
> *Gustavo Poyet*

Goals Resulting From

Key
🟦 Open Play 🟦 Corner ⬜ Indirect Free Kick
⬜ Direct Free Kick 🟦 Penalty

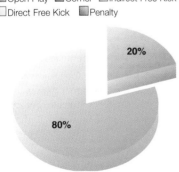

20%

80%

	Right Foot	Left Foot	Header
Open Play	4	2	2
Set piece	2	-	-

Goal Assists

Total number of goal assists	6

Teams Scored Against

Against	Home	Away
Arsenal	1	0
Bolton Wanderers	1	0
Charlton Athletic	0	1
Derby County	1	0
Fulham	0	1
Ipswich Town	0	1
Leeds United	0	1
Liverpool	1	0
Newcastle United	0	1
Sunderland	1	0
Total Goals Scored	**5**	**5**

 Fixtures, results and match reports – 4thegame.com

It's a fact

Les Ferdinand scored the 10,000th goal in the Premier League when he netted in the 4-0 win over Fulham. It was also the 400th goal of the season.

> **"When I scored the goal I heard a big cheer and Steffen Freund came up to me to congratulate me. I hope my dad had a bet on me because apparently I was 33-1 to get the goal."**
>
> *Les Ferdinand after scoring the 10,000th Premier League goal (December 2001)*

October saw three F.A. Barclaycard Premiership wins out of three while Spurs progressed in the Worthington Cup with a 4-0 thrashing of Tranmere. Sadly, midfielder Willem Korsten was forced to anounce his retirement.

Home wins over Derby – where Spurs scored three and forced a further 25 scoring opportunities – Middlesbrough and an impressive victory at Newcastle took them into seventh spot with the carrot of European qualification tantalisingly within their grasp.

Poyet was proving his worth with a string of valuable goals. Though November began with a 2-1 defeat at Leeds, Poyet netted his third goal in four League games and added another to steal a point in the North London derby.

Campbell returned and received a predictably hostile welcome. Taunted throughout, the Spurs fans could not contain their hatred and the Arsenal team bus was struck with missiles on its departure.

Tottenham lost Mauricio Taricco for three games after he was found guilty of misconduct following an incident at Everton, but continued to show a vast improvement with Darren Anderton beginning to rediscover his form of old thanks to a rare injury-free run.

F.A. Barclaycard Premiership
Goals By Position

Key
Forward | Midfield | League Position
Defence | Goalkeeper

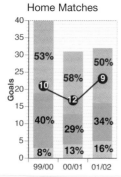

Home Matches

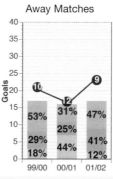

Away Matches

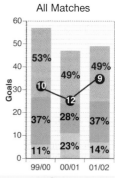

All Matches

Chart Analysis

statistics powered by **SUPERBASE**™

While Tottenham managed one more goal at home compared to the previous season, their return from away matches continued to disappoint.

Not only did they manage nearly twice as many goals at White Hart Lane as they did on their travels, they have now failed to score more than 20 goals away for the fourth year in a row.

The defenders and midfielders contributed just over half of all goals scored.

 Win Barclaycard Premiership tickets – 4thegame.com

Wins over West Ham and Bolton saw Spurs rise to the heady heights of fifth in the table, their highest placing for 14 months. They were also progressing nicely in the Worthington Cup, with a 2-1 win at Fulham at the end of November taking them into the fifth round.

In addition to impressive performances from Anderton and Poyet in midfield, King was coming of age in defence where Spurs were beginning to forget Campbell.

The Worthington Cup became more important to Spurs after they thrashed desperate Bolton 6-0. Les Ferdinand's hat-trick set up a semi-final with Chelsea.

Back in the League, form dipped going into Christmas but only after Ferdinand had struck a major landmark. His early strike in the 4-0 win over Fulham on 15 December was the 10,000th goal to be scored in the Premier League since its inception in 1992.

Disappointingly, Spurs were beaten 2-1 at home by Ipswich after losing Sheringham, sent off for striking out at John McGreal. Another loss, on Boxing Day at Southampton, was followed by a 1-1 draw at Villa where, inexplicably, Anderton handled and Villa levelled in the final minute from the penalty spot.

Spurs may have had one eye on the semi-final against Chelsea but they returned to winning ways against

F.A. Barclaycard Premiership
Team Performance Table

League Position	Team	Points won from a possible six	Percentage of points won at home	Percentage of points won away	Overall percentage of points won
1	Arsenal	1/6			
2	Liverpool	3/6			
3	Manchester Utd	0/6	47%	20%	33%
4	Newcastle Utd	3/6			
5	Leeds United	3/6			
6	Chelsea	0/6			
7	West Ham Utd	4/6			
8	Aston Villa	2/6	42%	33%	38%
9	**Tottenham H**	**50**			
10	Blackburn R	3/6			
11	Southampton	3/6			
12	Middlesbrough	4/6			
13	Fulham	6/6	67%	33%	50%
14	Charlton Athletic	0/6			
15	Everton	2/6			
16	Bolton W	4/6			
17	Sunderland	6/6			
18	Ipswich Town	0/6	80%	27%	53%
19	Derby County	3/6			
20	Leicester City	3/6			

The table shows how many points out of a possible six Tottenham Hotspur have taken off each of the teams in the four sections. The other columns show as a percentage how many points they have taken from those available.

Chart Analysis

statistics powered by SUPERBASE™

Spurs collected progressively less points against teams higher up the table.

However, they did manage wins over Liverpool, Newcastle and Leeds United to help them take a third of all points available against the top five. The only team they didn't take points off at the top was Manchester United.

As expected, they performed best against teams in the bottom half of the table, where they registered both their 'doubles', against Fulham and Sunderland.

Tottenham failed to take points off one team in each of the four sectors.

They were also one of only three teams along with Aston Villa and Blackburn Rovers to lose matches against both the bottom two. In fact, their form away from home against teams in the bottom sector was poor, picking up just four out of a possible 15 points.

➡ The heart of the Barclaycard Premiership – 4thegame.com

"I have a long-term plan but we all know what happens in football. If there are no trophies around in my third year, or we are not playing in Europe regularly, it might be a different story."

Glenn Hoddle
(March 2002)

Blackburn on New Year's Day. The jinx Chelsea held over them returned in the first leg of the Worthington Cup semi-final when, the run of games without a win against the Blues was extended to 26 thanks to two delightful goals from Jimmy Floyd Hasselbaink at Stamford Bridge. Steffen Freund also suffered a serious knee injury.

Ipswich completed a League 'double' over Spurs while a draw against Everton and successive defeats by Newcastle and Derby were clearly another sign of the pressure mounting.

Spurs knew the Worthington Cup was their one real chance of a trophy and, on a memorable night at White Hart Lane, they laid the jinx to rest with a 5-1 demolition of Chelsea to reach the final and set up a meeting with Blackburn. However, the trip to Cardiff was to end in disappointment with Rovers winning 2-1.

Spurs responded by beating Sunderland but a 4-0 defeat at Old Trafford, where Taricco was sent off, was followed by a 4-0 F.A. Cup defeat by Chelsea. The Blues were clearly in determined mood – they won 4-0 again in the home League meeting with Spurs and again Taricco was sent off.

Anderton was absent, suffering his first injury of the season, and Spurs were reeling from conceding 12 goals in

F.A. Barclaycard Premiership
Goals By Time Period

Key: ■ Goals Scored ■ Goals Conceded

Home Matches: 0-15: 5/4; 16-30: 4; 31-45: 7/3; 46-60: 4/4; 61-75: 5/4; 76-90: 7/9

Away Matches: 0-15: 2/4; 16-30: 3/3; 31-45: 4/2; 46-60: 5/3; 61-75: 8; 76-90: 3/9

All Matches: 0-15: 7/8; 16-30: 7/3; 31-45: 11/5; 46-60: 9/7; 61-75: 5/12; 76-90: 10/18

Chart Analysis

statistics powered by SUPERBASE™

While Tottenham outscored their opponents in the first half, they suffered in the last half-hour of matches when they conceded 30 out of 53 goals.

This hit them hard particularly away from home where they only managed to net three times in the last 30 minutes.

Their best spell came in the last 15 minutes of the first half when they outscored their opponents by more than two to one.

Tottenham Hotspur

F.A. Barclaycard Premiership

Goals Resulting From

Key ☐ Goals Scored ☐ Goals Conceded

	Six Yard Area				Inside Area				Outside Area				Total			
	Shots		Headers		Shots		Headers		Shots		Headers		**Shots**		**Headers**	
	Home	Away	Home	Away	Home	Away	Home	Away	Home	Away	Home	Away	**Home**	**Away**	**Home**	**Away**
Open Play	4	2	3	-	14	5	1	2	3	3	-	-	21	10	4	2
	2	-	2	2	7	14	2	-	3	5	-	-	12	19	4	2
Direct Free Kick									-	0			0	0		
									-	1			0	1		
Indirect Free Kick	-	-	-	-	1	0	1	1	-	-	-	-	1	0	1	1
	-	-	1	-	2	0	-	1	1	-	-	-	3	0	1	1
Penalty	-	-	-	-	1	2	-	-	-	-	-	-	1	2	0	0
	-	-	-	-	1	4	-	-	-	-	-	-	1	4	0	0
Corner	1	-	2	0	1	1	-	-	-	-	-	-	2	1	2	0
	1	-	1	1	-	-	1	-	-	-	-	-	1	0	2	2
Totals	5	2	5	0	17	8	2	3	3	3	0	0	25	13	7	3
	3	0	4	3	10	18	3	2	4	6	0	0	17	24	7	5

How Goals Were Scored
Home & Away Matches

6% 10% 6%
77%

Key
- ☐ Open Play
- ☐ Corner
- ☐ Indirect Free Kick
- ☐ Direct Free Kick
- ☐ Penalty

Charts do not include 1 own goal for.

How Goals Were Conceded
Home & Away Matches

2% 9% 9% 9%
70%

Goals Scored from
Key ☐ Open Play ☐ Set Piece

Home	Away
22% 78%	25% 75%

Goals Conceded from
Key ☐ Open Play ☐ Set Piece

Home	Away
33% 67%	28% 72%

Chart Analysis

Tottenham conceded five goals from each of Penalties, Corners and Indirect Free Kicks, nearly a third more in total than they managed to score from the same dead ball situations.

They were most successful with Shots from Open Play Inside Area.

Spurs conceded more goals from Headers and Direct Free Kicks than they scored.

WORST IN THE LEAGUE...
- **Most goals conceded from Penalties away**

statistics powered by SUPERBASE™

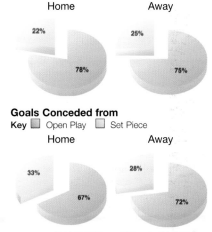

> **"Proving people wrong has always been a challenge. I never set out to play for Tottenham, Manchester United and England. No way. It's just that there has always seemed to be someone at my shoulder doubting me."**
>
> *Teddy Sheringham*
> *(April 2002)*

It's a fact

Stephen Clemence suffered the ignomiy of collecting the first F.A. Barclaycard Premiership caution of the season during Spurs' goalless draw against Aston Villa.

three games in March. Ferdinand and Ziege suffered injuries and the end of the season could not come quickly enough for the North Londoners.

King was beginning to tire towards the end of his first full season, his error allowing Charlton's Chris Powell to claim a 1-0 win at White Hart Lane.

Spurs bounced back, beating Leeds 2-1 at White Hart Lane before making the short trip across North London for a derby game which meant more than usual. Arsenal needed to win and took the lead early on, before a penalty converted by Sheringham pulled Tottenham level. The drama didn't end there with Lauren stealing a late winner for the Gunners with another penalty.

Tottenham then announced a new multi-million pound shirt sponsorship deal with holiday company Thomson.

Successive draws followed, at home to West Ham and at Bolton, and suddenly every Arsenal fan wanted Spurs to win. They played Liverpool at White Hart Lane where they had beaten the Reds in their last three outings. They made it four, thanks to another Poyet goal, and Arsenal had been nudged closer the title.

The season finished disappointingly, however. Tottenham were the last League visitors to Filbert Street, home of relegated Leicester, and left with a 2-1 defeat.

F.A. Barclaycard Premiership	Key
Shot Efficiency	■ Goals Scored ■ Other Shots On Target

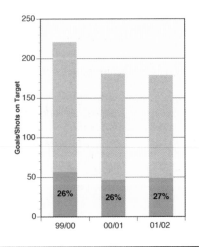

Season	Division	Shots Off Target	Shots On Target	Total Goals
1999 - 2000	P	n/a	221	57
2000 - 2001	P	n/a	181	47
2001 - 2002	P	215	179	49

Chart Analysis

While registering fractionally less Shots On Target than last season, Spurs upped their efficiency by 1%.

In fact, their 27% conversion rate was their highest ever in the Premier League in a year which saw them register their least amount of Shots On Target.

statistics powered by **SUPERBASE**™

→ **Win Barclaycard Premiership tickets - 4thegame.com**

Tottenham Hotspur

F.A. Barclaycard Premiership	Key
Team Discipline	■ Forward ■ Midfield ■ Defence ■ Goalkeeper

Total Number Of Bookings

Total number of red cards	4
Total number of yellow cards	58

Referee Performance

Referee	Games Refereed	Red Cards	Yellow Cards
M.A.Riley	2	2	4
D.R.Elleray	3	2	4
J.T.Winter	4	0	5

Type of Yellow Cards Received

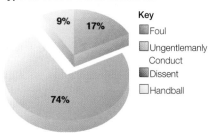

Key
- ■ Foul
- ☐ Ungentlemanly Conduct
- ■ Dissent
- ☐ Handball

9% 17% 74%

Bookings by Position 1999/2000 - 2001/2002

Home Matches	Away Matches	All Matches
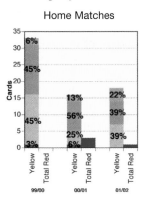	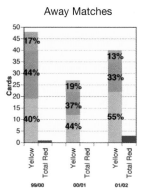	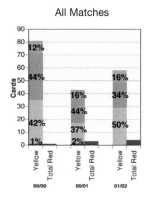

Chart Analysis

Spurs notched 15 more Yellow Cards overall than they did the previous season, although they were well below the 81 collected in 1999-00.

While the percentage contribution from midfielders dropped, that of the defenders rose to account for half of the cautions received.

Spurs picked up over twice as many Yellow Cards away from home as they did at White Hart Lane.

Red Cards rose to their highest number in three years.

"We'd never sack or even think about sacking Mauricio. He is not an assassin. Although he's made foolish mistakes we won't over-sensationalise his actions."

Director of Football David Pleat on Mauricio Taricco (March 2002)

statistics powered by SUPERBASE™

The heart of the Barclaycard Premiership - 4thegame.com

West Ham United

	F.A. Barclaycard Premiership Final standing for the 2001-2002 season							
Final Position		Games Played	Games Won	Games Drawn	Games Lost	Goals For	Goals Against	Total Points
6	Chelsea	38	17	13	8	66	38	64
7	West Ham United	38	15	8	15	48	57	53
8	Aston Villa	38	12	14	12	46	47	50

"We need strength in depth, because I am working with the smallest squad in the Premier League. There are probably only 13 or 14 players here who have played a dozen or more games."

Glenn Roeder (May 2002)

Club Honours and Records

Division 2 Champions: 1957-58, 1980-81

FA Cup Winners: 1964, 1975, 1980

European Cup Winners' Cup Winners: 1964-65

Record victory:

10-0 v Bury, League Cup 2nd Round (2nd leg), 25 October, 1983

Record defeat:

2-8 v Blackburn Rovers, Division 1, 26 December, 1963

League goals in a season (team):

101, Division 2, 1957-58

League goals in a season (player):

42, Vic Watson, Division 1, 1929-30

Career league goals:

298, Vic Watson, 1920 to 1935

League appearances:

663, Billy Bonds, 1967 to 1988

Reported transfer fee paid: £5,000,000 to Sunderland for Don Hutchison, August 2001

Reported transfer fee received: £18,000,000 from Leeds for Rio Ferdinand, November 2000

GLENN Roeder can be proud of his first season in charge of West Ham. He produced a team with an almost invincible home record, brought on Jermain Defoe, saw Joe Cole flourish, and finished seventh. It was the fourth time in five years that the Hammers had finished in the top ten.

Roeder had stepped in as cover for the departed Harry Redknapp at the end of the 2000-01 season but probably did not expect to be in charge at the start of the new campaign. Indeed, he was not the first choice of the Hammers' board; Alex McLeish, the Hibernian manager, was one target, while Steve McClaren opted for Middlesbrough rather than West Ham.

Alan Curbishley, the Charlton manager, was also considered but there was a growing feeling, particularly among the younger players, that Roeder should be given a chance. After Curbishley had signed a new contract at the Valley, the caretaker was upgraded, albeit with only a one-year contract. The board knew the decision might not appease all fans and even offered disgruntled season ticket holders a refund.

Frank Lampard had already left for Chelsea in a £11m move but Roeder insisted other stars such as Trevor Sinclair

 All the latest news, views and opinion – 4thegame.com

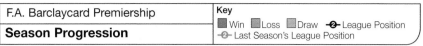

West Ham United

F.A. Barclaycard Premiership

Season Progression

Key
■ Win ■ Loss ■ Draw –②– League Position
–②– Last Season's League Position

All Matches

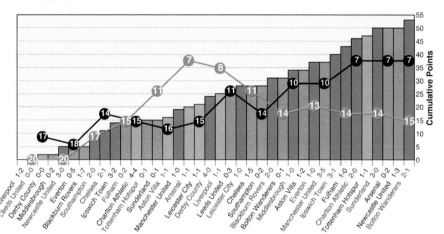

Home Matches

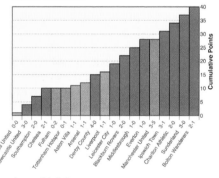

Away Matches

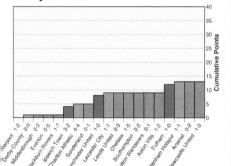

Chart Analysis

West Ham's fine campaign under rookie manager Glenn Roeder saw them finish seventh in the F.A. Barclaycard Premiership, their second best finish in nine years in the top flight.

Having been appointed to the post in the summer, Roeder endured a difficult opening to the new season. His new charges won just once in seven game run that ended with successive drubbings at the hands of Everton and Blackburn Rovers.

Three wins in quick succession starting in mid-October pulled them out of the danger zone before they slipped again, picking up just two points from their next five outings.

An inspired win at Manchester United in early December halted the decline as the Hammers' form stabilised in the run-up to the New Year.

From January onwards, their home form of eight wins in nine helped them rise up the table while away from home they managed just one win, at London rivals Fulham.

statistics powered by SUPERBASE™

> "I hope we can make some new signings as soon as possible because we are not playing in the Albanian League and will need a big squad to compete in the F.A. Barclaycard Premiership"
>
> *Paolo Di Canio*
> *(August 2001)*

It's a fact

When West Ham won 1-0 at Manchester United in December, it brought to an end a sequence of 11 successive League defeats at Old Trafford.

and Frederic Kanoute would not be following the midfielder out of Upton Park.

In came Villa goalkeeper David James and Frenchman Laurent Courtois to the squad, while Sebastian Schemmel's loan move from Metz was made permanent. However, a move to sign Atletico Madrid's Bosnian defender Mirsad Hibic fell through due to work permit problems.

James' debut was delayed after he suffered an injury playing for England against Holland and the start under Roeder was dismal. The first three games brought two draws, a defeat and just one goal.

The 2-1 opening day loss at Liverpool was followed by goalless draws against Leeds United and Derby County, while the Hammers' Worthington Cup aspirations were ended by Division Two Reading on penalties. West Ham signed former midfielder Don Hutchison from Sunderland but another failure to score, in the 2-0 loss at Middlesbrough, left them anchored at the foot of the F.A. Barclaycard Premiership. At the Riverside, West Ham had given a debut to Czech international Tomas Repka, signed for £5.5m from Fiorentina, and he started with a red card in an abject team performance.

There was some respite in the form of a 3-0 home win

F.A. Barclaycard Premiership
Half-Time/Full-Time Comparison

Key: ■ Win □ Loss ▨ Draw

Home				Away				Total			
Number of Home Half Time Wins	Full Time Result W	L	D	Number of Away Half Time Wins	Full Time Result W	L	D	Total number of Half Time Wins	Full Time Result W	L	D
10	9	-	1	2	2	-	-	12	11	-	1
Number of Home Half Time Losses	Full Time Result W	L	D	Number of Away Half Time Losses	Full Time Result W	L	D	Total number of Half Time Losses	Full Time Result W	L	D
2	-	1	1	8	-	7	1	10	-	8	2
Number of Home Half Time Draws	Full Time Result W	L	D	Number of Away Half Time Draws	Full Time Result W	L	D	Total number of Half Time Draws	Full Time Result W	L	D
7	3	2	2	9	1	5	3	16	4	7	5

Chart Analysis

statistics powered by ◆ SUPERBASE™

The Hammers were strong starters at home, going into the half-time break either in front or on level terms in 17 out of 19 matches.

Away from home, they held on to win in the two games they led at the break but struggled otherwise, losing 12 out of 17 matches they were either losing or drawing at half-time.

The one draw they did turn into a win on their travels was a memorable one, beating Manchester United 1-0 at Old Trafford.

 Win Barclaycard Premiership tickets - 4thegame.com

DATE	H/A	OPPONENT	H/T	F/T	POS	REFEREE	TEAM											SUBSTITUTES USED		
18-08	A	Liverpool	1-1	1-2	16	J.T.Winter	Hislop	Schemmel	Song	Dailly	Winterburn	Sinclair	Carrick	Moncur	Cole	Di Canio 29	Todorov ▲29	McCann ▲	Courtois ▲	Defoe ▲
25-08	H	Leeds Utd	0-0	0-0	17	P.A.Durkin	Hislop	Schemmel	Song ●	Dailly	Winterburn	Sinclair	Carrick	Moncur ●	Cole	Di Canio	Todorov	McCann ▲	Defoe ▲	
08-09	A	Derby County	0-0	0-0	17	C.R.Wilkes	Hislop	Schemmel	Song	Dailly	Winterburn	Sinclair	Carrick	Hutchison	Cole	Di Canio	Kanoute	Moncur ▲	Defoe ▲	Todorov ▲
15-09	A	Middlesbrough	0-2	0-2	20	M.A.Riley	Hislop	Repka ●	Song 53	Dailly 53	Winterburn	Winterburn ▲	Carrick	Moncur ▲	Cole	Di Canio	Sinclair	Soma ▲	Todorov ▲	Defoe ▲
23-09	H	Newcastle Utd	1-0	3-0	15	P.Jones	Hislop	Schemmel	Song	Dailly	Winterburn ●	Winterburn	Carrick	Hutchison 18	Courtois ▲18	Di Canio 53 82	Kanoute ▲82	Soma ▲	Todorov ▲	Defoe ▲
29-09	A	Everton	0-1	0-5	18	A.P.D'Urso	Hislop	Schemmel	Song	Dailly	Winterburn	Sinclair	Carrick	Hutchison	Courtois ●	Di Canio	Kanoute ▲82	Sinclair ●	Kitson ▲	Byrne ▲
14-10	A	Blackburn	1-3	1-7	19	A.P.D'Urso	Hislop	Repka ●	Soma	Dailly ▲	Winterburn 52	Hutchison	Carrick 39	Moncur ▲	Sinclair 39	Di Canio 80	Kanoute	Sinclair ●	McCann ▲	Foxe ▲
20-10	H	Southampton	0-0	2-0	15	N.S.Barry	Hislop	Schemmel	Repka	Dailly	Winterburn	Sinclair 4 12	Carrick	Hutchison	Courtois ▲	Di Canio 80	Kanoute 52 80	Moncur ▲	Defoe ▲	
28-10	H	Chelsea	2-1	2-1	14	D.J.Gallagher	Hislop	Repka	Foxe	Dailly	Winterburn	Sinclair 4 12	Carrick 4	Hutchison	Courtois ▲	Di Canio	Kanoute ▲12	Kitson ▲	Defoe ▲	
28-10	H	Ipswich Town	0-1	3-2	11	S.W.Dunn	Hislop	Repka	Foxe	Dailly	Winterburn	Sinclair 4 12	Carrick 90	Hutchison 21 72	Sinclair	Di Canio ▲21	Kanoute 72	Defoe ▲90		
03-11	A	Fulham	0-1	0-2	14	G.P.Barber	Hislop	Foxe ●	Winterburn	Dailly	Winterburn	Sinclair	Carrick	Hutchison	Courtois ●	Di Canio	Kanoute			
19-11	H	Charlton	2-2	4-4	15	A.G.Wiley	Hislop	Repka 84	Foxe	Dailly 84	Minto ▲30	Minto ▲30	Carrick	Hutchison ▲	Sinclair 64	Di Canio 3	Kitson ▲30 30 64	Lomas ▲30 30 64	Defoe ▲84	Cole ▲
24-11	A	Tottenham	0-0	0-1	15	D.R.Elleray	James	Schemmel	Repka	Dailly	Minto	Hutchison	Lomas ▲	Cole ▲	Sinclair	Kitson	Defoe	Moncur ▲		
01-12	A	Sunderland	0-1	0-1	16	P.Jones	James	Schemmel	Repka	Dailly	Minto ●	Hutchison	Carrick	Cole ▲	Sinclair	Kitson	Defoe	Moncur ▲		
05-12	H	Aston Villa	0-1	1-1	16	M.L.Dean	James	Schemmel	Repka	Dailly	Minto ●	Hutchison	Carrick 74 86	Cole 86	Sinclair	Defoe 90	Defoe 90	Todorov ▲	Moncur ▲	
08-12	A	Manchester Utd	0-1	0-0	16	P.A.Durkin	James	Schemmel ●	Repka	Dailly	Winterburn ●	Hutchison	Carrick 74 86	Cole 86	Sinclair ▲38	Defoe ▲74	Defoe	Kitson ▲		
15-12	H	Leicester City	0-1	1-1	15	E.K.Wolstenholme	James	Schemmel 35	Repka	Dailly	Winterburn	Hutchison	Carrick	Moncur	Cole 73	Di Canio 73	Defoe	Kitson ▲	Todorov ▲	
22-12	A	Leicester City	0-1	1-1	15	G.Poll	James	Schemmel 4	Repka	Dailly	Winterburn	Hutchison 4	Carrick 74 86	Hutchison	Cole 86	Di Canio ▲74	Kanoute ▲74	Moncur ▲	Defoe ▲89	
26-12	A	Derby County	1-0	4-0	11	R.Styles	James	Schemmel ●	Repka	Dailly	Winterburn ●	Hutchison	Carrick	Hutchison	Sinclair ▲38	Defoe	Kanoute	Kitson ▲		
29-12	H	Liverpool	0-2	0-3	11	S.W.Dunn	James	Schemmel 36	Repka ●	Dailly	Winterburn	Hutchison	Moncur ▲	Hutchison	Sinclair ▲	Di Canio 36	Kanoute	Garcia ▲	Fox ▲	Todorov ▲
01-01	A	Leeds Utd	1-0	1-5	12	D.J.Gallagher	James	Schemmel 88	Repka	Dailly	Winterburn	Hutchison	Carrick	Cole ●	Sinclair ▲	Di Canio ●	Kanoute	Courtois ▲	Defoe ▲88	
12-01	H	Chelsea	0-2	0-2	11	A.P.D'Urso	James	Schemmel	Repka	Dailly	Labant	Lomas	Carrick ●	Cole	Hutchison ▲16	Kanoute	Kanoute	Defoe ▲	Moncur ▲	
20-01	A	Southampton	0-1	0-2	14	P.Dowd	James	Schemmel ●	Repka	Dailly	Winterburn	Lomas	Lomas	Cole	Sinclair ●16	Di Canio 55	Kanoute ▲6 55	Labant ▲	Moncur ▲	Defoe ▲
30-01	H	Blackburn	1-0	2-0	11	P.Jones	James	Foxe ●	Foxe	Dailly	Minto ●	Labant	Foxe	Cole	Garcia ▲	Defoe	Defoe	Kitson ▲	Kishishev	
09-02	H	Bolton	0-1	1-0	12	D.Pugh	James	Lomas ▲	Repka	Dailly	Minto	Winterburn	Lomas	Cole	Sinclair 56	Kanoute 76	Kanoute 76	Garcia ▲	Labant ▲76	
23-02	A	Middlesbrough	0-1	1-0	10	C.J.Foy	James	Schemmel	Repka	Dailly	Pearce ●	Winterburn	Moncur ▲	Cole	Sinclair	Defoe 12	Defoe 12	Garcia ▲	Labant ▲76	
02-03	A	Aston Villa	1-1	1-2	13	G.P.Barber	James	Schemmel ▲	Pearce	Dailly	Pearce	Winterburn	Garcia ▲	Cole	Sinclair 56	Di Canio 12	Kanoute	Defoe ▲	Garcia ▲	
06-03	H	Everton	0-0	1-0	10	B.Knight	James	Schemmel ▲	Repka	Dailly	Pearce	Winterburn	Labant	Cole 56	Sinclair	Di Canio	Kanoute	Defoe ▲	Garcia ▲	
16-03	A	Manchester Utd	2-2	3-5	10	M.R.Halsey	James	Schemmel ▲19	Repka ●	Dailly	Winterburn ▲	Lomas 7	Lomas 7	Cole	Labant 7	Kanoute 19 78	Kanoute 19 78	Defoe ▲78	Defoe ▲85	
30-03	H	Ipswich Town	1-0	1-0	8	M.R.Halsey	James	Schemmel	Repka	Dailly	Winterburn ▲	Lomas 35	Carrick	Cole	Sinclair	Kanoute ▲35 73 85	Kanoute ▲35 73 85	Moncur ▲	Defoe ▲85	
01-04	A	Fulham	1-0	1-0	8	M.A.Halsey	James	Schemmel	Labant ▲	Dailly	Labant	Lomas	Carrick	Cole	Sinclair 45	Kanoute ▲45	Kanoute ▲45	Moncur ▲	Defoe ▲	Pearce ▲
06-04	H	Charlton	2-0	2-0	7	M.A.Riley	James	Schemmel 33	Repka	Dailly	Winterburn	Lomas	Carrick	Cole ●	Sinclair	Di Canio ▲22 22	Kanoute ▲22 22	Moncur ▲	Moncur ▲	
13-04	A	Tottenham	0-0	1-1	7	N.S.Barry	James	Schemmel	Repka	Dailly	Pearce 89	Sinclair	Carrick	Lomas 89	Sinclair	Defoe	Kanoute	Winterburn ▲		
20-04	H	Sunderland	1-0	3-0	7	S.G.Bennett	James	Schemmel ▲27	Repka ●	Dailly	Pearce	Winterburn	Carrick	Cole 51	Sinclair 27 51 76	Sinclair 27 51 76	Defoe ▲76	Labant ▲	Garcia ▲	
24-04	A	Arsenal	0-2	0-2	7	S.W.Dunn	James	Schemmel ▲	Repka	Dailly	Pearce	Winterburn	Carrick	Cole	Sinclair	Sinclair	Sinclair 20	Defoe ▲	Labant ▲	
27-04	A	Newcastle Utd	1-1	1-3	8	P.A.Durkin	James	Lomas	Repka ●	Dailly	Pearce	Labant ▲	Carrick	Cole	Sinclair	Defoe 20	Kanoute 20	Winterburn ▲	Garcia ▲	
11-05	H	Bolton	1-0	2-1	7	M.L.Dean	James	Lomas 43	Repka ●	Dailly	Pearce 88	Winterburn	Carrick ▲88	Cole ●	Sinclair	Defoe 43	Kanoute ▲	Moncur ▲	Garcia ▲	

F.A. Barclaycard Premiership

Squad List

Position	Name	Appearances	Appearances as Substitute	Goals or Clean Sheets	Goal Assists	Yellow Cards	Red Cards
G	S.Hislop	12		4			
G	D.James	26		9			
D	S.Byrne		1				
D	C.Dailly	38			2	4	
D	H.Foxe	4	2			2	
D	E.Iriekpen						
D	V.Labant	7	5		2	1	
D	S.Minto	5			1	1	
D	I.Pearce	8	1	2		3	
D	T.Repka	31				7	2
D	S.Schemmel	35		1	6	6	
D	R.Soma	1	2				
D	R.Song	5				1	
D	N.Winterburn	29	2		1	4	
M	M.Carrick	30		2	4	4	
M	J.Cole	29	1		4	5	
M	L.Courtois	5	2		1		
M	D.Hutchison	24		1	3	3	
M	S.Lomas	14	1	4	1	3	
M	G.McCann		3				
M	J.Moncur	7	12			6	
M	T.Sinclair	34		5	7	5	
F	T.Camara		1				
F	J.Defoe	14	21	10	2		
F	P.Di Canio	26		9	8	5	1
F	R.Garcia	2	6				
F	F.Kanoute	27		11	3	4	
F	P.Kitson	3	4	3			
F	S.Todorov	2	4		1	2	

over Newcastle at the end of September, where Hutchison capped his first game back at Upton Park with a goal. The relief was obvious with Roeder remarking: "I'm pleased for the whole club, from the tea lady up."

The lady with the urn could have been forgiven for wanting to pour it over Roeder's head as successive hammerings ensued at Everton and Blackburn.

Joe Cole was missing with a foot problem that would not go away and West Ham were unable to paper over the cracks of another dismal performance at Goodison Park where they lost 5-0. In their next game, the Hammers were on their travels again, and this time they left the North with a 7-1 defeat at Ewood Park. Their season, still in its infancy, was already becoming a nightmare. In addition, Repka was sent off for the second time in three games for the Hammers. As the storm clouds gathered, Roeder admitted he faced a battle to hold on to his job.

To add insult to injury, Sinclair demanded a move because, he claimed, he wanted to win trophies and improve his hopes of playing in the World Cup finals. Di Canio, never one to hide his emotions, criticised his teammates, saying they showed a lack of commitment.

West Ham needed to turn it around and they did just that, racking up three straight victories which took them to 11th. The good run began with a 2-0 home win over Southampton, Kanoute scoring both goals. They followed that with their best result so far, a 2-1 home win over Chelsea, which ended their London rivals' unbeaten start to the season. A 3-2 win at Ipswich was followed by a remarkable game, the 4-4 draw at Charlton, where Paul Kitson scored a hat-trick in his first start.

James made his belated debut in October against Spurs but could not

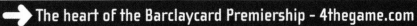

The heart of the Barclaycard Premiership – 4thegame.com

F.A. Barclaycard Premiership

Top Goal Scorer

Frederic Kanoute

Total Premier League Goals Scored:	Percentage Of The Team's League Goals:
11	**23%**

Goals Scored From

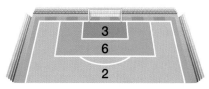

French striker Frederic Kanoute finished as the Hammers' leading marksman for the second year running, scoring 11 goals as he had the previous season, although this time he played five games less. Alongside him, young sensation Jermain Defoe gave Hammers fans a taste of things to come with ten goals, while captain Paolo Di Canio struck nine. The Italian also missed two penalties and the chance to finish level with the Frenchman on 11. Kanoute obviously enjoyed playing at Upton Park as nine of his 11 were scored at home. During the course of the season, he only managed to score more than one goal in a game once, when West Ham beat Southampton 2-0 at home in October.

"When Freddie is on form he is a big player for us – and certainly not one I would have liked to have played against."

Glenn Roeder

Goals Resulting From
Key

100%

	Right Foot	Left Foot	Header
Open Play	6	2	3
Set piece	-	-	-

Goal Assists

Total number of goal assists	3

Teams Scored Against

Against	Home	Away
Southampton	2	0
Arsenal	1	0
Blackburn Rovers	1	0
Charlton Athletic	1	0
Chelsea	1	0
Fulham	0	1
Ipswich Town	0	1
Manchester United	1	0
Middlesbrough	1	0
Newcastle United	1	0
Total Goals Scored	**9**	**2**

It's a fact

West Ham's 7-1 defeat at Blackburn in October equalled their worst Premier League defeat, the 7-1 thrashing at Old Trafford in April 2000.

"I was very fortunate to play here many times and I never came away with a victory. So to come here, bring a team here as a manager and to come away with a victory is special. It's definitely my best day in management."

Glenn Roeder after beating Manchester United (December 2001)

prevent a 1-0 home defeat, a result repeated at Sunderland. Things were definitely improving as the Hammers started an unbeaten run of six games in the F.A. Barclaycard Premiership, beginning with a 1-1 home draw against Villa in which Di Canio missed a penalty.

The Italian missed again three days later, at Old Trafford, but it did not prevent the Hammers from claiming another big scalp. The matchwinner was Jermain Defoe, the England Under-21 striker whose talents were ever more apparent as the season progressed. Successive draws against Arsenal and Leicester were followed by the 4-0 Boxing Day thrashing of Derby with Defoe and Di Canio both notching their fifth goal of the season.

While on the pitch the year ended with a 1-1 home draw against Liverpool, off it speculation linking Di Canio with a move to Old Trafford refused to go away. Finally, West Ham admitted they had rejected an offer from the Red Devils. Instead, Roeder made another signing, with Sparta Prague defender Vladimir Labant arriving in January after the 3-0 defeat at Leeds.

Michael Carrick, absent with a knee problem for three games, returned at Stamford Bridge but could not prevent

---

F.A. Barclaycard Premiership
Goals By Position

Key
■ Forward ■ Midfield –❷– League Position
■ Defence ■ Goalkeeper

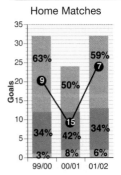

Home Matches

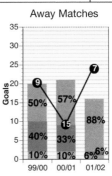

Away Matches

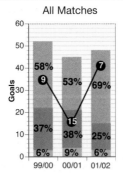

All Matches

Chart Analysis

statistics powered by **SUPERBASE**™

Despite scoring only three more goals overall compared to the previous season, the Hammers finished much higher up the final table.

As would be expected from a campaign in

which they managed just three wins on their travels, the number of goals scored away was half that scored at home and their lowest since 1998-99. Overall, just three goals out of 48 were scored by defenders.

 Fixtures, results and match reports - 4thegame.com

another bad away result, a 5-1 drubbing which was made worse by the sending off of Di Canio, the first of his Hammers career, after stamping on Jody Morris.

West Ham returned to the Bridge less than a week later in the F.A. Cup and held Chelsea to a 1-1 draw. Although they lost the replay 3-2 at Upton Park, Roeder was beginning to find some consistency in the League. After admitting in February that he had been only on a one-year 'trial', he was rewarded with a three-year contract.

His unexpected success was mainly due to a fine home record. Up to and including the 1-0 Upton Park win over Everton in early March, the Hammers had conceded just seven goals in 14 home games, by some distance the best home defensive record in the F.A. Barclaycard Premiership.

The Hammers received a cruel blow when Hutchison damaged cruciate knee ligaments during the 1-0 home win over Middlesbrough and it was predicted he could be out until the following Christmas.

At least West Ham were enjoying the best out of two other midfielders. Cole and Carrick – the former with his place on the plane to the Far East with England secured – were enjoying their best spells for West Ham and were instrumental in making Roeder's first season more than the relegation battle many had feared.

The impressive home record took a

F.A. Barclaycard Premiership
Team Performance Table

League Position	Team	Points won from a possible six	Percentage of points won at home	Percentage of points won away	Overall percentage of points won
1	Arsenal	1/6			
2	Liverpool	1/6			
3	Manchester Utd	3/6	40%	20%	30%
4	Newcastle Utd	3/6			
5	Leeds United	1/6			
6	Chelsea	3/6			
7	**West Ham Utd**	**53**			
8	Aston Villa	1/6	58%	8%	33%
9	Tottenham H	1/6			
10	Blackburn R	3/6			
11	Southampton	3/6			
12	Middlesbrough	3/6			
13	Fulham	3/6	80%	27%	53%
14	Charlton Athletic	4/6			
15	Everton	3/6			
16	Bolton W	3/6			
17	Sunderland	3/6			
18	Ipswich Town	6/6	100%	33%	67%
19	Derby County	4/6			
20	Leicester City	4/6			

The table shows how many points out of a possible six West Ham have taken off each of the teams in the four sections. The other columns show as a percentage how many points they have taken from those available.

Chart Analysis

statistics powered by **SUPERBASE**™

West Ham performed better away from home against teams in the top five than they did against teams in their own sector.

Overall, the percentage of points gained follows the pattern one would expect, with most points gained progressively rising down the table.

However, the split between points won at home and away is heavily weighted towards the former.

In particular, the Hammers only managed to take one point out of 12 available in encounters at the home of teams in their own sector.

West Ham took points off every team in the F.A. Barclaycard Premiership, doing the 'double' only over Ipswich Town.

➡ Win Barclaycard Premiership tickets - 4thegame.com

battering when Manchester United visited Upton Park. Twice the Hammers led, through a rare Steve Lomas header and Kanoute, and twice United responded, eventually netting five times to render Defoe's additional strike a scant consolation. Nevertheless, the month ended favourably, with Ipswich beaten 3-1 at Upton Park – Defoe scoring again with his 8th League goal of the season. The young striker was rewarded with a pay rise equivalent to 500 per cent.

The Hammers were finishing in impressive style and more than vindicating the decision to allow Roeder to take over from Redknapp. April began with another win, at Fulham, and then Charlton were defeated at Upton Park allowing West Ham to sit comfortably in seventh place.

Next was a trip to Tottenham and the London derby ended in dramatic fashion with Ian Pearce becoming West Ham's unlikely hero in his 100th game for the club with a spectacular equaliser in the closing moments.

Di Canio had been ruled out during the 2-0 win over Charlton with a knee injury which brought a premature end to his season. Against Sunderland at Upton Park United were also missing Kanoute, who had a cold, so the front line was led by Sinclair and Defoe. They won 3-0 with a fine display helped by poor resistance from the

It's a fact

West Ham conceded 43 away goals, the highest in the F.A. Barclaycard Premiership and the club's worst return in nine seasons in the Premier League.

> "You can't let one player unsettle the camp. No player is bigger than the club and they should just out him, get rid of him."
>
> *Former West Ham favourite Julian Dicks on Paolo Di Canio*
> *(April 2002)*

F.A. Barclaycard Premiership
Goals By Time Period

Key: ■ Goals Scored ☐ Goals Conceded

Home Matches

Time of Goal (mins)	Goals Scored	Goals Conceded
0-15	4	1
16-30	5	3
31-45	6	2
46-60	5	2
61-75	2	4
76-90	10	2

Away Matches

Time of Goal (mins)	Goals Scored	Goals Conceded
0-15	2	2
16-30	4	7
31-45	2	8
46-60	7	
61-75	4	6
76-90	4	13

All Matches

Time of Goal (mins)	Goals Scored	Goals Conceded
0-15	6	3
16-30	9	10
31-45	8	10
46-60	5	9
61-75	6	10
76-90	14	15

Chart Analysis

statistics powered by ◆ SUPERBASE™

Overall, the only time period in which West Ham outscored their opponents was in the opening 15 minutes of matches.

That was mainly due to a poor away scoring record which saw them outscored by nearly three to one.

At home, they started and finished matches very strongly, outscoring their opponents by four and five to one respectively.

→ The heart of the Barclaycard Premiership – 4thegame.com

F.A. Barclaycard Premiership
Goals Resulting From

Key
☐ Goals Scored ☐ Goals Conceded

	Six Yard Area				Inside Area				Outside Area				Total			
	Shots		Headers		Shots		Headers		Shots		Headers		Shots		Headers	
	Home	Away	Home	Away	Home	Away	Home	Away	Home	Away	Home	Away	Home	Away	Home	Away
Open Play	3	2	3	2	13	6	3	-	5	3	-	-	21	11	6	2
	3	7	-	1	5	19	1	4	1	4	-	-	9	30	1	5
Direct Free Kick									0	0			0	0		
									1	1			1	1		
Indirect Free Kick	1	-	-	-	-	-	-	-	-	-	-	-	1	0	0	0
	-	2	1	1	-	-	-	-	-	-	-	-	0	2	1	1
Penalty	-	-	-	-	1	3	-	-	-	-	-	-	1	3	0	0
	-	-	-	-	1	-	-	-	-	-	-	-	1	0	0	0
Corner	-	-	1	-	1	-	1	-	-	-	-	-	1	0	2	0
	-	-	1	-	-	2	-	-	-	-	-	-	0	2	1	0
Totals	4	2	4	2	15	9	4	0	5	3	0	0	24	14	8	2
	3	9	2	2	6	21	1	4	2	5	0	0	11	35	3	6

How Goals Were Scored
Home & Away Matches

8% 6% 2%
83%

Key
▪ Open Play
▪ Corner
☐ Indirect Free Kick
☐ Direct Free Kick
▪ Penalty

Charts do not include 2 own goals against.

How Goals Were Conceded
Home & Away Matches

2%
4% 5% 7%
82%

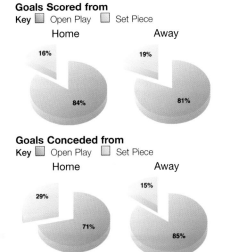

Goals Scored from
Key ☐ Open Play ☐ Set Piece

Home
16%
84%

Away
19%
81%

Goals Conceded from
Key ▪ Open Play ☐ Set Piece

Home
29%
71%

Away
15%
85%

Chart Analysis

West Ham scored exactly five times as many goals from Open Play as they did from Set Pieces.

Although they netted four Penalties, they managed just three goals from Corners and one from an Indirect Free Kick.

However, they proved equally adept at keeping their opponents out from Set Pieces, conceding just ten out of 57 from dead ball situations.

WORST IN THE LEAGUE...
• **Most goals conceded from Open Play away**

statistics powered by **SUPERBASE**™

➤ All the latest news, views and opinion - 4thegame.com

"It's been a much better season than last year. The team only finished with 42 points last year. We're on 50 and hopefully we can finish with a home win against Bolton in two weeks' time."

Glenn Roeder (April 2002)

It's a fact

West Ham's 3-2 win at Ipswich in October was the Hammers' first away success for eight months.

Black Cats.

West Ham were in good form and though their next port of call was Highbury, they were enjoying life and were hardly daunted by the prospect. Indeed, Kanoute thought he had given the Hammers the lead with a strike which, though the ball appeared to have crossed the line, was ruled out.

Arsenal went on to win 2-0 with two late goals. To add to West Ham's woes, Schemmel was injured in the early stages and he was ruled out for the last two games of the season after the defender fractured a bone in his foot.

The fixture list had not been kind to the Hammers. Having put them up against Arsenal at Highbury, they had to travel to the north and face a Newcastle side oozing confidence after qualifying for the Champions League.

Another goal from Defoe allowed West Ham to take the lead but the occasion was too much and Newcastle won 3-1.

Fittingly, West Ham finished in style with a 3-1 home win over Bolton to rise to seventh place, just missing out on a European place.

F.A. Barclaycard Premiership	Key
Shot Efficiency	■ Goals Scored ■ Other Shots On Target

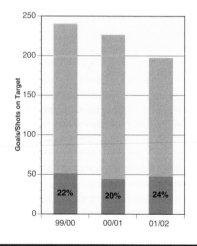

Season	Division	Shots Off Target	Shots On Target	Total Goals
1999 - 2000	P	n/a	241	52
2000 - 2001	P	n/a	227	45
2001 - 2002	P	213	198	48

Chart Analysis

Although West Ham managed less Shots On Target than in the previous two seasons, they equalled their best ever efficiency rating in the Premier League with 24%.

They still have room to improve given that more of their Shots were Off Target than On.

statistics powered by **SUPERBASE**™

➡ **Fixtures, results and match reports – 4thegame.com**

F.A. Barclaycard Premiership		Key
Team Discipline		Forward ■ Midfield
		Defence ■ Goalkeeper

Total Number Of Bookings

Total number of red cards	3
Total number of yellow cards	66

Referee Performance

Referee	Games Refereed	Red Cards	Yellow Cards
A.P.D'Urso	2	2	4
M.A.Riley	3	1	7
P.A.Durkin	4	0	8

Type of Yellow Cards Received

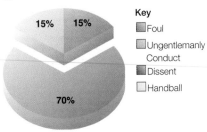

Key
- Foul
- Ungentlemanly Conduct
- Dissent
- Handball

15% 15% 70%

Bookings by Position 1999/2000 - 2001/2002

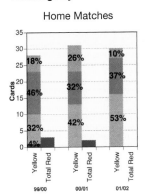

Home Matches

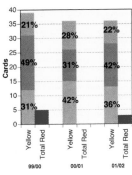

Away Matches

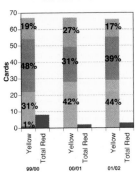

All Matches

Chart Analysis

West Ham failed to collect the same amount of Yellow Cards as in the previous two seasons by one.

While the share of cards picked up by forwards overall declined, those attributed to midfielders rose. Nearly a third of cards were shown for Dissent and Ungentlemanly Conduct.

All three Red Cards issued to West Ham players were away from home.

Two of the reds were brandished by referee A.P. D'Urso, who also issued four Yellow Cards to West Ham players in their two games he refereed in the League.

"I don't subscribe to this view that we should have video evidence, that we should be stopping the game to study every incident. You've still got to have that bit of excitement, mystery, romance or whatever you want to call it about the game."

Glenn Roeder (April 2002)

statistics powered by SUPERBASE™

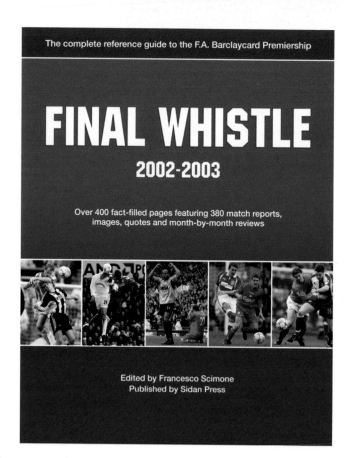

The complete reference guide to the F.A. Barclaycard Premiership

FINAL WHISTLE

2002-2003

Over 400 fact-filled pages featuring 380 match reports,
images, quotes and month-by-month reviews

Edited by Francesco Scimone
Published by Sidan Press

Match reports and statistics on every game in the 2001-02 F.A. Barclaycard Premiership.
Revealing quotes from the people involved. Photographs from every game. Team line-ups
and substitutes for every match. Statistics for every game including: attendance, referee,
form, shots, offsides, corners, fouls, bookings, assists and goals.

Division One Overview

The top flight welcomes two Premier League virgins in West Bromwich Albion and Birmingham City.

The Midlands duo join Division One Champions Manchester City in making the trip to the Promised Land.

Although City ran out comfortable winners in the end, the race for the title was much tighter than the final table suggests.

West Brom were the other side to clinch automatic promotion alongside City. The Baggies finished strongly to break the hearts of their fierce Midlands rivals Wolverhampton Wanderers.

Wolves were the early pace-setters and were still sitting pretty atop the table come the beginning of March. However, a dismal run-in in which they picked up just two wins in their last nine games saw them slip out of the top two.

Norwich City were were beaten in the play-off final in Cardiff by Birmingham City, the Blues finally making it into the Premier League.

At the other end of the table, the biggest shock was the demotion of Barnsley to Division Two for the first time in over 20 years.

Final Division One Table

Key: ☐ Promoted ☐ Relegated
P played, **HW** home win, **HD** home draw, **HL** home loss
HGF home goals for, **HGA** home goals against, **AW** away win
AD away draw, **AL** away loss, **AGF** away goals for
AGA away goals against, **PTS** points, **GD** goal difference.

	Team	P	HW	HD	HL	HGF	HGA	AW	AD	AL	AGF	AGA	PTS	GD
1	Manchester City	46	19	3	1	63	19	12	3	8	45	33	99	+56
2	West Brom	46	15	4	4	36	11	12	4	7	25	18	89	+32
3	Wolves	46	13	4	6	33	18	12	7	4	43	25	86	+33
4	Millwall	46	15	3	5	43	22	7	8	8	26	26	77	+21
5	Birmingham City	46	14	4	5	44	20	7	9	7	26	29	76	+21
6	Norwich City	46	15	6	2	36	16	7	3	13	24	35	75	+9
7	Burnley	46	11	7	5	39	29	10	5	8	31	33	75	+8
8	Preston	46	13	7	3	45	21	7	5	11	26	38	72	+12
9	Wimbledon	46	9	8	6	30	22	9	5	9	33	35	67	+6
10	Crystal Palace	46	13	3	7	42	22	7	3	13	28	40	66	+8
11	Coventry City	46	12	4	7	33	19	8	2	13	26	34	66	+6
12	Gillingham	46	12	5	6	38	26	6	5	12	26	41	64	-3
13	Sheffield Utd	46	8	8	7	34	30	7	7	9	19	24	60	-1
14	Watford	46	10	5	8	38	30	6	6	11	24	26	59	+6
15	Bradford City	46	10	1	12	41	39	5	9	9	28	37	55	-7
16	Nottm Forest	46	7	11	5	26	21	5	7	11	24	30	54	-1
17	Portsmouth	46	9	6	8	36	31	4	8	11	24	41	53	-12
18	Walsall	46	10	6	7	29	27	3	6	14	22	44	51	-20
19	Grimsby Town	46	9	7	7	34	28	3	7	13	16	44	50	-22
20	Sheffield Wed	46	6	7	10	28	37	6	7	10	21	34	50	-22
21	Rotherham Utd	46	7	13	3	32	29	3	6	14	20	37	49	-14
22	Crewe Alexandra	46	8	8	7	23	32	4	5	14	24	44	49	-29
23	Barnsley	46	9	9	5	37	33	2	6	15	22	53	48	-27
24	Stockport County	46	5	1	17	19	44	1	7	15	23	58	26	-60

➡ All the latest news, views and opinion - 4thegame.com

Birmingham City

Division One						Final standing for the 2001-2002 season	
Final Position		Games Played	Games Won	Games Drawn	Games Lost	Goals For	Goals Against	Total Points
4	Millwall	46	22	11	13	69	48	77
5	Birmingham City	46	21	13	12	70	49	76
6	Norwich City	46	22	9	15	60	51	75

"The supporters are the main reason I am here. We will now sell out week in, week out. And we are ready for it. The club has had nothing to shout about in 127 years and the supporters deserve this."

Steve Bruce (May 2002)

Club Honours and Records

Division 2 Champions: 1892-93, 1920-21, 1947-48, 1954-55, 1994-95

League Cup Winners: 1963

Record victory: 12-0 v Walsall T Swifts, Division 2, 17 December, 1892

Record defeat: 1-9 v Sheffield Wednesday, Division 1, 13 December, 1930

League goals in a season (team): 103, Division 2, 1893-94

League goals in a season (player): Joe Bradford, 29, Division 1, 1927-28

Career league goals: Joe Bradford, 249, 1920 to 1935

League appearances: Frank Womack, 491, 1908 to 1928

Reported transfer fee paid: £2,500,000 to Leicester City for Robbie Savage, May 2002

Reported transfer fee received: £2,500,000 from Coventry City for Gary Breen, January 1997

So often the bridesmaid in recent years, the Blues finally gatecrashed the Premier League party with a thrilling play-off final win over Norwich City. In doing so, they returned to the top flight – along with their Midlands neighbours West Brom – for the first time in 16 years.

After finishing in the top six without managing to progress past the play-off semi-finals in the previous three seasons, Birmingham qualified for the end of season bonanza once again after finishing fifth in Division One on 76 points, 13 adrift of automatic promotion and just one clear of seventh placed Burnley.

In the semi-finals, they drew 1-1 with newly-promoted Millwall at St Andrew's before Stern John's last-gasp winner at the New Den propelled Birmingham to a final date with Norwich City.

For the first time in four years, the play-off final went to a penalty shoot-out. After the game had finished 0-0 after 90 minutes – and then 1-1 after extra time – the Midlanders held their nerve to win 4-2 on penalties with one to spare.

The decisive kick which sent them up was struck by young midfielder Darren Carter after the Blues had come back from 1-0 down in extra time to level through former Fulham striker Geoff Horsfield.

➡ Fixtures, results and match reports – 4thegame.com

Winning promotion vindicated the club's decision to sack Trevor Francis in mid-October following a poor start which had left them languishing in 12th position with just 17 points from 11 games.

Getting rid of Francis was a brave step as he had taken them so close since his arrival in 1996, yet it was one that certainly had the desired effect.

There followed a stand-off between Birmingham and Division One rivals Crystal Palace while the Blues waited for the Eagles' boss to become available. He eventually took charge in December after, bizarrely, the man he was replacing – Trevor Francis – had already taken over at Selhurst Park.

He found a club which had been well looked after by joint caretaker managers Jim Barron and Mick Mills. Up to ninth with 36 points at the halfway stage – ten behind leaders Burnley – Bruce set his sights on securing his first promotion in four years of management.

Finally installed as manager, Bruce drafted in seven new players on permanent deals, five of whom started in the play-off final.

Striker Stern John, signed from Nottingham Forest for only £100,000 in February, was the most notable of these, his seven goals in 16 games firing them to the play-offs. Operating mostly from the midfield, Tommy Mooney notched 13 goals to finish top scorer in his first year following his move from Watford.

Following Bruce's arrival, Birmingham picked up 40 points and just five defeats in the second half of the campaign as they snatched a play-off spot on the final day of the season after beating Sheffield United 2-0. That win, against the club where Bruce had started his managerial career in 1998, concluded a run of ten League games unbeaten.

Squad List

Arkadiusz Bak 2 appearances (2 as substitute), **Ian Bennett** 18 (0),
Bjorn Otto Bragstad 3 (0), **David Burrows** 9 (3), **Darren Carter** 12 (1), **Paul Devlin** 11 (2),
Nicky Eaden 24 (5), **Carlos Ferrari** 0 (4),
Curtis Fleming 6 (0), **Paul Furlong** 3 (9),
Jerry Gill 14 (0), **Martin Grainger** 39 (1),
David Holdsworth 3 (1), **Geoff Horsfield** 33 (7),
Bryan Hughes 27 (4), **Michael Hughes** 4 (0),
Jonathan Hutchinson 1 (3),
Graham Hyde 1 (4), **Stern John** 17 (0),
Andrew Johnson 9 (14), **Damien Johnson** 5 (3),
Michael Johnson 30 (2), **Alan Kelly** 6 (0),
Jeff Kenna 21 (0), **Stan Lazaridis** 22 (9),
Tresor Luntala 9 (6), **Marcelo** 17 (4),
Jon McCarthy 3 (1), **Tommy Mooney** 29 (4),
Martyn O'Connor 24 (0), **Darren Purse** 35 (1),
Danny Sonner 10 (5), **Olivier Tebily** 7 (0)
Nico Vaesen 22 (1), Steve Vickers 13 (1),
Tom Williams 4 (0), **Curtis Woodhouse** 8 (10)

Four teams completed the League 'double' over Birmingham, although two of these were Manchester City and West Bromwich Albion who finished the season first and second respectively. In addition, only these two teams – along with Wolves who finished third – lost fewer games than the Blues.

After years of managerial stability – from August 1991 to October 2001 Birmingham had three managers – it is perhaps ironic that promotion finally came in a season when the Blues had four men at the helm.

Blues fans won't let that put them off celebrating their club's first season in the top flight for well over a decade.

Manchester City

Division One								Final standing for the 2001-2002 season

Final Position		Games Played	Games Won	Games Drawn	Games Lost	Goals For	Goals Against	Total Points
1	Manchester City	46	31	6	9	108	52	99
2	West Bromwich Albion	46	27	8	11	61	29	89
3	Wolverhampton W	46	25	11	10	76	43	86

> "Many of the same players were relegated last year. Winning the title will be sweeter for the players who came down with the club last season. The Championship is fantastic for all of them."
>
> *Kevin Keegan (April 2002)*

Club Honours and Records

Football League Champions:
1936-37, 1967-68
Division 1 Champions: 2001-02
Division 2 Champions: 1898-99, 1902-03, 1909-10, 1927-28, 1946-47, 1965-66
FA Cup Winners: 1904, 1934, 1956, 1969
League Cup Winners: 1970, 1976
European Cup Winners' Cup: 1969-70
Record victory: 10-1 v Huddersfield Town, Division 2, 7 November, 1987
Record defeat: 1-9 v Everton, Division 1, 3 September, 1906
League goals in a season (team):
108, Division 1, 2001-02
League goals in a season (player):
Tommy Johnson, 38, Division 1, 1928-29
Career league goals:
Tommy Johnson, 158, 1919 to 1930
League appearances:
Alan Oakes, 565, 1959 to 1976
Reported transfer fee paid: £13,000,000 to Paris St-Germain for Nicolas Anelka, May 2002
Reported transfer fee received: £4,925,000 from Ajax for Georgi Kinkladze, May 1998

Manchester City won promotion to the F.A. Barclaycard Premiership at the first time of asking and in some style. A year after suffering the ignominy of relegation under Joe Royle, they returned to the top flight under the tutelage of the Messiah.

Kevin Keegan was handed the reins at Maine Road last summer, his mission to steady the course of a once mighty club which, as recently as 1999, had plumbed the depths of Division Two football.

Throughout the campaign, City played to passionate sell-out crowds despite the previous season's relegation.

In winning promotion with City in his first full season in charge, the former England manager completed a remarkable hat-trick which had seen him previously steer both Newcastle United and Fulham to higher plains.

He led Newcastle to the promised land of the Premier League in 1993 on the back of an awesome campaign which had seen the Geordies storm the Division One title thanks to 96 points from 46 games. The following year they finished third behind Manchester United and Blackburn Rovers.

If anything, City have the potential to do even better. They took 99 points from 46 games, scoring an average of 2.3 goals per game. At home, they suffered just one

 The heart of the Barclaycard Premiership - 4thegame.com

defeat all season – 4-0 to Wimbledon in September – as well as winning their last ten fixtures at Maine Road.

Wimbledon were the only side to do the 'double' over City, adding a 2-1 win at Selhurst Park in February to their exploits earlier in the season. Stockport County and West Bromwich Albion were the only other teams they failed to beat. The latter were the only side to keep City from scoring in their two meetings.

Upfront, Shaun Goater notched 28 goals to finish top scorer in the Division. The Bermudan-born striker also made most starts for City with 42. Alongside him, former Newcastle and Coventry star Darren Huckerby racked up 20 League goals for the first time in his career.

At wing back, Sean Wright-Phillips – stepson of Highbury legend Ian – earned himself his first England Under-21 call-up thanks to some fine displays.

From mid-December onwards, City never took their foot off the pedal. Starting with a victory over fellow promotion-chasers Wolves, they took 60 points from a possible 72.

Even before the campaign had started, Keegan showed that he still had the charisma and the ability to draft in new faces to bolster the club's fortunes.

The free transfer signings of England veteran Stuart Pearce and Algerian international Ali Benarbia in June and September respectively were both shrewd bits of business, as was the acquisition of gifted Israeli attacking midfielder Eyal Berkovic from Celtic for £1.5m.

Keegan then splashed the cash to bring Jonathan Macken on board from Preston North End, setting a then new club record with the £5m purchase of the former Manchester United trainee.

True to type, Keegan packed the team with flair players, preferring the 5-3-2

Squad List

Eyal Berkovic 20 appearances (5 as substitute) **Ali Benarbia** 38 (0), **Laurent Charvet** 3 (0), **Simon Colosimo** 0 (6), **Paul Dickov** 0 (7), **Richard Dunne** 41 (2), **Richard Edghill** 9 (2), **Dickson Etuhu** 11 (1), **Shaun Goater** 42 (0), **Tony Grant** 2(1), **Danny Granville** 12 (4), **Alfie Haaland** 0 (3), **Kevin Horlock** 33 (9), **Steve Howey** 34 (0), **Darren Huckerby** 30 (10), **Niclas Jensen** 16 (2), **Sun Jihai** 2 (5), **Chris Killen** 0 (3), **Jon Macken** 4 (4), **Tyrone Mears** 0(1), **Lucien Mettomo** 17 (5), **Leon Mike** 1 (1), **Carlo Nash** 22 (1), **Christian Negouai** 2(3), **Stuart Pearce** 38, **Paul Ritchie** 0 (8), **Chris Shuker** 0 (2), **Danny Tiatto** 36 (1), **Alioune Toure** 0 (1), **Paulo Wanchope** 14 (1), **Nicky Weaver** 24 (1), **Jeff Whitley** 0 (2), **Gerard Wiekens** 24 (5), **Shaun Wright-Phillips** 31 (4)

formation with both Berkovic and Benarbia in midfield. He did so without sacrificing fight and determination.

City had started the campaign poorly, taking just 20 points from their opening 13 matches to leave them languishing in ninth position. In early March, they trailed leaders Wolves by eight points – albeit with three games in hand – yet they stuck to their task to run out worthy Champions.

Promotion means that City will spend their farewell Maine Road season in the top flight. Already, Keegan has been busy in the transfer market trying to ensure they won't be saying a second goodbye to the F.A. Barclaycard Premiership.

Peter Schmeichel signed on a free transfer from Aston Villa, while both Nicolas Anelka and Sylvain Distin have arrived from Paris St-Germain.

 All the latest news, views and opinion – 4thegame.com

West Bromwich Albion

	Division One				Final standing for the 2001-2002 season			
Final Position		Games Played	Games Won	Games Drawn	Games Lost	Goals For	Goals Against	Total Points
1	Manchester City	46	31	6	9	108	52	99
2	West Bromwich Albion	46	27	8	11	61	29	89
3	Wolverhampton W	46	25	11	10	76	43	86

> "We must strengthen the squad. It's no good just trying to play catch-up now we're being asked to mix it with the big boys. "
>
> *Gary Megson (April 2002)*

Club Honours and Records

Division 1 Champions: 1919-20
Division 2 Champions: 1901-02, 1910-11
FA Cup Winners: 1888, 1892, 1931, 1954, 1968
League Cup Winners: 1966
Record victory:
12-0 v Darwen, Division 1, 4 April, 1892
Record defeat:
3-10 v Stoke City, Division 1, 4 February, 1937
League goals in a season (team):
105, Division 2, 1929-30
League goals in a season (player):
William Richardson, 39, Division 1, 1935-36
Career league goals:
Tony Brown, 218, 1963 to 1979
League appearances:
Tony Brown, 574, 1963 to 1980
Reported transfer fee paid: £2,000,000 to Bristol Rovers for Jason Roberts, July 2000
Reported transfer fee received:
£5,000,001 from Coventry City for Lee Hughes, August 2001

West Bromwich Albion, founder members of the Football League in 1888, are back, in the top flight 16 years after dropping out of the old Division One following the worst season in the club's history, when they amassed four League wins and a total of just 24 points from 42 games.

There was to be further gloom at the Hawthorns five years later when, in 1990-91, they dropped again, to the then Division Two, for the first time ever with Bobby Gould at the helm.

Although they secured promotion back to Division One in 1992-93, West Brom struggled to find consistency and flirted with relegation on a number of occasions. In March 2000, Brian Little, who had been appointed manager at the start of the campaign, left and was replaced by Gary Megson.

The former Sheffield Wednesday midfielder managed to keep West Brom up – just – before embarking on a regeneration programme that would propel the Midlanders back to centre stage.

In 2000-01, they reached the Division One play-offs for the first time, losing out to eventually promoted Bolton Wanderers in the semi-finals. This time around, they

Fixtures, results and match reports - 4thegame.com

went one better, securing automatic qualification after finishing second behind Manchester City.

In doing so, they overhauled bitter local rivals Wolverhampton Wanderers who had led West Brom by ten points with eight games to go.

The Baggies' success was based on solid foundations. Just 29 goals were conceded throughout the campaign, 14 fewer than anyone else, and the least since Sunderland won promotion in 1998-99 a full 18 points clear of the opposition.

It should be noted that their solidity at the back was essential as West Brom finished with the least amount of goals scored in the top five. Summer signing Scott Dobie, their top scorer, scraped into double figures with 11 League goals.

In goal, former Leicester stopper Russell Hoult played a blinder. Not only did he start in all but one League game – a feat he shared with wing back Neil Clement and midfielder Derek McInnes – he then went on to keep 24 clean sheets. His efforts helped West Brom overcome a poor start to the season which saw them lying in 11th place after the 15 games with just 23 points.

By the turn of the year, they were moving in the right direction, up to 7th with 44 points from 27 games.

Promotion was clinched thanks to a great run in 2002 that saw the Baggies claim 45 of a possible 57 points. During that time, Millwall and Preston North End were the only teams to beat them – in addition, the former was the only side to do the 'double' over West Brom all season.

Nevertheless, the Baggies' meanness at the back was such that no side managed to score more than one goal against them in any League or Cup match from January until the end of the season.

Manager Gary Megson made limited

Squad List

Michael Appleton 18 appearances (0 as substitute), **Igor Balis** 32 (2),

Trevor Benjamin 1 (3), **Tony Butler** 14 (5),

Adam Chambers 24 (8), **James Chambers** 1 (4),

Neil Clement 45 (0), **Warren Cummings** 6 (8),

Danny Dichio 26 (1), **Scott Dobie** 32 (11),

Ruel Fox 2 (18), **Phil Gilchrist** 43 (0),

Russell Hoult 45 (0), **Brian Jensen** 1 (0),

Andy Johnson 28 (4), **Jordao** 19 (6),

Des Lyttle 13 (10), **Derek McInnes** 45 (0),

Darren Moore 31 (1), **James Quinn** 1 (6),

Jason Roberts 12 (2), **Uwe Rosler** 5 (0),

Larus Sigurdsson 42 (1), **Bob Taylor** 18 (16),

Stanislav Varga 3 (1)

changes to the personnel during the season despite the sale of striker Lee Hughes to Coventry in summer 2001 for £5m.

Although just 23 players were used – including some loan signings – new arrivals Scott Dobie, Andy Johnson and Danny Dichio quickly established themselves. Similarly, the capture of centre back Darren Moore from Portsmouth in September proved to be an inspired move.

In front of goal, where they would appear to have most work to do, West Brom missed more than their fair share of penalties during the campaign, although Igor Balis kept his nerve to score a crucial last-ditch winner against Bradford in the Baggies' penultimate game of the season.

They then hosted Crystal Palace on the last day of the season and it was fitting that West Brom veteran Bob Taylor should score the goal that ended 16 years in the wilderness.

All the charts and tables in this year's edition of KICK OFF have been generated by **SUPERBASE**™ our football database system.

SUPERBASE™ and is designed to help fans get closer to the game by providing detailed statistical analysis for every F.A. Barclaycard club, match and player.

powered by **SUPERBASE**™

If you have suggestions for other areas of team performance you would like to see covered, or to learn more about **SUPERBASE**™, please contact Sidan Press on: **info@sidanpress.com**